Bernaerts' Guide to the 1982 United Nations Convention on the Law of the Sea

Including the text of the 1982 UN Convention
&
Agreement concerning Part XI of 1994

Reprint of 1988 Edition

Arnd Bernaerts

© Copyright 2006 Arnd Bernaerts.
All rights reserved. No part of this publication may be reproduced, stored in a retrieval system, or transmitted, in any form or by any means, electronic, mechanical, photocopying, recording, or otherwise, without the written prior permission of the author.

Note for Librarians: A cataloguing record for this book is available from Library and Archives Canada at www.collectionscanada.ca/amicus/index-e.html
ISBN 1-4120-7665-x

Printed on paper with minimum 30% recycled fibre. Trafford's print shop runs on "green energy" from solar, wind and other environmentally-friendly power sources.

TRAFFORD
PUBLISHING

Offices in Canada, USA, Ireland and UK

Book sales for North America and international:
Trafford Publishing, 6E–2333 Government St.,
Victoria, BC V8T 4P4 CANADA
phone 250 383 6864 (toll-free 1 888 232 4444)
fax 250 383 6804; email to orders@trafford.com

Book sales in Europe:
Trafford Publishing (UK) Limited, 9 Park End Street, 2nd Floor
Oxford, UK OX1 1HH UNITED KINGDOM
phone 44 (0)1865 722 113 (local rate 0845 230 9601)
facsimile 44 (0)1865 722 868; info.uk@trafford.com

Order online at:
trafford.com/05-2560

10 9 8 7 6 5 4 3 2 1

Preface of the reprint in 2005

More than 15 years ago FAIRPLAY PUBLICATIONS Ltd, Coulsdon, Surrey, England, published the book "Bernaerts' Guide to the Law of the Sea – The 1982 United Nations Convention". The guiding potential of the book to find access to the 1982 Law of the Sea Convention is still given. Internet technology and publishing on demand invite to provide the interested reader, law student, and researcher with this tool again. Only the Status of the Convention (ratification etc) has been updated and instead of the Final Act, the reprint includes the "Agreement relating to the Implementation of Part XI of the United Nations Convention of the Law of the Sea" of 1994. The thorough Index of the 1988 edition is reproduced without changes.

Arnd Bernaerts, October 2005,

Foreword of the 1988 edition

by Satya N. Nandan
Special Representative of the Secretary-General of the United Nations
for the Law of the Sea
Office for Ocean Affairs and the Law of the Sea

Revolutionary changes have taken place in the International Law of the Sea since 1945. The process of change was accelerated in the last two decades by the convening in 1973 of the Third United Nations Conference on the Law of the Sea. The protracted negotiations, spanning over a decade, culminated in the adoption of the United Nations Convention on the Law of the Sea in 1982. By 9 December 1984, the closing date for signature, 159 signatures were appended to the Convention, the largest number for any such multilateral instrument in the history of international relations.

The Convention, which was adopted as a comprehensive package, introduced a new equity in the relationship among states with respect to the uses of the ocean and the allocation of its resources. It deals, inter alia, with sovereignty and jurisdiction of states, navigation and marine transport, over flight of aircraft, marine pollution, marine scientific research, marine technology, conservation and exploitation of marine living resources, the development and-exploitation of marine non-living resources in national and international areas, and unique provisions dealing with the settlement of disputes concerning the interpretation and application of the new regime.

There is no doubt that as we approach the 21st century, more and more attention will be paid to the uses of the oceans and the development of their resources. It is important, therefore, that these developments should take place within a widely accepted legal framework so that there is certainty as to the rights and obligations of all states. The United Nations Convention on the Law of the Sea provides that framework. It establishes a standard for the conduct of states in maritime matters. It is thus a major instrument for preventing conflicts among states.

The convention and its annexes contain over 400 articles. For many it may be a formidable undertaking to grasp the substance and structure of it without making a considerable investment in time and energy. Mr Bernaerts' guide, therefore, is a welcome addition to the growing body of literature on the convention. It provides a most useful reference tool which will benefit administrators and policy makers, as well as scholars. It makes the convention accessible to the uninitiated and refreshes, at a glance, the memories of the initiated. With meticulous references and graphic presentations of the provisions of the convention, Mr Bernaerts has given to the international community an invaluable guide to the understanding and implementation of the 1982 United Nations Convention on the Law of the Sea.

April 1988

Preface (extract) of 1988 edition

The reader will be aware that the 1982 United Nations Convention on the Law of the Sea is the first constitution of the oceans, a groundbreaking document in many respects. He or she might also have made the discovery that the full text of the Convention is immediately accessible only to experts. If the Convention were only a treaty consisting of straightforward technical regulatory provisions, it could be left to them with a clear conscience. But the Convention is to a large extent a political document and, as such, is expected to influence significantly the development of relations among the states in the world community; for this reason, a widespread knowledge of the scope, goals, and regulatory framework of the Convention can only serve to further the aims of the document and would surely follow the intentions of the many men and women who made this Convention their life-work, such as Arvid Pardo (Malta), Hamilton Shirtey Amerasinghe (Sri Lanka), Tommy T. B. Koh (Singapore), and Satya N. Nandan (Fiji), to name only a few of the hundreds who worked on the preparation of this Convention.

As the reader uses the Guide (Part II), he will find that many provisions of the Convention are much easier to understand if one knows the basic framework within which a particular regulation is placed. The Guide aims to provide this framework, with reference to the text of the Convention and, in addition, to the supporting Commentary of Part III, which describes the overall context of the major terms and concepts. The Introduction of Part I sketches the historical background of the Convention and some of the general effects. A detailed index at the end of the book will be of assistance in finding specific subjects.

About the author

As trained seaman and master mariner the author was shipmaster before he became lawyer and doctor of law in the 1970s, with a law office in Hamburg, and international consultant since 1980s. Recently he published his investigation on "Climate Change & Naval War – A Scientific Assessment -", Trafford Publishing - *on-demand* -, Victoria CANADA, 2005, which can be also found on www.seaclimate.com.

TABLE OF CONTENTS

I. INTRODUCTION TO THE EVOLUTION OF A NEW CONVENTION ON THE LAW OF THE SEA

A. Events Affecting the Law of the Sea from 1945-1973

1. The Reasons for International Maritime Conflicts — 2
2. The Truman Proclamations of 1945 — 3
3. Developments in the late 1940's and 1950's — 3
4. The First and Second United Nations Conferences on the Law of the Sea (1958 and 1960) — 4
5. Developments in the 1960's — 5
6. The Sea-Bed - "Common Heritage of Mankind" — 5
7. The Sea-Bed Committee 1967-1973 and the Preparations for the Third United Nations Conference — 6

B. The Third United Nations Conference on the Law of the Sea (1973-1982)

1. Participants, Sessions — 7
2. Initial Problems — 7
3. "Gentleman's Agreement" and "Package Deal" — 8
4. Negotiating Process — 8

C. The General Effects of the Convention

1. A Constitution for the Oceans — 9
2. Impact of the Four UN Conventions on the Law of the Sea of 1958 — 10
3. Significant Achievements — 10
4. Limits of Regulations — 11
5. "Equality" - Equal Rights for All? — 11
6. Major Objections to the Convention — 12
7. A New Economic Order? — 12
8. Provisions for Entry into Force — 13
9. The Importance of Having Signed the Convention — 13
10. Practice of the States in Recent Years — 14
11. What is the "Law of the Sea" Today? — 14
12. The Future of the Convention — 15

D. Ratification and Signature

Status of the four Geneva Conventions of 1958 and the UN Convention on the Law of the Sea of 1982 — 16

II. GUIDE TO THE CONVENTION

Preamble and Part I (Article 1)

1. Preamble	22
2. Introduction	22
3. Significant Content of the Preamble (Layout)	23

Part II (Articles 2-33)

1. Legal Status of the Territorial Sea	24
2. The Right of Foreign Nationals in Internal Waters and the Territorial Sea (Layout)	25
3. Baseline	26
4. Importance of Baseline (Layout)	27
5. Passage Through the Territorial Sea	28
6. Importance of the Concept "Innocent Passage" (Layout)	29
7. The Contiguous Zone	30
8. The Contiguous Zone (Layout)	31

Part III (Articles 34-45)

1. Straits Used for International Navigation	32
2. The Regime of Passage Through Straits (Layout)	33

Part IV (Articles 46-54)

1. Archipelagic States	34
2. Operations in Archipelagic Waters (Layout)	35

Part V (Articles 55-75)

1. Exclusive Economic Zone	36
2. Rights and Duties in the Exclusive Economic Zone (Layout)	37
3. Coastal State Fisheries	38
4. Fisheries in the Exclusive Economic Zone (Layout)	39

Part VI (Articles 76-85)

1. The Continental Shelf	40
2. Significant Rights of Others in the Economic Zone, Continental Shelf, and the High Seas (Layout)	41

Part VII (Articles 86-120)

1. The High Seas – General	42
2. The High Seas (Layout)	43
3. The Flag State's Obligations for Merchant Vessels	44
4. Vessels (Layout)	45
5. International Jurisdiction	46
6. Hot Pursuit	46
7. Special Jurisdiction on the High Seas (Layout)	47
8. Submarine Cables and Pipelines	48
9. Fisheries on the High Seas	48
10. Freedom of Fishing (Layout)	49

Part VIII (Article 121); Part IX (Articles 122-123)

1. The Regime of Islands 50
2. Enclosed or Semi-enclosed Seas 50
3. Regime of Islands (Layout) 51
4. Enclosed or Semi-enclosed Seas (Layout) 51

Part X (Articles 124-132)

1. Freedom of Transit 52
2. Freedom of Transit (Layout) 53

Part XI (Articles 133-191)

1. Principles Governing the Area 54
2. Principles Governing the Area (Layout) 55
3. Development of the Resources of the Area 56
4. Development of Resources (Layout) 57
5. The Sea-Bed Authprity 58
6. The Sea-Bed Authority (Layout) 59
7. The Organs of the Authority 60
8. The Organizations of the Sea-Bed Authority (Layout) 61
9. The Sea-Bed Disputes Chamber 62
10. The Sea-Bed Disputes Chamber (Layout) 63

Part XII (Articles 192-237)

1. Pollution Prevention Regulations in General 64
2. The Legal Framework for Prevention of Pollution (Layout) 65
3. Pollution Legislation Applicable to Vessels 66
4. General Jurisdiction for Vessels in Pollution Matters (Layout) 67
5. Enforcement of Pollution Laws Applicable to Vessels 68
6. General Enforcement Concept (Layout) 69
7. Port State Enforcement (Article 218) (Layout) 70
8. Coastal State Enforcement (Article 220) (Layout) 71

Part XIII (Articles 238-265)

1. Marine Scientific Research 72
2. Marine Scientific Research (Layout) 73

Part XIV (Articles 266-278)

1. Development and Transfer of Technology 74
2. Transfer of Marine Technology (Layout) 75

Part XV (Articles 279-299)

1. System for Settlement of Disputes 76
2. The Fora for the Settlement of Disputes (Layout) 77

Part XVI (Articles 300-304)

1. General Provisions 78
2. References to Peaceful Use of the Sea (Layout) 79

Part XVII (Articles 305-320)

1. Final Provisions	80
2. Entry into Force and Applicability of the Convention and Amendments (Layout)	81

Annexes I and II

1. Highly Migratory Species	82
2. Continental Shelf Commission	82
3. Continental Shelf Commission (Layout)	83

Annex III

1. Basic Conditions of Prospecting, Exploration and Exploitation	84
2. Authority - Contractor (Layout)	85

Annex IV

1. The Enterprise	86
2. Statute of the Enterprise (Layout)	87

Annex V

1. Voluntary Conciliation	88
2. Compulsory Conciliation	88
3. Conciliation Procedure (Layout)	89

Annex VI

1. The Tribunal for the Law of the Sea	90
2. 2. The Tribunal for the Law of the Sea (Layout)	91

Annex VII, Annex VIII

1. Arbitration	92
2. Special Arbitration	92
3. Arbitration - Special Arbitration (Layout)	93

Annex IX

1. International Organizations as "States Parties"	94
2. Participation of International Organizations (Layout)	95

Final Act, Annex I, Resolution I

1. Final Act	96
2. Preparatory Commission	96
3. Preparatory Commission (Layout)	97

Final Act, Annex I, Resolution II

1. The Regime for "Pioneer activities"	98

2. The "Pioneer Investors" (Layout)   99

III. COMMENTARY ON MAJOR SUBJECTS OF THE CONVENTION

A. States and Organizations

1. States and States Parties   102
2. Coastal States   102
3. Port states   103
4. Flag States   104
5. Register States   104
6. Flag of Convenience States   104
7. Archipelagic States   105
8. Geographically Disadvantaged States   105
9. Land-locked States   106
10. Transit States   107
11. Developing States   107
12. United Nations Organizations   108
13. Other International Government Organizations   109
14. Co-operaton – "Competent International Organization"   110
15. Govermental Organizations as Parties to the Convention   110

B. Zones and Areas

1. International Waters, "Historic Bays", and Ports   111
2. Territorial Sea   112
3. Contiguous Zone   112
4. Straits   113
5. Archipelagic Waters and Zones   114
6. Islands   114
7. Enclosed or Semi-enclosed Seas   114
8. Continental Shelf   115
9. Exclusive Economic Zone   116
10. The High Seas   117
11. The Area – The Deep Sea-Bed   117

C. Activities on the Oceans

1. Ships – Vessels   118
2. Navigation   119
3. Fisheries   119
4. Overflight   120
5. Marine Scientific Research   121
6. Deep-Sea Mining   121
7. Artificial Islands and structures   122
8. Cables and Pipelines   123
9. Dumping   123
10. Archeological and Historical Objects   124
11. Military use   124

D. Prevention Measures

    1. Safety of Shipping   125
    2. Preservation of the Marine Environment   126
    3. Indemnity   128

E. Measures for peace and Justice

    1. Establishing Peace   128
    2. Measures to Close the Economic Gap   129
    3. The Unification of the Law of the Sea   130
    4. Settlement of Disputes   131

- The 1982 UN Convention on the Law of the Sea, and the

- Agreement relating to the Implementation pf Part XI

Table of Contents (1982 UN Convention)   133

Convention & Agreement   152

Index   330

Introduction to the Evolution of a New Convention on the Law of the Sea

A. EVENTS AFFECTING THE LAW OF SEA FROM 1945 - 1973

1. The Reasons for International Maritime Conflicts

The most frequent and serious conflicts within the scope of the law of the sea used to arise from the clash of two opposing fundamental principles, territorial sovereignty and freedom of the seas, or, to put it more concisely, the interests of the states protecting their merchant, fishing, and naval fleets. On the one hand, coastal states had territorial sovereignty in their territorial seas, but the extent of this sovereignty and the enforcement of law over vessels using the territorial sea was often disputed. On the other hand, the principles of freedom of navigation and fishing were important for states under whose flags vessels sailed. Until the middle of this century, fishing and navigation were the only important economic uses of the sea, and conflicts were on the whole limited to questions in these matters; they were therefore more a legal matter involving particular incidents than one of wide-spread concern. International shipping was essential for coastal states as well as flag states, and countries were frequently active in both roles. This is surely one reason that the law of the sea, relying on three hundred year old principles, was in 1945 still an "unwritten" law and had not yet been codified; it applied as customary international law. Such law can be described as international custom, as evidence of a general and consistent practice by states which is generally accepted (whether duties or rights) as law. Codification attempts for the freedom of navigation, fisheries, submarine cables and pipelines, and airspace over the high seas in the period following the First World War did not succeed. At that time, an occupation of the sea-bed was considered beyond the capabilities of any state. General opinion tended towards the view that the legal status of the sea-bed should be governed by the same principles as the waters above it. But such a regulation was never codified and, with the exception of the laying of cables and pipelines, the sea-bed remained out of reach for any use.

As advances in technology increased the range for long-distance fishing vessels, fishing just outside the territorial waters of other states, but still within a few miles of the coast, began to increase, at first a cause of concern to coastal states. Beginning in 1945, some states began implementing measures to protect the living resources of the sea for their nationals beyond the limits of the territorial sea, then generally accepted as being three nautical miles in breadth. The principle of unlimited freedom of navigation was seriously called into question during the 1960s, when disastrous tanker accidents dramatically showed the effects of pollution-on the marine environment, and coastal states began to demand more rights to protect their coasts and coastal waters.

The narrowness of the law of the sea was also painfully illuminated by the growing use of the sea-bed. Shortly before World War II, when no one even knew of resources in the deep sea-bed, much less had the means or technology to explore or exploit them, off-shore drilling for oil and gas in waters near the coast and in shallow water had begun. With the immense growth in technology which accompanied the rapid expansion of these activities, exploration became possible in ever deeper waters. The question as to whether exploitation of resources from the seas beyond national jurisdiction should be subject to the principle of freedom of the high seas had forced its way into immediate relevance, and a generally accepted answer was needed.

Finally, the conflict between these opposing rights and interests was complicated by increasing awareness of questions of equality and equal use of, access to, and participation in the riches of the sea, as many countries did not have the means, know-how, or trained manpower which would enable them to compete on equal footing with the traditional industrialized states, whether in navigation, fishing, or mining. If these nations were to enjoy the right to participate in the resources of the sea and shoulder the responsibility of dealing with problems such as pollution, they had to be protected from the crush of overwhelming competition by being granted sole rights over resources and being given the opportunity to act together with the more advanced countries.

Sources of conflict on the seas, formerly restricted mainly to fishing and navigation on territorial seas, have thus increased in number and scope since the end of World War II.

2. The Truman Proclamations of 1945

By the mid-1940s, technological achievements in the United States had reached a level where prospects for exploration and exploitation of off-shore oil fields were beginning to generate wide-spread interest. At the same time, the country was embroiled in a controversy over fishery rights. The Roosevelt government therefore began (and continued throughout the war) preparing measures to be taken with regard to fishing and the continental shelf; the deliberations were concluded just before PresToent Roosevelt died in April 1945. Implementing the proposed measures as finalized, Roosevelt's successor as president. Harry S. Truman, issued in September 1945 the proclamation on "Coastal Fisheries in Certain Areas of the High Seas", which referred to the urgent need to protect coastal fishing resources from destructive exploitation and declared the need to establish a conservation zone and, on the same day, a proclamation concerning the "Natural Resources of the Subsoil and Sea-bed of the Continental Shelf", in which was stated:

> The government regards the natural resources of the subsoil and sea-bed of the continental shelf beneath the high seas but contiguous to the coast... (to be) subject to its jurisdiction and control.

These proclamations had far-reaching effects on fishing and exploration of the sea-bed. At the time, the continental shelf claim was not very controversial; the proclamation on the conservation of fisheries, by contrast, was. Other states such as Great Britain opposed any challenge to the traditional principles of the law of the sea, in particular the freedom of fishing and freedom of navigation. Time would show that this was precisely the significance the Truman Proclamations would have for the law of the sea; certain recent developments in this regime can be traced back to President Truman's actions.

3. Developments in the late 1940's and 1950's

In the wake of the Truman Proclamations of 1945, a number of states took measures for the protection of offshore resources. Mexico followed the Truman lead by issuing similar proclamations, and Argentina in 1946 and Chile in 1947 extended their sovereignty considerably beyond the territorial sea. Chile acted in particular to protect its whaling industry from the competition of foreign fleets. Within a few years, several South American states had claimed extensive rights, some demanding full sovereignty over coastal water zones extending up to two hundred nautical miles. These claims were generally rejected. The South American states were followed in moderate measure by some of the states bordering the Arabian Gulf, who declared the sea-bed adjacent to their territorial sea to be subject to their jurisdiction and control, a step necessary at that time to clarify the status of and control over drilling platforms in the Arabian Gulf. This trend was to continue. By 1958, about twenty states had made similar sea-bed claims. At that time, the right of the coastal states to make such claims on the continental shelf was not in question; instead, the disputes revolved around the definition of continental shelf and the resulting delimitation of the zone. These disputes must be regarded against the background of the legal point that possession or occupation is to some extent related to the ability to control or use the area, and technology had not yet advanced far enough to allow work in deeper waters. The basic "right" of a coastal state to the (exploitable) resources of the sea-bed off its coast was regarded as "natural." Freedom of fishing was not seriously threatened, although there were certainly local conflicts resulting from states' desires to protect the short-distance fishing industries of their nationals. A certain regulatory effect resulted from the establishment of international regional fishery commissions empowered to take necessary measures for conservation. However, the wide-spread belief that the living resources of the ocean were inexhaustible had not been proven false.

The work of the United Nations Organization, founded in 1945, was to have a different effect on relations involving the sea. A maritime body, the International Maritime Consultive Organisation (now the International Maritime Organisation, IMO), was established. The purpose of the organisation was to provide machinery for governmental regulations and practice concerning maritime safety regulations and efficiency of navigation.

Even more directly related to the codification of the law of the sea was the work of the International Law Commission of the United Nations. In 1949, the Commission decided to give its work on the law of the high seas top priority. The Commission was advised by the UN General Assembly on December 6, 1949, to include the regime of the territorial sea in its work. The Commission's report resulted in the convening of a conference in 1958. On February 21, 1957, the UN General Assembly resolved that not only the legal but also the technical, biological, economic, and political aspects of the problems should be the subject of the conference's deliberations.

4. The United Nations Conferences on the Law of the Sea I and II Geneva 1958 and 1960

At the 1958 conference, the eighty-six states in attendance adopted four conventions: the "Territorial Sea and the Contiguous Zone," the "High Seas," the "Continental Shelf", and "Fishing and Conservation of the Living Resources of the High Seas." These four conventions entered into force between 1962 and 1966. Progress had been made by codifying to a large extent customary -law, but agreement on substantive questions had not been reached. The second conference in 1960, convened to consider particular questions regarding territorial sea and fishing matters which had not been resolved in 1958, failed to adopt a convention. Developing countries wanted, mainly for surveillance and security reasons, a considerable extension of the territorial sea, then still generally recognized as being three nautical miles. The large shipping nations and naval powers, on the other hand, were deeply concerned about the effects any changes might have on the principle of freedom of navigation. It was requested that the limits of the territorial sea be set at twelve nautical miles. As far as the continental shelf was concerned, the regulations of the convention were not acceptable to the many states which had only a narrow continental shelf, as the convention defined the continental shelf as the sea-bed from the outer limits of the territorial sea to the 200-meter isobath and beyond this limit where the depth admitted exploration of natural resources. In addition, the problem of fishing rights beyond the territorial sea had not been solved for many coastal states. The negotiations of the 1960 Conference ended inconclusively.

Three of the 1958 conventions were ratified by about fifty states, thus gaining a certain measure of acceptance. The Convention on Fishing and Conservation of Living Resources of the High Seas, however, was ratified by only thirty-five states. This was due to the fact that conservation principles provided by the convention were already being practiced by fishing commissions which had been established in various regions, and the convention did not deal with the short-distance fishing interests of the coastal states.

5. Developments in the 1960's

As the United Nations Conferences I and II on the Law of the Sea in 1958 and 1960 failed to adopt substantive proposals on the breadth of the territorial sea and coastal state fishing rights in coastal waters not covered by the continental shelf regime of 1958, the widely diverging territorial sea claims of various states seriously challenged the unity of the law of the sea. Claims of territorial seas with a breadth of twelve nautical miles or more tripled from about twenty to sixty during the decade following the conferences.

Although every extension of a state's territorial sea necessarily means the extension of its exclusive fishing rights, even this quadruple expansion was seemingly insufficient. Many coastal states proclaimed a so-called exclusive fishing zone of varying breadth, although in most cases it did not exceed twelve nautical miles. More than thirty such claims had been made by the end of the 1960s. It was at this time, moreover, that the exhaustibility of the living resources of the sea became obvious. From 1955 to 1965, the world fish catch almost doubled and reached levels of overexploitation which seriously endangered the survival of the resources. Conservation measures, management, scientific research, and catch quotas on a large scale became essential. A further matter of growing concern was that the major fishing nations (about twenty states) harvested four times as much as the rest of the world together.

Extensive fishing to the point of overexploitation was undoubtedly a factor leading to an increase in the number of local controversies over fishing rights, such as the escalation of the "cod war" between Iceland and European countries to a high level of tension. Nevertheless, or perhaps because of such conflicts, many regional fisheries agreements were negotiated and concluded.

A combination of forces led to the call for a third conference on the law of the sea, in the hope that satisfactory solutions to the growing problems and legal uncertainties in maritime law could be found.

6. The Sea-Bed - "Common Heritage of Mankind"

Although in the 1960s deep sea exploitation was still a technology of the future, it was becoming evident that it would one day be possible, and scientists had discovered that there were enormous mineral resources in and on the sea-bed, particularly polymetallic nodules. Naturally, the question arose as to who would have the right to explore and exploit these resources. The awareness of the problem can be illustrated by the words of Lyndon Johnson, President of the United States, who stated in 1966:

Under no circumstances, we believe, must we ever allow the prospects of rich harvest and mineral wealth to create a new form of colonial competition among the maritime nations. We must be careful to avoid a race to grab and to hold the lands under the high seas. We must ensure that the deep sea and the ocean bottoms are, and remain, the legacy of all human beings.

The UN General Assembly began to act only on the initiative of the Ambassador of Malta to the United Nations, Arvid Pardo, who in 1967 recommended to the United Nations that the resources, other than fisheries, of the high seas beyond the territorial sea and the sea-bed beyond the continental shelf be proclaimed as belonging to the United Nations Organisation and as being subject to its jurisdiction and control, as otherwise militarization of the sea-bed and exploitation of its resources by highly developed countries to their national advantage and to the disadvantage of poor countries was probable. In addition to the important content of his suggestion, Pardo's efforts were of significance because they stirred the UN General Assembly to action. Within only a few weeks, the Assembly had established a Sea-Bed Committee to study this problem.

On December 17, 1970, the Assembly declared the sea-bed and ocean floor and the subsoil thereof, beyond the limits of national jurisdiction, as well as the resources to be the common heritage of mankind. A new concept had been established. As for the origin of the term itself, US President Truman is said to have presented a plan at the Potsdam Conference in 1945 according to which all large rivers would be governed by a regime of common heritage. The term "common heritage of mankind" is of immense political value, but at the same time it can hardly be called a legal term at present and, if used might well cause confusion rather than clarify a situation. Nonetheless, the expression could prove to have a major impact for the law of the sea and beyond in the future, and it will in any case be of value as a guideline for interpretation of the deep-sea mining provisions.

7. The Sea-Bed Committee 1967-1973 and the Preparations for a Third Conference on the Law of the Sea

In December 1967, the General Assembly of the United Nations established the Committee to Study the Peaceful Uses of the Sea-Bed and the Ocean Floor Beyond the Limits of National Jurisdiction; at the time it was established, the Committee consisted of thirty-five members, but was later enlarged to more than ninety. The Committee was instructed to study all aspects of international law concerning the deep sea, including provision of machinery for the exploitation of the resources in the interests of mankind, and other UN institutions were charged to support the Committee in its work by providing information on studies for the prevention of marine pollution, exploitation of resources, the needs of developing and land-locked countries, and long-term scientific considerations, including exchange of data and research capabilities.

On the basis of the Committee's proposals, the General Assembly in 1970 solemnly declared as the first of the principles governing the sea-bed area the concept of the "common heritage of mankind." The Assembly further decided that this and other principles included in the declaration should be embodied in an international treaty of universal character and that such a treaty should be drafted by a Third United Nations Conference on the Law of the Sea to be convened in 1973.

The Sea-Bed Committee was instructed to make preparations for the Conference and draft treaty articles embodying the international regime of the deep sea area. The Committee prepared a list of subjects and issues to be dealt with by the Conference, but failed to produce the text of a single preparatory document for the Conference. Although several members or groups of members had submitted various proposals to the Committee, a concensus could not be reached on basic texts.

B. THE THIRD UNITED NATIONS CONFERENCE ON THE LAW OF SEA (1973-1982)

1. Participants, Sessions

When in 1972 the UN General Assembly confirmed its decision to convene the Conference in 1973, it assumed the sessions would last through 1974, but finish no later than 1975. In the event, the first session of the Conference was opened on December 3, 1973, and the Conference concluded on September 24, 1982. During these nine years eleven sessions, including five resumed, sessions, were held, one in Caracas, five in Geneva, and ten in New York, With two exceptions, the sessions and resumed sessions lasted about one to two months each. A large number of the member states of the United Nations participated in the Conference: a total of 164 states were registered and an average of 140 delegations were represented at the sessions. More than one hundred observers from territories, organizations and specialized agencies of the United Nations, liberation movements, and other intergovernmental as well as non-governmental organizations also took part.

2. The Initial Problems

The Conference was confronted with a list of no fewer than twenty-five different topics, ranging from the broad areas discussed at the 1958 and 1960 conferences to a number of new fields such as land-locked states, shelf-locked states, marine environment, scientific research, archipelagoes, and a report of the Sea-Bed Committee consisting of six volumes, containing hundreds of individual proposals, but lacking a single negotiating text. The topics were often technical, of widely differing nature, and highly complex, such as the technical, commercial, scientific, and financial impact of deep sea mining. In addition, many specific national interests had to be considered, arising from reasons of security, strategy, and economic resources. The work was further hampered by the fact that many of the topics such as straits or the continental shelf were highly controversial or included novel concepts.

3. "Gentleman's Agreement" and "Package Deal"

Both the General Assembly and the Conference were well aware that the new Convention would be of value only if it found wide acceptance in the international community. In order to ensure such acceptance as far as humanly possible, the General Assembly approved a text which was later incorporated into a declaration appended to the Rules of Procedure of the Conference, adopted at the second session. According to this "Gentleman's Agreement,"

> The Conference should make every effort to reach agreement on substantive matters by way of consensus and there should be no voting on such matters until all efforts at consensus have been exhausted.

The unique rules of procedure consequently contained special provisions to avoid or delay the taking of decisions on substantive matters by voting. Delaying a vote was introduced to provide a cooling-off period and to avoid hasty voting, a further step to achieve the greatest possible unity among the participants.

In addition, the Conference agreed to work on the basis of a "package deal." This concept assumed that the Convention should meet the minimum interests of the largest possible majority, while at the same time accommodating the essential interests of the major powers and the dominant interest groups. It was also implicit that there would be trade-offs and reciprocal support between various claims.

4. The Negotiating Process

The negotiations during the Conference were conducted in several different types of groups, according to the nature of the topic under discussion. General issues and the subjects of peaceful use of the oceans and enhancement of the universal participation of states were dealt with in the plenary. Other subjects were delegated to the Main Committees as follows:

> First Committee: Regime of the sea-bed and ocean floor beyond national jurisdiction;
> Second Committee: The common regime of the law of the sea and related topics;
> Third Committee: Environment, scientific research and development, and transfer of technolgy.

There was also the General Committee, which acted as the Conference bureau, the Credentials Committee, and the Drafting Committee. The task of the latter was to formulate drafts and give advice on drafting upon request, without re-opening substantive discussion on any matter.

The Main Committees worked with various forms and methods of negotiations. There was a trend toward simplification of the negotiation process by reducing the number of delegations at times to even fewer than ten, while always taking care to include representation of divergent interests.

These interests were often related to well-known traditional groups such as the "Group of 77", which consisted of members from more than 100 developing countries, or regional groups such as the Arabian or Asian group. Informal groups - conference delegates meeting privately without officially acting together - also had an important impact on the negotiating process during the conference. There were even negotiating groups working in secret.

In 1975, due to the initiative of the President of the Conference, H. S. Amerasinghe, it was decided to prepare a single document. A so-called Single Negotiating Text was then drafted by the chairmen of the Main Committees, each writing that part of the Convention for which his Committee was responsible and acting entirely on his own, with the consequence that different methods of preparation were employed. The Main Committees themselves were not involve'd. These documents therefore had no further status than to serve as the basis for negotiations. Nonetheless, they represented a great step forward for the Conference. From 1976 on, the Conference worked toward an informal composite negotiating text, which after revision led to an Informal Draft Convention in 1980 and then to the Draft Convention in 1981. On April 30, 1982, the Conference voted on the Draft Convention and the following four resolutions, and they were adopted by 430 in favour, four opposed, and seventeen abstentions. The resolutions, which together with the Convention form an integral whole, are as follows:

> Resolution I: Establishment of a Preparatory Commission for the International Sea-Bed Authority and for the International Tribunal for the Law of the Sea;
> Resolution II: Preparatory Investment in Pioneer Activities relating to Poly-metallic Nodules;
> Resolution III and IV concern membership and observers.

After a further three day session in New York in September 1982 approving draft changes, the conference was closed in a formal meeting in Montego Bay/Jamaica on December 10, 1982, at which time participating states were given the opportunity to sign the "Final Act and Resolutions of the Third United Nations Conference on the Law of the Sea". 140 States signed the Final Act, and the Third United Nations Conference on the Law of the Sea had ended. The Convention now took on a life of its own, waiting for the acceptance of all the states in order to become the unrivalled and comprehensive law of the sea for the international community.

C. THE GENERAL EFFECTS OF THE CONVENTION

1. A Constitution for the Oceans

The Convention is a comprehensive political and legal work which includes directives for international politics, international relations, and international law. It is a new international order for the oceans of the world, which make up five-sevenths of the planet's surface. The Convention's 320 articles, which are divided into seventeen main parts, take into account all legal aspects of the ocean space; nine annexes dealing with specific matters are attached to the Convention, but are integral parts (Art. 318). In many areas the Convention does not lay down a detailed scheme of regulations; instead, it provides a general legal framework within which states parties are required to act (e.g.. Art. 194) or may act, (e.g., Art. 21) put other conventions or treaties into effect, (e.g., Art. 211, Para. 2) or conclude agreements (e.g., Art. 125, Para. 2). The Convention is designed and structured to be applied without prejudice for any laws or rules which may previously exist or which may be made in future, (e.g., Art. 237, Para. 1; Art.

304) while at the same time binding such laws, rules, and agreements of state to the general objectives and principles of the Convention, (e.g.. Art. 237, Para. 2; Art. 311, Para. 3-6) Moreover, the Convention distinctly manifests political principles and programmes such as, "The high seas shall be reserved for peaceful purposes," (Art. 88) "The Area and its resources are the common heritage of mankind," (Art. 136; Art. 311, para. 6) or, States have the obligation to protect and preserve the marine environment. (Art. 192) Its quality of general application and its basic impact on all matters concerning the ocean give the Convention the status of a constitution for the oceans.

2. Impact of the Four UN Conventions on the Law of the Sea of 1958

The subject matter of all four Geneva Conventions of 1958 was under discussion at the Conference. These conventions have all been incorporated into the 1982 Convention, with varying degrees of change and amendment for improvement and to make them more consistent with each other and the further provisions. For states parties to the 1982 Convention, the later Convention prevails over those of 1958 (Art 311, Para. 1)

3. Significant Achievements

During the course of its work, the Conference was able to solve highly controversial matters and make important innovations. Far-reaching innovations such as the "Dispute Settlement System" (Part XV) and the Sea-Bed Regime (Part XI) may even have revolutionary impact on relations between states in many other fields besides maritime operations. Other major achievement were

(1) Solving the question of the breadth of the territorial sea (Part II, Art. 3), which had remained open from the 1958/1960 conferences;
(2) Regulation of the fishing rights of coastal states by implementing the exclusive economic zone (Part V, Art. 56-57);
(3) Fundamental change in the continental shelf concept of the Convention of 1958 (Part. VI, Art. 76);
(4) Concept of transit passage through straits (Part III, Art. 38) and archipelagic waters (Part IV, Art. 53) for international navigation;
(5) The concept of archipelagic states (Part IV);
(6) The obligation to engage in international co-operation in general (e.g., Art. 118, conservation and management of living resources; Art. 242, marine scientific research) and the development and transfer of marine science and technology to developing countries (e.g. Art. 150, Subpara. (d); Art. 274, Area; Art. 202, prevention of pollution; Art. 275-277 scientific and technological centres);
(7) The concept of a comprehensive environmental law (Part XII).

Although this list is not complete, it does give some idea of the general magnitude of the achievements of the Conference. It is said that the Convention may, in addition to its technical and substantive regulations, affect other matters as well such as questions of disarmament and of a new international economic order. A provision which declares, "The sea-bed (Area) shall be open to use exclusively for peaceful purposes," (Art. 141) could influence military actions, and the concept by which an international authority such as the Sea-Bed Authority (Part XI, Section 4) is obliged to promote just and stable prices remunerative to producers and fair to consumers for minerals derived both from the Area and other sources (Art. 150, Subpara. (f); Art. 160, Para. 1) can challenge the concept of the free market economy.

4. The Limits of Regulations

The achievements mentioned above are without exception the result of long, tedious struggles for compromise. Even so, these compromises could quite often be reached only by leaving some questions open or by using vague, ambiguous, and even almost contradictory language. Thus the right of land-locked states to the sea is in practice weakened by the transit state's right to request an advance agreement on terms and modalities (Art. 125, Para. 2) and the supremacy of the transit state's "legitimate interests," while at the same time the meaning of the term is left open. (Art. 125, Para. 3) Other such examples are the term "innocent passage" (Art. 19) or the term straits used in international navigation; (Art. 37) in both cases, the articles were drafted so as to avoid a clear definition.

It is said that the Convention also employs the "technique of silence." This might be the case with respect to the polar areas and military actions, but whether this is actually "silence" or not will depend on the individual viewpoint. However, all matters not regulated by the Convention continue to be governed by the rules and principles of general international law. (Preamble, last paragraph)

5. "Equality" - Equal Rights for All?

The regime of the oceans established by the Convention brings about 40% of the ocean space partly or wholly under the national jurisdiction of coastal states. This space encompasses the most valuable and most easily accessible resources of the oceans; 100% of the presently exploitable hydrocarbon deposits in the sea (85% of all known deposits) and about 90% of the commercial living resources are to be found in this area. Of this 40% subject to the jurisdiction of individual states, about half will fall to only a dozen or so coastal or archipelagic states, while the remainder (about 20% of the ocean space) will be partitioned out to the remaining 120 coastal states, including the so-called geographically disadvantaged coastal states (there are about thirty of the latter). Of the dozen coastal states thus highly favoured, more than half, such as the USA, the USSR, Canada, Great Britain, France (including the Dominions), Japan, New Zealand, and Australia are highly developed countries. The approximately thirty land-locked states, fourteen of which are in Africa, receive no benefit from the ocean space under their jurisdiction. But all states share the same rights and obligations in the remaining 60% of the ocean space: the high seas, the deep sea area, and its resources.

In light of these figures, can the Convention be justified in claiming to be an equitable result of the Conference?

The Conference was instructed to deal with the establishment of an equitable international regime for the deep sea-bed area and its resources and, *inter alia,* with questions of the continental shelf and fishing on the high seas, including the question of the preferential rights of the coastal states. In coming to the conclusion that the rights of coastal states should take priority over about 40% of the ocean space and that all states should have equal rights in the remaining 60%, the Conference has done nothing but fulfil its task. The question could also be considered in the context of the Charter of the United Nations of 1945, which in Chapter I,

Purpose and Principles of the United Nations, requires that friendly relations among nations be developed, based on respect for the principle of equal rights, and that international cooperation be achieved in solving international problems of an economic, social, cultural, or humanitarian character. By convening the Conference on the basis of equal rights for all states, the General Assembly adhered to the principles of the Charter.

Another question is whether the economic effects resulting from the Convention are in the interest of mankind as a whole and, in particular, of the developing countries, a major objective of Ambassador Arvid Pardo's proposals in 1967.

6. Major Objections to the Convention

During the last two years of the Conference, the United States took a new approach to the negotiations after Ronald Reagan became President. On July 9, 1982, he announced in a statement that the USA would not sign the Convention. Attempts before and after this statement to alter the Convention so as to gain the support of the United States remained unsuccessful. The key concern of the United States at that time was to ensure the access of its nationals to deep sea mining, to avoid any deterrence to mining, and to prevent the monopolization of the resources (Reference: Art. 150) by the operating arm of the Sea-Bed Authority. Otherwise, the regime of the deep sea would become an unrealistic dream, and its centralized and anti-free market provisions, a set of precedents for the use of enormous power by an international institution, would be uneconomical. Later, certain problem fields such as tuna fishing (Reference: Art. 64; Annex I) and the compulsory transfer of deep sea mining technology (Reference: Annex III, Art. 5, Subpara. 3(b)) were also criticized. Great Britain and West Germany also objected to the regime of deep sea mining and concluded an agreement with France and the United States concerning interim arrangements relating to polymetallic modules of the deep sea in September 1982.

7. A New Economic Order?

The Convention is often mentioned in conjunction with the expression "new international economic order." This expression emerged in the mid-1970s as a result of the oil shortage and resultant price increases in those years and was the subject of UN resolutions. The central theme was "interdependence" and focused on the relationship between industrialized and nonindustrialized countries. One important aspect was transfer of technology. This has found its way into the Convention with respect to mining technology in the Area, (Art. 144) the development of marine technology and, more generally, the transfer thereof, (Part XIV) such as the specific case of the transfer of technology for the prevention of pollution. (Art. 202) Some regulatory impact on the ore commodity market can also be expected from the power delegated to the Sea-Bed Authority. (Art. 150-153) Detractors of the Convention are suspicious that these measures contain elements creating precedents for a new economic doctrine undermining democratic capitalism and the principles upon which that system is based. These elements would be the pacing of the development of the resources of the seabed according to market demand, the monopolization of the resources, and a system of compulsory transfer of technology.

It is almost impossible to conduct a fruitful discussion of criticism which is based more on ideological grounds than on factual evidence. Except for the concept of the common heritage of mankind, the systems of 'deep-sea mining and transfer of technology are more in the nature of political programmers than they are concrete plans readily subject to analysis or even predictions of how the system will work in the future. Democratic capitalism is itself static in practice, and neither the basic requirement of the Convention to co-operate nor any specific regulations undermine any principle. A negative attitude towards co-operation could have a greater impact on principles than any regulation of the Convention. In actual fact, an increased awareness on the part of the world's population of the importance of the oceans would in many cases be of advantage for industrialized countries. And have these countries not already benefited from the concept of the exclusive economic zone and the "package" deal in general? Although countless prognoses can be made with respect to mining in the Area and the impact of such operations, any such predictions concerning the use of the oceans in future can be only speculative and cannot be presented as unavoidable. The oceans themselves remain mysterious, relentless, and the source of constant surprise for the imagination of humanity.

8. Provisions, for Entry into Force

The Convention was open for signature (Art. 305, Para. 1) from December 10, 1982 to December 9, 1984. (Art. 305, Para. 2) 119 states signed the Convention on the opening day for signature at Montego Bay/Jamaica. As of the closing day, a total of 155 states and the Cook Islands, the European Economic Community, Namibia, and Niue had signed. (Art. 305, Subpara. l(b-f)) As of 1987, the Convention had been ratified by more than thirty states and Namibia, represented by the United Nations Council for Namibia. (Art. 305, Subpara. 1(b)) The ratifying states come from the following regions: eight from Asia, sixteen from Africa, eight from Latin America, and two from Europe (Iceland and Yugoslavia).

The Convention does not enter into force until twelve months after the date of deposit of the sixtieth instrument of ratification or accession. (Art. 308, Para. 1) Depository is the Secretary-General of the United Nations, (Art. 319, Para. 1) who is also responsible for preparing and circulating reports on issues related to the Convention. (Art. 319, Para. 2)

9. The Importance of Having Signed the Convention

The signing of the Convention between 1982 and 1984 has two effects for the signatory states. First, the states are obligated not to act in a manner which would defeat the object and purpose of the Convention unless the state makes clear that it does not intend to become a party to the treaty. Second, the signatory states obtain the right to participate as full members in the Preparatory Commission for the International Sea-Bed Authority and for the International Tribunal for the Law of the Sea, and under certain circumstances may commence preparatory work for deep sea mining before the Convention enters into force. States which have signed only the Final Act may act as observers, but they are not entitled to participate in the taking of decisions. The Preparatory Commission was to begin work when fifty states had signed the Convention, which was already the case on December 10, 1982. The Commission has indeed taken up its work.

10. Practice of the States in Recent Years

The states' practice of claiming sovereign rights in zones of varying sizes continued throughout the sessions of the Conference and into the 1980s. Today almost all coastal states have established a territorial sea (Art. 3) of twelve nautical miles or more. The number of contiguous zones (Art. 33) established is significantly lower, but exact figures are difficult to obtain, as many of the claims do not adhere to the applicable provision of the Convention, (Ibid) either in terms of the extent of such a zone or of the rights granted therein. The trend of the 1960s to claim exclusive fishing rights beyond the territorial sea was forgotten in the rush to establish an exclusive economic zone (Art. 56, 57) of up to two hundred nautical miles. By the end of the Conference, about seventy claims of exclusive economic zones had been made, and this number grew to about eighty-five by 1985 (including about twenty claims by territories, etc.). Continental shelf claims rose sharply during the 1970s, but only a few have been made in the 1980s. The coastal states' right to a continental shelf off its coast exists *ipso facto* today (as undisputed international law), and is not dependent on proclamation or occupation. (Art. 77, Para. 3)

In summary, it can be said that the most beneficial aspects of the Convention, namely the establishment of rights for the coastal states, have already "entered" into force.

11. What is the Law of the Sea Today?

As the 1982 Convention has not yet entered into force, the reluctance of the United States and other countries to act constructively and the self-serving "enactments" by the coastal states have created a legal environment which can only be described as gloomy and falling far short of the goal of law to provide stability, predictability, and justice. This preliminary note must be kept in mind in order not to be misled by the following generalization

In principle, the law that is in force today on any particular issue related to the oceans is still basically derived from the four 1958 Conventions and customary international law. To a large extent, this law is now represented in the provisions of the 1982 Convention. In other words, the 1982 Convention has absorbed (for the most part) the four 1958 Conventions on the Law of the Sea and unwritten customary law. The provisions which are not identical with the pre-1982 Conventions on the Law of the Sea, but which are practiced by the states, may become customary law, while other provisions of the 1982 Convention not practiced would only become applicable when the Convention enters into force. Day-to-day practice will not highlight any differences, and the 1982 Convention will be seen as representing the law of the sea. Thus the 1982 Convention serves as an excellent guideline to the regime of the law of the sea, but in any particular case it will continue to be necessary to weigh circumstances carefully in order to decide which source of law applies. In addition, the Convention contains new law fields, such as the deep-sea Area (Part XI), marine scientific research (Part XIII), development and transfer of technology (Part XIV), and settlement of disputes (Part XV). Some of these new regulations may have some impact on what is or what becomes international law, even prior to entry into force of the Convention.

The uncertainty for the field of the law of the sea will last until the Convention enters into force and is widely accepted.

12. The Future of the Convention

A reliable prediction of the significance of the Convention in the future cannot be expected at this point - but consideration of certain basic factors may indicate the probable direction events will take.

International conventions never enter into force until a certain period of time has passed, and experience in the last four decades has shown that the period needed today will be three or four times that required in the 1950s, if not even longer. The nations of the world can be expected to take a particularly long time with the 1982 Convention as it does not contain simple, straightforward technical regulations nor concern only one subject; instead, it is a unique and comprehensive law, with potentially far-reaching consequences for a broad range of subjects. Most of the coastal states which do not belong to the ten or so traditional shipping or fishing nations have only recently begun to think about making use of their "maritime rights", having previously had neither a reliable infrastructure nor the necessary means and knowledge of marine science to enable them to project the implications of the Convention or judge what effect its obligations would have on them, much less put it into practice. As there is presently no economic pressure to commence deep sea-bed mining, there will be quite a wait until the Convention enters into force.

The ratification process - as of this date (early 1988), slightly more than half of the required sixty instruments of ratification or accession have been deposited - will undoubtedly continue, and one day the Convention will formally enter into force. The more important question, however, is whether the Convention will be universally accepted.

The answer to this question depends on the attitude of the superpowers, particularly the United States, and the further development of political circumstances. The attitudes of the superpowers will have an immediate effect on their allies, with the result that larger groups of states may refuse to accept the Convention. If, however, only one of the superpowers withholds its acceptance, this state will more likely find itself increasingly isolated.

Other political circumstances or practices, such as ratification by groups (e.g., Group 77), incidents which occur during passage through straits, enforcement of coastal state laws in excess of the regulations of the Convention, economic recession, and military tensions, will favourably or adversely affect the implementation process or the position of the Convention. Indifference might also slow down the decision-making progress for a certain period of time, but a complete and final stop will not be possible, as the growing uncertainty and instability in legal, economical, and political matters concerning the oceans, already predictable, will continue to push the issue onto the order of business. It is already obvious that the 1982 Convention, whatever direction developments of the future take, has become an established guide for political, technical, and legal matters involving the oceans, and it will become obsolete only when it is replaced by its successor.

D. RATIFICATION AND SIGNATURE
Status of the 1982 UN Convention on the Law of the Sea and the Agreement Relating to the Implementation of Part XI of the Convention

The Table recapitulates the status of the Convention and Agreement as per January 2005[1] without indicating type of acceptance (e.g. by ratification; formal conformation, accession; succession), but whether the document has been signed (**X**) or any declaration or statement (**O**) has been made.

UN Convention on the Law of the Sea		State or Entity	Agreement relating to the Implementation of Part XI	
In force as from 16 November 1994			In force as from 28 July 1996	
	Bound by Ratification etc	X – Signature O – Declaration or Statement		Bound by Ratification etc
X		Afghanistan		
	23 June 2003	Albania		23 June 2003
O	11 June 1996	Algeria	X	11 June 1996
		Andorra		
O	5 December 1990	Angola		
X	2 February 1989	Antigua and Barbuda		
	1 December 1995	Argentina	X	1 December 1995
	9 December 2002	Armenia		9 December 2002
X	5 October 1994	Australia	X	5 October 1994
X	14 July 1995	Austria	X	14 July 1995
		Azerbaijan		
X	29 July 1983	Bahamas	X	28 July 1983
X	30 May 1985	Bahrain		
X	27 July 2001	Bangladesh		27 July 2001
X	12 October 1993	Barbados	X	28 July 1995
O		Belarus		
O	13 November 1998	Belgium	X	13 November 1998
X	13 August 1983	Belize		21 October 1994
X	16 October 1997	Benin		16 October 1997
X		Bhutan		
O	28 April 1995	Bolivia		28 April 1995
	12 January 1994	Bosnian and Herzegovina		
X	2 May 1990	Botswana		31 January 2005
O	22 December 1988	Brazil	X	
X	5 November 1996	Brunei Darussalam		5 November 1996
X	15 May 1996	Bulgaria		15 May 1996
X	25 January 2005	Burkina Faso	X	25 January 2005
X		Burundi		
X		Cambodia		
X	19 November 1985	Cameroon	X	28 August 2002
X	7 November 2003	Canada	X	7 November 2003
O	10 August 1987	Cape Verde	X	
X		Central African Republic		
X		Chad		
O	25 August 1997	Chile		25 August 1997
X	7 June 1996	China	X	7 June 1996
X		Colombia	O	
X	21 June 1994	Comoros		

---

[1] Source: UN Division for Ocean Affairs and the Law of the Sea. For more details consult: http://www.un.org/Depts/los/reference_files/chronological_lists_of_ratifications.htm

UN Convention on the Law of the Sea		State or Entity	Agreement relating to the Implementation of Part XI	
	Bound by Ratification etc	X – Signature O – Declaration or Statement		Bound by Ratification etc
X		Congo		
X	15 February 1995	Cook Islands		15 February 1995
O	21 September 1992	Costa Rica		20 September 2001
X	26 March 1984	Côte d'Ivoire	X	28 July 1995
	5 April 1995	Croatia		5 April 1995
O	15 August 1984	Cuba		17 October 2002
X	12 December 1988	Cyprus	X	27 July 1995
X	21 June 1996	Czech Republic	X	21 June 1996
X		Democratic People's Republic of Korea		
X	17 February 1989	Democratic Republic of the Congo		
X	16 November 2004	Denmark	X	16 November 2004
X	8 October 1991	Djibouti		
X	24 October 1991	Dominica		
X		Dominican Republic		
		Ecuador		
X	26 August 1983	Egypt	X	
X		El Salvador		
X	21 July 1997	Equatorial Guinea		21 July 1997
		Eritrea		
		Estonia		
X		Ethiopia		
O	1 April 1998	European Community	O	1 April 1998
X	10 December 1982	Fiji	X	28 July 1995
O	21 June 1996	Finland	X	21 June 1996
O	11 April 1996	France	O	11 April 1996
X	11 March 1998	Gabon	X	11 March 1998
X	22 May 1984	Gambia		
	21 March 1996	Georgia		21 March 1996
	14 October 1994	Germany	X	14 October 1994
X	7 June 1983	Ghana		
O	21 July 1995	Greece	X	21 July 1995
X	25 April 1991	Grenada	X	28 July 1995
X	11 February 1997	Guatemala		11 February 1997
O	6 September 1985	Guinea	X	28 July 1995
X	25 August 1986	Guinea-Bissau		
X	16 November 1993	Guyana		
X	31 July 1996	Haiti		31 July 1996
		Holy See		
X	5 October 1993	Honduras		28 July 2003
X	5 February 2002	Hungary		5 February 2002
X	21 June 1985	Iceland	X	28 July 1995
X	29 June 1995	India	X	29 June 1995
X	3 February 1986	Indonesia	X	2 June 2000
O		Iran (Islamic Republic of)		
O	30 July 1985	Iraq		
X	21 June 1996	Ireland	X	21 June 1996
		Israel		
O	13 January 1995	Italy	X	13 January 1995
X	21 March 1983	Jamaica	X	28 July 1995
X	20 June 1996	Japan	X	20 June 1996
	27 November 1995	Jordan		27 November 1995
		Kazakhstan		
X	2 March 1989	Kenya		29 July 1994

UN Convention on the Law of the Sea		State or Entity	Agreement relating to the Implementation of Part XI	
	Bound by Ratification etc	X – Signature O – Declaration or Statement		**Bound by Ratification etc**
	24 February 2003	Kiribati		24 February 2003
X	2 May 1986	Kuwait		2 August 2002
		Kyrgyzstan		
X	5 June 1998	Lao People's Democratic Republic	X	5 June 1998
	23 December 2004	Latvia		23 December 2004
X	5 January 1995	Lebanon		5 January 1995
X		Lesotho		
X		Liberia		
X		Libyan Arab Jamahiriya		
X		Lichtenstein		
	12 November 2003	Lithuania		12 November 2003
O	5 October 2000	Luxembourg	X	5 October 2000
X	22 August 2001	Madagascar		22 August 2001
X		Malawi		
X	14 October 1996	Malaysia	X	14 October 1996
X	7 September 2000	Maldives	X	7 September 2000
O	16 July 1985	Mali		
X	20 May 1993	Malta	X	26 June 1996
	9 August 1991	Marshall Islands		
X	17 July 1996	Mauritania	X	17 July 1996
X	4 November 1994	Mauritius		4 November 1994
X	18 March 1983	Mexico		10 April 2003
	29 April 1991	Micronesia (Federated States of)	X	6 September 1995
X	20 March 1996	Monaco	X	20 March 1996
X	13 August 1996	Mongolia	X	13 August 1996
X		Morocco	X	
X	13 March 1997	Mozambique		13 March 1997
X	21 May 1996	Myanmar		21 May 1996
X	18 April 1983	Namibia	X	28 July 1995
X	23 January 1996	Nauru		23 January 1996
X	2 November 1998	Nepal		2 November 1998
X	28 June 1996	Netherlands	O	28 June 1996
X	19 July 1996	New Zealand	X	19 July 1996
O	3 May 2000	Nicaragua		3 May 2000
X		Niger		
X	14 August 1986	Nigeria	X	28 July 1995
X		Niue		
X	24 June 1996	Norway		24 June 1996
O	17 August 1989	Oman		26 February 1997
X	26 February 1997	Pakistan	X	26 February 1997
	30 September 1996	Palau		30 September 1996
X	1 July 1996	Panama		1 July 1996
X	14 January 1997	Papa New Guinea		14 January 1997
X	26 September 1986	Paraguay	X	10 July 1995
		Peru		
O	8 May 1984	Philippines	X	23 July 1997
X	13 November 1998	Poland	X	13 November 1998
X	3 November 1997	Portugal	X	3 November 1997
O	9 December 2002	Qatar		9 December 2002
X	29 January 1996	Republic of Korea	X	29 January 1996
		Republic of Moldova		
X	17 December 1996	Romania		17 December 1996

UN Convention on the Law of the Sea		State or Entity	Agreement relating to the Implementation of Part XI	
	Bound by Ratification etc	X – Signature O – Declaration or Statement		Bound by Ratification etc
O	12 March 1997	Russian Federation		12 March 1997
X		Rwanda		
X	7 January 1993	Saint Kitts and Nevis		
X	27 March 1985	Saint Lucia		
X	1 October 1993	Saint Vincent and the Grenadines		
X	14 August 1995	Samoa	X	14 August 1995
		San Marino		
O	3 November 1987	Sao Tome and Principe		
X	24 April 1996	Saudi Arabia		24 April 1996
X	25 October 1984	Senegal	X	25 July 1996
	12 March 2001	Serbia and Montenegro	X	28 July 1995
X	16 September 1991	Seychelles	X	15 December 1994
X	12 December 1994	Sierra Leone		12 December 1994
X	17 November 1994	Singapore		17 November 1994
X	8 May 1996	Slovakia	X	8 May 1996
	16 June 1995	Slovenia	X	16 June 1995
X	23 June 1997	Salomon Islands		23 June 1997
X	24 July 1989	Somalia		
O	23 December 1997	South Africa	X	23 December 1997
O	15 January 1997	Spain	X	15 January 1997
X	19 July 1994	Sri Lanka	X	28 July 1995
O	23 January 1985	Sudan	X	
X	9 July 1998	Suriname		9 July 1998
X		Swaziland	X	
O	25 June 1996	Sweden	X	25 June 1996
X		Switzerland	X	
		Syria Arab Republic		
		Tajikistan		
X		Thailand		
	19 August 1994	The former Yugoslav Republic of Macedonia		19 August 1994
		Timor-Leste		
X	16 April 1985	Togo	X	28 July 1995
	2 August 1995	Tonga		2 August 1995
X	25 April 1986	Trinidad and Tabago	X	28 July 1995
X	24 April 1985	Tunisia	X	24 May 2002
		Turkey		
		Turkmenistan		
X	9 December 2002	Tuvalu		9 December 2002
X	9 November 1990	Uganda	X	28 July 1995
O	26 July 1999	Ukraine	X	26 July 1999
X		United Arab Emirates		
	25 July 1997	United Kingdom	X	25 July 1997
X	30 September 1985	United Republic of Tanzania	X	25 June 1998
		United States of America	X	
O	10 December 1992	Uruguay	O	
		Uzbekistan		
X	10 August 1999	Vanuatu	X	10 August 1999
		Venezuela (Bolivarian Republic of)		
X	25 July 1994	Viet Nam		
O	21 July 1987	Yemen		
X	7 March 1983	Zambia	X	28 July 1995
X	24 February 1993	Zimbabwe	X	28 July 1995
157 (35)	148	TOTALS - January 2005 -	79 (5)	121

Bernaerts' Guide to the Law of The Sea

Guide to the Convention

PREAMBLE

The significance of the Convention's opening statement, in addition to heightening the solemn character of the following document, can be found in its expression of the Conference's purposes, aims, desires, and beliefs which motivated the participating nations to conclude the agreement. The Preamble does not impose direct obligations on the states parties; but by showing the political, historical, and ideological context of the treaty, it imposes a certain obligation to interpret the treaty in good faith, in accordance with the ordinary meaning of the terms, and in the light of the object and purpose of the Convention.

The Conference itself was aware of the historic significance of and the need for a new and generally accepted Convention which would settle all issues of the law of the sea and hoped that the present effort would be a contribution to the maintenance of peace, justice, and progress for all peoples of the world. The Conference refers to the resolution of the General Assembly of the United Nations of December 17, 1970
[1] that

> "the area of the sea-bed and ocean floor and the subsoil thereof, beyond the limits of national jurisdiction, as well as its resources, are the common heritage of mankind, the exploration and exploitation of which shall be carried out for the benefit of mankind as a whole, irrespective of the geographical location of States."

Furthermore, the Conference recognized the desirability of establishing through the Convention a legal order for the seas and oceans which would facilitate international communication and promote the peaceful uses of the seas and oceans, aiding the equitable and efficient utilization as well as protection of living resources and the protection and preservation of the marine environment. If these goals could be achieved, the realization of a just and equitable international economic order would be a step closer to reality, and the Convention would contribute to the strengthening of peace, security, co-operation, and friendly relations among all nations and promote the economic and social advancement of all peoples of the world in accordance with the Purposes and Principles of the United Nations as set forth in the Charter.

The final paragraph of the Preamble states that matters not regulated by the Convention continue to be governed by rules and principles of general international law.

INTRODUCTION (DEFINITIONS)

The Introduction[2] defines several important, recurring terms. For the purposes of the Convention, the following definitions apply for the length of the document:
"Area" - Article 1, Subparagraph 1(1)
"Area" means the sea-bed and ocean floor and subsoil thereof, beyond the limits of national jurisdiction[3] The regime of the Area is subject to Part XI.
"Authority" - Article 1, Subparagraph 1(2)
"Authority" means the International Sea-Bed Authority, whose structure, rights, and duties are regulated at length in Part XI.[4]
"Activities in the Area" - Article 1, Subparagraph 1(3)"Activities in the Area" means all activities of exploration for, and exploitation of, resources in the Area. Resources are all solid, liquid, or gaseous

---

[1] See Preamble
[2] Art.1
[3] Art. 134, 56,76
[4] Art. 156-186
[5] Art. 133
[6] Reference: Part XII

Further readings: - Reference to Peaceful Uses of the Sea (Layot), Page 79
 - The Unification of the Law of Sea, Page 130
 - Equality – Equal Rights for All? Page 11

mineral resources *in situ* in the Area at or beneath the sea-bed, including polymetallic nodules[5]
"Pollution and Dumping" - Article 1, Subparagraphs 1(4) and 1(5)
These two terms are defined in considerably more detail, even at this early point. In short, pollution is the introduction of substances or energy by man into the marine environment and which may be a danger for the environment[6]. In summary, dumping means the deliberate disposal of waste, unless it is incidental to or derived from the normal operation of man-made devices or is placed for purposes other than mere disposal, provided this is not contrary to the aims of the Convention[1].
"States Parties" - Article 1, Paragraph 2
When the Convention refers to States Parties, it means all States and certain other entities (e.g., territories, international organizations)[2] for whom the Convention is internationally binding and in force.

---

[1] Reference: Art. 210, 216
[2] Art. 305, Para. 1; Annex IX

SIGNIFICANT CONTENT OF THE PREAMBLE

In accordance with the resolution of December 17, 1970, of the General Assembly of the United Nations which proclaims the resources of the seabed beyond national jurisdiction to be
– the common heritage of mankind –
the Convention's aims are to take the interests and need of mankind as a whole into account.

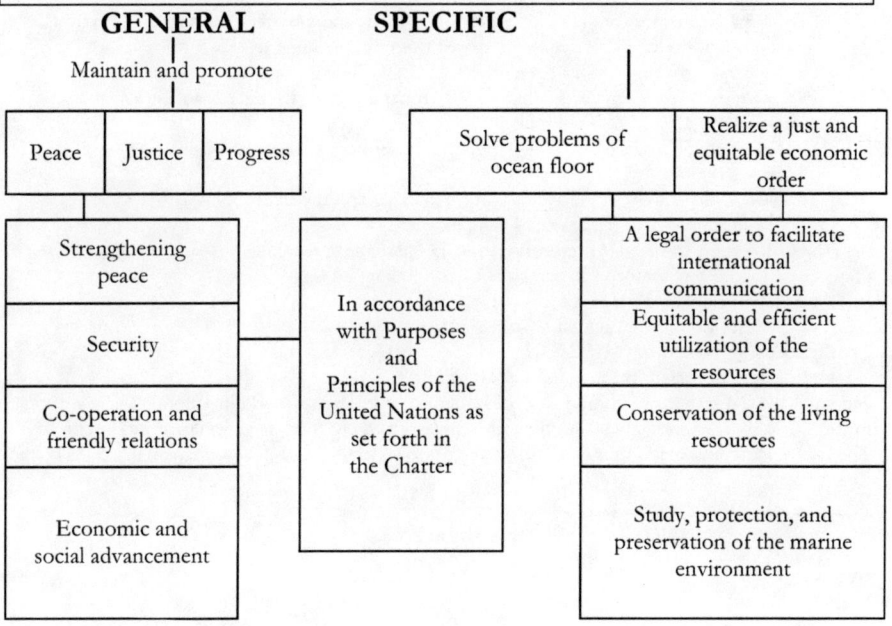

THE LEGAL STATUS OF THE TERRITORIAL SEA

The actions of states, whether on a national or an international scale, are based on the principle of sovereignty. When two or more sovereign subjects of international law meet, questions of jurisdiction arise, i.e., who has the right and obligation to act. The main purpose of the Convention is to define and regulate such questions relevant to the sea. A central point in this respect concerns how far from the coast the influence of a coastal state extends.

For the average person, the sea begins at the beach, the coastline of the mainland, where realization that another world begins is unavoidable: a different environment of wind, waves, tides, special means of communications, fishing, and so on. This perception of the sea is almost identical with that part of the planet which the Convention seeks to regulate. However, the Convention does not necessarily see the natural coastline as the limit of the sea; instead, an artificial line, the baseline, is drawn, as will be described in the next section. Within this artificial line all water areas (which are known as internal waters), the mainland, and islands are not subject to the Convention, and the state can exercise its sovereignty as provided elsewhere in international law. Adjacent to this baseline is a belt of sea known as the territorial sea, which falls within the area governed by the Convention. Every state can establish a territorial sea with a maximum breadth of twelve nautical miles, measured from the baseline[1]. Nonetheless, the importance of the Convention for this area is somewhat lessened by the fact that the Convention itself declares that the sovereignty of the coastal state extends over the territorial sea, including the air space over the sea as well as its bed and subsoil[2]. This also applies to archipelagic waters[3]. The sovereignty of a coastal state as well as that of an archipelagic state[4] is limited only by the fact that this sovereignty must be exercised in accordance with the Convention and with international law[5]. However, the Convention retains precedence with respect to matters of navigation which are of considerable importance:

(1) Technical regulations for drawing the artificial baseline and extending the territorial sea by a maximum of twelve nautical miles measured from the baseline (Articles 3-16);

(2) Passage through the territorial sea (Articles 17-32), including suspension of navigation in certain areas (Article 25, Paragraph 3); Safety zones around scientific research installations (Article 260);

(3) Passage through straits (Articles 34-45); using the territorial sea of states bordering the strait (Article 37)

(4) Passage through archipelagic waters (Article 2, Paragraph 1; Articles 52-54);

(5) Pollution from vessels (Articles 194, Subparagraph 3(b), 211, 217-234).

The Convention also retains precedence in pollution matters, requiring states parties to protect and preserve the marine environment[6] in particular by controlling

(1) Pollution from land-based sources (Article 207),

(2) Pollution from sea-bed activities (Article 208),

(3) Pollution by dumping (Article 209), and

(4) Pollution from and "through the air (Article 210),

and holds the coastal state responsible for the fulfilment of its international obligations[7]. There are some further regulations imposing limits on the state's sovereignty, but they are generally of less importance[8]. The Convention jurisdiction thus described is subject to compulsory dispute settlement provided by the Convention[9].

---

[1] Art. 3
[2] Art. 2, Para. 1&2
[3] Art.2; 49, Para.1
[4] Part IV
[5] Art.2, Para.3
[6] Art. 192, 194
[7] Art. 235
[8] e.g., Art. 131; 258
[9] Art. 297, Para. 1

Further Readings: - Territorial Sea, Page 112
- Internal Waters, 'Historic Bays' and Ports, Page 111
- The Reasons for International Maritime Conflicts, Page 2
- The I and II UN Conferences on the Law of the Sea, Page 4

THE RIGHTS OF FOREIGN NATIONALS IN INTERNAL WATERS AND THE TERRITORIAL SEA

NB: For vessels the flag state is in general obliged
- to exercise its jurisdiction and control in administrative, technical, and social matters (Article 94), and
- to ensure compliance with international pollution standards (Articles 211, 217).

ACTIVITY	INTERNAL WATERS	TERRITORIAL SEA
Navigation	Convention not applicable except where establishment of baseline encloses new internal waters (Article 8, Paragraph 2)	Convention applicable with regard to - Innocent passage of merchant vessels (Articles 17-28) - Innocent passage of warships (Articles 17-26, 29-32)
Overflight	Convention not applicable	Convention not applicable
Fishing	Convention not applicable	Convention not applicable
Scientific Research	Convention not applicable	Consent of coastal state required; conducted on conditions set by coastal state (Article 245)
Laying submarine cable	Convention not applicable	Convention not applicable
Mining	Convention not applicable	Convention not applicable
Imposition of environmental legislation	Convention not applicable	Only by coastal state (Article 21, 192 and following); must not hamper innocent passage (Article 211, Paragraph 4); 220 (2); Warships (Article 236)

THE BASELINE

The baseline is an artificial line from which zones of jurisdiction as provided by the Convention – territorial sea[1], contiguous zone[2], exclusive economic zone[3], and continental shelf[4]- are measured. The coastal state itself has to determine the baseline, which must then be shown on charts or defined by adequate geographical co-ordinates and given adequate publicity[5]. Particular care must be taken where the establishment of the baseline could have an effect on the rights of a state with an opposite or adjacent coast[6]; however, it should be noted that a state can declare its non-acceptance of dispute settlement procedures for disputes arising from the delimitation of sea boundaries[7]. The baseline can be determined by applying the technical provisions of the Convention in three steps:

First Step: The normal baseline is the low-water line along the coast[8] or, in the case of an island or atoll, the seaward low-water line of any reef[9] for delimiting the territorial sea, the outermost permanent harbour works which form an integral part of the harbour system are regarded as forming part of the coast[10];

Second Step: Certain appropriate outmost points and marks such as
- low-tide elevations no further than twelve nautical miles from the mainland[11]
- low-tide elevations upon which installations which are permanently above sea-level (e.g., lighthouses) have been built[12], even where the installations are more than twelve nautical miles from the mainland,
- mouths of rivers[13],
- low-water marks of the natural entrance points of bays if the distance between such marks does not exceed twenty-four nautical miles (except in cases of so-called historic bays)[14] and
- appropriate points along a deeply indented coastline or a fringe of islands close to the coast[15] can be used for establishing the baseline.

Third Step: The following significant circumstances must be taken into account:
- Roadsteads used for shipping and which would otherwise be wholly or partly outside the territorial sea are part of the same;
- low-water elevations without permanent installations[16] beyond the breadth of the territorial sea have no territorial sea of their own;
- islands have their own territorial sea[17]
- off-shore installations and artificial islands do not possess the status of islands and do not have any effect on the establishment of the baseline[18].

The coastal state is to deposit charts or lists showing the baseline with the Secretary-General of the United Nations[19].

---

[1] Art. 3
[2] Art. 33
[3] Art. 57
[4] Art. 76
[5] Art. 16
[6] Art. 15
[7] Art. 298, Subrapa. 1 (a)

[8] Art. 5
[9] Art. 6
[10] Art. 11
[11] Art. 13, Para.1
[12] Art. 7, Para. 4
[13] Art. 9
[14] Art. 10 (Art. 10, Para. 6)

[15] Art. 7 , Para. 1;Art12
[16] Art. 7, Para. 4, Art. 13
[17] Art. 121, Para. 2 indirectly also Art. 6, Art. 13, Para. 2
[18] Art. 11; Art. 60, Para. 8; Art. 80; Art. 147, Subpara. 2 (e); Art. 259
[19] Art. 16, Para. 2

Further Readings: - Internal Waters, Historic Bays and Ports. Page 111

Bernaerts' Guide to the Law of The Sea

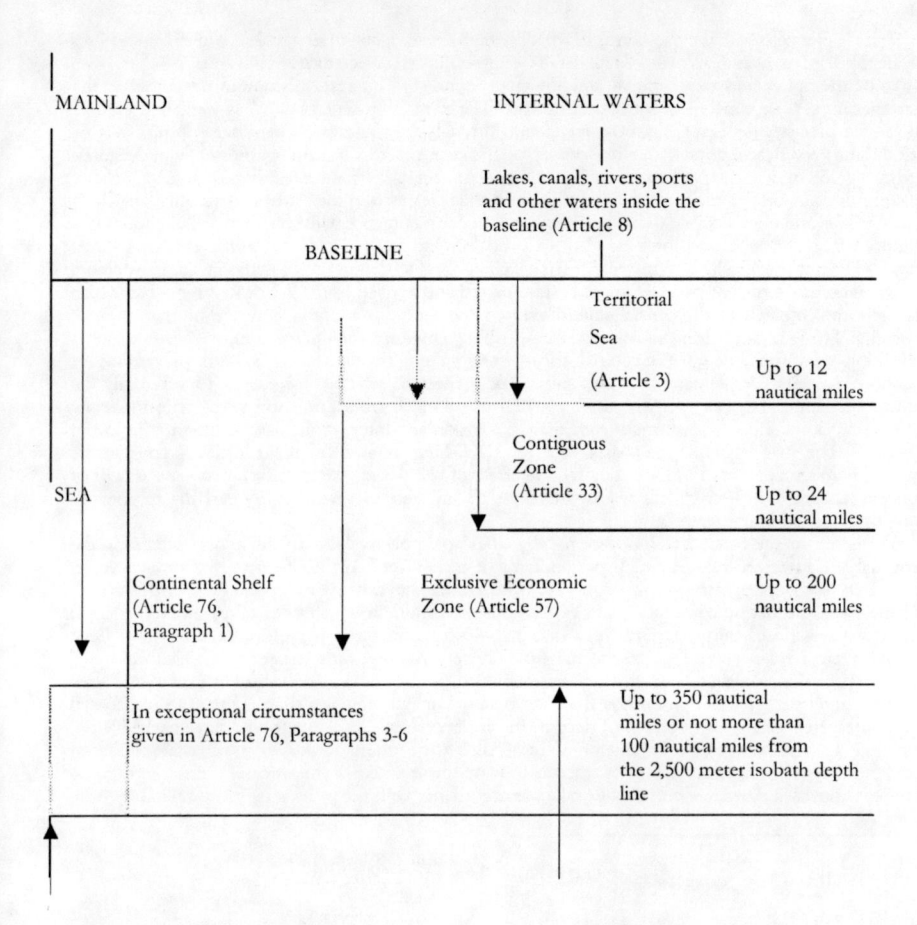

IMPORTANCE OF THE BASELINE

MAINLAND | INTERNAL WATERS

Lakes, canals, rivers, ports and other waters inside the baseline (Article 8)

BASELINE

Territorial Sea (Article 3) — Up to 12 nautical miles

Contiguous Zone (Article 33) — Up to 24 nautical miles

SEA

Continental Shelf (Article 76, Paragraph 1) | Exclusive Economic Zone (Article 57) — Up to 200 nautical miles

In exceptional circumstances given in Article 76, Paragraphs 3-6 | Up to 350 nautical miles or not more than 100 nautical miles from the 2,500 meter isobath depth line

AREA (Article 1, Paragraph 1; Article 134, Paragraph 3)
- The Area starts where the jurisdiction of the coastal state over the continental shelf ends (Article 76)
- The Area beyond 200 nautical miles is subject to contributions to the Sea-Bed Authority (Article 82)

HIGH SEAS (Article 86)
- If an exclusive economic zone is established, the high seas start at the outer limits of this zone (Article 86)
- otherwise, they begin from the outer limits of the territorial sea (Article 86)
- A contiguous zone alone does not affect the status as high seas

PASSAGE THROUGH THE TERRITORIAL SEA

This chapter deals with the question as to what extent the sovereignty[1] of a coastal state in its territorial sea may be restricted or set aside to permit unhindered passage of foreign vessels through this zone.

In its attempt to find an acceptable solution to the conflict of interests inherent in this question, the Convention uses the concept of innocent passage[2]. The term "innocent passage" is vaguely described rather than precisely defined. Transitory navigation through the territorial sea -passage[3] - must not be prejudicial to the peace, good order or security of the coastal state[4]. A catalogue of activities[5] can be used as a guide in determing whether passage is innocent or not. With the exception of a general clause which reads, "any other activity not having a direct bearing on passage[6] the clauses cover activities which pose a serious and unacceptable threat to the coastal state (e.g., practice with weapons, wilful and serious pollution). The general clause must be read with this in mind and applied only in the case of a threat which, while not specifically listed, would be of a weight equal to that of the activities given. In addition, the general term "innocent passage" must be interpreted and applied in the light of national law which has been implemented by the coastal state. Every coastal state can adopt laws regarding the safety of navigation, laying of submarine cables, resources, fishing, environmental protection, scientific research, prevention of infringement of customs, fiscal, immigration, or sanitary laws[7] and prevention of pollution[8] as well as implement sea lanes and traffic separation schemes[9] or suspend temporarily the right of innocent passage in specified areas of its territorial sea[10], subject only to the restriction that any such measures must be in conformity with the Convention and international law relating to "innocent passage"[11]. The sovereignty of the coastal state in establishing law is also limited to the extent that the imposed requirements may not have the practical effect of hampering, denying, or impairing the right of innocent passage[12] or discriminate against the ships of any state or against ship's carrying cargoes to, from, or on behalf of any state[13].

Furthermore, the concept of innocent passage does not apply to ships which are only present in the territorial sea, however innocent such presence might be. As the term itself states, the foreign vessel must be in passage, i.e., in transit through the territorial sea between any two points not in this zone[14] and the passage must be continuous and expeditious[15] a condition which does not, however, exclude stops for navigational purposes and other acceptable reasons[16]. Even if these conditions have been fulfilled, there remain exceptions to the right of innocent passage with respect to criminal and civil jurisdiction of the coastal state on foreign vessels, which can be summarized as follows: a coastal state may not exercise its jurisdiction on board a foreign vessel unless there is a serious threat to the coastal state[17], measures for the suppression of drug traffic are necessary[18], requests for aid have been made[19], or there is a particular situation in which the vessel has left the internal waters of the coastal state[20] and is still in the territorial sea and action by the coastal state is warranted[21]. If the vessel cannot be stopped in the territorial sea, further action may be taken in accordance with the provisions for hot pursuit[22]

---

[1] Art. 2
[2] Art. 17; Part II, Sec. 3
[3] Art. 18
[4] Art. 19, Para. 1
[5] Art. 19, Subpara. 2 (a-1)
[6] Art. 19, Subpara. 2 (1)
[7] Art. 21
[8] Ibid; Art. 211, Para. 4

[9] Art. 22
[10] Art. 25, Para.3
[11] Art. 21, Para 1
[12] Art. 24, Subpara. 1 (a)
[13] Art. 24, Subpara. 1 (b)
[14] Art. 18, Para. 1
[15] Art. 18, Para. 2
[16] Art. 18, Para 2

[17] Art. 27 Subpara. 1(a-b) (Art. 27, Para. 5; Art. 73; Art. 220)
[18] Art. 27, Subpara. 1 (d)
[19] Art. 27, Subpara. 1 (c)
[20] Art. 27, Para.2; Art. 28, Para. 3;
[21] Ibid
[22] Art. 111

Further Readings:
- Navigation, Page 119
- Military Use, Page 124

IMPORTANCE OF THE CONCEPT "INNOCENT PASSAGE"

SOVEREIGNTY OF THE COASTAL STATE (Article 2)	RIGHT OF INNOCENT PASSAGE (Article 17)
First Restriction The coastal state may only adopt laws as given in Article 21 *Second Restriction* The coastal state may not regulate the design, construction, manning, or equipment of foreign vessels (Article 21, Paragraph 2), but may implement other pollution measures (Article 194, Subparagraph 3(b) *Third Restriction* Coastal state is to make public all applicable laws (Article 21, Paragraph 3) and any dangers to navigation (Article 24, Paragraph 2) *Fourth Restriction* Regulations may not be adopted for the purpose of or have the effect of hampering innocent passage (Article 24, Subparagraph 1(a)); 214 (4). *Fifth Restriction* Coastal state is to abstain - in form or fact – from discriminatory measures against any ship (Article 24, Subparagraph 1(b)) *Sixth "Restriction* Coastal state may exercise its jurisdiction in criminal and civil cases only as specified in Articles 27 and 28; see also 220(2). *Seventh Restriction* Charges may not be levied by reason only of passage (Article 26, Paragraph 1) *Eighth Restriction* - Warships and other government non commercial vessels are immune (Article 32) - Coastal state required to allow these vessels passage if they comply with law and regulations of coastal state (Article 30) - If laws and regulations disregarded by these vessels, coastal state must request compliance before acting (Article 30)	*First Restriction* Vessel must be in passage, continuous and expeditious (Article 18) *Second Restriction* A certain number of activities and activities not having a direct bearing on passage are not regarded as innocent (Article 19) *Third Restriction* Coastal statp may adopt regulations in the areas enumerated in Article 21 (Article 211, Paragraph 4, Pollution; Article 260, Safety Zones) *Fourth Restriction* Coastal state may establish sea lanes and traffic . separation schemes (Article 22) *Fifth Restriction* Nuclear-powered ships and ships carrying dangerous materials must carry documents and take established precautions (Article 23) *Sixth Restriction* Temporary suspension of passage in specific areas must be accepted (Article 25,Paragraph 3) *Seventh Restriction* Coastal state may prevent passage which is not innocent (Article 25, Paragraph 1); may prevent breach of conditions for admission to its internal yaters (Article 25, Paragraph 2) *Eighth Restriction* Arrest and investigation can take place as specified in Articles 27 and 28 (e.g., Art, 73: 220) *Ninth Restriction* Charges may be levied for specific services rendered (Art 26, Paragraph 2) *Tenth Restriction* Submarines must navigate on surface and show flag (Article 20) *Eleventh Restriction* Warships, etc., must upon request of coastal state leave territorial sea immediately - if they do not comply with laws and Regulations - and have been requested to do so (Article 30)

THE CONTIGUOUS ZONE

By means of a formal proclamation made public to the international community, a coastal state may establish a zone contiguous to the territorial sea and extending a maximum of twenty-four nautical miles from the baseline.[1] Consequently, the breadth of the contiguous zone itself depends on the distance proclaimed and on the breadth of the territorial sea. If the territorial sea of the coastal state has the maximum breadth of twelve nautical miles[2], then the contiguous zone can have a maximum breadth of only twelve nautical miles.

The contiguous zone enjoys independent legal status only as long as the coastal state has not proclaimed an exclusive economic zone[3] exceeding the outer limits of the contiguous zone. If an exclusive economic zone is established, it begins beyond and adjacent to the territorial sea[4], with the resultant effect that the contiguous zone becomes a part of the exclusive economic zone, and all provisions which apply to the latter also apply completely and fully (as there are no exceptions) in the contiguous zone. The principle of freedom of navigation applies in this zone as well as elsewhere[5] outside the territorial sea, but other states are to have due regard for the rights of the coastal state in the exclusive economic zone and to comply with its laws and regulations[6].

The rights derived from this provision are of two types: "prevention"[7] and "extended power"[8]. Rights of "prevention" mean that the coastal state exercises police force limited to "control" necessary to prevent infringements of customs, fiscal, immigration, or sanitary laws in the territorial sea or territory of the coastal state, including boarding and searching and even prohibiting the foreign vessel from entering the territorial sea. If there is no such infringement, the coastal state has no further rights. "Extended power" to apply national criminal law goes into effect if there has been an infringement of the laws listed above within the territory or territorial sea of the coastal state. In many instances of such infringements, coastal states would also be able to exercise the right of hot pursuit.[9] There seems to be hardly any need for the concept of a contiguous zone, particularly now that the territorial sea has been extended from three to twelve nautical miles.

Finally, it is worthy of mention that the Convention unexpectedly and rather curiously grants' special status to the contiguous zone in one other area: in order to control traffic in historical and archaeological objects, the coastal state may presume that the removal of any such objects from the contiguous zone without the state's approval would violate the laws mentioned in Article 33, and the state may act accordingly.[10] The law of salvage and other international rules and agreements remain unaffected[11].

---

[1] Art. 33, Para. 2; Art. 5-14
[2] Art. 3
[3] Art. 57
[4] Art. 55
[5] Art. 58, 87
[6] Art. 58, Para. 3
[7] Art. 33, Subpara. 1 (a)
[8] Art. 33, Subpara. 1 (b)
[9] Art. 111
[10] Art. 303, Para. 2
[11] Art. 303, Para. 3-4

Further Readings: - Contiguous Zone, Page 112
    - Archaeological and Historical Objects, Page 124

THE CONTIGUOUS ZONE

Within the contiguous zone, the coastal state is invested with the power
- to prevent infringement of its customs, fiscal, immigration, or sanitary laws and regulations within its territory or territorial sea (Article 33, Subparagraph 1(a));
- to punish infringement of the above laws and regulations committed within its territory or territorial sea (Article 33, Subparagraph 1(b)).

Activity	Rights of Foreign Nationals in the Contiguous Zone
Navigation	Full navigation rights if compatible with Convention (Articles 58, Paragraph 1, and 87; 58, Paragraph 2, and 88-115) Restricted by Article 33 (see above) in, general only; boarding and search by coastal state only to prevent and punish infringement of specific coastal state laws Removal of historical and archaeological objects only with approval of coastal state (Article 303, Paragraph 2)
Over-flight	Full rights of over-flight
Fishing	No rights after establishment of exclusive economic zone (Exceptions: Article 62, Paragraph 2)
Scientific Research	Consent of coastal state is required when economic zone has been established (Article 246)
Laying of Cable	Full rights (Article 58, 79), consent of coastal state for routing required (Article 79, Paragraph 5)
Mining	No rights (Rights of coastal state over continental shelf need not be claimed) (Article 76, Paragraph 3)
Observance of environmental legislation	Must observe sanitary laws of coastal state (Article 33); must observe pollution laws (Part XII) applicable in exclusive economic zone

STRAITS USED FOR INTERNATIONAL NAVIGATION

The regime of passage through straits used for international passage is entirely independent of the regime of the territorial sea; to the extent to which it is applicable, the former takes precedence over any other regulations of the Convention.[1] Applicability of the provisions is dependent on two conditions: (1) there must be a recognized strait used for international navigation[2] which is not regulated by long-standing international conventions[3] and (2) the vessel must be in transit passage, continuous and expeditious traversing[4] without delay[5] of the strait. Other activities or vessels not in "transit passage" are treated in accordance with the provisions applying to the territorial sea[6].

The Convention does not define the term "strait". Any geographical formation commonly understood to be a navigable strait would therefore fall under these provisions. However, Part III applies only to those straits which are used for international navigation[7] unavoidable for convenience of navigation[8] and provide access from one part of an exclusive economic zone or the high seas to another part of an exclusive economic zone or the high seas[9]. As the exclusive economic zone commences twelve nautical miles from the baseline, the regime of the passage of straits will generally apply only in straits with a width of twenty-four nautical miles or less, for when there is within the strait an equally convenient route which is part of the high seas or the exclusive economic zone, the regime of passage through straits does not apply, just as it is not applicable if one end of the strait opens only into the territorial sea of a third state[10].

The concept of transit passage takes its place midway between "freedom of navigation"[11] and "innocent passage,"[12] while being related more closely in structure to the latter. Transit passage includes provisions of conduct[13] and the use of sea lanes and traffic separation schemes;[14] states bordering straits are obligated not to hamper any passage[15] and they have no right to suspend transit passage temporarily even in specifically designated areas as is possible for innocent passage in the territorial sea[16]. The jurisdiction of states bordering straits is restricted to administration: navigation (including sea lanes and traffic separation schemes)[17] pollution, fishing, loading and unloading[18]. However, it also includes the fields for which the state has jurisdiction in the contiguous zone[19] namely the prevention of infringement of customs, fiscal, immigration, and sanitary laws[20]. Any such regulations may not be discriminatory nor may they have the practical effect of abolishing the right of transit passage[21]. Vessels may not conduct research and survey activities without the consent of the states bordering the strait[22]. Aircraft may overfly the straits[23]. Both vessels and aircraft must comply with coastal state regulations[24] refrain from threats[25], and respect international regulations regarding safety at sea and pollution[26], regulations for prevention of pollution are to be established by agreement[27]. It should be emphasized that the Convention provisions in respect to pollution from vessels[28] do not affect or apply within the regime of straits; only if there is major damage or the threat of major damage may the bordering states act[29].

The right of transit passage also applies without restriction to warships and government-owned commercial vessels, but the flag state in each case is responsible for any damage caused by vessels which are entitled to sovereign immunity[30].

---

[1] Art. 34, 45
[2] Art. 37; 38, Para. 1; 45
[3] Art. 35, Subpara. (c)
[4] Art. 38, Para. 2
[5] Art. 39, Subpara. 1 (a)
[6] Art. 38, Para. 3
[7] Art. 37
[8] Art. 38, Para. 1
[9] Art. 34; 45
[10] Art. 45; 36; 38
[11] Art. 87
[12] Art. 17-26
[13] Art. 39; 40; 42, Para.4
[14] Art. 41;, Para. 7
[15] Art. 44
[16] Art. 44; 25, Para. 3
[17] Art. 41.
[18] Art. 42, Para. 1
[19] Art. 33
[20] Art. 42, Subpara. 1(d)
[21] Art. 42, Para.2
[22] Art. 40
[23] Art. 39, Para. 3
[24] Art. 42, Para. 4
[25] Art. 39
[26] Art. 39, Para. 2
[27] Art. 43
[28] Art. 233 (Art. 211-232)
[29] Art. 233
[30] Art. 42, Para. 5; Art. 236

THE REGIME OF PASSAGE THROUGH STRAITS

I. *STRAITS FOR WHICH THE PROVISIONS GOVERNING PASSAGE THROUGH STRAITS ARE APPLICABLE*

Prinple: Article 37

	Bordering State	
High Seas or Exclusive Economic Zone	Territorial Sea Strait Being Used for Navigation Territorial Sea	High Seas or Exclusive Economic Zone
	Bordering State	

Including: Internal waters which have become such only as a result of the application of provisions of the Convention for drawing baseline (Article 35, Subparagraph (a))

Unless: (1) Strait is not used for international navigation (Article 37)
(2) Passage through the strait is regulated by a long-standing international convention
(3) Another route of similar convenience through the strait exists in the high seas or exclusive economic zone (Article 36; Article 38, Paragraph 1; Article 45, Subparagraph 1(a)); but the right of innocent passage may not be suspended (Article 45, Para. 2)
(4) Strait connects the high seas or exclusive economic zone with the territorial sea of a third (foreign) state (Article 45, Subparagraph 1(b)); but the right of innocent passage may not be suspended (Article 45, Paragraph 2)

II. *THE IMPACT OF THE CONCEPT OF "TRANSIT PASSAGE"*

Sovereignty and Jurisdiction of the State Bordering the Strait	Right of Transit Passage for Vessels
1st Restriction: State may adopt laws and regulations only as enumerated in Article 42	*1st Restriction:* Vessels must observe laws adopted, in accordance with Article 42 (Article 42, Paragraph 4)
2nd Restriction: Laws may not be discriminatory nor undermine the right of transit passage (Article 42, Paragraph 2)	*2nd Restriction:* Vessels must comply with duties enumerated in Article 39 (e.g., refrain from threats or use of force), passage must be continuous and expeditious (Article 38, Paragraph 2) and comply with international safety and pollution regulations (Article 39, Paragraph 2)
3rd Restriction: Transit passage may not be hampered or suspended (Article 44)	
4th Restriction: Co-operation with other states with regard to navigational aid and pollution prevention (Article 43)	*3rd Restriction:* Vessel must refrain from research and surveys (Article 40)
5th Restriction: No restrictions on warships (Article 38 - all ships enjoy the right of transit passage)	*4th Restriction:* Vessel must observe sea lanes and traffic separation schemes (Article 41, Paragraph 7)
6th Restriction: Provisions on prevention of pollution from vessels (Part XII, Sections 5, 6, 7, Articles 211-232) are not applicable, unless major damage or threat of major damage (Article 233)	*5th Restriction:* Flag states-are liable for vessels entitled to immunity (Article 42, Paragraph 5; Article 236)
NB: Any activity not an exercise of the right of transit passage is subject to regime of territorial sea (Article 38, Paragraph 3)	*6th Restriction:* Must comply with international safety and pollution regulations (Articles 38 and 42)

ARCHIPELAGIC STATES

The impact of the Convention on those states which can claim status as archipelagic states[1] due to the fact that they consist of a group of islands forming an intrinsic geographical, economic, and political entity[2] is considerable, as all of the water area between the islands (the archipelagic waters) is under the sovereignty of the state[3], regardless of the depth of the water or the distance from the coast[4] One of the consequences of this assignment of sovereignty is that passage of vessels through these areas is basically innocent passage[5]. Sea lanes and air routes[6] through archipelagic waters are governed by specific regulations, including certain provisions of the regime of passage through straits[7]. Vessels are to respect sea lanes and traffic separation schemes[8]. As long as the archipelagic state has not designated sea lanes as provided by the Convention, the routes normally used for international navigation may be used as "sea lanes,"[9] with the status of "archipelagic sea lane passage"[10]. If necessary for the security of the state, navigation may be suspended temporarily in specified areas of the archipelagic waters, but this may not result in a suspension of sea lane passage[11].

An archipelagic state may draw straight archipelagic baselines of a maximum of 125 nautical miles in length to join the outermost points of the outermost islands and drying reefs,[12] provided that the ratio of land to water is not more than 1:1 and not less than 1:9[13]. These baselines are to be shown on charts and given due publicity.[14] The waters enclosed by the archipelagic baselines are the archipelagic waters and are under the sovereignty of the state[15].

The legal concept of archipelagic waters is without prejudice for the right of the state to draw lines for the delimitation of internal waters in accordance with Articles 9, 10, and 11[16] for the mouths of rivers, bays, and ports. Such lines of delimitation are known as closing lines rather than baselines as in the territorial sea concept,[17] as they serve only as the boundary for waters completely outside the jurisdiction of the Convention (internal waters) and do not act as the starting point for establishing zones. There is no right of innocent passage in internal waters enclosed by closing lines, even if they were not considered internal waters previously, a further contrast to the territorial sea concept[18].

The territorial sea, contiguous zone, exclusive economic zone, and continental shelf are measured from the archipelagic baselines, not from the closing lines drawn to delimit internal waters[19]. An archipelagic state may designate sea lanes through its archipelagic waters and through the adjacent territorial sea as well, and establish air routes there above[20].

An archipelagic state is to respect existing agreements and to recognize legitimate activities by neighbouring states in its archipelagic waters; this includes existing submarine cables passing through the archipelagic waters. An archipelagic state is to permit the maintenance and replacement of such cables[21].

In respect to pollution matters, there is a curious situation which might raise some concern in practice. Archipelagic sea lane passage is obviously intended to have a status similar to that of transit passage through straits."[22] But whereas the general enforcement regulations for pollution from vessels referred to in Part XII (Pollution) are not applicable in straits[23], a corresponding exclusion for archipelagic sea lane passage, either *expressis verbis* or by reference, does not exist. Archipelagic states may therefore apply Part XII to the full extent if not contrary to specific provisions of Part IV[24].

---

[1] Art. 46, Subpara. (a)
[2] Art. 46, Subpara. (b)
[3] Art. 2, Para.1
  Art. 49, Para. 1
[4] Art. 49, Para. 1
[5] Art. 52
[6] Art. 53
[7] Art. 53, Para. 2-3; Art. 54
[8] Art. 53, Para. 11
[9] Art. 53, Para.12
[10] Art. 53, Para. 1-3
[11] Art. 52, Para. 2; 54; 44
[12] Art. 47, Para. 1-2
[13] Art. 47, Para. 1, 3-7
[14] Art. 47, Para. 8-9
[15] Art. 49, Art. 2, Para. 1
[16] Art. 50
[17] Art. 5
[18] Art. 8, Para. 2
[19] Art. 48
[20] Art. 53, Para. 1
[21] Art. 51
[22] Art. 54
[23] Art. 233
[24] e.g. Art. 42; 44

Further Readings: - Archipelagic States, Page 105
  - Archipelagic Waters and Zones, Page 114

OPERATIONS IN ARCHIPELAGIC WATERS

I. DETERMINING ARCHIPELAGIC SEA LANES FOR VESSELS

(1) The archipelagic state may establish sea lanes which traverse the archipelagic waters and the adjacent territorial sea (Article 53, Paragraph 4)
(2) These routes are to include all normal passage routes and all normal navigational channels within such routes
   Unless: this would lead to duplication of routes of similar convenience (Article 53, Paragraph 4)
(3) A sea lane is defined as a series of continuous axis lines from entry point of passage routes to the exit point (Article 53, Paragraph 5)
(4) Vessels must not deviate more than twenty-five nautical miles to either side of the axis line during passage
   But: they must not navigate closer to the coast than 10% of the distance between the nearest points on islands bordering the sea lane (Article 53, Paragraph 5)
(5) The archipelagic state may prescribe traffic separation schemes for sea lanes to ensure safe passage of vessels through narrow channels (Article 53, Paragraph 6)

II. RIGHTS OF FOREIGN STATES IN ARCHIPELAGIC WATERS

Activity	Rights
Navigation	- Foreign vessels' enjoy rights of innocent passage through archipelagic waters, but these may be suspended temporarily for security reasons (Articles 52, 54) - Designated sea lanes are to be respected (Article 53, Paragraph 11); in such sea lanes vessels have right of "archipelagic sea lane passage" (Article 53, Paragraph 2) - Sea lane passage may not be hampered or suspended (Articles 54, 44) - Traffic separation schemes are to be respected (Article 53, Paragraph 11)
Overflight	Foreign aircraft have right of overflight, but must follow designated corridors (Article 53, Paragraph 2); must observe Rules of the Air and monitor the assigned radio frequency (Articles 54; 39, Subparagraph 3)
Fishing	Can be obtained by agreement; archipelagic state must recognize traditional fishing rights (Article 51)
Scientific Research	Consent of archipelagic state is required (Articles, 54, 40)
Submarine cables	Foreign states have rights only with regard to existing cables (Article 51)
Mining	Foreign states have no rights
Environmental Legislation and Enforcement	Archipelagic state may adopt laws and regulations to give effect to international regulations to prevent, reduce and control pollution in sea lanes, but restricted to "discharge" (Article 54, Article 42, Subparagraph 1(b)). Passage outside sea lanes is passage through territorial sea (Article 52)

EXCLUSIVE ECONOMIC ZONE

The Convention gives coastal states the right to establish by proclamation an exclusive economic zone beyond and adjacent to the territorial sea[1]. This zone can extend to a maximum of 200 nautical miles, measured from the baseline used for determing the breadth of the territorial sea[2]. If the sea is not open for this distance, agreements are to be made with opposite or adjacent coastal states, a matter which can be excepted from compulsory dispute settlement.[3] The coastal state is to publish charts showing the zone and deposit a copy with the UN Secretary-General.[4] Within this zone of a maximum breadth of 188 nautical miles, the coastal state has sovereign rights for specific purposes,[5] but does not have sovereignty comparable with that which it enjoys in its territory or in the territorial sea; rather, it has - in the scope of the Convention provisions -sovereign rights related to resources and jurisdiction in respect to artificial installations, marine scientific research, and marine environment protection[6]. In granting these rights, however, the Convention also charges the coastal states with certain responsibilities and duties. Many of the regulatory provisions governing this section are not to be found here at all; instead, they are in other sections of the Convention, most notably in Part XII, regulations for the prevention of pollution, and in Part XIII, which regulates scientific research. Rights with respect to the seabed and its subsoil[7] are to be exercised in accordance with the regulatory provisions of Part VI, Continental Shelf[8]. Part V contains three groups of provisions: (a) general rights as mentioned and the corresponding duty to give due regard to the rights and duties of other states[9] (b) fisheries (see next chapter), and (c) a detailed provision concerning artificial islands (see below). The greatest impact comes from the sovereign rights of the coastal state to explore and exploit all living and non-living resources, from the subsoil to the wind[10].

However, the interests of other states are of no lesser significance, particularly with regard to navigation. Part V therefore includes provisions for the freedom of navigation and overflight, for the laying of submarine cables and pipelines, and other lawful uses of the sea related to these freedoms[11]. These freedoms can basically be exercised as on the high seas[12] but always in a manner compatible with applicable provisions of the Convention[13] and states must respect the coastal state's rights and duties when acting in its exclusive economic zone[14]. Consequently, the exclusive economic zone has to be treated as an ocean area which "shall be reserved for peaceful purposes[15].

The coastal state has the exclusive right to construct and to authorize and regulate the construction, operation, and use of artificial islands, installations, and structures[16], including jurisdiction in respect to customs, fiscal, health, safety, and immigration laws[17]. Due care is to be given to navigation matters[18].

Conflicts arising from the failure of the Convention to attribute rights or jurisdiction to a coastal state or to designate areas as being governed by the "freedom of the seas" are to be solved on the basis of equity and in the light of all the relevant circumstances[19], bearing in mind that matters not regulated by this Convention continue to be governed by rules and principles of general international law[20] But the common uses of the ocean (navigation, overflight, laying of cables) are always subject to compulsory dispute settlement[21].

---

[1] Art. 55
[2] Art. 57; Art. 5-16
[3] Art. 74; Art. 298 (1)(a)
[4] Art. 75, Para. 2
[5] Art. 55, 56
[6] Art. 56, Para. 1
[7] Art. 56, Subpara. 1 (a)
[8] Art. 56, Para. 3
[9] Art. 56, Para. 2; Art. 59
[10] Art. 56, Subpara. 1 (a)
[11] Art. 58, Para. 1
[12] Art. 58, Para. 2; Art. 88-115
[13] Art. 58, Para. 1-2
[14] Art. 58, Para. 3
[15] Art. 58, Para. 2 ; Art. 88
[16] Art. 60, Para. 1
[17] Art. 60, Para. 2
[18] Art. 60, Para. 3-7; Art. 260-262
[19] Art. 59
[20] Preamble, last paragraph
[21] Art. 297, Para. 1

Further Reading: - Coastal state, Page 102
- Exclusive Economic Zone, Page 116
- Artificial Islands and Structures, Page 122
- Marine Scientific Research, Page 121

RIGHTS AND DUTIES IN THE EXCLUSIVE ECONOMIC

I. THE RIGHTS OF THE COASTAL STATE

Activity	Regulations	Significant Impact on Rights and Duties
Management	Of the natural resources (Article 56, Subparagraph 1(a))	Coastal state must act with due regard for rights apd duties of other states (Article 56, Paragraph 2)
Living Resources	Fishing (Article 56, Subparagraph 1(a), Articles 61-67) sedentary species (Article 77, Paragraph 3)	Participation of land-locked and geographically disadvantaged states and others (Article 62, Paragraphs 2 & 3)
Non-living resources superjacent to sea-bed and subsoil	Production of energy from water, current, wind, and other activities (Article 56, Subparagraph 1(a))	None
Non-living resources of sea bed and subsoil	Mining (Article 56, Subparagraph 1(a)), 56, Para 3 (Part VI, Articles 76-85)	None
Use of artificial islands	Article 56, Paragraph 2, Article 60	Due regard to shipping, including safety zones (Article 60), Paragraphs 3-5, 260-262)
Marine scientific research	Article 56, Paragraph 2 (Part XIII, Articles 246-262)	- International co-operation (Article 242) - Peaceful purposes only (Article 246. Paragraph 3) - Non-interference with shipping (Article 260-262) by artificial islands
Law Enforcement	Fishing, inspection, arrest, proceedings (Article 73)	- Release vessel upon security (Article 73) - No imprisonment in fishing cases (Article 73, Paragraph 3)
Other uses of sed-bed	Sovereign rights in drilling (Article 81), tunnelling (Article 85)	Coastal state has to accept cables and pipelines (Article 79)

II. THE DUTIES OF THE COASTAL STATE

Conservation	Natural Resources (Article 56, Subparagraph 1(a)), in particularly fish (Article 61)	Contribution and exchange of data (Article 61 Paragraph 5)
Utilisation	Of living resources (Article 62)	Coastal state must regulate fishing by other states (Article 62, Paragraph 4)
Marine Environment protection	Article 56, Subparagraph 1(a), Part XII, Articles 192-237	Coastal state is responsible and liable (Article 235, Vessels, Article 232, 304)
Resolution of conflict	Article 59, Part XV, Settlement of Disputes (297-298)	Limitation of applicability (Article 297) Release of fishing vessels (Article 292)
Delimitation of zone	Articles 74, 75	Dispute procedure with opposite/adjacent states if not otherwise settled (Article 74, Paragraph 2, Art 298(I)(a)

Further Readings: - Significant Rights of other States (Layout), Page 41

COASTAL STATE FISHERIES

Aside from possible exploration of oil fields, the most valuable resource for coastal states in their exclusive economic zone is the sovereign right of fishing[1]. The fishing rights within the exclusive economic zone are almost exclusive and are nearly equivalent to total sovereignty. The general obligation to conserve and the right to utilize[2] the living resources as well as the obligation to invite countries which traditionally fish there[3] or are land-locked or geographically disadvantaged states[4] to participate in fishing only if there is a surplus of catch and agreements or arrangements have been reached[5] are not conditions under which fishing rights of other states can easily be exercised. In addition, the coastal state need not accept compulsory dispute settlement procedure in many substantive fishing matters and is subject to compulsory conciliation[6] in only three instances. Nonetheless, the coastal state has to exercise its rights in the light of the general provision of "good faith and non-abuse of rights"[7].

Conservation includes the determination by the coastal state of the allowable catch[8], which is to be based on the best scientific evidence available; where appropriate, the coastal state is to co-operate with the competent international organization to avoid over-exploitation[9]. Measures must be designed to restore and maintain the population[10] and must take into account the effects of harvesting on associated or dependent species in order to prevent the endangering of such species[11]. Where the same stocks or associated stocks occur in the exclusive economic zones of two or more states or in the high seas as well as the zones, the states concerned are to seek to co-operate to ensure that the species is conserved and developed[12].

For particular species, the coastal state must especially emphasize co-operation when exercising its rights[13]. Primary responsibility for anadromous stocks and for catadromous species rests with the states where the stocks originate[14] or spend the greater part of their life cycle[15]. In general, harvesting of these species is to take place only within the exclusive economic zone boundaries of the state of origin[16].

The coastal state is to aim for optimum utilization of the resources in its zone[17] and, in particular, to allow land-locked, geographically disadvantaged, and developing states[18] to participate in the surplus its national capacity cannot harvest[19]. The coastal state is to give land-locked states and geographically disadvantaged states preference[20]. Even if the capacity of the coastal state approaches a point which would enable it to harvest the entire allowable catch, arrangements must be established permitting developing land-locked states and geographically disadvantaged states to participate in the harvest[21]. These provisions do not apply only in the event that the coastal state depends overwhelmingly on the catch for its own economy[22]. Participation by other states in the harvest of living resources, if not regulated by agreement[23], is to be regulated by laws and regulations of the coastal state[24], including enforcement procedure[25].

Vessels arrested for violation of coastal state fishing laws and regulations for the fulfilment of this state's obligations must be released upon payment of reasonable security[26]. Imprisonment or corporal punishment of crew is not permitted[27].

1 Art. 56, Subparagraph 1 (a)
2 Art. 61, Para. 2-3; Art. 62; Para. 1
3 Art. 62, Para. 3
4 Art. 62, Para. 3 ; Art. 69, Art. 70
5 Art. 62, Para. 2-3
6 Art. 297, Para. 3
7 Art. 300
8 Art. 61, Para. 1
9 Art. 61, Para.2
10 Art. 61, Para. 3
11 Art. 61, Para.4
12 Art. 63; 64; 116(b)
13 Art. 64-67
14 Art.66, Para.1
15 Art. 67, Para. 1
16 Art. 66, Para.3; Art. 67, Para. 2
17 Art. 62, Para. 1
18 Art. 62, Para. 3
19 Art. 62, Para. 2
20 Art. 69, Para. 3; Art. 70, Para. 4
21 Ibid
22 Art. 71
23 Art. 62, Para. 2; Art. 72
24 Art. 62, Para. 4-5
25 Art. 62, Subpara. 4 (k)
26 Art. 73, Para. 2
27 Art.73, Para. 3

Further Readings: - Fisheries, Page 119

FISHERIES IN THE EXCLUSIVE ECONOMIC

I. Conservation and Utilization

Conservation (Article 61)	Utilization (Article 62)

includes
(1) Determination of allowable catch on the basis of
  - best scientific evidence available
  - duty to maintain and restore stocks
  - avoidance of serious threat to species
  - where appropriate, co-operation with international organizations
(2) Available scientific information is to be contributed and exchanged
  - through international organisations
  - to states concerned -
(3) For stocks/species not only in one economic zone, co-operative efforts required (Articles 63, Paragraph 2; 64-67, 116, Subparagraph (b))
High Sea Fisheries (Article 116)
  - Fisheries on the high seas must observe rights, duties and interests of coastal states
	Coastal state is to
	(1) Promote, without prejudice to conservation, optimum utilization
	(2) Determine the capacity of its fish industries
	(3) Allow, "harvesting capacity approaches catch allowance, developing land-locked/ geographically disadvantaged states to participate (Articles 62, Paragraph 3; 69, Paragraph 4; 70, Paragraph 4; 71)
	(4) Allow, if there is surplus in allowable catch, traditional fisheries, land-locked and geographically disadvantaged states to participate (Articles 62, Paragraph 3, 69; 70, 72)
	(5) Determine the conditions for fishing by other states (Article 62, Paragraph 4)
	(6) Release arrested vessels upon payment of security; imprisonment and corporal punishment of crew not permitted (Article73)

II. Measures in Regard to Stocks and Species

TYPE	GENERAL	THIRD STATES	INTERNATIONAL ORGANIZATIONS
Stocks and associated species (Article 63)		Coastal state is to co-operate with states concerned	Involvement of sub-regional or regional organizations
Highly migratory species (Article 64)	Species designated in Annex I	Co-operation directly with states concerned	(1) With existing organizations (2) Otherwise establish organization
Marine mammals (Article 65)	Stricter measures than in Part V may be taken	States are to co-operate	Work through appropriate organizations, especially for cetaceans
Anadromous stocks (Article 66)	States where stock originate responsible for stock	(1) Fishing primarily reserved for responsible state (2) Co-operate with states concerned	Involvement where appropriate
Catadromous species (Article 67)	State where species spends greater part of life cycle responsible	(1) Fishing primarily reserved for responsible state (2) Co-operation when fish as juveniles or mature migrate to other zones	None
Sedentary species (Articles 68, 77)	Are treated as natural resources of the sea-bed	None	None

THE CONTINENTAL SHELF

The continental shelf concept emerged primarily in 1958, the concept of the exclusive economic zone at the 1973-1982 Conference. Provisions derived from both concepts expressly state that the coastal state has sovereign rights to the non-living resources of the sea-bed and its subsoil within the area of each of the zones[1]. But whereas the continental shelf concept is dependent on the rise of the continental shelf and can basically be applied only up to a certain depth of the sea-bed, the exclusive economic zone's outer limits are determined solely in terms of a distance from the coast (baseline), regardless of the depth of the water (and whether there is a continental shelf or not)[2]. A distinction between the exclusive economic zone and the continental shelf zone is therefore necessary for two reasons:

(a) a state party has to proclaim an exclusive economic zone, whereas the continental shelf rights exist for the coastal state independent of any proclamation or occupation, etc.[3] Consequently, a coastal state may exercise sovereign rights to resources of the sea-bed beyond the territorial sea, even where an exclusive economic zone has not been established or where it has not been established to the full extent permitted;

(b) if an exclusive economic zone has been established to the full extent permitted, a continental shelf subject to the coastal state's jurisdiction exists beyond the 200 nautical mile limit, if the topography of the sea-bed displays shelf character. The shelf may not exceed 350 nautical miles from the baseline from which the territorial sea is measured or 100 nautical miles from the 2,500 meter isobath, a line connecting the depth of 2,500 meters.[4]

If an exclusive economic zone has been established - and this will be the general rule - two legal regimes exist with regard to the sea-bed subject to coastal state sovereign rights. Part of the shelf (sea-bed) is then subject to the regime of the exclusive economic zone and is governed generally by its provisions, which include reference to continental shelf provisions.[5] To avoid confusion, one should speak of the "sea-bed of the exclusive economic zone" or, synonymously, the "primary sea-bed," and call the sea-bed beyond the limits of the exclusive economic zone the "outer shelf." The "outer shelf" would be governed by an independent legal regime under the application of the provisions of Part VI for the "continental shelf" only.

The sovereign rights of the coastal state always include the exploitation of living organisms belonging to sedentary species,[6] drilling,[7] tunneling,[8] and the use of artificial islands, installations, and structures.[9] On the outer shelf beyond the 200 mile limits, the coastal state has no rights with regard to the superjacent waters to the sea-bed and the air space above those waters[10]. It must avoid interference with navigation and other rights and freedoms of other states[11] as laid down in the regime of the high seas.[12] The coastal state must make annual payments or contributions to the Sea-Bed Authority for resources exploited from the outer shelf, beginning five years after the start of production and increasing yearly to a maximum of seven percent of the value or volume of production at the site.[13] The delimitation of the outer shelf is to be undertaken by the coastal state on the recommendation of the Commission on the Limits of the Continental Shelf;[14] corresponding charts and relevant information are to be deposited with the Secretary-General of the United Nations[15] or the Secretary-General of the Authority (charts showing outer limits) and published[16]. The coastal state can exclude compulsory settlement of disputes[17] which might arise from delimitation of the outer shelf where other states have opposite or adjacent coasts[18].

---

[1] Art. 56(1)(a); 77(1)
[2] Art. 57, 76
[3] Art. 77, Para. 3
[4] Art. 76, Para 5
[5] Art. 56, Para. 3
[6] Art. 77, Para. 4; Art. 68
[7] Art. 81(Art. 56, Para. 3)
[8] Art. 85(Art. 56, Para. 3)
[9] Art. 60, 80
[10] Art. 78, Para. 1
[11] Art. 78, Para 2
[12] Part. VII
[13] Art. 82
[14] Annex II
[15] Art. 76, Para. 8-9, Art. 84
[16] Art. 84, Para. 2
[17] Art. 298, Subpara. 1(a)
[18] Art. 76, Para. 10; Art. 83

Further Readings: - The Truman Proclamation of 1945, Page 3
- Developments in the late 1940s and 1950s, Page 3
- UN Conferences 1958 and 1960, Page 4
- The Continental Shelf, Page 115

RIGHTS OF FOREIGN NATIONALS IN THE EXCLUSIVE ECONOMIC ZONE, ON THE CONTINENTAL SHELF, AND ON THE HIGH SEAS

(1) Exclusive Economic Zone including its sea-bed, the "Primary Sea-bed" (see text)
(2) Continental Shelf/"Outer Shelf" (see text)
    (A) If no exclusive economic zone has been established, then beyond territorial sea, and
    (B) If exclusive economic zone has been established, then only "outer shelf"
(3) High Seas: As defined in Article 86

ACTIVITY	(1) EXCLUSIVE ECONOMIC ZONE, INCL "PRIMARY SEA-BED"	(2) CONTINENTAL SHELF OR "OUTER SHELF"	(3) HIGH SEAS
Navigation	Free, if compatible with Convention (Articles 58, Paragraph 1, 87, 58, Paragraph 2, 88-115	Equal rights for all (Article 87)	Equal rights for all (Articles 87 and 90)
Overnight	Free, if compatible with Convention (e g , Article 222, Pollution)	Equal rights for all (Article 87)	Equal rights for all (Article 87)
Fishing	Access through agreements (Article 62) Land-locked, geographically disadvantaged states (Articles 69,70)	Equal rights (Articles 87,116-120), except sedentary species (Article 77, Paragraph 4)	Equal rights (Articles 87, 116-120)
Scientific research	Consent necessary (Article 246)	Water column: Equal rights (Article 87) Sea-bed. Consent (Article 246)	Equal rights (Article 87) Except, on the — "outer shelf" (Article 246) — Area. requires co-operation (Article 143)
Cables	Free, consent for routing required (Articles 56, Paragraph 3, 58, 1; 79, 112-115)	Free, consent for routing required (Article 79)	Equal rights (Articles 87, 112-115)
Mining	No rights	No rights	Equal rights (Article 141) management by Sea-Bed Authority (Article 137)
Marine Environment	Jurisdiction as provided by Convention (Article 56, Subparagraph 1(b); Part XII)	Rights of coastal states (Articles 192, 208) with regard to sea-bed activities	Equal responsibility (Article 192); activities in Area (Articles 209, 215), flag state (Articles 211, 217), port state jurisdiction (Article 218)

THE HIGH SEAS – GENERAL

Beyond the limits of national jurisdiction, the water column and the air space above the oceans are governed by the regime of the high seas.[1] When coastal states have established exclusive economic zones - and that is already (or will in future be) the rule - the high seas are the ocean space beyond the 200 nautical mile limit of this zone.[2]

The high seas are to be open and freely available for use by all states, regardless of their location Their use is to be governed by the principle of equal rights for all[3]. No state may validly purport to subject any part of the high seas to its sovereignty;[4] in agreeing to the Convention, all states acknowledge that these oceans are reserved for peaceful purposes.[5] These are, after all, merely the logical consequences of the Convention's aim to maintain peace, justice, and progress for all people of the world.[6]

Within this context, the regime of the high seas is based on the freedom to use the oceans. In exercising its right of use of the high seas, no state may interfere with the justified and equal interests of other states[7] or act in a manner which would constitute an abuse of the rights recognized by the Convention.[8] States are also to respect the activities on the sea-bed in the Area, which are managed by the Sea-Bed Authority in the interests of mankind as a whole[9]. A similar attitude shall be required from coastal states undertaking activities on the "outer shelf," and the coastal state is to avoid any unjustified interference with the rights of other states.[10]

The Convention establishes freedom of activity in six general fields: (1) navigation, (2) overflight, (3) laying of cables and pipelines, (4) artificial islands and installations, (5) fishing, and (6) marine scientific research.[11] This is not intended as a conclusive list, nor does this listing in any way prejudice possible rights of coastal states.[12]

Freedom of navigation is of utmost importance for all, for the shipping community and naval forces as well as for the fishing industries and marine scientific research. Every state has the right to sail ships and participate in navigation[13] by granting its nationality to vessels which are registered with the state and which fly its flag.[14] Such flag states have the right and duty to exercise their exclusive jurisdiction on ships on the high seas.[15] This includes administrative, technical, social,[16] and pollution[17] matters. Other states are generally excluded from exercising any jurisdiction, e.g., penal, disciplinary, arrest, or detention matters in collision cases,[18] although there are exceptions;[19] furthermore, there are activities generally considered reprehensible[20] (see following pages). Government-owned non-commercial vessels and warships are under no circumstances subject to the jurisdiction of other states.[21]

For the use of artificial installations in and airplanes over the high seas, the Convention provides only regulatory provisions in respect to scientific research and pollution. For these freedoms and those of fishing, cables, and pipelines, see *Further Readings*.

---

[1] Art.86
[2] Art. 57
[3] Preamble;87-90
[4] Art. 89
[5] Art. 88
[6] Preamble
[7] Art. 87, Para. 2; 301
[8] Art. 300
[9] Art. 87, Para. 2; Part XI(Art. 137, Para. 2)
[10] Art. 78, Para. 2
[11] Art. 87, Para. 1
[12] Art. 63; 64; 116(b); 77, Para. 1
[13] Art. 90
[14] Art. 91
[15] Art. 92, Para. 1
[16] Art. 94
[17] Art. 194, 211, 217
[18] Art. 97
[19] e.g. Art. 97, 221
[20] Art. 99-110
[21] Art. 95, 96

Further Readings:
- Fisheries, Pages 48, 119
- Marine Scientific Research, Pages 72, 121
- Submarine Cables and Pipelines, Pages 48, 123
- Artificial Islands and Structures, Page 122
- Overflight, Page 120
- The High Seas, Page 117

THE HIGH SEAS

I. GENERAL PRINCIPLES

(1) Justice and equal rights for all (Preamble) to be exercised in good faith and with no abuse of rights of others (Article 300)
(2) Freedom of all types of activities (Article 87, Paragraph 1) with due regard for the interests of other states
(3) Reserved for peaceful purposes (Article 88)
(4) State sovereignty over any part of the high seas is excluded (Article 89)

II. PARTICULAR FREEDOMS

List of Freedoms (Article 87)	Regulations governing the high seas

Navigation	*Basics*
	1) Nationality of Vessels; Article 91
	2) Vessels in service of international organizations. Article 93, Annex IX
	3) Warships, etc : Articles 95, 96
	Jurisdiction
	1) Exclusive jurisdiction; flag stage. Article 92
	2) Administrative, technical, social; flag state. Article 94, Paragraphs 1-5
	3) Collisians on the high seas
	   - Inquiry each state. Article 94, Paragraph 7; cooperation with flag state "
	   - Penal jurisdiction; to this effect, disciplinary, arrest, detention; flag state. Article 97
	4) Pollution; flag state. Articles 192, 194, 211, 217
	5) Pollution, port state. Articles 218, 232 (flag state; Article228)
	6) International offences; other states, Articles 99-110
	Other items: Search and rescue service by coastal states; Article 98, Paragraph 2; Render assistance; Article 98; Hot pursuit. Article 111; Civil pollution claims; Article 229

Overflight	Pollution; state of registry. Articles 212, 222
Submarines cables and pipelines	1) Subject to Part VI (Continental Shelf); Article 87 2) General right; Article 112 3) Liability for damage; Articles 113-114; Indemnity for loss incurred avoiding damage; Article 115
Construction of artificial islands	1) In accordance with international law; Article 87 2) Subject to Part VI (Continental Shelf); Article 87 3) For scientific research in general; Articles 258-262; In the Area; Articles 143, 256
Fishing	Articles 116-120
Scientific research	1) Subject to Part VI (Continental Shelf); Article 87 2) Subject to Part XIII (Marine Scientific Research); Article 87 3) Scientific research in the Area; Article 143 4) Development and transfer of marine technology; Part XIV

THE FLAG STATE'S OBLIGATIONS FOR MERCHANT VESSELS

Every state has the right to have a merchant fleet under its flag, and the vessels in this fleet are entitled to use the high seas.[1] But this right is coupled with obligations. As there is no sovereign authority of a state or other agency to maintain law and order on the high seas, there must be some tie to the jurisdiction of a state. According to common international law, which is confirmed by the Convention, the flag state in general exercises exclusive jurisdiction over a vessel on the high seas.[2] The Convention's provisions are part of a complicated network of public international laws, rules, and regulations, but they also represents the general rules which serve as basic principles for the entire network of international public law of the sea.[3]

The flag state's initial obligation is to maintain a registry of all ships entitled to fly its flag[4] and to issue documents to this effect to such ships.[5] As a result of this procedure, the ship has the nationality of the country whose flag it flies.[6] However, states are permitted to grant their nationality to vessels only when there is a "genuine link"[7] between vessel and state, a term not defined by the Convention, but which is to be interpreted as a strong economic tie between nationals of the flag state and the vessel with regard to ownership, management, and manning of the ship. In order to prevent changes of flag for convenience, vessels sailing under the flags of two or more states may be assimilated to a ship without nationality.[8]

Upon registering the vessel, the flag state must ensure that the ship complies with international safety standards. It must exercise its jurisdiction and control in administrative, technical, and social matters over vessels flying its flag.[9] A broad listing of measures to be taken would include construction of equipment, seaworthiness, manning, labour conditions, training of crew, means of communication, prevention of collisions, and regulations and inspections.[10] In taking these measures, the state is obliged to conform to generally accepted international regulations, procedure, and practice,[11] which means for all practical purposes applying IMO (International Maritime Organization) and ILO (International Labour Organization) conventions and standards. Where there are clear grounds for believing that proper Jurisdiction and control are not being exercised over a ship, other states may report the facts to the flag state.[12]

In cases of collision or incident on the high seas involving loss of life or serious injury or serious damage, other states may cause an inquiry to be held,[13] although penal or disciplinary procedures remain basically under the jurisdiction of the flag state[14] as does also the right to arrest or detain vessels in such cases (e.g., for penal or investigative purposes).[15] The flag state and the other state are to co-operate in the conduct of any inquiry.[16] It should be emphasized that the regulations of the Convention do not affect private law and civil claims and rights,[17] e.g., application in court for arrest of a ship arising from a claim for compensation for damages caused by the ship.

Finally, the flag state must require masters of vessels of its nationality to render assistance to any person in danger of being lost or in distress in so far as this can be done without serious danger to his own ship.[18] In the case of involvement in a collision, assistance to the other ship is to be provided.[19]

---

[1] Art. 90
[2] Art. 92, Para. 1
[3] Art. 311; 304
[4] Art. 94, Subpara. 2(a).
[5] Art. 91, Para. 2
[6] Art. 91, Para. 1
[7] Art. 91, Para. 1

[8] Art. 92, Para. 2; see Art. 110, Subpara1 (d)
[9] Art. 94, Para. 1
[10] Art. 94, Para. 3-4
[11] Art. 94, Para. 5
[12] Art. 94, Para. 6
[13] Art. 94, Para. 7

[14] Art. 97, Para. 1-2
[15] Art. 97, Para. 3
[16] Art. 94, Para. 7
[17] Art. 304 (e.g. Pollution 229); Preamble, last paragraph
[18] Art. 98
[19] Art. 98, Subpara. 1(c)

Further Readings:
- Flag States, Register States, Flag of Convenience State, Page 104
- Ships-Vessels, Navigation, Pages 118, 119
- Safety of Shipping, Page 125

VESSELS

Issue	Flag State Obligations - Merchant Vessels	Other Circumstances
Jurisdiction	*General* Vessels are subject to exclusive jurisdiction of flag state on the high seas (Article 92, Paragraph 1) (For pollution measures in general, see Articles 194, Subparagraph 3(b); 211; 217) *Particular* Flag state required to assume jurisdiction under its internal law with respect to administrative, technical, and social matters *Collision incidents on the high seas* - In respect to penal jurisdiction: arrest/detention flag state (Article 97, Paragraph 3) - Penal and disciplinary matters exclusive jurisdiction of flag state (Article 97, Paragraph1) *except:* withdrawal of certificates issued by other states (Article 97, Paragraph 2) - Inquiry (Administrative jurisdiction) (Article 94, Paragraph 7)	Except in cases expressly provided for in international treaties and this Convention (Article 92, Paragraph 1; e g , Articles 99-111, Articles 218 and 221) - In penal cases, home state can institute proceedings against its nationals (Article 97, Paragraph 1) - Inquiry by other states possible (Article 94, Paragraph 7)
Administration	*Registration* - Fix conditions for grant of nationality (Article 91, Paragraph 1) - Maintain a register of ships (Article 94, Subparagraph 2(a)) - Inspect before registration (Article 94, Subparagraph 4(a)) - Issue flag documents (Article 91, Paragraph 2) *Other measures* - Require master to help persons in danger or distress (Article 98, Subparagraphs 1 (a-b)) and assist in collision cases - Investigate allegations of improper control (Article 94, Paragraph 6)	- Registration may take place only where "genuine link" (Article 91, Paragraph 1) - Nationality follows flag (Article 91, Paragraph 1) - "Treatment" as ship without nationality (Article 92, Paragraph 2)
Technical Matters	Required to ensure - Construction, equipment, seaworthiness, manning, training of crew, use of signals, maintenance of communication, collision prevention (Article 94, Paragraph 3) - Inspection at intervals (Article 94, Subparagraph 4(a)) - Charts, nautical publications, navigational equipment is on board (Article 94, Subparagraph 4(a))	Flag state measures are to - Comply with generally accepted international regulations, procedure and practice (Article 94, Paragraph 5) - Ensure appropriate crew qualification and numbers of crew (Article 94, Subparagraph 4(b)) - Ensure that crew is conversant with and required to observe international regulations. safety, collision, pollution, radio communication (Article 94, Subparagraph 4(c))
Social Matters	- Labour conditions (Article 94, Paragraph 3)	

WARSHIPS, etc.: Immunity (Articles 89-90), Pollution (Articles 236, 304)
VESSELS OF UNITED NATIONS, etc. Article 93

INTERNATIONAL JURISDICTION

The exclusive jurisdiction of the flag state[1] is not absolute. There are several exceptions by which other states are granted in varying degrees a share of legislative or enforcement jurisdiction with the flag state. This sharing of jurisdiction is related in four cases to offences and in two cases to the nationality of vessels. These provisions are not derived from a common structure, although some of them are of ancient origin.

Only two basic principles in these provisions find some general application. One is that the states are required to co-operate in the repression of the offences of piracy,[2] illicit drug trade,[3] and unauthorized broadcasting;[4] co-operation is not, on the other hand, expected for the prevention of transport of slaves.[5] Secondly, warships and other vessels and aircraft clearly on government service[6] have a right of visit on foreign vessels suspected of involvement in piracy, the slave trade, or unauthorized broadcasting.[7] Government vessels also have a right of visit on vessels without nationality (important in the case of vessels which sail under the flags of two or more states[8]) and on vessels of apparently the same nationality as the government ship, even though flying a different flag or refusing to show any flag at all,[9] in reality a question of flag state jurisdiction. In the case of ships involved in illicit drug trade, the jurisdiction of the flag state remains in this respect unchallenged.[10] But the flag state may request co-operation from another state, including the conducting of a visit on board.[11]

The jurisdiction of other states on foreign vessels as granted in the right to visit by duly authorized government vessels is limited to cases of suspicion of certain activities (piracy, slave trade, unauthorized broadcasting, sailing without nationality, practicing deception with regard to nationality);[12] the boarding vessel may verify the right of the ship to fly the flag, by checking its documents and, if suspicion remains, proceed to a further investigation.[13] Only in cases of piracy and unauthorized broadcasting are the rights of other states considerably extended.[14] It is significant that the definition of piracy presumes the involvement of at least two vessels, a pirate vessel and a victim vessel,[15] thus excluding hijacking as it has been practiced in recent years from being treated as piracy. Piracy is the only case in which every state's official vessels may carry out a seizure[16] and the state exercises full jurisdiction with regard to penalties to be imposed and action to be taken.[17] Actions of arrest and seizure due to unauthorized broadcasting, on the other hand, may be carried out only by states affected by unlawful broadcasting.[18]

HOT PURSUIT

The right of hot pursuit[19] has developed of itself. It allows an official vessel to extend the sovereignty of the coastal state beyond the territorial sea by maintaining an uninterrupted chase of a fleeing merchant vessel. The pursuing vessel must be authorized to make arrests. Hot pursuit may commence when the coastal state has good reason to believe that the foreign vessel has violated the state's laws and regulations and the vessel has disobeyed a clear order to stop. The chase must begin within the limits of the territorial sea or, where relevant rights have been violated, in zones further out. The right of hot pursuit ceases when the chase is interrupted or the vessel reaches the territorial sea of its own state or a third state.

---

[1] Art. 92, Para. 1
[2] Art. 100
[3] Art. 108, Para. 1
[4] Art. 109, Para. 1
[5] Art. 99
[6] Art. 110, Para. 1, 4, 5
[7] Art. 110, Subpara. 1(a-c)
[8] Art. 92, Para. 2 (110, 1(d))
[9] Art. 110, Subpara. 1(e)
[10] Art. 108, 110
[11] Art. 108, Para. 2
[12] Art. 110, Para. 1
[13] Art. 110, Para. 2
[14] Art. 101-107; 109
[15] Art. 101
[16] Art. 107
[17] Art. 105
[18] Art. 109, Para. 3-4
[19] Art. 111

SPECIAL JURISDICTION ON THE HIGH SEAS

I. ARTICLES 99-110

Activity	General	"Right to Visit" (Article 110)
Slave trade (Article 99)	Flag state shall take measures to prevent	- Any warship has right to board
Piracy (Article 100-107)	- *Piracy* Illegal acts of crew or passenger or support of such for private ends by or on commercial or official vessels against another vessel (Articles 101-103) - Seizure by official vessels (Article 107) - Retention-or loss of nationality (Article 104) - Jurisdiction of state seizing vessel (Article 105) - Liability for unjustified seizure (Article 106) All states co-operate in repression of piracy (Article 100)	- Must be reasonable grounds - Action which can be taken: 1) Verify the right ship to fly flag 2) Document check 3) If suspicion remains, inspection of ship - Compensation for loss or damage if unjustified - Applicable for official aircraft and vessels (Article 110, Paragraphs 4 and 5)
Vessels without nationality, e.g.. Article 92, Paragraph 2		
Unauthorized broadcasting (Article 109)	Arrest of person and vessel and seizure of broadcasting apparatus; prosecution by state with jurisdiction for boarding	Boarding only by state affected by undertaking (Article 109, Paragraph 3)
Refusal to show flag (Article 110)		Boarding only by warship which in reality same nationality as boarded ship
Illicit traffic in narcotic drugs or psychotropic substances (Article 108)	- All states must co-operate in repression - Flag state may request co-operation from other states in suspicious cases	No boarding

II. ARTICLE 111: HOT PURSUIT

Principles:
1) By vessels or aircraft in government service
2) Clear visual or auditory signal to stop must be given
3) Pursuit must not be interrupted
4) Right of hot pursuit ceases by reason of
    a) Interruption
    b) Vessel reaching territorial sea of flag state or other state
5) Hot pursuit must begin in zone where the vessel violated applicable coastal state law
    - In internal waters and territorial sea - at the latest in the territorial sea
    - Violation of customs, fiscal, immigration, and sanitary law (Article 33) applicable for continuous zone - at the latest in contiguous zone (also for exclusive economic zone and continental shelf)
6) Liability for unjustified measures

SUBMARINE CABLES AND PIPELINES

The freedom to lay submarine cables and pipelines on the bed of the high seas beyond the continental shelf is guaranteed,[1] but states must have due regard for cables and pipelines already in position.[2] The provisions serve to protect such installations and require states to implement laws and regulations as follows:
1) Injury or obstruction of installations done wilfully, through culpable negligence, or intentionally are to be treated as punishable offences, unless the act was committed in a distress situation;[3]
2) Cable or pipeline owners who, in laying or repairing that cable or pipeline, cause damage to or break another cable or pipeline are to bear the costs of repair;[4]
3) Owners of cables or pipelines are to indemnify owners of ships who have sacrificed equipment in order to avoid damage to a cable or pipeline.[5]

FISHERIES ON THE HIGH SEAS

Until the middle of this century, the traditional international law of fisheries provided for a territorial sea of three nautical miles and the remainder of the oceans, the high seas, for which there was freedom of fishing. Although the Convention retains freedom of fishing on the high seas,[6] the results are considerably different.

Of greatest impact is the fact that the coastal states have the right to establish an exclusive economic zone which extends for 200 nautical miles from the coast[7] within which they have fishing rights.[8] About 90% of the commercially exploitable fish stocks can be found in such zones if they are universally established.

Consequently, the Convention requires measures for the high seas supplementary to those for the exclusive economic zone. These measures can be summarized as conservation measures implemented by the state for its nationals[9] and measures for co-operation between the states for conservation and management of resources in the high seas.[10] The guidelines which apply for determining allowable catch and establishing conservation measures are similar to those for the coastal states in their exclusive economic zones;[11] furthermore, such measures must avoid the discrimination of fishermen of any other state.[12] States must also have due regard for stocks and species which move from coastal state zones to the high seas and back and consider whether these stocks are subject to coastal state conservation and management measures[13]. In particular, coastal states and states concerned with fishing on the high seas are to co-operate in respect to highly migratory species[14] listed in Annex I.

The limited resources of the high seas, together with the various measures to be taken, make it essential to reach a balance between the conflicting principles of freedom of fishing and cooperative conservation and management of the resources of the high seas.[15] The Convention provides for the establishment of subregional or regional fisheries organizations to achieve this end.[16]

---

[1] Art. 112; 87 Subpara. 1(c)
[2] Art. 112, Para. 2; Art. 79, Para. 5
[3] Art. 113
[4] Art. 114
[5] Art. 115
[6] Art. 87, Subpara. 1(e)
[7] Art. 57
[8] Art. 56, Subpara. 1 (a)
[9] Art. 117, 119, 120
[10] Art. 117, 119, 120
[11] Art. 119, 61
[12] Art. 119, Para. 3
[13] Art. 116, Subpara. (b); 63, Para. 2; 64-67
[14] Art. 64
[15] Art. 117
[16] Art. 118

Further Readings: - Cables and Pipelines, Page 123
- Fisheries, Page 119

FREEDOM OF FISHING
ARTICLE 87, SUBPARAGRAPH 1(e)

subject to

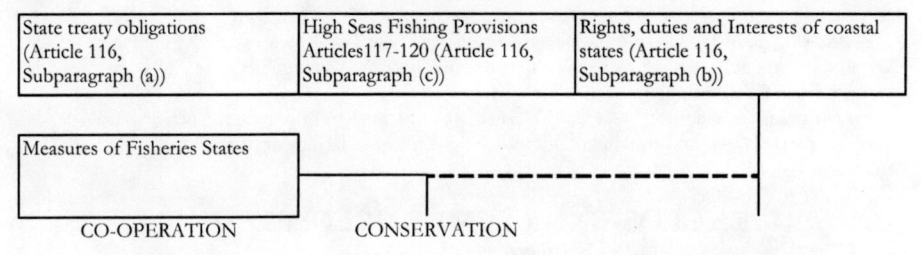

State treaty obligations (Article 116, Subparagraph (a))	High Seas Fishing Provisions Articles 117-120 (Article 116, Subparagraph (c))	Rights, duties and Interests of coastal states (Article 116, Subparagraph (b))

Measures of Fisheries States

CO-OPERATION

Article 117
- As necessary for the conservation of living resources

Article 118
- In conservation and management
- Negotiations between states where nationals exploit identical or different living resources in the same area
- Establish subregional or regional organizations

Article 119, Paragraph 2
- Exchange data with states concerned

Articles 120, 65
- States together with international organizations

Article 64, Annex I
- Co-operation between flag state and coastal state in respect to highly migratory species

CONSERVATION

Article 119
In determining the allowable catch (alone or with other states) and establishing other conservation measures the the states are to
- use the best scientific evidence
- consider relevant factors maintaining and restoring populations of stocks
- take due regard for developing countries
- take into account nternational standards, whether subregional, regional, or global
- avoid serious treat to species
- exchange data and information
- avoid in form or fact discrimination of fisherman from other other states

Article 120, 65
- May restrict the exploitation of marine mammals more strictly the provided by Convention

Article 63, Paragraph 2
- States concerned are to seek, either directly or through organizations, to agree upon the measures necessary for the conservation of these stocks in the adjacent area (here: high seas)

Articles 65-67
- Marine mammals
  Article 65
- Anadromous stocks
  Article 66
- Catadromous species
  Article 67

Article 64, Annex I
- Co-operation required in respect to highly migratory species

THE REGIME OF ISLANDS
Article 121

With respect to resources in exclusive economic and continental shelf zones, the regime of islands has quite an impact. An island which can maintain human habitation or economic life of its own has the right to establish the zones laid down by the Convention: territorial sea,[1] contiguous zone,[2] exclusive economic zone,[3] and continental shelf.[4] Archipelagic states[5] are an exception; in this case, the waters between the islands are the archipelagic waters.[6] A distinction must be made for rocks which cannot maintain human habitation or economic life of their own;
they do not have an exclusive economic zone or a continental shelf, but (on the condition that they are above water at high tide[7]) they may have a territorial sea and contiguous zone.[8] This corresponds to the criteria for determining the baseline of the territorial sea.[9]

Artificial islands are not "a naturally formed area of land."[10] Consequently, such artificial islands and other installations and equipment do not have the status of islands or of rocks.[11]

ENCLOSED OR SEMI-ENCLOSED SEAS
Articles 122-123

An "enclosed or semi-enclosed sea" is a gulf, bay, basin, or sea surrounded by two or more states which has a narrow outlet to the ocean or whose waters consist entirely or primarily of the territorial seas or exclusive economic zones of no fewer than two states. The Baltic Sea, the Mediterranean, the Red Sea, and the Arabian Gulf are undoubtedly such seas, but according to this definition the Gulf of Mexico and the North Sea are semi-enclosed seas as well.

States bordering on enclosed or semi-enclosed seas are expected to co-operate with each other in exercising their rights and performing their duties under the Convention[12] and, where appropriate, to invite other interested states or international organizations to co-operate in furthering the aims of the Convention.[13] Furthermore, they are to co-ordinate their activities with regard to fisheries, marine environment, and scientific research.[14] These requirements are derived to some extent from similar provisions to be found elsewhere in the Convention. Coastal states have to co-operate with other states where both are concerned with the same living resources.[15] The provisions for the protection of the marine environment even include two complete sections regulating co-operation,[16] including a directive for regional and global co-operation,[17] a call for studies, research programmes, and exchange of information and data,[18] and the requirement of notification of imminent or actual damage and provision of appropriate contingency plans against pollution.[19] States bordering enclosed or semi-enclosed seas may in particular apply the Convention provisions for co-operation in all marine scientific matters.[20]

[1] Art. 3
[2] Art. 33
[3] Art. 55, 57
[4] Art. 76
[5] Art. 46, Subpara. (a)
[6] Art. 47-49
[7] Art. 121, Para. 1
[8] Art. 121, para.3
[9] Art. 7, Para. 4; Art. 13
[10] Art. 121, Para. 1
[11] Art. 11 ; 60; Para. 8; 147, Subpara. 2 (e); 259
[12] Art. 123, Subpara. (a-c)
[13] Art. 123, Subpara. (d)
[14] Art. 123, Subpara. (a)-(c
[15] Art. 63, 1; Art. 64-67
[16] Art. 197-201, 204-206
[17] Art. 197
[18] Art. 200-201
[19] Art. 198-199
[20] Art. 242-244

Further Readings: - Island, Page 114
- Enclosed or Semi-enclosed Seas, Page 114

REGIME OF ISLANDS
ARTICLE 121

1. Islands	- Naturally formed area of land - Surrounded by water; above high-tide mark - Human habitation and economic life is possible	Territorial Sea (Art. 3) Contiguous Zone (Art. 33) Exclusive Economic Zone (Art. 56, 57) Continental Shelf (Art. 76)
2. Rock	- Naturally formed area of land - Surrounded by water; above high-tide mark - Cannot maintain human habitation or economic life on its own	Territorial Sea (Art. 3) Contiguous Zone (Art. 33)
3. Artificial islands, installations and equipment		Do not posses the status of islands (or rocks) (Art. 11; 60, Para. 8; 147, Subpara. 2(e); 259

ENCLOSED OR SEMI-ENCLOSED SEAS
ARTICLES 122-123

1. *Definition (Article 122)*

   A gulf, basin, or sea
   - surrounded by two or more states
   - connected to another sea or ocean by a narrow outlet
   OR
   - consisting of zones of jurisdiction of two or more coastal states

2. *Areas of Co-operation (Article 123)*
   - Management, conservation, exploration and exploitation of the living resources
     Closely related provisions: Articles 61, Paragraph 2; 63, Paragraph 1; 64-67
   - Protection and preservation of the marine environment
     Closely related provisions: Articles 193; 197-201; 204-206
   - Scientific research programs and joint scientific research
     Closely related provisions: Articles 242-244; 246, Paragraph 3

FREEDOM OF TRANSIT

The Convention defines land-locked states as those states which have no sea-coast.[1] These states are at a definite disadvantage in comparison with those states which have their own coast and consequent access to their own ports and the sea for transportation. But they have the right to sail vessels flying their flag on the high seas,[2] and they are free to carry on activities on the high seas, enjoying equal rights with all other states.[3]

Furthermore, land-locked states are barred from claiming parts of the sea for the benefit of the state. They do have a rather weak right to participate in the living resources of the exclusive economic zone of coastal states of the same subregion or region.[4] However, even this right is limited to developing land-locked states when the harvesting capacity of a coastal state approaches a point which would enable it to harvest the entire allowable catch.[5] Preferential treatment is granted developing land-locked states with regard to activities in the Area.[6] All land-locked states are denied rights for participation in sea-bed activities on the continental shelf or in the exclusive economic zone of other states, but they must be given the opportunity to participate in marine scientific research in these zones of neighboring coastal states.[7]

As far as their use of the ocean in any way is concerned, land-locked states are at the mercy of other states, especially neighbouring states with a coastline, willing to grant the land-locked states access to seaports under reasonable conditions. The Convention provides a minimum of protection for the interests of land-locked states by guaranteeing the right of access to and from the sea and freedom of transit[8] as well as equal treatment of ships flying the flag of a land-locked state.[9] Freedom of transit is ensured by provisions of the Convention which prohibit the levying by the transit state[10] of customs duties, taxes, and other charges on traffic in transit [11]or subjecting means of transport in transit to higher taxes or charges than those customary in the transit state;[12] preferential treatment of certain nations is prohibited.[13] Transit states are obligated to take all appropriate measures to avoid delays or other difficulties of a technical nature in transit,[14] and in the event that such difficulties arise, the authorities responsible in the transit states and land-locked states concerned are to co-operate in eliminating such difficulties quickly.[15] Naturally, these minimum requirements do not in any way preclude agreements between transit states and land-locked states providing facilities for the convenience of traffic in transit,[16] co-operation in the construction and improvement of means of transport,[17] or the granting of greater transit facilities, either now or in future, than those provided for by the Convention.[18] In addition to the means of transport listed in the Convention (railway rolling stock, sea, lake and river craft, road vehicles, porters and pack animals),[19] the states concerned may agree to include pipelines and gas lines as well as other means of transport.[20] But all of the "rights of transit" mentioned above must be considered in light of the condition that the transit state exercises full sovereignty over its territory and may act to protect its "legitimate interests" as well as insist that agreements be made regarding terms and conditions for exercising the freedom of transit.[21]

---

[1] Art. 124, Subpara. 1 (a)
[2] Art. 90
[3] Art. 87
[4] Art. 69, Para. 1
[5] Art. 69, Para. 3
[6] Art. 148
[7] Art. 77; Art. 254
[8] Art. 125
[9] Art. 131
[10] Art. 124(1(b)), definition
[11] Art. 127, Para. 1
[12] Art. 127, Para. 2
[13] Art. 126
[14] Art. 130, Para. 1
[15] Art. 130, Para. 2
[16] Art. 128
[17] Art. 129
[18] Art. 132
[19] Art. 124, Subpara. 1(d)
[20] Art. 124, Para. 2
[21] Art. 125, Para. 2-3

Further Readings: - Land-locked States, Page 106
 - Equality"-Equal Rights for All? Page 11

PRINCIPLES OF "FREEDOM OF TRANSIT"

CONTINENT

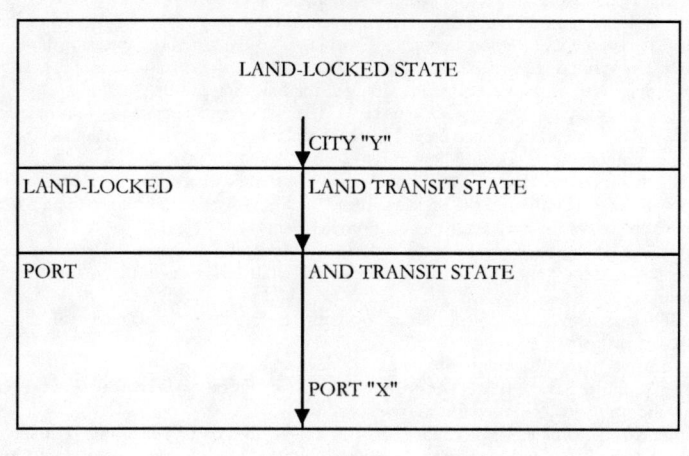

LAND-LOCKED STATE	
	↓ CITY "Y"
LAND-LOCKED	LAND TRANSIT STATE
PORT	AND TRANSIT STATE
	↓ PORT "X"

SEA

"Traffic in Transit" means movement of passengers or goods from City "Y" to Port "X" or vice-versa
(Article 124, Subpara. 1(c))

Rights of Transit States
(Article 125, Paragraphs 2-3)
- Can exercise full sovereignty over their territory
- Rights of land-locked states are not to infringe in any way on the legitimate interests of the transit states

Rights of Land-Locked States
(Article 125, Paragraph 1)
- Have the right of access to and from the sea for the purpose of exercising their rights under the Convention
- Enjoy freedom of transit

(Article 125, Paragraph 2)
The terms and modalities for exercising freedom of transit are to be agreed between the states concerned through bilateral, subregional, and regional agreements

Further regulations Articles 124, 126-132

PRINCIPLES GOVERNING THE AREA

Principal Articles: 133-149

The Area is defined as the sea-bed and ocean floor and subsoil thereof, beyond the limits of national jurisdiction;[1] in other words, it consists of the entire ocean floor which is not subject to sovereign rights of coastal states in an exclusive economic zone or the continental shelf ("the outer shelf").[2] The water surface above the area is the high seas.[3] While the latter is governed by the principle of freedom of the seas, the Area has been declared the common heritage of mankind.[4] Although this expression is an important political manifest, it is not a recognized legal term which would be directly applicable. The declaration of the common heritage is to be put into effect according to the following principles:

First: All rights to the resources, which means all solid, liquid, or gaseous minerals, including polymetallic nodules,[5] *in situ* in the Area,[6] and to archaeological and historical objects[7] are vested in mankind as a whole.[8] An international organization, the Sea-Bed Authority,[9] is to act on behalf of mankind;[10]

Second: All activities of exploration for and exploitation of the resources from the Area are to be carried out for the benefit of mankind[11] and the benefits shared on a non-discriminatory basis which is to provide for the equitable sharing of financial and other economic benefits;[12]

Third: The Area is open to use by all states exclusively for peaceful purposes.[13] The states are to adhere to the Convention and the principles of the Charter of the United Nations in the interest of maintaining peace and security;[14]

Fourth: All states are to be given the opportunity to participate in activities in the Area, and monopolization must be avoided;[15]

Fifth: In particular, special attention is to be paid to developing countries;[16]

Sixth: The Authority has the power necessary to exercise its functions as set forth in Part XI and is to adopt all rules and regulations required for this purpose[17].

The Authority is responsible for promoting and encouraging the conduct of marine scientific research in the Area[18] and the acquisition and transfer to developing countries of technology and scientific knowledge[19]. Furthermore, the Authority must with respect to activities in the Area adopt rules for the protection of the marine environment and human life[20] and the use of installations[21] States Parties may, in accordance with their obligation to act according to the Convention and international law[22], conduct marine scientific research in the Area, and are in any case obligated to promote international co-operation in such research[23] States are responsible for ensuring that any activities in the Area, whether they themselves or natural or juridical person of their nationality carry them out, are effectively controlled and that any such undertakings are carried out in conformity with Part XI[24]. States Parties and entities of the same status[25] are liable for damages caused by their failure to carry out their responsibilities under the Convention[26].

---

[1] Art. 1 Subpara. 1(1)
[2] Art. 57, 76, 134, 142
[3] Art. 135, 86
[4] Art. 136, Preamble
[5] Art. 133, Subpara. (a)
[6] Art. 1, Subpara. 1(1-3)
[7] Art. 149
[8] Art. 137, Para. 2
[9] Art. 156
[10] Art. 137, Para. 2; Art. 153, Para.1
[11] Art. 140, Para. 1
[12] Art. 140, Para. 2
[13] Art. 141
[14] Arzt. 138; Art. 301
[15] Art. 150, Subpara. (g)
[16] Art. 140, 143-144, 148
[17] Art. 157, Para. 2; Annex III, Art.17; (145-147)
[18] Art. 143, Para. 2; 256
[19] Art. 144; 274; Annex III, Art. 5
[20] Art. 145-146
[21] Art. 147
[22] Art. 138
[23] Art. 143, Para. 3
[24] Art. 139, Para. 1
[25] Art. 1, Para., 2; Annex IX, Art. 6
[26] Art. 139, Para. 2; Art. 304, Annex III, Art. 4, Para. 4

Further Readings: - Sea-Bed- Common Heritage of Mankind", Page 5
- New Economic Order? Page 12
- The Area-The Deep Sea-Bed, Page 117

PRINCIPLES GOVERNING THE AREA

Articles 133-149

> The Area and its resources are the common heritage of mankind
> (Article 136)

> All rights to the resources of the Area are vested in mankind as a whole
> (Article 137, Paragraph 2)

Area means the sea-bed and ocean floor and subsoil there-of, beyond the limits of national jurisdiction (Article 1, Subparagraph (1))	*Activities in the Area* means all activities of exploration for and exploitation of the resources of the Area (Article 1, Subparagraph 3)	*Resources* means all solid, liquid, or gaseous mineral resources, including polymetallic nodules, which have been recovered from the Area (Article 133, Subparagraph (a))
		Minerals are resources which have not been recovered from the Area (Article 133, Subparagraph (b))

International Organizations and States		Sea-Bed Authority (Article 156)

Specific Provisions	*General Provisions*	*Specific Provisions*
- No state is to claim sovereignty over any part of the Area and its resources (Article 137, Paragraph 1) - No State is to claim rights with regard to minerals (Article 137, Paragraph 3) - States are to use the Area and installations exclusively for peaceful purposes (Articles 141; 147, Subparagraph 2(d); Article 143) - Conduct of states in the Area is to be in accordance with Convention AND Principles of UN Charter (Article 138) - States are to ensure compliance with Convention (Article 139, Paragraph 1) - States liable for damages (Article 139, Paragraph 2)	- The Area is to be open exclusively for peaceful purposes (Article 141) - Activities are to be carried out for the benefit of mankind (Article 140, Paragraph 1) - Developing countries are to be supported (Articles 140, Paragraph 1; 143, Subparagraph 3(b); 144, Paragraph 2; 148) - Due regard is to be given to coastal state rights (Article 142) - Historical finds can be preserved for the benefit of of mankind (Article 149)	- The Authority is to act for mankind as a whole to the resources (Article 137, Paragraph 2) - Is to provide for an equitable sharing of financial and other benefits (Article 140, Paragraph 2) - Is to require transfer of technology and knowledge to developing states and assist them (Article 144) - Implement regulations for installations (Article 147) - Implement regulations for protection of human life (Article 146) - Implement regulations for protection of marine environment (Article 145) - Carry out marine scientific research (Article 143)

DEVELOPMENT OF THE RESOURCES OF THE AREA

Articles 150-155

Activities in the Area are to be organized, carried out, and controlled by the Sea-Bed Authority.[1] The Authority is to conduct its undertaking in such a manner as to foster healthy development of world economy and balanced growth of international trade[2] and to promote both just and stable prices remunerative to producers and fair to consumers as well as a long-term equilibrium between supply and demand.[3] These goals are inherent in the provisions on production policy as well,[4] and are the logical and consistent development of the overriding principle that the Area and its resources are to be developed for the benefit of mankind as a whole.[5] Further policies to be followed are[6] *inter alia* (a) responsible conduct in the Area and on the world mineral markets, (b) acquisition and transfer of technology, (c) raising and use of all kinds of revenues from activities in the Area, (d) enhancement of opportunities for activities for all states, and (e) taking at each step the interests and needs of particular states or particular groups of states into consideration. These general policy aims are to be accepted and supported by all states, their nationals, and the Enterprise when conducting activities in the Area[7] under the organization and control of the Authority, and are regulated in particular in Annexes III (Basic Conditions of Prospecting, Exploration, and Exploitation) and IV (Statute of the Enterprise).[8]

For an interim period of up to twenty-five years (beginning five years before first commercial production),[9] the Authority must adhere to a detailed production policy for polymetallic nodules, which is to be calculated on the basis of the projected world nickel consumption.[10] Production authorizations for operators are also to be issued in accordance with these projections.[11] The Authority has further the power to limit the production of minerals other than those in polymetallic nodules[12] and may implement compensation schemes or take economic measures for developing countries which might suffer adverse effects as a result of the production policy issued.[13]

The performance of the Authority is to be reviewed by the Assembly[14] at intervals of five years[15] with the aim of improving the practice of the deep-sea mining regime. In addition, the Assembly is to convene a Review Conference fifteen years after commercial production commences.[16]

In summary, it can be said that the duties entrusted to the Authority go beyond those of simple administrative nature. The Authority is to take any measures necessary to promote the growth, efficiency, and stability of markets of commodities produced from minerals derived from the Area[17] and can enforce such policies by means of the right to participate in any commodity conference and the right to become a party to any arrangement or agreement resulting from such a conference.[18] The Authority's duties and rights are intended to enable management with political effect, but it must avoid discrimination in the exercise of its power and functions[19] and monopolization of activities in the Area.[20]

---

[1] Art. 153, Para. 1
[2] Art. 150
[3] Art. 150, Subpara. (f)
[4] Art. 151, Subpara. 1 (a)
[5] Art. 140(1; Art. 150(i)
[6] Art. 150
[7] Art. 138, 150; Art. 153, Para. 2
[8] Art. 153, Para. 1; Art. 162, Subpara. 2(i-l)
[9] Art. 151, Para. 3
[10] Art. 151, Para. 2-9
[11] Art. 151, Para. 2(165, 2(n))
[12] Art. 151, Para. 9
[13] Art. 150(h); 151(10)
[14] Art. 159-160
[15] Art. 154
[16] Art. 155
[17] Art. 151, Subpara. 1(a)
[18] Art. 151, Subpara. 1(b)
[19] Art. 152, Para. 2
[20] Art. 150, Subpara. (g); Annex III, Art. 7, Para. 5

Further Readings: - Deep Sea Mining, Page 121
- Governmental Organizations as Party to the Convention, Page 110

DEVELOPMENT OF RESOURCES

POLICIES RELATING TO ACTIVITIES, ARTICLES 150 AND 151

Activities in the Area are to promote

In General:
- Healthy development of world economy
- Balanced growth of international trade
- International co-operation

In Particular: - Development of resources and orderly, safe and, rational management
- Participation of all states in all opportunities, avoiding monopolization
- Support of developing countries
- Efficient and reasonable involvement in the mineral market
- Development of the common heritage of mankind

PRODUCTION POLICY, ARTICLE 151

Principles of Policy
- Growth, efficiency, and stability of mineral market
- Prices remunerative for producer
- Prices fair for consumer

External Policy of Authority
- Act through fora which include producers and consumers
- Participate in commodity conferences,

Internal Policy of Authority for Interim Period (Paragraph 3)
- Establish annual production ceiling based on nickel consumption (Paragraph 4) for the exploitation of polymetallic nodules
- Issue for each operator production authorization (Paragraph 2) for no more than 46,500 metric tons of nickel per year (Subparagraph 6(b))
- May limit production of minerals other than those found in polymetallic nodules (Paragraph 9)
- Take measures to counteract adverse effects for developing producer states (Paragraph 10)

SYSTEM OF, EXPLORATION AND EXPLOITATION, ARTICLE 153

- The Authority is to organize, carry out, and control activities
- The Authority is to issue rules, regulations, and procedures to this effect (Annex III, Article 17)
- Activities are to be carried out in accordance with a formal written plan of work approved by the Council (Article 162, Subparagraph 2(j)) (and a production authorization (151, 2; 165, 2(n)) by
- the Enterprise, the organ of the Authority (Article 170; Annexes III and IV)
- (a) states parties, (b) state enterprises, (c) natural persons, (d) juridical persons who meet the requirements of Part XI (Art. 153) and Annex III (Art 3-7)

PERIODIC REVIEW AND REVIEW CONFERENCE, ARTICLES 154-155

- Periodic review every five years by Assembly to improve the manner of practice of the regime of the Area
- Review Conference fifteen years after beginning of commercial production. The Conference is to develop the system and adopt amendments by means of consensus (Article 314)

THE SEA-BED AUTHORITY

The Convention provides for the establishment of the International Sea-Bed Authority[1] at the time the Convention goes into effect. As this date was not known at the time of the conclusion of the Conference, it was decided to establish a Preparatory Commission to make the necessary arrangements for the commencement of the functions of the Authority.[2] The Commission, which was established in December 1982, is to remain in existence until the conclusion of the first session of the Sea-Bed Authority Assembly.[3]

The Authority thus established has international legal personality and such legal capacity as may be necessary for the exercise of its functions and the fulfillment of its purposes.[4] The Authority and certain persons connected with it enjoy diplomatic status in the performance of their duties.[5] Members of the Authority are those states and entities which are "states parties."[6] The Authority is based on the principle of the sovereign equality of all its members[7] and is the organization through which the States Parties organize and control activities in the Area with the view of administering the resources[8] for the benefit of mankind as a whole, on whose behalf the Authority is to act.[9]

The long-term goal is for the Sea-Bed Authority to become self-supporting. Until that time, the Authority is to receive contributions from its members, the amount of which is to be fixed in accordance with the regular budget of the United Nations.[10] Further funds necessary for operation are to come from activities in the Area, i.e., from royalties paid by operators in the Area,[11] from payments by the Enterprise,[12] or from coastal states for exploration of the outer shelf.[13] The Authority may also raise money by other means, particularly in the initial phase.[14] It also has the right to borrow funds, for which the States Parties are not liable.[15]

The Convention establishes four organs to enable the Authority to fulfil its tasks, three of which are the Assembly, the Council, and the Secretariat.[16] The fourth organ established by the Convention is the Enterprise, through which the Authority carries out activities in the Area directly in accordance with a formal written plan of work as well as transporting, processing, and marketing minerals recovered from the Area.[17] Further subsidiary organs may be established by the Authority as necessary.[18] Except for the Enterprise (which enjoys a special status), these organs act through the Authority. The Authority is the body which concludes contracts with mining operators[19] and which is liable for damage caused by wrongful acts or omissions by the organization[20] or its staff.[21] While actions against the Authority are to be submitted to the Sea-Bed Disputes Chamber[22] certain violations by staff members[23] are considered by a special tribunal of the Authority.[24]

---

[1] Art. 156, Para. 1
[2] Final Act, Annex I, Resolution I
[3] *Ibid* (Para. 13)
[4] Art. 176
[5] Art. 177-183
[6] Art.156, Para. 2; Art. 1, Para. 2; 306-307
[7] Art. 157, Para.3
[8] Art. 157, Para.1
[9] Art. 137, Para. 2; Art. 153, Para. 1
[10] Art. 171, Subpara. (a); Art. 160, Subpara. 2(e)
[11] Art. 171(b); Annex III, Art. 13
[12] Art. 171(c); Annex IV, Art.10
[13] Art. 82
[14] Art. 171, Subpara. (d-f)
[15] Art. Art. 174, Para. 4
[16] Art. 158, Para. 1
[17] Art. 158, Para. 2; Art.153, Para. 2; Art. 170, Para. 1
[18] Art. 158, Para. 3; Art. 160, Para. 2(d)
[19] Annex III, Art. 3; Art. 6
[20] Annex III, Art. 22
[21] Art. 168, Para. 3
[22] Art. 187, Subpara. (e)
[23] Art. 168, Para. 2
[24] Art. 168, Para. 3

Further Readings: - Developing States, Page 107
 - Measures to Close the Economic Gap, Page 129

SEA-BED AUTHORITY

Articles 171-175

SEAT: JAMAICA (Article 156, Paragraph 4)

OTHER LOCATIONS: Yes, for regional centres and offices (Article 156, Paragraph 5)

MEMBERS: All States Parties and those bodies which are entitled to ratify or accede to the Convention (Article 305, Subparagraphs l(a-f); Articles 306-307)

SUSPENSION OF RIGHTS FOR STATE PARTIES:
- Voting rights: State Party in arrears of payment of contribution (Article 184)
- Exercise of rights and privileges: Gross and persistent violations of Part XI, The Area (Article 185)
- State parties which have transferred rights to an international organization may not exercise themselves rights transferred (Annex IX)

OBSERVERS: Those observers of the Conference who have signed the final act of the Conference (Article 156, Paragraph 3); African National Congress, Netherlands Antilles, Palestine Liberation Organization, Pan Africanist Congress of Azania, South West Africa People's Organization.

FUNDAMENTAL PRINCIPLES (ARTICLE 157): The Authority - Is the organ through which states parties administer the resources of the Area - Has powers and functions expressed in the Convention and any incidental powers consistent with the Convention necessary for conduct of activities in the Area - Is based on the sovereign equality of all members - All members are to act in good faith	
Legal Status, Privileges and Immunities, Articles 176-183	Financial Arrangement of the Authority, Articles 171-175
Legal Status, Article 176 - The Authority has international legal personality Privileges and Immunity, Articles 177-182 - for the Authority - for certain persons connected with the Authority; Representatives of States, the Secretary-General, and the staff of the Authority Exemption from taxes and customs duties, Article 183	Funds of the Authority, Article 171 - assessed contributions of members funds received from activities in the Area - funds transferred for the enterprise - borrowed funds - voluntary contributions - payment to a compensation fund for specific developing countries Annual Budget, Article 172 Expenses, Article 173 Borrowing power, Article 174 Annual Audit, Article 175

THE ORGANS OF THE AUTHORITY

The Assembly is the supreme organ of the Authority and has the power to establish general policy[1]. It consists of all members of the Authority, each member having one representative.[2] The Assembly meets in regular annual sessions,[3] if not otherwise decided, at Jamaica, the seat of the Authority.[4] The Assembly adopts its rules of procedure and elects its president and other officers as required, who hold office until their successors are elected at the next regular session.[5] The Assembly has the power to establish general policies on any question or matter within the competence of the Authority[6] as well as powers and functions expressly stated in the Convention.[7] Decisions on questions of procedure, including special sessions, are taken by a majority vote of the members present and voting;[8] decisions on all other questions (questions of substance) can -in general - be taken only by a two-thirds majority of the members present and voting.[9]

The Council is the executive organ of the Authority and has the power to establish, in conformity with the Convention and the general policies established by the Assembly, the specific policies to be pursued by the Authority on any question or matter within the Authority's competence.[10] The Council consists of thirty-six members, who are elected by the Assembly in accordance with a detailed directive designed to ensure that states parties with certain interests and from certain regions are represented.[11] The electoral term is four years,[12] and each member of the Council has one vote.[13] The council meets as often as the business of the Authority requires, but not less than three times a year, at the seat of the Authority.[14]

Two organs are established to advise and aid the Council:[15] an Economic Planning Commission, and a Legal and Technical Commission. Each Commission has fifteen members who are elected by the Council from among the candidates nominated by the states parties.[16] The candidates are expected to be highly qualified in the fields appropriate for the position,[17] and they are elected to serve a five-year term.[18] The commissions' responsibilities cover a wide field, but they have no independent directive power and can act only through the Council or on behalf of the Authority (e.g., issue production authorizations).[19]

The Secretariat is established to fulfil the administrative functions of the Authority. The Secretary-General is elected by the Assembly for a term of four years.[20] The staff is appointed by the Secretary-General and employed in accordance with the regulations of the Authority.[21] The Secretary and his staff are obligated to secrecy.[22]

The Enterprise is organized with elements of a private company, with a director general and a governing board of fifteen members[23] and has to operate in accordance with sound commercial principles.[24] But its position remains that of an organ of the Authority, and as such it envoys certain privileges and must fulfil specific duties.[25] The Enterprise is subject to direction and control by the Council[26] and must after an initial period of a maximum of ten years transfer income to the Authority[27].

---

[1] Art. 160(1), e.g. Art. 150
[2] Art. 159, Para. 1
[3] Art. 159, Para. 2
[4] Art. 159, Para. 3; 156, 4
[5] Art. 159, Para. 4
[6] Art. 160, Para. 1
[7] Art. 157, Para. 2
[8] Art. 159, Para. 7
[9] Art. 159, Para. 8-10
[10] Art. 162, Para. 1
[11] Art. 161, Para. 1-2
[12] Art. 161, Para. 3
[13] Art. 161, Para. 7
[14] Art. 161, Para. 5
[15] Art. 163, Para. 1
[16] Art. 163, Para.2
[17] Art. 163, Para. 3
[18] Art. 163, Para. 5
[19] art. 164-165 (165, 2(n))
[20] Art. 166
[21] Art. 167, Para. 3
[22] Art. 168, Para. 2
[23] Annex IV, Art. 4-7
[24] Annex IV, Art. 1, Para. 3
[25] Art. 170
[26] Art.170, Para. 2; Art. 162, Subpara. 2(i)
[27] Annex IV, Art. 10, Para. 1&3

THE ORGANIZATION OF THE AUTHORITY
Articles 158-170

THE ASSEMBLY (Article 159)
MEMBERS: All State Parties (Article 156, Paragraph 2) and others (Articles 305-307)
MEETINGS: In regular annual sessions (Article 159, Paragraph 2)
PLACE: Seat of the authority (Article 159, Paragraph 3)
VOTE: Each member has one vote (Article 159, Paragraph 6)
DECISSIONS: 1. Questions of procedure and special sessions = Majority vote (Article 159, Paragraph 7)
2. Questions of substance = Two-thirds majority (Articles159, Paragraphs 8-10)

ELECTS
(Article 160, Paragraph 2)

In accordance with
Article 161, Paragraph 1-2

In accordance with
Annex IV, Article 5

THE COUNCIL
Articles 161-165

Members: 36
Applicable criteria for the election of members from those states with
- high imports of minerals = 4
- largest investment in the Area = 4
- Major exports of minerals = 4
- Developing countries with specific interests = 6
- Equitable representation of regions = 18

Meetings: as often as required, but not less than three times a year

THE SECRETARY-GENERAL
Articles 166-169

The Secretary-General is chief administrative office of the authority

elects → The Economic Planning Commissions (15 Members) Article 163

Advice to the Council Article 164

elects → The Legal and Technical Commissions (15 Members) Article 163

Advice to the Council Article 165

THE ENTERPRISE
Article 170

1. Director General
2. Governing Board
15 Members

The Council is the executive organ of the Authority; it establishes, in conformity with the Convention and the general policies established by the Assembly, the specific policies to be pursued by the Authority on any question or matter within the competence of the Authority, Article 162, e.g.:
- issue directives to the Enterprise
- make recommendations to the Assembly
- review the collection of payments
- submit the proposed annual budget
- approve plan of work (Annex III, Art.6)

The Enterprise carries out activities in the Area directly, including transporting, processing, and marketing of minerals recovered from the Area, Article 170 and Annex IV, Article 1

THE SEA-BED DISPUTES CHAMBER

ARTICLES 186-191

Disputes arising from deep-sea mining activities[1] in the Area are to be settled by compulsory procedures which basically do not give the parties a choice of courts or tribunals.[2] In interpreting or applying provisions related to the sea-bed Area and related Annexes, jurisdiction is to be exercised in such a manner as to ensure that rulings are uniform. The essential device for achieving this goal is the Sea-Bed Disputes Chamber, a special chamber of the Tribunal for the Law of the Sea.[3] This Tribunal elects eleven of its twenty-one members[4] to the Sea-Bed Disputes Chamber[5] for a three-year term; a quorum of seven members is required to constitute the Chamber. [6]The Chamber has jurisdiction in the following cases:

(1) States parties in dispute may submit cases to a three-member *ad hoc* chamber formed from the members of the Sea-Bed Disputes Chamber[7] or to a special chamber of the Tribunal for the Law of the Sea;[8]

(2) Contractual disputes, including those involving the plan of work, with respect to interpretation or application[9] and financial terms in general and in particular with respect to transfer of technology[10] are to be submitted to binding commercial arbitration (if the parties to the dispute do not agree otherwise).[11] But tribunals for commercial arbitration have no jurisdiction on questions of the interpretation of the Area provisions and the Annexes; such questions must be referred to the Sea-Bed Disputes Chamber.[12] In summary: questions on interpretation of the Convention which are related to the interpretation of Part XI (Activities in the Area) cannot be referred to or decided by commercial arbitration;[13]

(3) The Sea-Bed Disputes Chamber has no jurisdiction with regard to the exercise by the Authority of its discretionary powers; furthermore, it does not pronounce itself on the question of whether any rules, regulations, and procedures of the Authority are in conformity with the Convention, nor does it declare invalid any such rules, regulations, and procedures.[14] This limitation of the Chamber's jurisdiction should be regarded in light of the majority requirements for taking decisions on questions of substance in the Assembly[15] and of the possibility for the Assembly to request opinions from the Chamber.[16]

The Chamber gives advisory opinions at the request of the Assembly or the Council on legal questions arising within the scope of their activities and treats such requests as matters of urgency.[17]

The procedure of the Sea-Bed Disputes Chamber is governed by the provisions applicable for the International Tribunal for the Law of the Sea. [18] In cases where a natural or judicial person is a party to a dispute, the sponsoring state[19] has the right to participate in the proceedings by submitting written or oral statements. [20]

---

[1] Art, 1, Subpara. 1(3)
[2] Art. 187; Art. 288, Para. 3; Art. 287, Para. 1
[3] Art. 287, Subpara. 1(a); Annex VI, Art. 35
[4] Annex VI, Art. 2
[5] Annex VI, Art. 35
[6] Annex VI, Art. 35, Para. 7
[7] Art. 188, Subpara 1 (b); Annex VI, art. 36
[8] Art. 188, Subpara. 1(a); Annex VI, Art.15
[9] Art. 187, Subpara. (c)(i)
[10] Annex III, Art. 13 (15); Art. 5, Para. 4
[11] *Ibid*; Art. 188, Para. 2
[12] Art. 188, Subpara. 2(a-b); Art. 288, Para. 3
[13] *Ibid*. Art. 286
[15] Art. 159, Para. 8
[16] Art. 159, Para. 10
[17] Art. 191
[18] Part. XV, (Art. 289-296); Annex VI, Art. 40
[19] Art. 153, Para. 2(b); Annex III, Art. 4, Para. 3
[20] Art. 190, Para. 1

Further Readings: - Authority-Contractors (Layout), Page 85
                   - Tribunal of the Law of the Sea, Page 90

THE SEA-BED DISPUTES CHAMBER

	LAW OF THE SEA TRIBUNAL (Annex VI, Articles 1-19) Members: 21 Term of Office: 9 years		
Ad Hoc Chamber (Annex VI, Art. 36) Members: 3	*Sea-Bed Disputes Chamber* (Art. 186-191; Annex VI, Art. 14, 35-40) MEMBERS 11 (elected from the members of the Tribunal); 7 members constitute a quorum TERMS OF OFFICE: 3 years	Special Chamber (Annex VI, Art. 15) Members: 3 or more	Chamber of Summary Procedure (Annex VI, Art. 15) Members: 5

PRINCIPLES OF THE SEA-BED DISPUTES CHAMBER'S JURISDICTION WITH RESPECT TO ACTIVITIES IN THE AREA

Obligatory Jurisdiction of Sea-Bed Dispute Chamber on Non-Contractual Matters

Disputes between States Parties concerning Part XI, including Annexes, Art. 187(a) - which can, however, be submitted instead:
   1. to a special chamber of the Tribunal (Art. 188, Para. 1(a)); or
   2. to an *ad hoc chamber* (Art. 188, Para. 1(b))

Disputes between a State Party and the Authority (Art. 187(b)) concerning alleged violation by State Party or Authority with the limitation that the Chamber has no jurisdiction with regard to the Authority's discretionary power (Art. 189)

Obligatory Jurisdiction of Sea-Bed Disputes Chamber on Contractual Matters

Disputes between States Parties, the Authority or the Enterprise, state enterprise, and natural and judicial persons in cases of omission, refusal, or liability affecting contractual relations (Article 187, Subpara. (c)(ii), (d), (e))
but not in   (1) disputes concerning the interpretation or application of the contract or plan of work Art. 188, Subpara. 2(a) with further reference);
   (2) Disputes over financial terms of contracts (Annex III, Art. 13, Para. 15);
   (3) Disputes related to transfer of technology - commercial terms and conditions – (Annex III, Art. 5, Para. 4).

   Such disputes shall be referred to binding commercial arbitration.

Other Tasks of the Sea-Bed Disputes Chamber

- On submission of a commercial arbitral tribunal, decide any question of interpretation of Part XI and Annexes (Article 188, Subparagraph 2(b))
- Advisory opinions at the request of the Assembly on conformity of proposals before the Assembly with the Convention (Art. 159, Para. 10)
- Decisions on suspension of membership (Art. 185)
- Advisory opinions at the request of the Assembly and Council on legal questions (Art. 191)

POLLUTION PREVENTION REGULATIONS IN GENERAL

This Part represents a constitution for the prevention of pollution of the seas on a global, regional, and local basis. Any obligations assumed by states under special conventions and agreements related to the protection and preservation of the marine environment are to be carried out in a manner consistent with the general principles and objectives of the Convention;[1] consequently, these provisions should not be viewed solely as a text of law, as they are also a political document. This thread of thought can be found in many of the provisions, which require the states to undertake efforts to create a reliable and effective global system for the protection of the marine environment by means of international co-operation, including technical assistance and environment observation,[2] and the application of international regulations and standards.[3]

All states have the obligation to protect and preserve the marine environment[4] and can be held liable for failure to fulfil their obligations,[5] e.g., if pollution spreads beyond the area where a state exercises its sovereign rights.[6] They are obliged to take measures to reduce to the fullest possible extent pollution from all sources, whether land-based sources, sea-bed activities, dumping, the atmosphere, or vessels;[7] furthermore, plans must be made to prevent accidents and deal with emergencies that may occur during the operation of vessels and installations and devices used for exploration and exploitation.[8] However, these provisions affect mostly the coastal states and the flag states; only those provisions dealing with the Area,[9] dumping,[10] and the atmosphere[11] (which includes air navigation) affect all states, as these fields are either partly or wholly related to the high seas. A corollary to these provisions is the granting of investigative power to port states, which may even initiate proceedings in respect of unlawful discharge beyond their general jurisdiction against any vessel, which is voluntarily within a port or at an off-shore terminal of the port state.[12]

The main responsibility for the protection of the marine environment lies with the states, which have a coastline. These states, which enjoy the benefits of being granted sovereign rights over living and non-living resources within the limits of an exclusive economic zone[13] and a continental shelf,[14] have also been given the corresponding duty to protect and preserve the marine environment within these areas.[15] Significant in this context are the duties not to transfer damage or hazards,[16] to provide necessary information,[17] and control land-based sources of pollution,[18] sea-bed activities,[19] and vessels.[20] The Convention distinguishes among varying levels of intensity of involvement, e.g., "taking into account," "not less effective," and "giving effect." This results from the Conference's aim of unifying pollution regulations on a global basis[21] without overburdening the capabilities of developing states.[22] However, the urgency of controlling marine pollution also caused the Conference to provide for scientific and technical assistance[23] and preferential treatment for developing countries in their efforts to prevent, reduce, or control pollution and its effects on the environment.

---

[1] Art. 237, Para. 2
[2] Art. 197-206
[3] Art. 207(1), 208(3), 209(2); 210(6), 211(2), 212(1)
[4] Art. 192
[5] Art. 235, Para. 1
[6] Art. 194, Para. 2; Art. 195
[7] Part. XII, Sec. 5-6
[8] Art. 194, Para. 3
[9] Art. 209, 215
[10] Art. 210, 216
[11] Art. 212, 222
[12] Art. 218
[13] Art. 56-57
[14] Art. 76
[15] Art. 193, 207-208
[16] Art. 195
[17] Art. 206
[18] Art. 207
[19] Art. 208
[20] Art. 194, Para. 3
[21] Art. 237
[22] Art. 207, Para. 4
[23] Art. 202; Art. 203

Further Readings: -Preservation of the Marine Environment, Page 126
 -Indemnity, Page 128
 -Dumping, Page 123

FRAMEWORK FOR POLLUTION PREVENTION

The general application of the Convention: The Provisions of the Convention are without prejudice for other obligations assumed by the states to prevent pollution; however, all obligations are to be earned out in a manner consistent with the general principles and objectives of the Convention (Art 237).

GENERAL OBLIGATION	PARTICULAR OBLIGATION		
States have the obligation to protect and preserve the marine environment (Art 192) and must incorporate international law to various degrees, see column. *Legislation* below	States are responsible and liable with regard to their international Obligations (Art. 235)	States are to cooperate on global and regional Basis (Art. 197-201)	States are to monitor and report (Art. 204-206)
	States must not transfer hazard or transform one type of pollution to another (Art. 195-196)	States must render technical assistance to developing states (Art. 202)	
Source of Pollution	Legislation Art. 207-212, 237	Enforcement Art. 213-222	Responsibilty and Liability General: Art 304
Land-based source	207, State (taking into account)	213, Coastal state	Art 235
Sea-bed activities territorial Sea Exclusive Economic Zone	208(1), Coastal state 208(2-3), States (not less effective)	214, Costal state	Art. 235
Area	209(1), Authority Annex III, Art 17 209(2), States (not less effective)	215, Authority in accordance with Part XI, Annex III, Art.47	Art 235
Dumping	210, States (not less effective)	216(a), Coastal State 216(b), Flag state 216(c), Any state for loading of wastes or other matters occurring in territory	Art. 235
Vessel	194, 3, States 211, 2, Flag State (at least to the same effect) 211, 4, Coastal state 211, 5, Coastal state (giving effect) 211, 6, Coastal State	For details, including safeguards, see next two diagrams Warship immunity, Art 236	Art 232, 235-236
Atmosphere	212, States (taking into account)	222, States	Art 235
Ice-covered area	234, Coastal state (non-discriminatory)		Art. 235-236

POLLUTION LEGISLATION APPLICABLE TO VESSELS

ARTICLE 211

Whereas a flag state grants a vessel its nationality[1] and therefore exercises sovereignty on board, a coastal state enjoys sovereignty in its territorial sea[2] and jurisdiction in regard to pollution matters in the exclusive economic zone.[3] During the last few decades, coastal states have become increasingly reluctant to accept common flag state jurisdiction and the consequent problems of enforcement and have sought more influence and control in pollution matters related to navigation, effective exercise of jurisdiction, and rights for prevention measures. The Convention therefore obliges shipping states to establish international rules and standards through competent organizations or diplomatic conferences.[4] As far as agreements and standards have been established and practiced,[5] they form the backbone of a legal framework for prevention of pollution. The Convention provisions in this Part contain the general principles, which the legal framework is to apply[6] and according to which it will, if necessary, be re-examined from time to time.[7]

The basic principles of the 1982 Convention concerning pollution matters provide that the primary responsibility for establishing measures for the prevention of pollution by vessels lies with the flag state. The flag state is to adopt laws and regulations for the prevention of pollution which are to have at least the same effect as generally accepted international rules and standards established through the competent organization[8] (competent organization here means International Maritime Organization - IMO -) and take measures to ensure to the fullest possible extent the safety of operations at sea, including the regulation of design, construction, equipment, operation and manning of vessels, prevention of accidents, and prevention of intentional and unintentional discharges, and is to provide emergency measures.[9] As the coastal states which cooperate in regional pollution prevention agreements may require information from foreign vessels navigating in their territorial sea,[10] the flag state is to ensure that the master of a vessel flying its flag furnishes information as to whether his destination is a port of that region and, if so, whether his ship complies with port entry requirements.[11] There is further the obligation to render information required in order to determine if a violation has occurred.[12]

In exercising sovereignty in the territorial sea, the coastal states can take measures in regard to accidents, emergencies, safety of operations and discharge, and so on, except with respect to design, construction, manning, or equipment of foreign vessels on innocent passage.[13] National measures may not hamper the right of innocent passage through the territorial sea.[14] Where a ship is exercising its right of transit passage[15] through straits, the bordering states may adopt laws only in respect to discharge of oil and similar substances[16] and can only in part apply the provisions of Part XII.[17] Archipelagic states, on the other hand, can apply Part XII[18] for vessels in archipelagic sea lane passage, [19] but in adopting laws have to keep in mind that the regulations for sea lane passage refer only to discharge. [20]For its exclusive economic zone, a coastal state may adopt only laws which give effect to generally accepted international rules, [21] but may also tighten such rules for a particular, clearly defined area of the exclusive economic zone[22] and in ice-covered areas. [23]

---

[1] Art. 91
[2] Art. 2
[3] Art. 56, Subpara. 1 (b) (iii)
[4] Art. 211, Para. 1
[5] e.g. Convention for the Prevention of Pollution from Ships(MARPOL)
[6] Art. 237
[7] Art. 211, Para. 1
[8] Art. 211, Para. 2
[9] Art. 194, Subpara. 3(b)
[10] Art. 211, Para. 3
[11] Art. 211, Para. 3
[12] Art. 220, Para 4, Art. 211, Para. 7
[13] Art. 21, Subpara. 1 (f); Art. 211, Para. 4; Art. 194, Subpara. 3 (b)
[14] Art. 211, Para. 4, Art. 24
[15] Art. 38
[16] Art. 42, Subpara.1 (b)
[17] Art. 233, Art. 192-206; remain applicable
[18] Art. 233 applicable only to straits
[19] Art. 53
[20] Art. 54 and 42, Subpara. 1 (b)
[21] Art. 211, Para. 5
[22] Art. 211, Para. 6
[23] Art. 234

Further Readings: -Ships-Vessels, Page 118
-Preservation of the Marine Environment, Page 126

Bernaerts' Guide to the Law of The Sea   67

GENERAL JURISDICTION FOR VESSELS

Note: (1)   The regulations of the Convention for the prevention of pollution do not apply to warships and other vessels owned by governments and in non-commercial service. However, states are to ensure that such ships act, as far as reasonable and practicable, in a manner consistent with the Convention (Art. 236).
      (2)   The provisions of the Convention do not affect
            - the institution of civil proceedings in respect of any claim for loss or damage resulting from pollution of the marine environment (Art. 229), or
            - the rights of states to take and enforce measures to, avoid pollution arising from maritime casualties (Art. 221).

STATES   - Are obligated to protect and preserve the marine environment (Art. 192)
            - Are to take measures to prevent pollution by vessels (Art. 194, Subpara. 3(b))

THE COASTAL STATE		*THE FLAG STATE ,*	
- is sovereign in the territorial sea (Art 2) - has jurisdiction in marine environment matters (Art 56, Subpara 1(b)(iii), Art 192) - deals with emergencies and safety of operation of vessels (Art 194, Subpara 3(b)), but not for construction, etc (Art 21, Para 2)		- has in general jurisdiction and control in administrative, technical, and social matters (Art 94, Para 1) - takes pollution measures for emergencies, design, etc (Art 194, Subpara 3(b)) - must adopt pollution regulations which have at least the same effect as that of international rules (Art 211, Para 2)	
High Seas	Port State Enforcement (218)	Exclusive Jurisdiction (92, (1))	must ensure at all times the compliance with applicable international rules and standards (Art 217, 194, Subpara 3(b), 211) effective enforcement (Art 217, Para 1) - detain vessel which is not seaworthy (Art 217, Para 2) - ensure inspection (Art 217, Para 3) - conduct investigations, institute proceedings (Art 217, Para 4) - information upon request (Art 217, Para 5) - provide adequate penalties (Art 217, Para 8) - ensure that masters give adequate information (Art 211, Para 3) - air pollution matters (Art 212, Para 1) - ensure that masters give information whether pollution has occurred (Art 220, Para 3)
Exclusive economic zone	- May adopt laws, giving effect to generally accepted international rules and standards (211, (5)) - may adopt special mandatory measures for clearly defined areas (211, (6), 234)	- Exclusive jurisdiction (58, 87-94) if compatible with other provisions of the Convention - (See Art 228)	
Territorial Sea	- may in the exercise of its sovereignty adopt laws which do not hamper innocent passage (211, (4), 21, (1)(f)) - Not with respect to design, construction, etc (21, (2))	flag state can enforce physically its general jurisdiction through coastal state only (with respect to Innocent passage See Art 27 Subpara 1(c))	
Archipelagic Waters	Sea lane passage (53, 54, 42, 1(b))		
Straits	- are to give effect to international pollution regulations regarding discharge (Art 42, Subpara 1(b)) - further pollution regulations by special agreements (Art 43, Subpara (b)) as Art 207-232 not applicable (Art 233)	See above, Territorial Sea	
Archipelagic Sea Lanes	- are to give effect to international pollution regulations regarding discharge (Art 42, Subpara 1(b), 54)	See above Territorial Sea	
Inland waters, ports	These waters are not subject to the Convention	See above Territorial Sea	

ENFORCEMENT OF POLLUTION LAWS APPLICABLE TO VESSELS

ARTICLES 217-233

The provisions of enforcement are carefully designed to balance the opposing interests of the flag states and the coastal states. Just as the flag state has primary legislative jurisdiction over its vessels, it also bears the primary responsibility for ensuring that its vessels comply with international law.[1] In the event of a violation, the flag state is to institute investigations and proceedings.[2] Penalties provided by the laws and regulations of the flag state must be sufficiently severe to discourage violations, wherever they might occur. [3]Although official vessels are not subject to these Convention provisions, similar measures are to be implemented for such ships by each state,[4] which is also liable for any damage caused by its vessels.[5]

The coastal state, on the other hand, has been vested with rights (in varying degrees) to enforce pollution laws, although safeguards have been built in to ensure that this power can be exercised only to a limited extent. The measures, which can be taken,[6] depend on the exact nature of the violation with regard to two sets of factors:

1) Location of violation: territorial sea, exclusive economic zone; location of vessel: territorial sea, exclusive economic zone, voluntarily in port
2) Intensity of violation: substantial discharge, major damage, any violation; reasons for acting: warranted by evidence, clear grounds for believing.

The measures the coastal state may take include request for information, physical inspection, proceedings, and even detention[7]. With some generalization, it can be said that the coastal state jurisdiction is strongest when the vessel is voluntarily in port[8] and weakens with increasing distance of the location of the violation from the coast (zone by zone) and the impact of the damage or the threat of damage.

All measures must be taken in compliance with the safeguards given in Articles 223 to 233, which prohibit undue delay of a foreign vessel, excessive physical inspection, and general disregard for accepted international rules[9] and provide for the release of vessels, subject to reasonable procedures such as bonding or appropriate financial security.[10] If a detaining state has not released a vessel, the question is subject to compulsory dispute settlement.[11]

Finally, coastal states taking measures have obligations to other affected states, particularly the flag state,[12] and to international organizations.[13] The flag state must be notified of measures taken (although not in all circumstances), and all official reports concerning the measures must be submitted to the flag state.[14] The flag state can institute proceedings itself, thus suspending -with certain exceptions - the proceedings in the coastal state.[15] If a vessel has been detained, e.g., due to lack of seaworthiness,[16] the flag state must be informed promptly.[17]

States are liable for damages or loss resulting from such measures if the measures are unlawful or unreasonable.[18] This provision also applies to a port state, which investigates or institutes proceedings against a vessel based on an allegation of unlawful discharge on the high seas or in zones of other states (on request).[19] Investigation reports are to be transmitted to the flag state or the coastal state upon request and instituted proceedings suspended.[20]

---

[1] Art. 217, Para. 1
[2] Art. 217, Para. 4
[3] Art. 217, Para. 8
[4] Art. 236
[5] *Ibid.*; Art. 31; 42; Para. 5; 235, 304
[6] Art. 219-221
[7] Art. 219; 220, (2)&(6)
[8] Art. 220, Para. 1
[9] Art. 226, Subpara. 1(a)
[10] Art. 220(7); 226(1)
[11] Art. 292; 297(1)(c)
[12] Art. 223, 231
[13] Art. 223
[14] Art. 231
[15] Art. 228
[16] Art. 219
[17] Art. 226, Subpara. 1(c); 231
[18] Art. 232
[19] Art. 218, Para. 2-3
[20] Art. 218, Para. 4

GENERAL ENFORCEMENT CONCEPT
ARTICLES 217-220 (ENFORCEMENT): 223-233 (SAFEGUARDS)

Abbreviations TS = Territorial Sea, EEZ = Exclusive Economic Zone

COASTAL STATE: Rights and Obligations	FLAG STATE- Rights and Obligations
General - Promptly notify flag state of any measures taken and submit reports (Art. 231) - Minimum standards of proceedings (Art 223) - Enforcement by officials only (Art. 224) - Safety of navigation must not be endangered (Art 225) - Foreign vessels may not be discriminated (Art 227) - Liability for unlawful measures (Art. 232, 304) - Release of detained vessels on appropriate security (Art 220(7), 226(l)(b))	- Ensure compliance of vessels with international law (Art. 217) see. previous layout - Must be informed (in cases of proceedings from matters in TS) and given official reports (Art 218-220,231) Must exercise penal jurisdiction and institute investigations (Art 217 (4-8))
Information - Vessels navigating in TS or EEZ which have possibly committed violation in EEZ must provide information (Art 220(3))	- Must ensure that vessels give required information (Art 220(4))
Physical Inspection (examination of certificates only, for more extensive inspection, see Art 226(l)(a)) - Vessels navigating in TS (Art 220(2) - Vessels navigating in TS or EEZ and substantial discharge in EEZ and refusal to give information or case justifies inspection (Art. 220(5))	
Investigations by "port state" - Vessel voluntarily in port and discharge on high seas (elsewhere, on request) (Art 218(3))	- Records on request (Art. 218(4))

Proceedings
- For possible violation by vessels voluntarily in port
  (a) violation in TS and EEZ of law in accordance with Convention (Art. 220(1))
  (b) discharge on high seas and evidence to warrant proceedings (Art 218(1)) or on request (Art 218(2))
- Vessel navigating in TS and evidence to warrant proceedings (Art 220 (2))
- Vessel navigating in TS or EEZ and major damage or threat of such in EEZ (220(6))
	- *Suspension* (Art 228)
	If violation beyond TS, proceedings to be suspended if flag state institutes proceedings *unless* e.g. major damage in EEZ
	- Port state proceedings (Art 218) to be suspended on request of affected coastal state (Art. 218(4); subject to Art 228)
	- Right of attendance (Art 223)

Detention - Vessel navigating in TS and evidence so warrants - Navigating in TS or EEZ and major damage or threat of such in EEZ (Art. 220(6)) - Violation affecting the seaworthiness of vessel (Art 219, 226(1)(c))	- Release of vessels (Art 226(l)(b-c), 220(7), 292) - Prompt notification (Art. 226(l)(c), 231)
Penalties - Only monetary penalties can be imposed (Art 230) except in cases of wilful and serious act of pollution in TS (Art 230(2))	-Suspension in case of violation beyond TS (see above: Proceedings) (Art, 228)
Maritime casualties - Take measures (Art. 221)	

PORT STATE ENFORCEMENT
(ARTICLE 218)

1st Condition: Vessel must be voluntarily in port
2nd Condition: There must be a violation of applicable international rules and standards established through the competent international organization or diplomatic conference

Discharge (as defined by the Convention for the Prevention of Pollution from Ships (MARPOL), 1973) means, in relation to harmful substances or effluents containing such substances, any release howsoever caused from a ship and includes any escape, disposal, spilling, leaking, pumping, emitting, or emptying (Three exceptions related to dumping, activities in the Area, and scientific research are not given here.)

Abbreviations TS = Territorial Sea, EEZ = Exclusive Economic Zone

PROCEEDINGS *Where evidence so warrants*

Location of Violation	Location of Damage or Threat of Same	Basis for Institution of Action	Suspension
Any place	Any place	Request of flag state	Art 228
High seas	—	Rights of port state	Art 228
Internal waters, TS, or EEZ of foreign state High seas or	Affecting the internal waters, TS or EEZ of port state	Rights of port state	Art 228
Internal waters, TS, or EEZ of any state	In internal waters, TS, or EEZ of another state	Request of affected or threatened state	Art 218(4) (Art 228)
Internal waters, TS, or EEZ of a state	—	Request of state where violation occurred	Art 218(4) (Art 228)

INVESTIGATION: *Believed to have occurred in, caused, or threatened damage to*

Any place	Any place	Request of flag state	
High seas	—	Rights of port state	
Internal waters, TS, or EEZ	—	Request of state where violation occurred	Records of investigation are to be transmitted to flag state or state requesting action Art 218, Para 4
—	Internal waters, TS, or EEZ	Upon request of affected state	

Further Readings: - Port States, Page 103

COASTAL STATE ENFORCEMENT (ARTICLE 220)

Location of		Applicable Law	Type of charge or facts	Measures
Vessel	Violation			
Voluntarily in port (Art 220(1))	TS EEZ	Laws and regulations of coastal state - in accordance with the Convention (Art. 21 (2)(f), Art 211(4-7), Art 234) or - applicable international rules and standards	Any violation	Proceedings
TS (Art. 220(2))	TS		1) Clear grounds for belief, *but* without prejudice to right of innocent passage 2) Where evidence so warrants	- Physical inspection (Art 226(I)(a)) or - Further physical inspection (Art 226(I)(a)(i-iii)) - Proceedings - Detention
TS or EEZ (Art. 220(3))	EEZ	International rules and standards (or national law conforming with or giving effect to)	Clear grounds for belief	Give information as listed in Art 220(3) - Identity - Registry - Last port - Next port - Information in respect to incident
TS or EEZ (Art. 220(5))	EEZ	International rules and standards (As above)	Clear grounds for belief *and* substantial discharge causing or threatening significant pollution *and* vessel has refused to give information *or* information supplied obviously incorrect	Physical inspection (Further physical inspection (Art.226(I)(a))
TS or EEZ (Art. 220(6))	TS or EEZ	International rules and standards (As above)	Clear objective evidence and discharge is - causing major damage - or threat of major damage to - coastline or - resources of TS/EEZ *and* provided that evidence so warrants	- Proceedings - Detention (Release Art. 220(7))
TS or EEZ (Art. 220(8))	EEZ (clearly defined area)	National law giving effect to generally accepted rules (Art. 211(5))	Applicable in cases of Art. 220(3-6) accordingly	Measures accordingly (Art. 220(3-6))

MARINE SCIENTIFIC RESEARCH

All states and competent international organizations may conduct marine scientific research[1]; they are, however, obligated to promote international co-operation in marine research for peaceful purposes[2] and to make known all pertinent information about such projects and the results available[3]. States are therefore to promote actively the flow of information and scientific data and the transfer of knowledge resulting from research, with particular emphasis on the transfer to developing states and the strengthening of the autonomous marine scientific research capabilities of such states[4]. Unless otherwise agreed, communications concerning projects are to be made through appropriate official channels[5], and the states are to seek through competent international organizations the establishment of general criteria and guidelines to assist the former in ascertaining the nature and implications of marine research[6].

All research on the high seas, i.e., in the water column over the Area and continental shelf beyond the limits of the exclusive economic zone[7] the water surface, and the atmosphere above, is open to all, on the condition that the basic premises of research for peaceful purposes only[8] and some general principles, including those of co-operation[9] are observed.

In the Area, the Sea-Bed Authority may carry out marine research on its own[10], just a s all states and competent international organizations[11]. The Authority is obligated to take measures to acquire technology and scientific knowledge as far as deep sea mining activities[12] are concerned, and to promote and encourage transfer to developing states of such knowledge and technology so that all States Parties benefit[13]. Other scientific research projects are to be undertaken with the co-operation of all states and organizations[14].

Within the exclusive economic zone and on the continental shelf (the "outer shelf"), the coastal states have been given control over marine scientific research[15] with very little influence left for other states and international organizations. Consent of the coastal state is required for any type of research carried out in these zones, and any states or international organizations planning marine research must provide the coastal state with a detailed description of the project at least six months before the anticipated commencement of the research activities[16]. The research must be conducted in accordance with certain requirements, in particular the right of the coastal state to participate in the project if it so desires[17] and to suspend any research activities in progress if they are not being conducted in accordance with the information provided[18] on which the consent of the coastal state was based[19] or if the state or organization conducting the research fails to comply with minimum conditions[20]. Only if the coastal state has not raised any objections or refused approval of the project within four months after receipt of the required information[21] may the project proceed after six months[22]; however, this procedure will not appear as much of an improvement in the eyes of the scientific community.

The long-term solution to such problems will be found in co-operation[23] global and regional agreements[24] and the establishment of guidelines[25].

---

[1] Art. 238 (Art. 87 (1. f.))
[2] Art. 242, Para. 1
[3] Art. 244, Para. 1
[4] Art. 244, Para. 2
[5] Art. 250
[6] Art. 251
[7] Art. 257
[8] Art. 240, Subpara. (a), Art. 88
[9] Art. 240-244
[10] Art. 143, Para. 2
[11] Art. 256
[12] Art. 274
[13] *Ibid*; Art. 144, Subpara. 1 (b)
[14] Art. 143, Para. 2-3
[15] Art. 246, Para. 2; 56, 1 (b)
[16] Art. 248
[17] Art. 249
[18] Art. 253, Subpara. 1 (a); Art. 248
[19] *Ibid.*
[20] Art. 249; Art. 253, Subpara. 1 (b)
[21] Art. 248
[22] Art. 252; Art. 247
[23] Art. 242
[24] Art. 243
[25] Art. 251

Further Readings: - Marine Scientific Research, Page 121

MARINE SCIENTIFIC RESEARCH

NB: The Convention has no jurisdiction over scientific research in the territorial sea (Art. 245)

General Provisions (Art. 238-241):
- All states and competent international organizations may conduct research (Art. 238)
- Research may be conducted for peaceful purposes only (Art. 240(a), 246, (3), 301)

International Co-operation (Art. 242-244):
- Flow of knowledge must be promoted (Art. 244(2))

Installations or equipment in the marine environment (Art. 258-262)	Responsibility and liability (Art. 263, 304)	Settlement of disputes (Art. 264, 265)
- Installations are subject to provisions in Art. 246-255 (see Art. 258) - Installations do not possess status of islands (Art. 259)	- Measures in accordance with the Convention (Art. 263(1)) - Liable for damage by pollution (Art. 263(2), 235)	- In accordance with Part XV, (Art. 264)

High Seas (Art. 238, 87(1.f))	*Area* and water column beyond exclusive economic zone (Art. 256, 143 (1), 87 (l.f))

Research in the exclusive economic zone and on the continental shelf (Art. 246-255) with limitation of Art. 246 (6,7) and Art. 257

Coastal States (Art. 56, (1)(a); 77 (2))
- Have the right to regulate, authorize, and conduct research (Art. 246 (1))
- Obligated to adopt reasonable rules to facilitate research (Art. 255)
- do not have to accept compulsory dispute settlement in matters of Articles 246 and 253 (Art. 297, Para. 2)
- Suspension of specific project conciliation (Art. 297, 2(b); 265)
- Responsible for installations (Art. 60; 80; 258-262)

Consent of coastal state is assumed if no objections within four months - required information has been given (Art. 252) - project by (competent) international organization (Art. 247)	Particular Research Applications and conditions (Art. 248-253) - Provide information (Art. 248) - Comply with conditions (Art. 249) - Implied consent (Art. 252) - Suspension (Art. 253)	Coastal state is to make arrangement for participation by neighbouring land-locked or geographically disadvantaged state upon request (Art. 254, Para. 3)

DEVELOPMENT AND TRANSFER OF TECHNOLOOGY

The Convention refers to "marine technology" chiefly in terms of exploration, exploitation, conservation, and management of marine resources, the protection and preservation of the marine environment, marine scientific research, and other activities in the marine environment[1] although in the greater sense it includes "all kinds of technology"[2]. The aim of this part of the Convention is to promote and develop knowledge, technology, the necessary technological infrastructure for the transfer of such technology, training and education, and co-operation on all levels[3] as well as to develop the marine scientific and technological capacity of such states, particularly developing states, which may need and request assistance to accelerate their social and economic development[4]. In particular, the Convention hopes to stimulate and advance the conduct of marine research by developing coastal states and to enhance their national capabilities to utilize and preserve their marine resources for their economic benefit[5], especially with regard to their exclusive economic zone and continental shelf. The transfer of technology is to take place on fair and reasonable terms and conditions[6], with due regard for all legitimate interests, including *inter alia* the rights and duties of holders, suppliers, and recipients of marine technology[7].

In addition to the Sea-Bed Authority[8] competent international organizations are, either at the request of states[9] or directly or in close co-operation among themselves[10] to ensure the efficiency of the transfer of technology, although states may promote such activities on their own initiative[11]; however, with regard to the transfer of technology to developing states, they are obligated to cooperate with the international organizations so as to assure efficient co-ordination[12].

Support can be provided directly[13] through bilateral, regional, or multilateral programmes[14], or by the establishment or strengthening of established national[15] or regional[16] centers. The measures to be taken should include programmes of co-operation, conclusion of agreements and contracts, conferences and seminars, exchange of scientists and technological and other experts, and joint ventures[17].

The national centres are to stimulate and advance the conduct of marine research[18] whereas the functions of the regional centres include *inter alia* training and educational programmes, management studies, publicizing of national policies with regard to the transfer of marine technology, and statistical work[19].

These provisions on transfer of technology also have an impact on other parts of the Convention related to the support of developing states, such as participation in activities in the Area[20], the flow of scientific research data[21] technical assistance for pollution management[22] and participation of neighbouring land-locked and geographically disadvantaged states in scientific research in the exclusive economic zone[23].

---

[1] Art. 266, Para. 2
[2] Art. 269, Subpara. (a)
[3] Art. 268
[4] Art. 266, Para. 2
[5] Art. 275, Para. 1
[6] Art. 266, Para. 1
[7] Art. 267
[8] Art. 274
[9] e.g., Art. 266(1); Art. 271
[10] Art. 278
[11] e.g. Art. 269, Para.1; Art. 275, Para. 1
[12] Art. 272-273
[13] Art. 269
[14] Art. 270
[15] Art. 275
[16] Art. 276
[17] Art. 269
[18] Art. 275
[19] Art. 277
[20] Art. 143-144; AIII, Art. 5 and 15
[21] Art. 244
[22] Art. 202-203
[23] Art. 254, Para. 3

Further Readings: - Measures to Close the Economic Gap, Page 129
 - Co-operation—"Competent International Organizations", Page 110

Bernaerts' Guide to the Law of The Sea 75

TRANSFER OF MARINE TECHNOLOGY

(1) Activities in the Area - Objectives. Of the Authority (Art. 274)
- Marine scientific research (Art. 143)
- Transfer of Technology (Art. 144; Annex III, Art. 5, 15)

(2) Marine scientific research - Flow of data, etc. (Art. 244)
(3) Protection of environment - Technical assistance (Art. 202, 203)
(4) Fish resources - Participation (Art. 69 (3); 70 (4)); Information (Art. 119 (2))

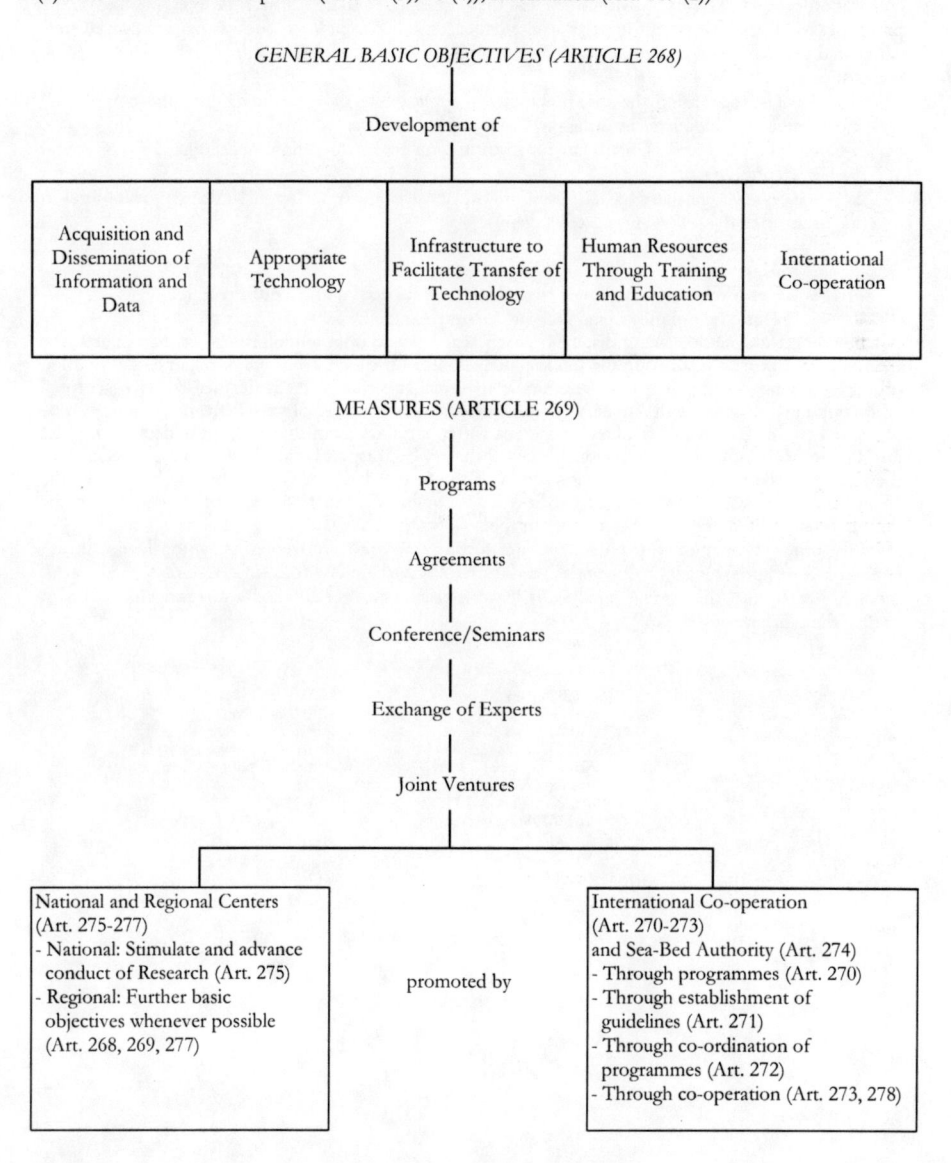

GENERAL BASIC OBJECTIVES (ARTICLE 268)

Development of

Acquisition and Dissemination of Information and Data	Appropriate Technology	Infrastructure to Facilitate Transfer of Technology	Human Resources Through Training and Education	International Co-operation

MEASURES (ARTICLE 269)

Programs

Agreements

Conference/Seminars

Exchange of Experts

Joint Ventures

promoted by

National and Regional Centers (Art. 275-277)	International Co-operation (Art. 270-273)
- National: Stimulate and advance conduct of Research (Art. 275) - Regional: Further basic objectives whenever possible (Art. 268, 269, 277)	and Sea-Bed Authority (Art. 274) - Through programmes (Art. 270) - Through establishment of guidelines (Art. 271) - Through co-ordination of programmes (Art. 272) - Through co-operation (Art. 273, 278)

SYSTEM FOR SETTLEMENT OF DISPUTES

Part XV of the Convention itself includes only provisions for the conduct of the states parties, procedures, and jurisdiction, while the whole structure of the dispute settlement system includes four of the Annexes to the Convention: Conciliation (Annex V), Statue of the International Tribunal for the Law of the Sea (Annex VI), Arbitration (Annex VII), and Special Arbitration (Annex VIII). States Parties must exhaust all local remedies before resort is made to the procedures provided in this section of the Convention[1].

The basic tenent underlying the settlement of disputes is that the parties are bound to use only peaceful means[2] exchange their views without delay[3] behave in accordance with the requirements of the United Nations Charter[4] and seek a solution by negotiation, enquiry, mediation, conciliation, arbitration, and judicial settlement[5] in good faith[6]. The final effort prior to official proceedings is a non-binding conciliation procedure[7]. But it is necessary that the parties agree to conciliation proceedings and to the procedure to be applied[8] except in cases where conciliation is compulsory[9] such as when a coastal state is required to submit certain marine scientific research disputes[10] and fisheries disputes[11] to non-binding conciliation.

For disputes concerning the interpretation or applicability of the Convention, the compulsory procedures entailing binding decisions apply[12] with two exceptions:

1. Cases where the coastal state has jurisdiction with regard to central questions of fisheries and marine scientific research[13];
2. Those cases where states have declared that they will not accept dispute settlement procedures in one or more of the following causes of dispute:
    - sea boundary delimitations[14];
    - military activities[15]
    - law enforcement activities of coastal state for fisheries and scientific research;
    - disputes before the United Nations Security Council[16].

For procedural settlement of disputes[17], the parties may choose among four fora: two courts (the International Court of Justice and the International Tribunal for the Law of the Sea) and two arbitration tribunals[18]. If no declaration to the contrary is in force, the state party is deemed to have accepted arbitration in accordance with Annex VII[19]. Disputes involving release of vessels from detention can be submitted to the Tribunal of the Law of the Sea within ten days from the time of the detention, if the jurisdiction of no other court or tribunal is established[20]. For disputes with respect to interpretation of the Area provisions of Part XI, the jurisdiction of the Sea-Bed Disputes Chamber, a chamber of the International Tribunal for the Law of the Sea[21] is compulsory[22], unless States Parties request that the dispute be submitted to a special chamber[23] or to an *ad hoc* chamber[24].

Of some importance for procedure are further provisions covering provisional measures[25], applicable law[26], preliminary proceedings[27], and the finality and binding force of decisions[28]. At all times of the dispute, the guiding principle is that the parties are free to choose any peaceful means of settling their differences[29].

---

[1] Art. 295
[2] Art. 279
[3] Art. 283, Para. 1
[4] Art.279
[5] UN Charter, Art.33, Para. 1
[6] Art. 300
[7] Art. 284, Annex V
[8] Art. 284, Para. 2
[9] Art. 297; Annex V, 11-14
[10] Art. 297, Para. 2

[1] Art. 297, Para. 3
[12] Art. 286
[13] Art. 297, Para. 2-3
[14] Art. 298, Subpara. 1 (a)
[15] Art. 298, Subpara. 1 (b)
[16] Art. 298, Subpara. 1 (c)
[17] Art. 288, Para. 1-2
[18] Art. 287, Subpara 1 (a)
[19] Art. 287, Para. 4
[20] Art. 292, Para. 1

[21] Annex VI, Art, 14 and 35
[22] Art. 287, Para. 2; Art. 288, Para. 3
[23] Art. 188, Subpara. 1 (a)
[24] Art. 188, Subpara. 1 (b)
[25] Art. 290
[26] Art. 293
[27] Art. 294
[28] Art. 296
[29] e.g. Art. 280, 299(2)

Further Readings: - Settlement of Disputes, Page 131
 - What is the Law of the Sea Today? Page 14

THE FORA FOR THE SETTLEMENT OF DISPUTES
GENERAL OVERVIEW

I. *FORA FOR DISPUTES NOT RELATED TO JUDGEMENTS INVOLVING INTERPRETATION OF THE CONVENTION*

(1) Special Arbitration, Annex VIII, Article 5, Fact-Finding
(2) Conciliation Procedure, Annex V, Section 1 Pursuant to Part XI, Section 1, Settlement of Disputes (General Provisions)
(3) Binding Commercial Arbitration
    - Interpretation of contracts and plan of work. Art. 188, Subpara. 2(a)
    - Financial terms. Annex III, Art. 13, Para. 15
    - Financial terms of technology transfer. Annex III Art. 5, Para. 4

II. *CHOICE BETWEEN ONE OR MORE OF FOUR FORA IN CASES OF COMPULSORY PROCEEDINGS (ART 287, PARA 1)*

States Parties are free to choose among the fora (No. 4-7) for the settlement of disputes concerning the interpretation or applicability of the Convention (for limited court/tribunal jurisdiction on matters (a) sovereign rights of coastal states; (b) military; (c) boundaries; (d) Security Council, see Art. 297-298)

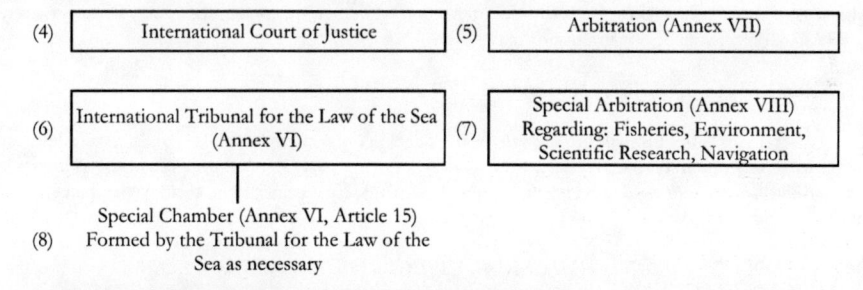

(4) International Court of Justice
(5) Arbitration (Annex VII)
(6) International Tribunal for the Law of the Sea (Annex VI)
(7) Special Arbitration (Annex VIII) Regarding: Fisheries, Environment, Scientific Research, Navigation
(8) Special Chamber (Annex VI, Article 15) Formed by the Tribunal for the Law of the Sea as necessary

NB: If a State Party has not made a declaration or if the parties of the dispute have not agreed to a forum, the dispute is to be submitted to Arbitration (Annex VII). The parties can agree otherwise (Art. 287, Paras. 3-5). A question of the detention of a vessel may be submitted to the court or tribunal of the choice of the parties; otherwise, to the Tribunal for the International Law of the Sea (Art. 292, Para. 1)

III. *COMPULSORY FORA*
(9) Sea-Bed Disputes Chamber (Annex VI, Article 3)
    - Compulsory (Art. 287, Para. 2; Jurisdiction: Art, 288, Para. 3; Activities in the Area, Art. 187)
(10) *Ad Hoc* Chamber of the Sea-Bed Disputes Chamber (Annex VI, Article 36)
    - May be formed at the request of States Parties (Art. 188, Para. 1) with respect to seabed activities (Article 187)
(11) Conciliation Procedures (Annex V, Section 2, Articles 11-14)
    - Compulsory (Annex V, Section 2); On matters stated in Part XV, Section 3
    - Article 297, Paragraph 2 (Certain matters of marine scientific research)
    - Article 297, Paragraph 3 (Certain matters of fisheries)

GENERAL PROVISIONS

INTRODUCTION

Each of these provisions covers a different area, and it is not possible to summarize the articles from a standpoint of principles common to all of them. It is even questionable whether the heading "General" can be applied to all five of the provisions; it is clearly applicable only to the first two on "good faith" and "peaceful use," as the last three are of more regulatory nature.

GOOD FAITH AND ABUSE OF RIGHTS (Article 300)

Pacta sunt servanda. This principle implies the condition that every party to an agreement has to recognize and to fulfil the obligations of the contract in good faith.

PEACEFUL USES OF THE SEA (Article 301)

The Conference took place under the auspices of the United Nations. The principle aim of the Charter of the United Nations is to maintain international peace and security, and, to that end, to take effective collective measures for the prevention and removal of threats to peace[1]. In the on-going effort to maintain peace, the Convention is intended as a contribution giving new impulse to the strengthening of peace and security[2]. The obligation of the states parties to refrain from any threat or use of force against the territorial integrity or potential independence of any state is merely a logical consequence of this intention.

DISCLOSURE OF INFORMATION (Article 302)

It is not the intention of the Convention to infringe upon or impair a state's sovereignty or integrity in any manner whatsoever; for this reason, no state party may be obliged, in the fulfillment of its obligations under the Convention, to disclose any information which is contrary to the essential interests of the state party[3].

ARCHAEOLOGICAL AND HISTORICAL OBJECTS FOUND AT SEA (Art. 303)

Whereas all objects found in the Area are to be preserved or disposed of for the benefit of mankind as a whole[4], this provision establishes the duty of all states to protect such objects and to co-operate for this purpose. Coastal states are given control over the removal of objects from the contiguous zone[5].

RESPONSIBILITY AND LIABILITY FOR DAMAGE AT SEA (Article 304)

This article ensures that the provisions of the Convention concerning responsibility and liability cannot be used to subvert or hinder the application of existing rules or development of further rules regarding responsibility and liability under international law.

---

[1] UN Charter, Art. 1, Para.2
[2] Preamble
[3] For activities in the Area, see Annex III, 14; Art. 168(2)
[4] Art. 149
[5] Art. 303, Para. 2; Art. 33

Further Readings: - Archaeological and Historical Objects, Page 124
 - Indemnity, Page 128

REFERENCES TO PEACEFUL USES OF THE SEA

UNITED NATIONS CHARTER 1945

Article 1:   - maintain peace and security
             - prevention and removal of threats to peace
             - strengthen universal peace
Article 2:   - refrain from the threat and use of force against the territorial integrity or political independence of any state

CONVENTION ON THE LAW OF THE SEA 1982

Article 301: - refrain from any threat or use of force against the territorial integrity or political independence of any state

Territorial Sea
- Innocent passage (Art. 19, Para. 2)
- Criminal jurisdiction (Art. 27, Para. 1(b))

Straits
- Transit passage (Art. 39, Subpara. 1(b))

High Seas (Article 88)
Area (Articles 138; 14 147,2(d))

Marine Scientific Research
(Art. 240, Subpara, (a))

Disputes (Article 279))

Exclusive Economic Zone
The coastal state is to act in a manner consistent
with the provisions of the Convention
(Art. 56, Para. 2)
but
Freedom of navigation in the exclusive economic zone must be exercised in accordance with the principle that the "high seas are reserved for peaceful purposes". (Art. 58, Para. 2)

Marine Scientific Research
Coastal states are expected to give their consent
for peaceful research in their exclusive
economic zone or continental shelf
(Art. 246, Para. 3)

Further Readings: - Military Use, Page 124
                    - Establishing Peace, Page 129

FINAL PROVISIONS

The entry into force of the Convention follows common procedure for international conventions; it is open for signature[1], and subject to ratification, formal confirmation[2], and accession[3]. The Convention will not enter into force until twelve months after the deposit of the sixtieth instrument of ratification or accession[4] with the Secretary-General of the United Nations, who is the depository of the Convention and any amendments thereto[5]. After its entry into force, the Convention will be binding on all states which have ratified or acceded to it, and they will be obligated to apply the provisions of the Convention to the relations among themselves[6], the rights and obligations of states parties arising from other agreements will not be affected by the entry into force of the Convention, as long as such agreements are not incompatible with the Convention and do not hinder other states parties in the enjoyment of their rights or the performance of their obligations under the Convention[7]. Agreements between states parties which modify or suspend operation of provisions of the Convention are even possible as long as such agreements do not hinder effective execution of the object and purpose of the Convention[8]. Reservations or exceptions are permitted only when expressly allowed by the Convention[9], ensuring equitable application of the Convention. States may, when signing, ratifying, or acceding to the Convention, make declarations or statements as long as such declarations or statements do not purport to exclude or to modify the legal effect of the provisions of the Convention in their application to that state[10]. States are to ensure full application of the Convention principles, including that of the common heritage of mankind[11].

All other states, whether they signed the Convention (possible until December 9, 1984[12]) or not, cannot be forced to apply the Convention, although this does not exclude the possibility that provisions of the Convention might acquire the force of customary international law and would therefore find application as such. In addition, all states which signed the Convention (as of the final deadline in 1984, there was a total of 159 signatures, not all of them from states) must refrain from acts which are contrary to the objectives of the Convention, unless they declare they are no longer willing to be bound by their signature or behave in a manner which would be tantamount to such a declaration. However, the state's signature means that the state is allowed to participate in the Preparatory Commission[13] which is to prepare the installation of the Sea-Bed Authority and the Tribunal for the Law of the Sea. The Authority will acquire international legal personality[14] at the moment the Convention enters into force and can immediately thereupon begin to operate in accordance with the Convention[15]. The Tribunal is then constituted[16].

A state party may at any time denounce the Convention, either with or without indication of its reasons; the denunciation takes effect one year after the date of notification unless a later date is specified in the notification[17].

The Convention includes provisions for amending or establishing alternatives to present regulations contained in the Convention[1].

---

[1] Art. 305
[2] Art. 306
[3] Art. 307
[4] Art. 308, Para. 1
[5] Art. 306-307; 319, Para. 1
[6] Art. 1, Subpara. 2(1)
[7] Art. 311, Para.2
[8] Art. 311, Para. 3
[9] Art. 309
[10] Art. 310 (Disputes: 297-298)
[11] Art. 311, Para.3-6
[12] Art. 305, Para.2
[13] Final Act, Res. I
[14] Art. 156, 176
[15] Art. 308, Para.3-5
[16] Annex VI, Art. 1(1)
[17] Art. 317
[18] Art. 312-316

Further Readings : - The General Effects of the Convention, Pages 9-15
 - State and States Parties, Page 102
 - United Nations Organization Page 108

ENTRY INTO FORCE AND APPLICABILITY OF THE CONVENTION AND AMENDMENTS

GENERAL	APPLICABILITY OF THE CONVENTION	EFFECT ON THE STATES
Signature (Article 305) - Open for signature until December 9, 1984 - For all states - For bodies mentioned in Article 305, subparagraphs l(b-f)	In Principle NONE but. - The high number of signatures (159) has a significant effect on customary law - There is a difference in understanding between industrialized and developing countries on this point	A state which has signed must refrain from acts which are contrary to the Convention
Ratification (Article 306) *Accession* (Article 307) - The Secretary-General of the United Nations is the Depository	Until deposit of 60th instrument, same as above	Ratification can have an immediate effect on national law
	As of deposit of 60th instrument Convention enters into force 12 months after deposit (Article 308, Paragraph 1), binding all ratifying and acceding States	The Convention becomes international law and is applicable law among all states parties
Reservations (Article 309)	Possible only when expressly permitted by other articles of the Convention	
Declarations (Article 310)	Permitted as long as applicability of Convention is not affected	
Other Conventions (Article 311)	Principles of Convention, including "common heritage of mankind", may not be suspended	Prevails over 1958 Conventions on Law of the Sea
Denunciation (Article 317)	Possible at any time, goes into effect at earliest 1 year after date of notification	State must fulfil any obligations of the Convention to which it would be subject under international law (Article 317, Paragraph 3)
Amendments (Article 312-316) - upon request of a State Party (a) On questions besides those concerning activities in the Area, after 10 years (Articles 312, 313) (b) On questions concerning activities in the Area at any time (Article 314)	Entry into force 30 days after ratification by 2/3rds of the States Parties or 60, whichever greater (Article 316, Paragraph 1) Entry into force 1 year after ratification by 3/4ths of States Parties (Article 316, Paragraph 5)	Amendments adopted open for signature for 12 months (Article 315) Effect see above
Authentic Texts (Article 320)	The Arabic, Chinese, English, French, Russian, and Spanish texts are equally authentic	

HIGHLY MIGRATORY SPECIES

Annex I is a list of seventeen species which are related to coastal state conservation and utilization rights and duties[1] when these species are found in the exclusive economic zone. In this respect, all fishery provisions of this zone apply[2]. The coastal states are obliged to co-operate, whether directly with the flag states of fishing vessels or through international organizations, with other states to ensure conservation and optimum utilization by all states concerned. The purpose of giving these species a separate classification is to assure them a particular position with respect to freedom of fishing on the high seas and, in so doing, further co-operative actions

CONTINENTAL SHELF COMMISION

The Commission on the Limits of the Continental Shelf has no decision-making power; it can only make recommendations[3]. The delineation of the outer limits of the continental shelf is the responsibility of the coastal state concerned if that shelf exceeds the limits of the exclusive economic zone[4]. As the sovereign rights over the shelf[5] do not depend on a proclamation or occupation[6], the establishment of the border with the Area[7] is necessary. Although the Convention gives instructions for drawing the limits[8], these instructions are not and could not be so precise that the exact limits could have been established beyond a doubt on this basis alone, but the coastal state is held to apply these criteria in establishing the limits[9] and, if of any help, request the Commission to provide scientific and technical advice[10] for this task. The Commission itself may co-operate with the Oceanic Commission of UNESCO[11] and other competent organizations[12]. The coastal state is to submit data and other material concerning the delineation of the continental shelf to the Commission, which considers the information[13] and submits its recommendations[14] in writing to the coastal state and the Secretary-General of the United Nations[15]. If the coastal state disagrees with the recommendation, it is to make a revised or new submission to the Commission[16]. After a second recommendation has been made, the coastal state establishes the limits of the shelf on the basis of the recommendation[17]. These limits, to be deposited with the UN Secretary-General[18], are final and binding except in cases of delimitation of shelf between states with opposite or adjacent coasts[19]. Copies of the charts and lists showing the outer limit lines of the continental shelf are also to be deposited with the Secretary-General of the Sea-Bed Authority[20].

A coastal state is to institute the procedure described above within ten years after the entry into force of the Convention[21]. This procedure is without prejudice to delimitation measures between states with opposite or adjacent coasts[22], which are subject to agreements between the states concerned or to dispute settlement as provided by the Convention[23] (provided the state has not declared its non-acceptance of dispute settlement in such questions[24]).

---

[1] Art. 64
[2] Art. 64, Para.2
[3] Art. 76, Para. 8; AII. Art. 3, Para. 1
[4] Art. 76, Para. 7
[5] Art. 77, Para. 1
[6] Art. 77, Para. 3
[7] Art. 1, Subpara. 1(1); Art. 134, Para. 4
[8] Art. 76, Para. 3-6
[9] Art. 76(4-7); AII, Art. 7
[10] AII, Art. 3, Subpara.1(b)
[11] UN Educational, Scientific and Cultural Organization
[12] AII, Art. 3, Para. 2
[13] AII, Art. 3, Subpara. 1 (a)
[14] Ibid.; Art. 76, Para.8
[15] Art. 76, Para. 8; AII, Art. 6, Para.3
[16] AII, Art. 8
[17] Art. 76, Para.8
[18] Art. 76, Para. 9
[19] Art. 76, Para. 10; AII, Art.9
[20] Art. 84; Para.2
[21] AII, Art. 4
[22] Art. 76, Para. 10 AII, Art. 9
[23] Art. 83, Para. 2
[24] Art. 298, Subpara. 1(a)

CONTINENTAL SHELF COMMISSION

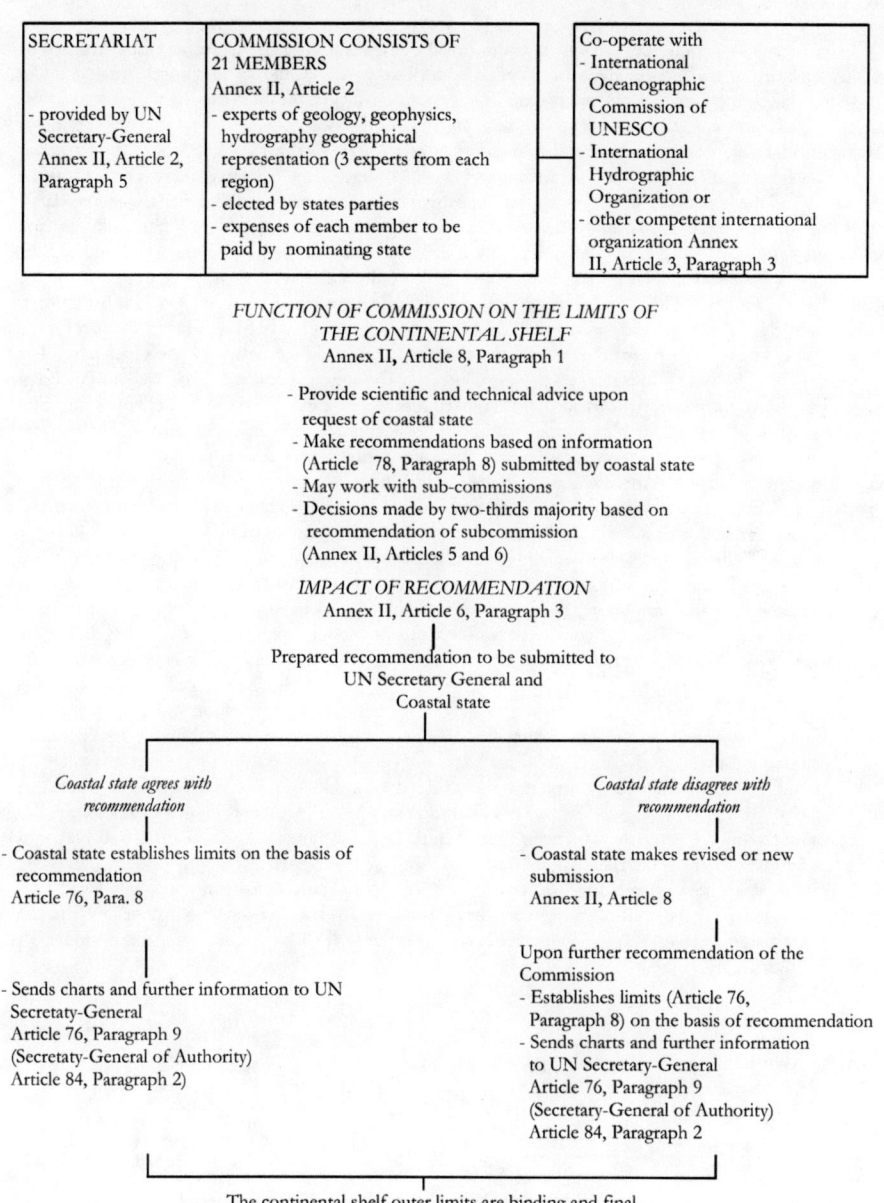

SECRETARIAT	COMMISSION CONSISTS OF 21 MEMBERS Annex II, Article 2	Co-operate with
- provided by UN Secretary-General Annex II, Article 2, Paragraph 5	- experts of geology, geophysics, hydrography geographical representation (3 experts from each region) - elected by states parties - expenses of each member to be paid by nominating state	- International Oceanographic Commission of UNESCO - International Hydrographic Organization or - other competent international organization Annex II, Article 3, Paragraph 3

FUNCTION OF COMMISSION ON THE LIMITS OF THE CONTINENTAL SHELF
Annex II, Article 8, Paragraph 1

- Provide scientific and technical advice upon request of coastal state
- Make recommendations based on information (Article 78, Paragraph 8) submitted by coastal state
- May work with sub-commissions
- Decisions made by two-thirds majority based on recommendation of subcommission (Annex II, Articles 5 and 6)

IMPACT OF RECOMMENDATION
Annex II, Article 6, Paragraph 3

Prepared recommendation to be submitted to
UN Secretary General and
Coastal state

Coastal state agrees with recommendation

- Coastal state establishes limits on the basis of recommendation
Article 76, Para. 8

- Sends charts and further information to UN Secretaty-General
Article 76, Paragraph 9
(Secretaty-General of Authority)
Article 84, Paragraph 2)

Coastal state disagrees with recommendation

- Coastal state makes revised or new submission
Annex II, Article 8

Upon further recommendation of the Commission
- Establishes limits (Article 76, Paragraph 8) on the basis of recommendation
- Sends charts and further information to UN Secretary-General
Article 76, Paragraph 9
(Secretary-General of Authority)
Article 84, Paragraph 2

The continental shelf outer limits are binding and final
Article 76, Paragraph 8
(Exception: Article 76, Paragraph 10)
The UN Secretary-General gives due publicity thereto
Article 76, Paragraph 9

BASIC CONDITIONS OF PROSPECTING, EXPLORATION AND EXPLOITATION

Basic conditions for a deep-sea mining contract will be the regulations of this Annex, supplemented by the particular rules, regulations, and procedures to be adopted by the Authority[1] and which are now under consideration by the Preparatory Commission[2]. In general, activities in the Area may be undertaken by the organ of the Authority, the Enterprise (see next chapter), or by others, who can be a state party or its nationals, including state enterprises an natural or Juridical persons[3]. Sponsorship of a state party is obligatory for the latter[4]. The basis for mining rights is a contract to be concluded between the Sea-Bed Authority and the applicant[5]. The Authority is to approve applications, provided that they are in accordance with the uniform and non-discriminatory requirements set forth in the regulations of the Authority and consistent with the Convention[6]. Each application is to indicate one or more areas which in total are sufficiently large to allow two mining operations[7]. Half of the indicated area is to be reserved for the Enterprise (or for developing states), it is the responsibility of the Authority to designate which within forty five (ninety) days[8]. When on the basis of such an application a contract has been concluded, the part for the Enterprise is known as a reserved area, and the contractor has exclusive rights for the other part[9]. The application is to be based on a plan of work[10], which must include the applicant's pledge[11] to (a) accept rules, regulations, and Authority decisions, (b) accept the control of the Authority[12], (c) fulfil the contract in good faith, and (d) comply with provisions for transfer of technology The financial terms of the contract are regulated and provide for application and minimum annual fees and a production charge (but negotiations over financial terms are not completely excluded)[13]. The contractor has the option of paying a flat-rate "socialist" production charge of 5% annually of commercial production for the first decade and 12% annually thereafter or a "capitalist" charge, described in great detail, based on a combination of a percentage of production and a share of net proceeds[14]. These two modes of contribution were established out of deference to the two economic systems of East and West A contractor's calculations should take two basic conditions into account (a) the mining site is to be of sufficient estimated value and of a size to satisfy the objective[15], and (b) the contractor is obligated to obtain a production authorization before he commences work[16]. A production authorization establishes a fixed amount of nickel which may be recovered from mining operations under the contract[17]. A general production ceiling is to be fixed annually[18], which is of importance when selection is made among applicants for a production authorization[19]. (General production ceiling less amount of production authorizations issued equals possible amount for new production authorizations.)

A transfer of technology to the Enterprise or to developing countries takes place only if required by the Authority, if the technology is used to carry out activities in the Area, and if such technology is not available on the open market, the contractor must then make the technology available on reasonable terms and conditions[20.] Training programmes may be established as contractual conditions or as regulations[21]. The contract may be suspended or terminated only if a contractor persistently and wilfully violates fundamental terms of the contract or ignores final dispute settlement decisions, and monetary penalties may be imposed instead[22]. Both the contractor and the Authority are liable for wrongful acts or omissions for which they are responsible[23].

[1] AIII, Art. 17
[2] RI, Art. 5, Subpara. (g)
[3] Art. 153, Subpara. 2 (b);
AIII, Art. 3, Para. 1
[4] AIII, Art. 4, Para. 1&3
[5] AIII, Art. 3, Para. 5
[6] Art. 153, Para.1;
AIII, Art. 3, Para. 4;
AIII, Art. 6, Para. 3
[7] AIII, Art. 8;
AIII, Art. 17, Subpara. 2 (a)
[8] AIII, Art. 8 ; (Art.9, Para. 4)
[9] AIII, Art. 8-9; 16
[0] AIII, Art. Art. 3, Para. 3;
AIII, Art. 6
AIII, Art.4, Para.6
[2] e.g., AIII, Art. 17,
Subpara. 1(b)(viii)
[3] AIII, Art. 13, Para. 1, 2-4
[4] AIII, Art. 13, Para. 5-6
[5] AIII, Art. 8; AIII, Art. 17,
Subpara. 2(a)
[6] Art. 151, Subpara. 2 (a)
[7] Art. 151 Subpara. 2 (b)
[8] Art. 151, Para. 4-7
[9] AIII, Art. 7
[20] Art. 144; AIII, Art. 5
[2] AIII, Art. 15; AIII, Art. 17,
Subpara.1(b)(xi)
[22] AIII, Art. 18
[23] AIII, Art. 22; Art. 139

AUTHORITY – CONTRACTOR

NB: For an interim period (Article 151 (3)) contracts must be conducted in accordance with a production authorization (Article 151 (2)) based on a production ceiling (Article 151 (2(d))) determined according to trends on the nickel market (Article 151 (4)) by applying the Production Policy as provided by the Convention (Article 151)

Subject Matter	Provisions of Convention	Basic Conditions of Annex III	Dispute Settlement Convention/Annex III
Power of Authority	157;160;153	Rules regulations and procedure to be issued by Authority (Article 17)	Not applicable in respect to discretionary power of Authority (Article 189)
Applicants Except Enterprise	Article 153 (2)	Application (Article 3 (1)) - plan of work (Art 6) undertakings (Art 4 Para 6), proposed area (Art 8) Qualification (Art 4 Para 1-3) financial/technical capability - sponsorship by state party Application fee (Art 13 Para 2) (US$500 000)	Dispute Chamber (Article 187(d))
Contract	Article 153 (3) Article 153 (6)	- Contract concluded between Authority and applicant (contractor) (Article 3 (5)) approved by Council (Article 162 (2(j)) - Joint venture with Enterprise (Article 11) - Suspension (serious persistent and wilful violations) (Article 18 (1)) - Revision (conduct inequitable impracticable impossible) (revisable only by consent) (Article 19) - Transfer of rights and obligations (Article 20) consent required	- In general Commercial arbitration (Article 188 (2) Article 187(c)(i)) - Dispute Chamber acts or omissions related to Area activities (Article 187(c)) and others (Article 187(f))
Reservation		Of the proposed area - One half reserved for Enterprise (Articles 8-9) - Contractor granted exclusive rights for one half (Article 16 Art 3(4c))	
Production Authorization	Article 151 (2)	Selection of Applicants (Article 7)	Disputes Chamber (Article 187(c)(ii))
Financial Terms		Minimum annual contribution US$1 million (Article 13 (3)) or production charge (Article 13 (4)) whichever is greater (Article 13 (3))	Commercial arbitration AIII (Article 13 (15))
Transfer of Technology	Article 144	Transfer of technology (Article 5) - Training program (Article 15)	AIII Article 5 (4) - In general Commercial terms and conditions commercial arbitration (Article 187 187(c)(i))
Liability	Articles 139 and 304	- Contractor and Authority (Article 22) - Authority for its staff (Article 168 (2))	Dispute Chamber (Article 187(e)) Liability of Authority
Monetary penalties		- Imposed by Authority proportionate to seriousness of violation (Article 18 (2))	Dispute Chamber AIII, Article 18 (3)

THE ENTERPRISE

The Enterprise is a unique undertaking. On the one hand, it is an organ of the Sea-Bed Authority[1] and is to act in accordance with the general policy of the Assembly and the directives of the Council[2]. On the other hand, it is to enjoy autonomy in the conduct of its operations[3], operate in accordance with sound commercial principles[4], and make its decisions on the basis of commercial considerations only[5]. As an organ of the Authority, it has legal personality and such legal capacity as is necessary to achieve the aims expected from it[6], such as providing funds for the Authority[7], providing technology and training for personnel from developing countries[8], and, last but not least, supporting the mineral policy of the Authority[9]. For this purpose, the Enterprise is entitled to act as any other operator in carrying out activities in the Area, including transporting, processing, and marketing of minerals[10], after obtaining approval of a plan of work[11] and a production authorization[12]. But the Convention also permits joint ventures of the Enterprise, either with developing or developed countries[13]. The Enterprise is to have title to all minerals and processed substances produced by it[14].

The Enterprise is expected to become self-supporting. As it can be assumed that this will take considerable time, the Enterprise is exempt from payment of contributions to the Authority for ten years[15]. In addition, funds are to be raised by various means so that it can commence operations as soon as possible[16]. As it is unlikely that the necessary funds will be raised by voluntary contributions from states parties or from the financial resources of the Authority, states parties are obliged to lend money to the Enterprise on a long-term interest-free basis for half of the funds and to guarantee debts incurred by the Enterprise in raising the other half; each state party's share is to be calculated in accordance with the scale of assessments for the United Nations regular budget[17]. Further measures can be taken if the necessary funds are not raised in this way[18]. In order to assure an early and effective entry into operation of the Enterprise, the Preparatory Commission is to establish a subcommission to deal with any questions which may arise[19]. The amount of the funds for initial operation mentioned above and the criteria and factors for the adjustment of the same are to be included by the Preparatory Commission in the draft rules, regulations, and procedure of the Authority[20]. The Enterprise is to have its principal office at the seat of the Authority. The Enterprise may establish offices and facilities in other states[21].

One of the main tasks of the Enterprise is to act as a "medium" to ensure the effective participation of developing states. For this purpose, it may apply for approval of a plan of work in any part of the Area or in reserved areas[22], and if it does not intend to carry out activities in a reserved area (either alone or together with states), developing states may apply to conduct activities in that reserved area[23]. Applications for production authorizations in a reserved area can be of advantage to the Enterprise (developing state) in comparison with applications for other parts of the Area, as the former enjoy priority if fewer reserved areas than non-reserved areas (being worked by operators with exclusive rights) are under exploitation[24]. Furthermore, the Enterprise is the arm of the Authority for the acquisition and transfer of technology as well as the training of personnel of developing countries[25].

---

[1] Art. 158, Para.2; Art. 170
[2] AIV, Art. 2, Para. 1; (162(2i))
[3] AIV, Art. 2, Para. 2
[4] AIV, Art. 1, Para. 3
[5] AIV, Art. 12, Para. 7
[6] Art. 170, Para. 2; AIV, Art. 13
[7] Art. 171, Subpara. (c); AIV, Art. 10
[8] Art. 144; AIII, Art. 5
[9] Art. 150-152
[10] AIV, Art. 1, Para. 1
[11] AIII, Art. 12; (170(2); 162(2)(k))
[12] Argument: AIII, Art. 12; Art. 151, (5); AIII, Art. 7, (6)
[13] AIII, Art. 9; Art. 11
[14] AIV, Art. 12, Para. 4
[15] AIV, Art. 10, Para. 3
[16] AIII, Art. 11, Para. 1
[17] AIV, Art. 11, Subara.3 (b)
[18] AIV, Art. 11, Subpara. 3 (c)
[19] RI, Para. 8
[20] AIV, Art. 11, Subpara. 3 (a)
[21] AIV, Art. 8; Art. Para. 13, Para. 2
[22] AIII, Art. 3 (2); Art. 9
[23] AIII, Art. 9, Para. 4
[24] AIII, Art. 7, Para. 6
[25] Art. 144; AIII, Art. 5(3-6)

STATUTE OF THE ENTERPRISE

The Enterprise is the organ of the Sea-Bed Authority

ASSEMBLY COUNCIL
Articles 170, 162;
AIV, Article 2

The Enterprise is to act in accordance with the general policy of the Assembly and the directives of the Council

GOVERNING BOARD

COMPOSITION (AIV, Article 5)
- 15 members elected by Assembly
- Two-thirds of members constitute a quorum
- One member - one vote
- Decision by majority

POWER AND FUNCTION (AIV, Article 6)
- Direct operation of the Enterprise
- Submissions to Assembly and Council
- May delegate power to Director General

Director General (AIV, Article 7)
- Elected by Assembly
- Legal representative and chief executive of the Enterprise
- Responsible to the Board for conduct of Enterprise

The Enterprise is to
- Carry out activities in the Area directly, including transporting, processing, and marketing (AIV, Article 1)
- Work on approved formal written plan of work (AIV, Article 12, Paragraph 1)
- Sell its products on a non-discriminatory basis according to commercial considerations only (AIV, Article 12, Paragraphs 5 & 7)

Staff of Enterprise
(AIV, Article 7)
Appointed and dismissed by Director General

The Enterprise may
- Carry out activities under joint arrangements (AIII, Articles 9, 11)
- Purchase goods and services when required (AIV, Article 12, Paragraph 3)
- Require transfer of technology (AIII, Article 5, Subparagraph 3(c-d))
- Choose reversed areas (AIII, Articles 8&9)
- Apply to conduct activities in other parts of the Area (AIII, Art. 3(2))

Legal Status, Privileges, and Immunities
AIV, Article 13

Budget and Finances
- For ten years no contribution to Authority (A IV, Art. 10(3))
- Funds to be raised *inter alia* by system of interest-free loans and debt guaranties of states parties (AIII, Article 11, Paragraph 3)

Liability
Article 139, Paragraph 2; AIII, Article 22; Article 304

VOLUNTARY CONCILIATION

States are urged to settle disputes concerning the interpretation or application of the Convention by peaceful means[1], by exchanging their views, and by negotiations[2]. As an additional or alternative step, a state may invite the other party to institute conciliation proceedings[3], which will be held only if the invited state accepts[4]. Conciliation proceedings instituted before a five-member conciliation commission[5] can solve the dispute only by means of an agreement between the parties[6], as the power of the commission is restricted to hearing the parties, examining their claims and objections, and making proposals to the parties with the view of reaching an amicable settlement[7]. Such proposals may be made at any time during the proceedings, but if this is not possible (or reasonable), the commission is to prepare a report within twelve months of its constitution for deposit with the Secretary-General of the United Nations; the report is to include any recommendations the commission may consider appropriate for an amicable settlement of the dispute[8]. The Secretary-General then notifies the parties concerned, who have three months to accept the commission's recommendations[9]. In any case, the report is to record any agreements reached and, failing agreement, the commission's conclusion on all questions of fact or law relevant to the matter in dispute[10].

COMPULSORY CONCILIATION

Compulsory conciliation[11] is established as obligatory for settlement of disputes in only two areas, namely coastal state sovereign rights in respect to marine scientific research and fisheries, as enumerated by the Convention. The Convention arrives at this result in the following way: although dispute settlement procedure is actually obligatory in these matters as in others, states need not accept this procedure where basic principles are concerned (in fact the most important questions)[12]. However, if a coastal state does not comply with the regulations of the Convention in a variety of matters (in summary: a specific research project in accordance with Articles 246 and 253; fish conservation and management measures; refusal to determine the allowable catch; refusal to determine the surplus in accordance with Articles 62, 69, and 70)[13], the Convention requires at least the institution of compulsory conciliation[14].

The general principles of compulsory conciliation procedure are the same as those for voluntary conciliation given above, but there are two significant differences. First, the conciliation commission is constituted and the proceedings held, regardless of whether the other party to the dispute attends or replies[15]; second, the report of the commission (or its recommendation for an amicable settlement) in fishery cases is to be communicated to the appropriate international organizations[16], a measure which could apply at least some pressure on parties to participate in any conciliation proceedings instituted. But in no case is the conciliation commission to substitute its discretion for that of the coastal state[17]. If the parties disagree as to whether the commission has competence, the commission is to decide the question[18].

Compulsory conciliation procedure can also be chosen as an option in certain types of disputes involving boundary delimitations with opposite or adjacent states in that a state declares in writing that it does not accept dispute settlement procedure for such cases; this declaration is only possible if the state accepts compulsory conciliation procedure in such questions if agreement is not reached in a reasonable time by other methods[19]. It should be noted that the Convention's overriding goal is for states parties to arrive at a peaceful and amicable solution to their disputes, and the parties are given almost complete freedom in their choice of procedure for all kinds of disputes[20].

---

[1] Art. 279
[2] Art. 283
[3] Art. 284, Para. 1
[4] Art. 284, Para. 3
[5] AV, Art.3, Subpara. (a)
[6] AV, Art. 7, Para. 2
[7] AV, Art. 5-6
[8] AV, Art. 7
[9] AV, Art. 7, Para. 1; AV, Art.8
[10] AV, Art. 7, Para. 1
[11] AV, Art. 11-14
[12] Art. 297, Subpara.2 (a), 3 (a)
[13] Art. 297, Subpara. 2 (b), 3 (b)
[14] *Ibid.*; AV, Art. 11-14
[15] AV, Art. 11-12
[16] Art. 297, Subpara. 3 (b)
[17] Art. 297, Subpara. 3 (c)
[18] AV, Art. 13
[19] Art. 298, Subpara. 1 (a)
[20] Art. 280; 299

CONCILIATION PROCEDURE

POWER OF THE PARTIES
AV, Article 10

The parties to the dispute may by agreement applicable solely to that dispute modify any provision of Annex V

LIST OF CONCILIATORS
Annex V, Article 2

- Every state party may nominate up to four conciliators
- Names of nominated conciliators are drawn up in a list by the UN Secretary-General

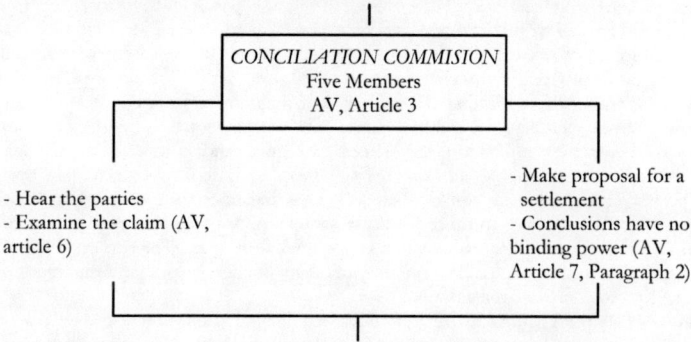

CONCILIATION COMMISION
Five Members
AV, Article 3

- Hear the parties
- Examine the claim (AV, article 6)

- Make proposal for a settlement
- Conclusions have no binding power (AV, Article 7, Paragraph 2)

First step
A state party institutes conciliation proceedings by notifying other party or parties to the dispute (Article 284; AV, Article 1); appoints two conciliators, preferably from list, one of whom may be national of state party.

Second Step
(a) If other state party or parties to the dispute refuses conciliation, no further action takes place (Article 284, Paragraph 3)
(b) If invitation is accepted or compulsory conciliation is required (Article 297, Paragraphs 2 & 3; AV, Articles 11-14);
    (aa) this state party appoints two conciliators, preferably from list, one of whom may be its national, within twenty-one days; if no appointment within this period,
    bb) UN Secretary-General appoints third and fourth conciliators.

Third Step
The four conciliators appoint fifth member as chairperson.

Fourth Step
If chairperson has not been chosen within thirty days, UN Secretary-General makes

Settlement	Report	Termination	Fees
AV, Article 5	AV, Article 7	AV, Article 8	AV, Article 9
- Commission may draw attention of parties to measures to facilitate agreement	- To be made within twelve months - Recording of agreements, etc. - Recommendations for settlement	- By settlement - Recommendations rejected or not accepted within three months	- Expenses and fees to be borne by Parties

THE TRIBUNAL FOR THE LAW OF THE SEA

The Tribunal is one of the four fora among which state parties may choose within the compulsory dispute settlement system of the Convention[1] whenever the interpretation or application of the Convention is in question[2]; parties may also call upon the Tribunal in a dispute arising from treaties or conventions already in force concerning subject matters covered by this Convention, if the parties agree to do so[3]. The Tribunal's position will ultimately depend upon the reputation it earns for itself, but its greatest significance from the beginning will be related to the compulsory jurisdiction in matters concerning deep-sea mining in the Area for its sub-chamber, the Sea-Bed Disputes Chamber[4], to which all concerned (state parties, the Sea-Bed Authority, the Enterprise, state enterprises, and natural or juridical persons) have access[5], and its final jurisdiction in matters of release from detention of crews and vessels, if the states concerned have not otherwise agreed[6].

The Tribunal has twenty-one members[7] elected by the states parties[8] for nine-year terms; in order to provide for staggered terms, at the first election seven of the members will be elected for only three years and another seven members for only six years.[9] The members are to be elected from among persons enjoying the highest reputation for fairness, integrity, and competence[10] and are to be independent and avoid incompatible activities.[11] Each member is to declare solemnly that he will exercise his power impartially and conscientiously.[12] Due regard is to be given to geographical representation in the Tribunal and no more than one national of any one state may be elected. [13] The Tribunal elects its President and Vice-President and appoints a Registrar. [14] The sessions of the Tribunal are to be held as far as possible with all twenty-one members in attendance, but a minimum of eleven members is necessary to constitute the Tribunal.[15]

Proceedings before the Tribunal are instituted when a dispute is submitted to the Tribunal either by notification of a special agreement or by written application. [16] If the dispute concerns interpretation or application of this Convention, the Registrar notifies all states parties; if an international agreement is in question, he notifies all parties to the agreement[17]. The Tribunal itself is responsible for laying down rules of procedure; [18] the Convention provides that the hearings are to be public and under the control of the President of the Tribunal. [19] The Tribunal may prescribe provisional measures[20] and is to make orders for the conduct of the case.[21] If one of the parties does not appear or refuses to participate, the other party may request that proceedings continue. [22] Every state which has a legal interest in a decision may submit an intervention request.[23] Decisions of the Tribunal are made by majority vote[24] and the reasons on which the judgement is based must be given; the judgement must be read in open court. [25] Decisions other than in provisional matters are final and are binding on the states parties of the dispute[26] and for an intervening state in so far as the decision relates to matters in respect of which that state intervened. [27]

---

[1] Art. 287
[2] AVI, Art.21; Art. 286; Art. 288, Para 1
[3] AVI, Art.22
[4] AVI, Art. 35-40; Art. 288, Para. 2
[5] Art. 187
[6] Art. 292
[7] AVI, Art. 2
[8] AVI, Art. 4
[9] AVI, Art. 5
[10] AVI, Art. 2
[11] AVI, Art. 7-9; AVI, Art. 17
[12] AVI, Art. 11
[13] AVI, Art. 2-3
[14] AVI, Art. 12
[15] AVI, Art. 13, Para. 1
[16] AVI, Art. 24
[17] AVI, Art. 32
[18] AVI, Art, 16
[19] AVI, Art. 26
[20] AVI, Art. 25; Art. 290
[21] AVI, Art. 27
[22] AVI, Art. 28
[23] AVI, Art.; AVI, Art. 32, Para.3
[24] AVI, Art. 29
[25] AVI, Art. 30
[26] AVI, Art. 33; Art. 296
[27] AVI, Art. 31, Para. 3

TRIBUNAL FOR THE LAW OF THE SEA

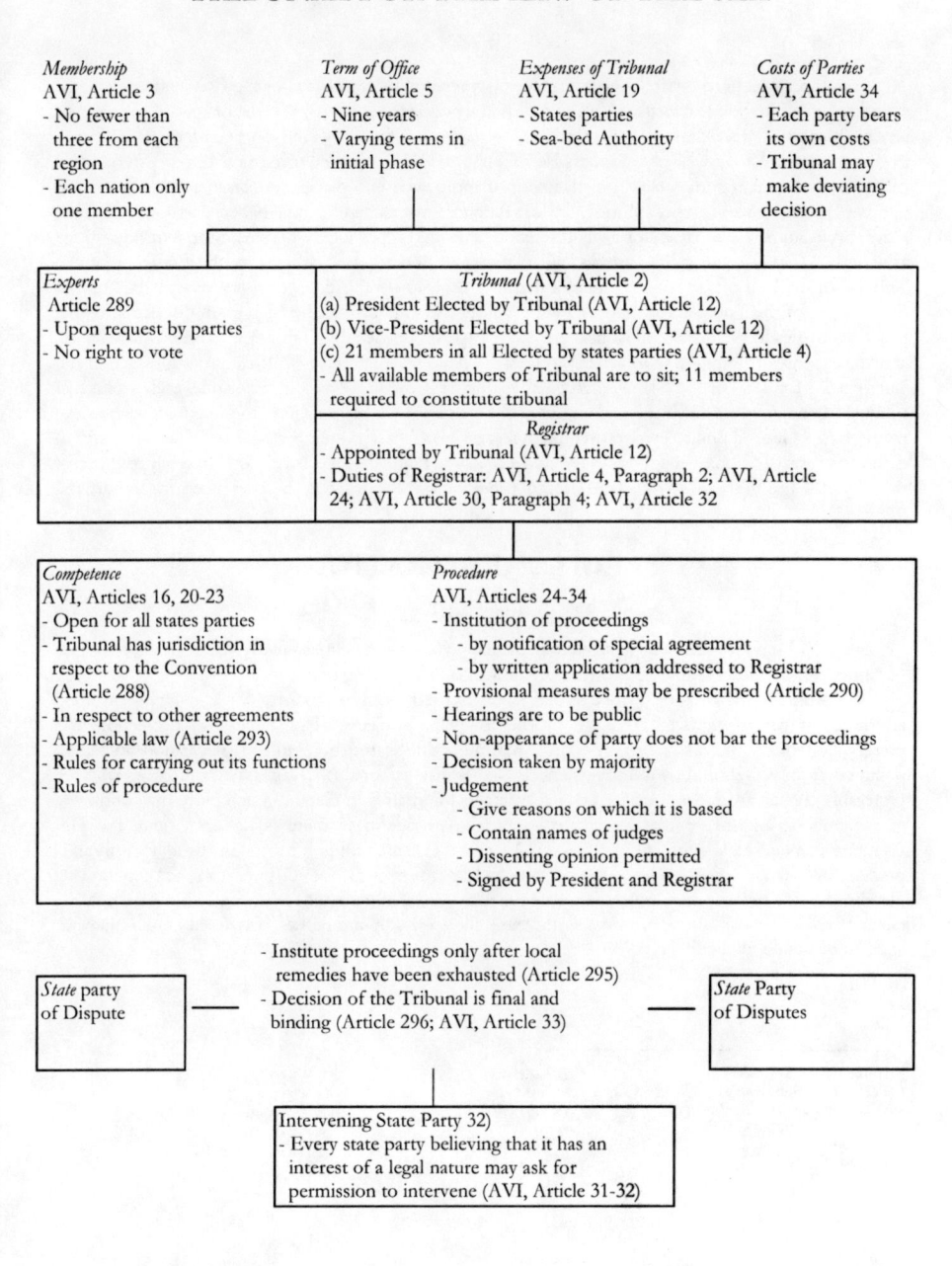

Membership
AVI, Article 3
- No fewer than three from each region
- Each nation only one member

Term of Office
AVI, Article 5
- Nine years
- Varying terms in initial phase

Expenses of Tribunal
AVI, Article 19
- States parties
- Sea-bed Authority

Costs of Parties
AVI, Article 34
- Each party bears its own costs
- Tribunal may make deviating decision

Experts
Article 289
- Upon request by parties
- No right to vote

Tribunal (AVI, Article 2)
(a) President Elected by Tribunal (AVI, Article 12)
(b) Vice-President Elected by Tribunal (AVI, Article 12)
(c) 21 members in all Elected by states parties (AVI, Article 4)
- All available members of Tribunal are to sit; 11 members required to constitute tribunal

Registrar
- Appointed by Tribunal (AVI, Article 12)
- Duties of Registrar: AVI, Article 4, Paragraph 2; AVI, Article 24; AVI, Article 30, Paragraph 4; AVI, Article 32

Competence
AVI, Articles 16, 20-23
- Open for all states parties
- Tribunal has jurisdiction in respect to the Convention (Article 288)
- In respect to other agreements
- Applicable law (Article 293)
- Rules for carrying out its functions
- Rules of procedure

Procedure
AVI, Articles 24-34
- Institution of proceedings
    - by notification of special agreement
    - by written application addressed to Registrar
- Provisional measures may be prescribed (Article 290)
- Hearings are to be public
- Non-appearance of party does not bar the proceedings
- Decision taken by majority
- Judgement
    - Give reasons on which it is based
    - Contain names of judges
    - Dissenting opinion permitted
    - Signed by President and Registrar

State party of Dispute

- Institute proceedings only after local remedies have been exhausted (Article 295)
- Decision of the Tribunal is final and binding (Article 296; AVI, Article 33)

State Party of Disputes

Intervening State Party 32)
- Every state party believing that it has an interest of a legal nature may ask for permission to intervene (AVI, Article 31-32)

ARBITRATION

Annex VII

Any disputes between states concerning the interpretation or application of the Convention are to be submitted to arbitration if the states have not chosen by declaration the same court or tribunal or reached an agreement otherwise.[1] For this reason, arbitration might become one of the most common procedures - in theory. Practice may well prove otherwise. If only two parties are involved in a dispute, the arbitral tribunal consists of five members[2] (involvement of more than two parties can cause an increase in the number[3]), preferably to be chosen from a list of arbitrators maintained by the UN Secretary-General. Each party may nominate one arbitrator at its discretion, and the parties jointly nominate the remaining three arbitrators[4]. If one or all of the parties fail to nominate the required arbitrators, the President of the Tribunal of the Law of the Sea is to appoint them.[5] The arbitral tribunal has only one-quarter the number of members of the Tribunal for the Law of the Sea (twenty-one[6]). A further significant distinction is that the states parties to the dispute must bear the entire expense of the arbitral tribunal,[7] both their own costs and the expenses of arbitration in general (otherwise, only their own costs[8]). While procedure before the Tribunal for the Law of the Sea is determined by the Tribunal itself[9] as a general code, each arbitration tribunal determines its own procedure, and the parties may even agree to determine procedure themselves.[10] General principles of procedure in respect to effect of non-appearance or failure of a party to defend its case, decision by majority, award, and a final and binding award correspond basically to those of the Tribunal for the Law of the Sea.[11] Even provisional measures may be prescribed by the arbitral tribunal.[12]

SPECIAL ARBITRATION

Annex VIII

Special arbitration differs from arbitration in only two respects; consequently, the general provisions of Annex VII apply accordingly for procedure under Annex VIII.[13]

The arbitral tribunal is distinctive with respect to the lists of arbitrators. A list of highly-qualified arbitrators is to be prepared for each of the following subjects: (1) fisheries, (2) protection and preservation of the marine environment, (3) marine scientific research, and (4) navigation, including pollution from vessels and by dumping. The special arbitral tribunal is to consist of arbitrators who are preferably chosen from the list of experts relevant to the matter in dispute. Each party may nominate two members, and the parties nominate jointly the president. If there is no agreement, the UN Secretary-General makes the appointment.[14] The second distinction is a provision for a "fact-finding" procedure,[15] according to which the facts which gave rise to the dispute can be conclusively determined.[16] However, the parties to the dispute can agree that the results of the procedure have only the effect of recommendations which serve as the basis for review by the parties, just as they would have to agree to be bound by the findings.[17]

---

[1] Art. 287, Para. 1, 3, & 5
[2] AVII, Art. 3, Subpara. (a)
[3] AVII, Art. Subpara. (g)-(h)
[4] AVII, Art. 3, Subpara. (b-d)
[5] AVII, Art. 3, Subpara. (e)
[6] AVI, Art. 2, Para. 1
[7] AVII, Art. 7
[8] AVI, Art. 19; AVI, Art. 34
[9] AVI. Art. 16
[10] AVII, Art.5
[11] AVII, Art.8-12; AVI, Art. 24-33
[12] Art. 290
[13] AVIII, Art. 4
[14] AVII, Art. 2-3
[15] AVIII, Art. 5
[16] AVIII, Art. 5, Para.2
[17] AVIII, Art. 5, Para.3

ARBITRATION - SPECIAL ARBITRATION

TRIBUNAL

5 Members
Preferably to be chosen from list of arbitrators AVII, Article 3, Subpara (a);
A VIII, Art. 3, Subpara (a)

Procedure
AVII, Articles 5 and 9
- If desired, parties may choose procedure
- Non-appearance or failure to defend does not bar proceedings

Duties of Parties
AVII, Articles 6-7
- Provide documents, information, etc.
- Enable tribunal to call witnesses or experts
- bear all costs and expenses in equal shares

Tribunal Duties
AVII, Articles 8, 10, 12
- Make decisions by majority
- Make an award
- State reasons on which an award is based (dissenting opinion possible)
- Settle questions of interpretation or manner of implementation of award upon request

LIST OF ARBITRATORS

Arbitration
- Each state may nominate four arbitrators
- List drawn up and maintained by UN Secretary-General
- If necessary, appointments are the made by President of Tribunal for the Law of the Sea

Special Arbitration

(1) Fishery (2) Marine Environment (3) Marine Scientific Research (4) Navigation, Pollution/Dumping from vessels

- Each state party may nominate two experts in each field whose legal, scientific, or technical competence in the field is recognized
- The list is to be drawn up and maintained by

(1) UN Food and Agricultural Organization FAO

(2) UN Environment Program UNEP

(3) Inter-governmental Oceanographic Commission IOC

(4) International Maritime Organization IMO

- If necessary, appointments are made by the UN Secretary General

INTERNATIONAL ORGANIZATIONS AS "STATES PARTIES"

The term "international organizations" in this context refers only to intergovernmental organizations, meaning that two or more governments have concluded an agreement for general or specific purposes (e.g., the European Economic Community (EEC) or the Saudi-Sudanese Red Sea Joint Commission, which was founded for the purpose of exploring and exploiting the non-living resources beyond the 1000 meter depth isobath in the Red Sea). Such organizations can obtain the status of a state party[1] and thus become a member of the Sea-Bed Authority[2] on two conditions:

First: The member states of an intergovernmental organization must have transferred partially or wholly their competence over matters governed by the Convention, including the competence to enter into treaties in respect to matters governed by the Convention.[3] A state party may - in theory - transfer all of its rights of voting, decision-making, and presentation and nomination to an organization. Although the provisions allow for the transfer of "obligations,"[4] it is not clear to what extent a state can transfer obligations laid upon it by the Convention. To what extent does the term "transfer of competence"[5] include obligations? The Annex mentions that the organization is to comply with obligations,[6] but this might be easier said than done. In any case, state parties to an organization carrying out activities in the Area are to ensure that appropriate legislation for indemnity is implemented in respect to such organizations.[7]

Second: An organization may deposit an instrument of formal confirmation or accession only if (a) a majority of its members have deposited their instruments of ratification or accession,[8] (b) a declaration is deposited specifying the competence which has been transferred,[9] and (c) the instrument of the organization contains an undertaking accepting the rights and obligations of states in respect of matters relating to which competence has been transferred.[10] Under no circumstances may the participation of an organization create more or new rights. For this reason, there may be no increase in representation,[11] rights under the Convention may not be transferred to member states which are not states parties to the Convention,[12] nor may the obligations arising from the agreement establishing the organization prevail over the obligations under the Convention;[13] finally, the instrument of formal confirmation or accession of an international organization is not taken into account in determining when the Convention enters into force.[14]

With respect to responsibility, liability, and settlement of disputes, regulatory provisions are provided[15] to place membership of organizations on equal footing with membership of states. The participation of organizations appears to be a simple matter, but if a larger number of organizations take advantage of the opportunity, it might prove very problematic if, for example, not all member states of an organization are states parties to the Convention, or with respect to "obligations" of the Convention for states parties.

The European Economic Community is so far the only international intergovernmental organization to have even signed the Convention,[16] but it or other organizations might yet confirm or accede to the Convention.[17]

---

[1] Art. 1, Subpara. 2(2)
[2] Art. 156, Para. 2
[3] AIX, Art. 1
[4] AIX, Art. 4, Para. 1&3
[5] AIX, Art.1
[6] AIX, Art. 6, Para. 1; cf. AIX, Art. 4, Para. 1
[7] Art. 139, Para. 3
[8] AIX, Art. 3; Art. 306-307
[9] AIX, Art. 5, Para. 1-2
[10] AIX, Art. 4, Para. 2
[11] AIX, Art. 4, Para. 4
[12] AIX, Art. 4, Para. 5
[13] AIX, Art. 4, Para. 6
[14] AIX, Art. 8, Subpara. (a)
[15] AIX, Art. 6-7
[16] AIX, Art. 2; Art. 305
[17] AIX, Art. 3; Art. 307

Further readings: - Governmental Organizations as Parties to the Convention, Page 110

PARTICIPATION OF INTERNATIONAL ORGANIZATIONS

MEANING OF INTERNATIONAL ORGANIZATION
(AIX, Article 1)

A participating organization must be one which has been constituted by states and to which its members have transferred competence over matters governed by the Convention, including the competence to enter into treaties in respect to those matters.

STATUS OF PARTICIPATING ORGANIZATIONS

(AIX, Article 4, Paragraph 2; Article 1, Subparagraph 2(2))
- Such an entity is a state party to the extent it has competence
- The term states parties refer to those entities.

Entry Requirements	*Effect of entry of Organization*	*Obligations of Organization*
Formal Confirmation (Articles 305-306; AIX, Article 3) - Signature (until December 9, 1984) but only if more than half of the members of the organization had signed - Declaration specifying competence transferred - Formal confirmation, but only if more than half of the members have deposited instruments of ratification or accession *Accession* (Article 307; AIX, Article 3) - Declaration of competence - More than half of the members must have deposited instruments of ratification or accession	Any participation of an organization may not - Increase representation of its members in respect to the Convention (AIX, Article 4, Paragraph 4) - Confer any rights on non-states parties (AIX, Article 4, Paragraph 5) - Affect obligations under the Convention (AIX, Article 4, Paragraph 6) - Be regarded as entry into force of Convention (AIX, Article 8, Subparagraph (a)) Paragraph 2) *Further effects* - In respect to amendments (AIX, Article 8, Subparagraph (b)) - In respect to denouncement (AIX, Article 8, Subparagraph (c))	The organization is to - Undertake to accept the rights and obligations of membership (AIX, Article 4, Paragraph 1) - Exercise the rights and perform the obligations transferred (AIX, Article 4, Paragraph 3) - Promptly notify depository of any changes in distribution of competence (AIX, Article 5, Paragraph 4) - Give information as required (AIX, Article 5, Paragraph 5; AIX, Article 6, - Assume responsibility for failure to comply with obligations or for any violations (AIX, Article 6, Paragraph 1; Article 139)

OBLIGATIONS OF STATES PARTIES AS MEMBERS OF ORGANIZATIONS

- May not exercise any competence which they have transferred (AIX, Article 4, Paragraph 3)
- Are to give all information required (AIX, Article 5, Paragraph 5; AIX Article 6, Paragraph 2)
- Are to implement indemnity legislation in respect to such organizations (Article 139, Paragraph 3)

FINAL ACT

The "Final Act" document is self-explanatory; it records the organization and operation of the Conference, beginning with the UN General Assembly decision of December 17, 1970, continuing through the convening of the Third UN Conference on the Law of the Sea in 1973, and finishing with the signing of the Final Act by 140 representatives of states and other Conference participants in Montego Bay on December 10, 1982. (This must not be confused with the signing of the Convention itself in accordance with Article 305, an act performed by 117 states on the same day.) In general, the signing of the Final Act is purely formal and does not create any treaty obligations. The Resolutions I-IV contained in Annex I to the Final Act, however, are an exception, as the Conference considered the resolutions to be an integral whole with the Convention,[1] especially in regard to the "Preparatory Commission" and "Pioneer Activities" discussed below.

PREPARATORY COMMISSION

As it was clear that considerable time would pass between the closing of the Conference and the entry into force of the Convention, it was seen as desirable to establish the *Preparatory Commission for the International Sea-Bed Authority and for the International Tribunal for the Law of the Sea* to make use of the interim period. The Commission's work was to commence as soon as fifty states had signed the Convention,[2] which, as previously mentioned, was already the case in Montego Bay on December 10, 1982. All states which have signed the Convention have the right to participate through their representatives in the Commission, including the right of participation in the taking of decisions; states which have signed only the Final Act may participate fully in deliberations, but not in the taking of decisions.[3] The Commission held its first meeting in March 1983 and its first session in August/September 1983; it has since been working continuously. Five special committees were established with the following tasks:

(a) Dealing with problems of developing land-based producers of nickel, copper, cobalt, and manganese which might be affected by deep-sea mining;[4]
(b) Preparing rules, regulations, and other measures for an early commencement of operations by the Enterprise;[5]
(c) Preparing a sea-bed mining code;[6]
(d) Making preparations for the Tribunal for the Law of the Sea.[7]
(e) Preparations for the Assembly, Council, Commission, and Secretariat of the Sea-Bed Authority[8] and for matters concerning pioneer activities[9] are made by the plenary session or its general committee.

As the Preparatory Commission is to follow the rules and procedure of the Third UN Conference 1973-1982, it attains the importance - within the scope of its task - of a "continuous mini-conference", although with the significant distinction that states which have not signed the Convention have the status only of observers. The Commission is to remain in existence until the conclusion of the first session of the Assembly of the Sea-Bed Authority,[10] at which time the Preparatory Commission is to present a final report to the Assembly on all matters within its mandate.[11] When the Convention enters into force, the rules, regulations, and procedures drafted by the Commission are to apply provisionally pending their formal adoption by the Authority.[12]

A separate report is to be prepared regarding the Tribunal for the Law of the Sea, containing recommendations for a meeting of the states parties for the nomination and election of the members of the Tribunal.[13] The Commission's report could possibly include the recommendation to choose another seat in place of Hamburg[14] for the Tribunal if the Federal Republic of Germany has at that point not yet become state party to the Convention.

---

[1] Final Act, Para. 42
[2] RI, Para. 1
[3] RI, Para.. 2
[4] RI, Para. 9; Subpara. 5(i)
[5] RI, Para. 8
[6] RI, Para. 7, Subpara. 5(g)
[7] RI, Para. 7&10
[8] RI, Subpara. 5(a-f)
[9] RI, Subpara. 5(h)
[10] RI, Para. 13
[11] RI, Para. 11
[12] Art. 308, Para. 4
[13] RI, para. 10
[14] AVI, Art. I

PREPARATORY COMMISSION

NB: The schematic layout includes the established sub-commissions.

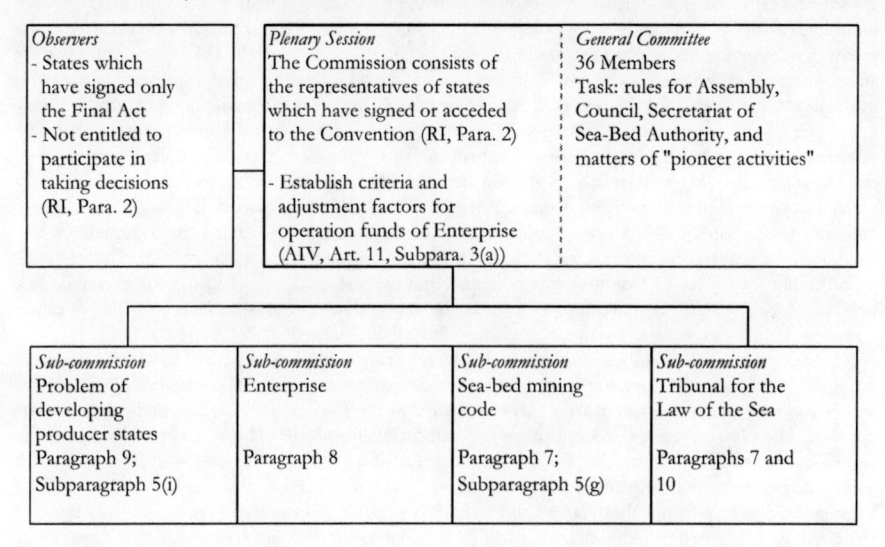

Observers	*Plenary Session*	*General Committee*
- States which have signed only the Final Act - Not entitled to participate in taking decisions (RI, Para. 2)	The Commission consists of the representatives of states which have signed or acceded to the Convention (RI, Para. 2) - Establish criteria and adjustment factors for operation funds of Enterprise (AIV, Art. 11, Subpara. 3(a))	36 Members Task: rules for Assembly, Council, Secretariat of Sea-Bed Authority, and matters of "pioneer activities"

Sub-commission	*Sub-commission*	*Sub-commission*	*Sub-commission*
Problem of developing producer states Paragraph 9; Subparagraph 5(i)	Enterprise Paragraph 8	Sea-bed mining code Paragraph 7; Subparagraph 5(g)	Tribunal for the Law of the Sea Paragraphs 7 and 10

- The Authority and its organs are to recognize and honor the rights and obligations arising from Resolution I and the decisions of the Commission taken pursuant thereto (RII, Para. 13; Art. 308, Para. 5);
- Until formal adoption by the Sea-Bed Authority, rules, regulations, and procedure drafted by the Commission are to apply provisionally (Art. 308, Para. 4)

THE REGIME FOR "PIONEER ACTIVITIES"

The regime for "pioneer activities" was established to permit investments for activities in the Area[1] and to ensure immediate commencement of mining activities upon entry into force of the Convention. It emerged from the requests of industrialized states for a safeguard for the considerable investments which had already been made by some companies and consortia, with the intention of giving these pioneers priority with respect to other - non-pioneer - investors for the recovery of investments as soon as possible after the conclusion of the 1973-1982 Conference. Other states, especially from among the developing countries, were keenly interested in preserving the main principles of the regime for the deep-sea Area. The pioneer regime is to remain in effect until the entry into force of the Convention,[2] although the events of this interim period will continue to have an influence long after that point.[3] The resolution provides that companies, consortia, state enterprises, and the like which invested at least US$30 million before 1983 or, in particular cases, before 1985[4] may under certain conditions apply to the Preparatory Commission for registration as a "pioneer investor" and for registration of a "pioneer area"[5] which may not exceed 150,000 square kilometers.[6] The conditions for registration concern the status of the sponsoring state as a signatory to the Convention,[7] a certification of the level of pioneer expenditures[8], and the assurance that claims of applicants do not overlap[9]. Three years after allocation of a "pioneer area", 20% of the same reverts to the Area, an additional 10% within another two years, and an additional 20% later on.[10]

Once a pioneer investor has been registered, he may carry out pioneer activities, which include all preliminary measures for exploitation,[11] but exclude commencement of commercial production, which may only take place when, after entry into force of the Convention, the Sea-Bed Authority has approved the plan of work[12] and issued a production authorization[13]. The Authority must give due regard to decisions made by the Preparatory Commission.[14] Only pioneer investors from states which are parties to the Convention will be approved to begin operations in the Area.[15] The "rights" of pioneer investors from other states will be terminated after a short time;[16] however, this lapse of rights can be prevented if the pioneer investor changes its nationality and sponsorship to a state party to the Convention within a certain period of time.[17] Prior to the commencement of commercial operations, the pioneer investor is required to pay a certain fee[18] and, at the request of the Preparatory Commission, carry out exploration (costs to be reimbursed) in the reserved area, provide training, and perform Convention obligations related to the transfer of technology[19] in order to ensure that the Enterprise is able to keep pace with states and other entities with respect to activities in the Area.[20] Every state which has certified the level of pioneer expenditures is to ensure that the necessary operating funds for the Enterprise are made available when the Convention enters into force,[21] an obligation to which all states parties will be subject to one degree or another on that future day[22].

---

[1] Preamble of RII
[2] RII, Para.14
[3] Art. 308, Para. 5
[4] RII, Subpara. 1(a)
[5] RII, Para. 2-3
[6] RII, Subpara. 1(e)
[7] RII, Para.2
[8] RII, Subpara. 2 (a)
[9] RII, Para. 5
[10] RII, Subpara. 1(e)
[11] RII, Subpara. 1(b)
[12] RII, Para. 8; AIII, Art. 6
[13] RII, Subpara. 9(a)(Art. 151)
[14] RII, Para. 13 (Art. 308, Para. 5)
[15] RII, Subpara. 8(a); Para. 9
[16] RII, Subpara. 8(c)
[17] RII, Para. 10
[18] RII, Subpara. 7(a-b)
[19] RII, Para. 12
[20] Preamble of RII
[21] RII, Subpara. 12(b)
[22] Art. 170, Para. 4; AIV, Art. 11

THE "PIONEER INVESTORS"

The following states can apply for registration of pioneer investors (RII, Subpara. 1(a)(i-iii)

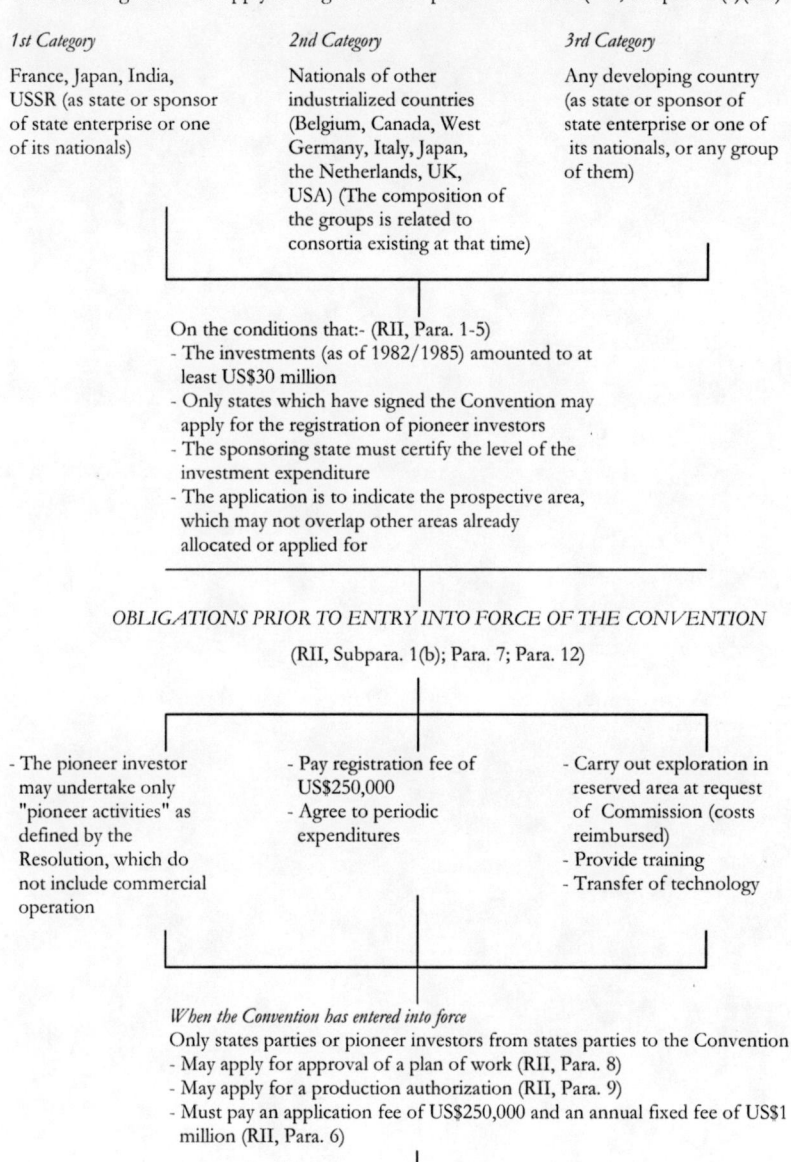

1st Category
France, Japan, India, USSR (as state or sponsor of state enterprise or one of its nationals)

2nd Category
Nationals of other industrialized countries (Belgium, Canada, West Germany, Italy, Japan, the Netherlands, UK, USA) (The composition of the groups is related to consortia existing at that time)

3rd Category
Any developing country (as state or sponsor of state enterprise or one of its nationals, or any group of them)

On the conditions that:- (RII, Para. 1-5)
- The investments (as of 1982/1985) amounted to at least US$30 million
- Only states which have signed the Convention may apply for the registration of pioneer investors
- The sponsoring state must certify the level of the investment expenditure
- The application is to indicate the prospective area, which may not overlap other areas already allocated or applied for

OBLIGATIONS PRIOR TO ENTRY INTO FORCE OF THE CONVENTION
(RII, Subpara. 1(b); Para. 7; Para. 12)

- The pioneer investor may undertake only "pioneer activities" as defined by the Resolution, which do not include commercial operation

- Pay registration fee of US$250,000
- Agree to periodic expenditures

- Carry out exploration in reserved area at request of Commission (costs reimbursed)
- Provide training
- Transfer of technology

When the Convention has entered into force
Only states parties or pioneer investors from states parties to the Convention
- May apply for approval of a plan of work (RII, Para. 8)
- May apply for a production authorization (RII, Para. 9)
- Must pay an application fee of US$250,000 and an annual fixed fee of US$1 million (RII, Para. 6)

Rights of pioneer investors from other states
- Are terminated (RII, Subpara. 8(b); Para. 10)

COMMENTARY ON MAJOR SUBJECTS OF THE CONVENTION

A. STATES AND ORGANIZATIONS

1. STATES AND STATES PARTIES

Every state acknowledged as such by the community of nations (about 160) can become a party to the 1982 Convention by ratification or accession. (Art. 306-307) Instruments of ratification or accession must be deposited with the Secretary-General of the United Nations, who is the depository of the Convention. (Art. 319, Para. 1) Once the Convention has entered into force, a state becomes a State Party (Art. 1, Subpara. 2(1)) and internationally bound with respect to other States Parties on the thirtieth day following the deposit of its instrument of ratification or accession. (Art. 308, Para. 2) States which deposit their instruments of ratification or accession before the entry into force of the Convention become State Parties and contractually bound to other States (Parties) twelve months after the date of deposit of the sixtieth instrument of ratification or accession, as this is the point in time at which the Convention enters into force. (Art. 308, Para. 1)

The Convention mentions "States" alone, e.g., "States shall...", but also generalized ("All States", "Every State", "State Party") and specified ("Coastal State", "Flag State", "Archipelagic State", "Developing State", and so on). But in spite of this variety of expressions, the Convention speaks to and means only States Parties, i.e., states which have consented to be bound by the Convention (Art. 1, Subpara. 2(1)) until there is a formal denunciation. (Art. 307) Applicable law of the sea between states party to the Convention and states which are not party to the Convention must be determined according to legal sources other than the 1982 Convention.

2. COASTAL STATES

Coastal states have one of the most significant positions in the 1982 Convention. That should come as no surprise as they not only make up three-quarters of the community of nations (about 120 of 160 states), but also have an overwhelming share (over 90%) of world industry, world trade, and world population. The naval forces of the world are exclusively in the hands of the coastal states. Then, too, there is tradition: coastal states have historically had sole influence in matters of the sea.

Whereas the coastal states' interests five decades ago had been reduced to little more than questions concerning foreign vessels in a territorial sea with a breadth of three nautical miles and sometimes, on a small scale, matters related to fishing, the picture today has changed considerably. The coastal states have become the "owners" of about 70% of the known non-living and 90% of the known living resources of the oceans; in addition, they have been vested with more administrative power with respect to prevention and control of pollution (Art. 56; Part XII) and marine scientific research. (Art. 56; Part XIII)

The fact that such a large part of the ocean's riches is now in the hands of the coastal states is the result of a zone system established by the Convention (Part II-Part VI) The extension of administrative power is related to protection and security interests of coastal states. As far as pollution is concerned, it is only necessary to call to mind the disastrous tanker accidents which have occurred since the 1950's.

The 1982 Convention provides the necessary framework for the coastal states' rights and obligations as well as the limits thereof for the protection of other states' interests. Other states' interests can be summarized as follows:

(a) Coastal states have to exercise their powers with respect to pollution and marine scientific research in a manner which protects and develops the use of the oceans (Art. 192; Art. 239; Art. 246) and which is conducted with due regard to the rights and duties of other states; (Art. 56, Para. 2)
(b) The deep-sea Area is reserved for mankind as a whole; (Art. 136-137)
(c) The high seas (Part VII) or any part thereof cannot in general be subject to the sovereignty of any state; (Art. 89)
(d) The regime of navigation, which is sub-divided into
  (aa) navigation in the territorial sea,
  (bb) navigation in the exclusive economic zone, with the further subdivision of navigation in the contiguous zone, and
  (cc) freedom of navigation on the high seas, can be exercised on an equal non-discriminatory basis (Art. 24-26; Art. 42; Art. 52; Art. 227) around the globe. (Part II-VII)

Almost every Part or section of the Convention has a direct or indirect impact or reference to the position of coastal states (See e.g. Art. 116, Subpara. (b); Art. 142), many of them ensuring that coastal states do not extend their interests beyond the limits laid down by the Convention.

3. PORT STATES

The Convention, which has no jurisdiction over the internal waters and ports of a coastal state, refers to "Port State" only once with respect to certain investigative and procedural powers in pollution cases and, most significantly, for cases of discharge from vessels on the high seas (Art. 218; Para. 1.) or, at the request of the flag state or the state affected by the violation, in the zones of other states. (Art. 218, Para. 2) The term Port State is derived from the fact that a state can institute investigations of such matters which have occurred outside its own internal waters, territorial sea, or exclusive economic zone only when the vessel is voluntarily within a port of that state.

The Convention does not define what is meant by discharge, but in conducting an investigation a port state has to apply international rules; such an applicable rule might be the definition of the Convention for the Prevention of Pollution from Ships 1973 (MARPOL), which establishes that:

> 'Discharge' in relation to harmful substances or effluents containing such substances, means any release, however caused, from a ship and includes any escape, disposal, spilling, leaking, pumping, emitting, or emptying. (Three exceptions are not given here.)

This delegation of power to all states, regardless of whether they have been affected by such discharge, is significant in light of the exclusive jurisdiction of the flag state on the high seas, (Art. 92) even if such investigations might be suspended at the request of the flag state (Art. 228) or of the state within whose zones the violation occurred. This establishes the principle that other states may take action against vessels polluting the oceans in spite of the reluctance or hesitation of the flag state. This global investigative machinery may have a great influence on the further evolution of the law of the sea.

4. FLAG STATES

A flag state is a state which grants vessels using international waters, regardless of type and purpose, the right to fly its flag (Art. 91, Para. 1) and, in so doing, gives the ships its nationality. (Art. 91, Para. 1) This right is to be documented by the flag state. (Art. 91, Para. 2) The term "flag state" is generally used in conjunction with non-official vessels (merchant, fishing, etc.), but it is also used for warships and other official vessels e.g., (Art. 31; 95) and in reference to installations, structures, or other devices, e.g., (Art. 209, Para. 2) and would also apply to ships employed by the United Nations, related organizations, (Art. 93) or other entities. (Art. 1, Subpara. 2(2); Annex IX, Art. 1)

The interest of flag states in exercising their right of navigation (Art. 90) has always been quick to conflict with the interests of the coastal states. Whereas the former want their vessels to be able to sail the seas with the greatest freedom and the least interference possible, the latter seek the greatest possible legislative and enforcement power in order to further their national interests in the waters near the coast. Until recently, the flag state's freedom of navigation took priority over all of the ocean surface except for a small section close to the coastal state's coastline; under the 1982 Convention, however, the situation has changed. The flag state's position is affected most by three regimes of passage ("innocent passage" (Art. 17-32) through the territorial sea, "transit passage" (Art. 37-44) through straits, and "archipelagic sea lane passage" (Art. 53-54) through archipelagic waters) and regulations for the prevention of pollution. (Part XII, Sec. 5-7) Nonetheless, there is no change of the flag state's principal responsibility for and jurisdiction over vessels of its nationality. The provisions governing the topics mentioned above exemplify various attempts to strike a balance between opposing interests, e.g., (Art. 24, 27, 41; Part XII, Sec. 7).

5. REGISTER STATE

The Convention uses the term "State of Registry" in regard to, among other things, installations used for unauthorized broadcasting from the high seas, (Art. 109, Para, 3) aircraft, (Art. 212, 216, 222) marine scientific research installations, (Art. 262) or other structures and devices. (Art. 209, Para. 2) With the exception of a few pollution regulations, e.g., (Art. 212, Para. 1; Art. 222) the Convention uses the terms "flag state" or "flying a state's flag" when referring to vessels, although the flag state is always to register the vessel, (Art. 91; Art. 94, Subpara. 2(a)i) and is consequently also a State of Registry. For the purposes of this Convention, "Flag State" and "Register State" are therefore the same.

As the Convention requires that all states fix conditions for the registration of ships in their territory, (Art. 91, Para. 1; Art. 94, Subpara. 2(a)) a United Nations conference held under the auspices of the United Nation Conference on Trade and Development (UNCTAD) adopted in 1986 a convention on conditions for registration of ships. One of the aims of this registration convention is of a political and economic nature and related to the topic of "flag of convenience".

6. FLAG OF CONVENIENCE STATE

The term "flag of convenience" refers to a state which registers foreign-owned vessels, granting the vessel its nationality and the right to fly its flag, giving the vessel the benefit of registration fees, annual fees, and taxes which are considerably less than in other states. In addition to the detrimental effect on fee scales, such registrations can have negative results in terms of social benefits and wages of the crew and the safety standards of the vessel. About 30% of the world merchant shipping tonnage navigates under three to four flags of convenience such as Liberia, Panama, and Cyprus. This situation has long been unacceptable for many developing countries, who believe that it hinders them in their efforts to build up their own merchant fleets, and has been criticized by seamen's trade unions in industrialized countries. The Convention attempts to require a "genuine link" between the register state and the vessel, (Art. 91, Para. 1) but does not go into detail. However, the Convention does permit a ship sailing under two or more flags according to convenience to be assimilated to a ship without nationality, (Art. 92, Para. 2) depriving such a vessel of the protection of any state. (Art. 92, Para. 1; Art. 110, Subpara. 1(d)) The meaning of a "genuine link" is described by the UN Convention on Conditions for Registration of Ships, 1986, which requires participation of nationals of the flag (register) state in ownership, manning, and management of the vessel. The register state may choose between "manning" and "ownership", but at least one of these conditions must be met.

7. ARCHIPELAGIC STATES

An archipelago is a "group of islands" which in some way forms an intrinsic unit. (Art. 46, Subpara. (b)) As early as the 1930's, questions about the treatment of groups of islands arose in conjunction with discussions of the territorial sea concept, but this had more to do with the inclusion of coastal islands than the status of a mid-ocean group of islands. The discussion focused on the problem of where the baseline dividing the internal waters from the territorial sea should be drawn. The 1958 and 1960 Conferences on the Law of the Sea did not recognize mid-ocean archipelagos, although the states concerned were even then seeking a specific solution. A global solution could be found only after an economic zone of two hundred nautical miles had been accepted. The two leading proponents of a concept of a mid-ocean archipelago, Indonesia and the Philippines, then received the-solution they had long urged. During the early stages of the 1973-1982 Conference, the Indonesian foreign minister declared:

> "Indonesia has always considered its land, water, and people to be inseparably linked to each other; the survival of the Indonesian nation depended on the unity of these three elements".

Indonesia in 1957 and the Philippines in 1961 had passed laws declaring the waters between the islands to be inland waters.

The Convention has now created a new legal concept (Part IV) which is based on two principal elements: the unity doctrine of archipelagic states (Art. 49) and the concept of archipelagic sea lane passage through the archipelagic waters. (Art. 53-54)

The following countries already apply (or might be interested in applying) the archipelago concept: Indonesia, Philippines, Tonga, Fiji, Mauritius, Bahamas, Papua New Guinea, Madagascar, West Samoa, Maldives, and Micronesia (non-exclusive list).

8. GEOGRAPHICALLY DISADVANTAGED STATES

Geographically disadvantaged states are those states which have direct access to the sea, but which because of geography (e.g., a relatively short coastline) feel that they are at a disadvantage in comparison with other states. In the context of fishing rights in the exclusive economic zone, the Convention defines "geographically disadvantaged states" as coastal states, including states bordering enclosed or semi-enclosed seas, whose geographical situation makes them dependent upon other coastal states (which are not disadvantaged) in the subregion or region, and coastal states which can claim no exclusive economic zone of their own. (Art. 70, Para. 2) Prior to the Conference and during the Conference itself, these states worked together closely with the land-locked states, as they were annoyed by the blunt manner in which the non-disadvantaged coastal states (a group of about eighty states) pushed for an exclusive economic zone with a limit of two hundred nautical miles. In spite of this, they found themselves in a weak position in the Convention. To be sure, they have the right to participate on an equitable basis with the coastal state of the same region or subregion in the exploitation of an appropriate part of the surplus of the living resources. (Art. 70, Para. 1) But this right is only very rarely enforceable. (Art. 70, Para. 5; Art. 71; Art. 297, Para. 3) Geographically disadvantaged states are also to be given the opportunity to participate in proposed marine scientific research projects of coastal states. (Art. 254) For all practical purposes, the geographically disadvantaged states were unable to achieve any more. The situation does improve slightly if the state is also a developing country, e.g., (Art. 70, Para. 4; Art. 148; Art. 269, Subpara. (a))

At the time of the 1973-1982 Conference, the following states considered themselves to be geographically disadvantaged (list not necessarily complete):

Africa: Algeria, Ethiopia, Gambia, Egypt, Sudan, United Republic of Cameroon, Zaire America: Jamaica

Asia: Singapore

Europe: Belgium, Bulgaria, Finland, German Democratic Republic, Greece, Federal Republic of Germany, Netherlands, Poland, Romania, Sweden, Turkey

Middle East: Bahrain, Iraq, Jordan, Kuwait, Qatar, Syria, United Arab Emirates

9. LAND-LOCKED STATES

There are about thirty land-.locked states, which means that roughly one-fifth of the members of the community of nations have no direct access to the sea, or, as defined by the Convention, are states which have no sea-coast. (Art. 124, Subpara. 1(a)) Although this number is high, the actual impact of these states on global economic and population figures is rather slight. But this basic disadvantage forces them to find reasonable and reliable access to regional or global communication and transport systems on the basis of established international law. The first efforts on the part of these states to carve out a niche for themselves in this respect (other than certain bilateral agreements) were made at the Barcelona Conference of 1921, later at a United Nations Conference on Trade and Employment, in Havana in 1948, then at various conferences, including the 1958 Conference on the Law of the Sea, which adopted the first small step for establishing a global legal framework for transit. (1958 Convention on the High Seas, Art. 3)

When as a result of the Ambassador Arvid Pardo proposal in 1967 the Sea-Bed Committee was instructed to discuss the future of the sea-bed, the land-locked states were anxious to place their problems on the agenda as well. In 1970, the UN General Assembly instructed the Secretary-General to prepare a study on the question of free access to the sea of land-locked countries, with a report on the special problems of land-locked countries relating to the exploration and exploitation of the resources of the sea-bed and the ocean floor.

As far as the sea-bed is concerned, the land-locked states did not get preferential access to sea mining, not even in the Area. (See Art. 141; Art. 148, 152, and 160, Subpara. 2(k) apply only to developing countries) The right of participation in coastal states fisheries (Art. 69) is weak, (Art. 69, Para. 3; Art. 71) and the right of transit Part X still depends to a considerable extent on the willingness of the transit state to co-operate; (Art. 125, Para. 2-3) nonetheless, the Convention includes some improvements compared to the period prior to 1982. Land-locked states may also participate in marine scientific research. (Art. 254)

The only guarantees for land-locked states found in the Convention are the right of navigation (Art. 90) or participation in the freedom of the high seas (Art. 86) and the right to equal treatment of their vessels in maritime ports. (Art. 131) The following is a list of land-locked states:

Africa:	Botswana, Burkina Faso, Burundi, Central African Republic, Chad, Lesotho, Malawi, Mali, Niger, Rwanda, Swaziland, Uganda, Zambia, Zimbabwe
Asia:	Afghanistan, Bhutan, Laos, Mongolia, Nepal,
Europe:	Austria, Czechoslovakia, Hungary, Luxembourg, Switzerland
South America:	Bolivia, Paraguay

10. TRANSIT STATES

Transit state means a state, with or without a sea-coast, situated between a land-locked state and the sea, through whose territory traffic in transit passes. (Art. 124, Subpara. 1(b)) The Convention does not use the term in any other context than the right of access of land-locked states to and from the sea and freedom of transit. (Part X)

11. DEVELOPING STATES

Of the approximately 160 state members of the United Nations, more than 100 are developing states. The answer to the question of who is a developing state depends on the judgement of each state itself, on whether it feels comparable or competitive with or as developed as the industrialized or developed states. The Convention does not offer any help in this respect; it refers only to developing states in general, and, rarely, to developing geographically disadvantaged or land-locked states, e.g., (Art. 148; Art. 140; Art. 69, Para. 3; Art. 70, Para. 4) In December 1967, the United Nations General Assembly instructed its Secretary-General to study the interests and needs of developing states with respect to the deep-sea area and the proposed Mining Authority, a consideration of preferential treatment which was made part of the 1970 Assembly Declaration of Principles governing the sea-bed. (Preamble)

The Convention provides numerous provisions designed to promote and support the growth of developing countries. Three broad themes intended for the benefit of developing states can be found in the Convention: co-operation (a), training (b), and preferential treatment (c).

(a) Although the Convention requires states in general to co-operate, (e.g., Preamble, Art. 118, 138, 197, 242, 270) it implies the need for particular care for and co-operation with developing countries. The most significant examples can be found in the provisions governing the Area, as they are applicable for all states, (e.g., Art. 140, Para. 1) and marine scientific research, whether conducted in the Area (Art. 143, Para. 3) or in general to strengthen the coastal state's own technological and research capabilities through development and transfer of marine technology. (Art. 266-278)

(b) In addition to the benefits of co-operation aimed at closing the technological gap, developing countries are to receive technical assistance to aid them in setting up programmes for the full and satisfactory protection of the marine environment. (Art. 202-203) Furthermore, adequate education and training of scientific and technical personnel is to be provided, (Art. 244, Para. 2) including the establishment of national and regional marine scientific and technological centres. (Art. 275-277)

(c) The most effective and supportive provisions for developing states might one day turn out to be those vesting the Sea-Bed Authority with powers and obligations for preferential treatment of developing states. These powers cover several aspects. In addition to support to be given by all states (and by the Sea-Bed Authority), (Art. 143, 148) the Authority is to acquire technology and training programmes from contractors operating in the Area (Art. 144, Subpara. 1(a); Annex III, Art. 5, Para. 3&15) and transfer it to developing countries. (Art. 144, Subpara. 1(b)) The Authority is to show preference to these countries when considering the use of revenues (Art. 150, Subpara. (f); Art. 82, Para. 4; Art. 160, Subpara. 2(f)) and pay compensation to those developing countries which suffer serious adverse effects on their export earnings as a result of the mineral policy of the Authority or of exploitation of minerals from the Area. (Art. 150, Subpara. (h); Art. 151, Para. 10; Art. 160, Subpara. 2(l)) A general clause of the Convention is open enough to allow further supportive measures for developing countries on the part of the Authority (Art. 148, Art. 274) as long as such measures can be covered by the term "activities in the Area". (Ibid; Art. 1, Subpara. 1(3))

Apart from these broad themes, developing countries which are land-locked, (Art. 124, Subpara. 1(a)), geographically disadvantaged, (Art. 70, Para. 2) or border enclosed or semi-enclosed seas (Art. 122; Art. 70, Para. 2) have only weak preferential access to fishing in exclusive economic zones of developed coastal states located in the same area. (Art. 69, Para. 3; Art. 70, Para. 4; Art. 71) But there is another, small supportive measure by the Convention which cannot be found directly in the text. Some provisions are a compromise between the "desirable standard" and the "obtainable standard", e.g., in the provision defining the flag state duties which requires only compliance with generally accepted regulations (Art. 94, Para. 5) or for pollution from land-based sources (taking into account), (Art. 207, Para. 4) so that developing states will not be overburdened with excessive investments for the time being.

12. UNITED NATIONS ORGANIZATION

The United Nations has been deeply involved in the development of the law of the sea since the organization's founding in the 1940's. It is doubtful that the community of nations would have reached the present standard of law governing the sea if there had not been a system of international organizations able and willing to act on the proposals of its members, such as that of the Malta delegate, Arvid Pardo, in 1967. One can also wonder whether an international conference such as the 1973-1982 Conference would have been held, much less succeeded, if it had not been for the United Nations and the support of its administrative machinery. The active participation of various United Nations organs or conferences in certain fields or their studies and recommendations will have had an impact on the drafting of the Convention. Particular mention should be made of the UNEP (United Nations Environmental Program) for its work on regional action plans, (Art. 197; in particular, Art. 123, Subpara. (b)) e.g., Kuwait Regional Convention for Co-operation on the Protection of the Marine Environment on Pollution 1978, and UNCTAD (United Nations Conference on Trade and Development) for its work concerning registration of ships and the "genuine link" (Art. 91; Art. 92, Para. 2) and the transfer of technology, e.g., (Art. 266)

The United Nations is in charge of conducting the administrative part of the Convention. One of its organs, the Secretary-General, is the depository of the Convention (Art. 319) and denunciations are to be addressed to him. (Art. 317) The Secretary-General is to communicate with the States Parties, the Authority, and competent international organizations (Art. 319) concerning all matters relevant to the Convention and is to take the necessary steps concerning amendments in due time and in accordance with the Convention. (Art. 312-314) The Secretary-General is to be supplied with charts and lists which show limit lines or geographical co-ordinates drawn by coastal states. (Art. 16; Art. 47, Para. 9; Art. 75; Art. 76, Para. 9; Art. 84) The United Nations may employ vessels in its service, and these can fly the flag of the United Nations. (Art. 93)

13. OTHER INTERNATIONAL GOVERNMENTAL ORGANIZATIONS

The international governmental organizations can be divided into two groups. One group works on a global basis, as Organs of the United Nations or are related to it in some degree. The latter are basically independent, have constitutions of their own, and states become members only by means of a separate procedure for each organization. The other group is often established only for regional or specific purposes and is open only to certain countries, but such organizations can also have global character. Many such organizations attended the 1973-1982 Conference as observers. (See Appendix to Final Act) The importance of three organizations will be described below.

International Maritime Organization (IMO) This is by far the most important organization for all matters concerning vessels, and this fact can be seen quite clearly in the Convention. The most important regulations which can be traced backed to IMO conventions are those concerning the safety of ships, including manning, signal and radio communication, and qualification of crew, (Art. 94, Para, 3-4) search and rescue, (Art. 98, Para. 2) prevention of collisions (Art. 21, Para 4; Art. 39, Para. 2; Art. 94, Subpara. 3(c)) including traffic separation schemes (Art. 22; Art. 41; Art. 53) and the involvement of the organization in the implementation of such schemes, (Art. 22, Subpara. 3(a); Art. 41, Para. 4; Art. 53, Para. 9) documents and precautionary measures by nuclear-powered merchant vessels and vessels carrying dangerous cargo, (Art. 23) and last but not least prevention of pollution e.g., (Art. 211, Para. 2)

International Labour Organization (ILO) A large number of ILO conventions, which make up the International Seafarer's Code, are concerned with working conditions of seamen. The 1982 Convention honours these conventions by urging States Parties to take measures governing labour conditions which conform to generally accepted international regulations. (Art. 94, Subpara. 3(b), Para. 5)

United Nations Food and Agriculture Organization (FAO) This organization and its committees on fisheries influenced to a large extent the provisions on utilization and conservation of fish resources. (Art. 61-68; Art. 117-120)

14. CO-OPERATION - "COMPETENT INTERNATIONAL ORGANIZATIONS"

The 1982 Convention contains numerous directives for co-operation between states, (e.g., Art. 123) between states and international organizations, (e.g.. Art. 199) and between international organizations, (e.g.. Art. 278) Apparently the co-operation required between states and international organizations will ultimately be of greatest importance for the effectiveness of the Convention, as this enhances the prospects of efficient enforcement of the Convention as well as unification and development of the law of the sea. Terms often used in this context include "States and competent international organizations shall...", (e.g., Art. 242, Para. 1) "States, in co-ordination with the competent international organization", (e.g., Art. 276, Para. 1) and "States, acting through the competent international organization". (e.g.. Art. 211, Para.1)

The competent international organizations for the various parts of the 1982 Convention are as follows (non-exhaustive list):

	Activities	Competent Organization(s)
Part XVII	Convention	United Nations Secretariat
Part VII	Shipping and Navigation	a) International Maritime Organization
		b) UN Conference for Trade and Development
Part VII	Marine Labour	International Labour Organization
Part VII	Marine Health	World Health Organization
Part V	Living Resources	Food and Agriculture Organization
	Non-living Resources	Ocean economic and technology branch of UN
Part XI	Non-living Resources	International Sea-Bed Authority
Part XII	Marine Environment	a) UN Environment Programme
		b) International Maritime Organization
		c) International Atomic Energy Agency
Part XIII	Marine Science	a) UN Educational, Scientific, and Cultural Organization
		b) Intergovernmental Oceanographic Commission
Part XIV	Marine Technology	UN Industrial Development Organization

15. GOVERNMENTAL ORGANIZATIONS AS PARTIES TO THE CONVENTION

The Convention provides the opportunity for inter-governmental organizations to become "states parties" to the Convention. (Art. 305, Subpara. 1(f) (306-307); Annex IX, Art. 3) This possibility was implemented under pressure from the member states of the European Economic Community (EEC). This move came about as a result of the fact that EEC institutions have certain powers, such as the conclusion of treaties and the establishment of internal rules in fisheries and in certain pollution matters.

The prospect of sea-bed mining gives the so-called "EEC clause" an even more interesting feature. The status of an acceding organization will more likely be that of a principal and agent rather than of a "state party," as a state party remains a "state party to the Convention" regardless of how much competence in matters governed by the Convention (AIX, Art. 1) it might have transferred to the organization, although corresponding rights (e.g., voting) will be affected accordingly. The handling of the "EEC clause" might prove to be somewhat difficult. The European Economic Community was the only inter-governmental organization to sign the Convention.

B. ZONES AND AREAS

1. INTERNAL WATERS, "HISTORIC BAYS", AND PORTS

Internal waters are the waters of lakes, rivers, and bays landward of the baseline of the territorial sea. (Art. 5-14) A "historic bay" based on a historical title (Art. 15) is part of the internal waters, even if not on the landward side of a baseline drawn according to the principle rules provided by the Convention. (Art. 10, Para. 6) Wherever there is a port, the baseline is always drawn in such a manner as to include it in the internal waters. (Art. 11) An archipelagic state may draw the so-called "closing line" (Art. 50) accordingly, which should not be confused with the "archipelagic baseline", (Art. 47) which serves the same function as the territorial sea baseline.

The baseline is the boundary between the territorial sovereignty of the coastal state and the regime of the oceans covered by the Convention, which to some extent includes the territorial sea zone of the coastal state. But the Convention does not ignore completely the landward side of the baseline; there are regulations establishing rights of land-locked states to transit passage through other states in general (Part X) and in particular guaranteeing them the right to equal treatment in maritime ports. (Art. 131) The Convention further authorizes coastal (port) states to undertake investigations and proceedings against vessels in pollution matters, depending on circumstances such as location of the vessel and the type and scope of the pollution, (Art. 218; Art. 220) and requires that laws and regulations be implemented for access to their ports and assistance for marine scientific research vessels. (Art. 255)

A further regulatory framework for matters such as access to ports or jurisdiction over ships in ports or internal waters is not provided by the Convention. This can be derived from national law of the coastal state in conjunction with international common law and treaties, for example, from the Convention on the International Regime of Maritime Ports, 1923, which, although ratified by only a small number of states, reflects largely customary rules of international law, or the various conventions of the International Maritime Organization (IMO) with respect to safety of ships and ship pollution matters. In a few words, it can be generally said that a foreign merchant vessel which is voluntarily in a port is fully subject to the administrative civil and criminal jurisdiction of the coastal state unless applicable conventions, treaties, bilateral agreements, or international common law provide particular regulations.

2. TERRITORIAL SEA

The extent of coastal state jurisdiction in waters near the coast has been a central theme of the law of the sea since the Middle Ages. While the superpowers of the Middle Ages, Spain and Portugal, regarded "conquered" ocean space as similar to a land mass, their successors were more interested in a "free" sea for commercial, communication, and naval power purposes. The result was rather limited control by coastal states of waters adjacent to their coasts, embodied in the concept of the territorial sea. As of the beginning of this century, the breadth of this zone had been determined for almost three hundred years by the "cannon shot doctrine", which in time had led to the rule of three nautical miles; the United States Neutrality Act of 1794, for example, translated the cannon shot doctrine into the three-mile rule. In any case, the establishment and long survival of this rule was more a result of superior British naval power and British colonial policy than of any consensus of the states.

The degree of general acceptance of this rule began declining after the First World War, and this process accelerated rapidly after the Truman Proclamation in 1945. The 1982 Convention sets the breadth of the territorial sea at twelve nautical miles. (Art. 3) The twelve mile mark emerged from a number of different factors, the simplest of which was doubling (from three to six to twelve miles). A more serious factor is the "package" of zones provided by the Convention. (Part II-Part VI) These zones were designed to satisfy the interests of all states concerned, and to a considerable extent they take into account the problems such as fishing, customs, sanitation, security, and, more recently, protection of the marine environment. The latter was closely tied to the discussion of more control over foreign vessels in pollution matters.

Today's concept of the territorial sea foresees full sovereignty of the coastal state in this area (Art. 2) with the restriction that the right of "innocent passage" for foreign ships as provided by the Convention (Art. 17-32) must be accepted. But other provisions of the Convention also affect the full sovereignty of the coastal state. Specifically, these include the regulations on the protection of the marine environment (Part, XII) and provisions such as those that require that research installations in any area of the marine environment be subject to Convention conditions. (Art. 258)

3. CONTIGUOUS ZONE

The concept of the contiguous zone is derived from the long-established concept of a territorial sea with a breadth of three miles. Ever since the Middle Ages, coastal states have, for one reason or another, taken measures of control over space beyond the territorial sea. The more typical of these reasons have found their way into the 1982 Convention: enforcement of customs, fiscal, immigration, and sanitary laws. (Art. 33, Subpara. 1(a)) Smuggling in particular was one of the earliest concerns. In 1736, Great Britain implemented an act against smuggling, claiming jurisdiction in such cases for a distance of up to twenty-four nautical miles. In 1935, the United States established a customs enforcement area of fifty nautical miles in order to enforce its "liquor" legislation. The 1855 Chilean Civil Code, as well as the laws of other South American states, contained provisions for policing waters beyond the territorial sea if customs and security were concerned. But these and other cases remained isolated instances and did not lead to a separate concept until after the Second World War.

It was not until a quick solution to the problems of the concept, baseline, and breadth of the territorial sea was delayed in the 1930's and early 1950's that the concept of a contiguous zone was able to emerge at the 1958 Conference in an attempt to provide "compensation"for those states which had pressed for rights of control for security reasons. As the regime of the law of the sea has changed considerably since then, it is doubtful that there is really a further need for this concept.

4. STRAITS

The establishment of a regime for straits was a major concern of the two naval superpowers and, with less intensity, of the shipping community. The difficulties are closely connected with the breadth of the territorial sea. International shipping routes through strategically important narrow straits within which the waters have the status of the territorial sea were subjects of disputes, litigation, and treaties prior to the 1973-1982 Conference. Such straits include the Dardanelles and Bosporus, the Sound and Belts of Denmark, the Strait of Magellan (Argentina and Chile), and, in the 1950's, the Straits of Tiran, which give Jordan and Israel access to the Red Sea. One case concerning the Corfu Channel was submitted to the International Court of Justice and decided in 1949.

Although the principle of a territorial sea with a breadth of three nautical miles remained unaltered at the 1958 and 1960 Conferences on the Law of the Sea, only the prohibition of suspension of innocent passage for foreign vessels through straits (1958 Territorial Sea Convention, Art. 16, Para. 4) was codified. This guarantee of "free passage" was no longer adequate assurance for the superpowers when it became obvious during the 1970's that the territorial sea would be extended to twelve nautical miles, as this would bring an even larger number of international navigation routes under the jurisdiction of coastal states. The negotiations centered in on the condition that a consensus for a territorial sea of twelve nautical miles would be reached only if an acceptable regime for passage through straits could be agreed on. This led to the emergence of the concept of transit passage. (Art. 37-44)

Some of the important navigation routes which became straits under the 1982 Convention are as follows:

Name of Strait	Breadth of Strait in Nautical Miles	Bordering States
Bering	9	USA - Soviet Union
Dover	18	Great Britain - France
Gibraltar	8	Morocco - Spain
Hormuz	20	Oman - Iran
Malacca	8	Indonesia - Malaysia
Saint Lucia Channel	22	Saint Lucia - Saint Vincent
Western Chosen	23	South Korea - Japan

A strait such as that of the Strait of Tiran which only gives access to a territorial sea does not possess the status of a "strait for international navigation"; consequently, only the principle of innocent passage (but which cannot be suspended) applies. (Art. 45, Subpara. 1(b) & Para. 2)

There is considerable reason to doubt that "straits" to and from archipelagic waters such as those in Indonesia (Sunda, Limbic, Makassar) are governed by the regime of straits and not solely by the compulsory concept of archipelagic sea lane passage. (Art. 53, Para. 2) It would make little sense for a vessel to be on archipelagic sea lane passage (Art. 53, Para. 1 & 12) before entering the strait between two islands, within the strait to be in strait transit passage, (Art. 37-44) and then to navigate again under the concept of archipelagic sea lane passage. (Art. 53)

5. ARCHIPELAGIC WATERS AND ZONES

An archipelago (Art. 46, Subpara. (b)) and the waters between the individual islands have a particular status. (Art. 46, Subpara. (b)) The Convention provides for the drawing of archipelagic baselines, (Art. 47) granting the waters within such lines the legal status of archipelagic waters, (Art. 49) with the resultant effect on navigation, which had previously been exercised in such areas as on the high seas. Although the large maritime powers had long opposed any attempt to restrict the freedom of navigation in these waters, the introduction of these concepts no longer raised any serious opposition when it had become evident during the mid-1970's that a 200 nautical mile wide exclusive economic zone would find its way into the Convention. When this wide economic zone was combined with the concept of islands, (Art. 121) the result was that almost all of the waters within island groups such as Indonesia fell under the corresponding sovereign rights of such "group of islands" states. However, a significant distinction remains between the archipelagic concept and the situation of coastal states: whereas the coastal state has only enumerated sovereign rights within it exclusive economic zone, (Art. 56) the archipelagic state has sovereignty over the archipelagic waters (Art. 1, Para. 2; Art. 49) (the waters between the islands and within the archipelagic baselines (Art. 47)) similar to that of the coastal state in its territorial sea. (Art. 2) Using the archipelagic baseline as a starting point, the archipelagic state may then establish a territorial sea, a contiguous zone, and an exclusive economic zone towards the high seas, and has rights to the resources of the continental shelf as provided by the Convention. (Part II-Part VI) In order to ensure freedom of navigation, the archipelagic state must accept the concept of archipelagic sea lane passage; (Art. 53) it was only under this condition that general acceptance of an archipelagic concept could be achieved.

6. ISLANDS

The regime of islands, which allows the establishment of all zones provided by the Convention if only an island can sustain human habitation or an economic life of its own, (Art. 121) has a significant effect on the colonization of the oceans. The "island effect" may well bring more ocean space under the jurisdiction of states than a 200 nautical mile zone as measured from the coastline of the continents. In quite a number of cases, a tiny island with a small population can now acquire rights to the resources in an area almost as large as France. The Republic of Kiribati (formerly Gilbert Islands) with its population of about sixty thousand has a claim on marine resources in an area bigger than that to which the People's Republic of China with its one billion people is entitled.

7. ENCLOSED AND SEMI-ENCLOSED SEAS

The very term "enclosed and semi-enclosed seas" (Art. 122) is not a traditional concept of international law. At the 1958 Conference, only a weak attempt was made to establish a special regime for navigation in certain areas, but it did not meet with any serious response until the time of the 1973-1982 Conference. By that point, it was well-known to all concerned that such seas faced immediate and serious threats to their marine environment. The states bordering the Baltic Sea signed a Marine Environment Protection Convention in 1974. In 1973, the Convention for the Prevention of Pollution from Ships (MARPOL), which provided a stricter regime for protection of "special regions", including the Mediterranean, the Baltic Sea, the Black Sea, the Red Sea, and the Arabian Gulf, was prepared for ratification. Further action was undertaken during the 1970's by the United Nations Environment Program (UNEP), which together with the affected states developed programmes for, among other areas, the Arabian Gulf, the Caribbean, and the Mediterranean. It soon became obvious that the measures would have the desired effect only if they could be taken on the basis of intense co-operation among the states bordering seas. The essential quality of the Convention provisions is that it requires the states to engage in this kind of co-operation. (Art. 123)

8. CONTINENTAL SHELF

The regime of the continental shelf is clearly a post-World War II development. Prior to that, practically the only cases involving rights to resources of the sea-bed were related to pearl fisheries of Bahrain and Ceylon in the last century. If European legal experts had drafted a doctrine of the rights to resources of the sea-bed before World War II, they might have required two conditions, "claim" and "exploitation", and referred to the principle of freedom of the seas. The Truman Proclamation of 1945 changed the direction, but the European approach survived partly into the 1958 Conference, which defined the continental shelf as the sea-bed to a depth of 200 meters or, beyond that, to where the depth of the superjacent waters admits of the exploitation of the natural resources. (1958 Continental Shelf Convention, Art. 1) However, instead of granting all interested states the right to a "claim", the 1958 Conference granted the coastal states exclusive sovereign rights over the natural resources on the continental shelf adjacent to their coasts, although in the 1950's the state of technology did not permit exploitation of the sea-bed at a depth even approaching two hundred meters. This caused concern for coastal states whose continental shelf to the two hundred meter depth limit was very narrow. When surveys in the Red Sea discovered vast mineral resources at a depth of about 2,500 meters, Saudi Arabia in 1968 claimed sovereign rights to all mineral resources up to the mid-line of the Red Sea.

The Saudi oil minister, Sheikh Ahmed Zaki Yamani, stated (excerpt):

> Those vast mineral resources have attracted several companies from distant countries who are now laying claims to the ownership of these resources. We have found it necessary to issue a law declaring (our) ownership.
> This development is analogous to what happened in the United States during President Truman's administration, when the United States declared its title to the hydrocarbon resources in its off-shore areas. Several nations followed the example of the United States, and it has now become an established international rule that every nation has the right to exercise sovereignty over the- subsoil resources of its continental shelf. This time it was Saudi Arabia that took the lead in establishing another fair and equitable rule in international law.

The barrier of "two hundred meter depth" or "exploitation beyond" of 1958 was threatened. Although the Red Sea is a unique situation, it was quite obvious that other coastal states would soon follow suit if the community of nations did not agree on clear and enforceable rules. The 1982 Convention found a generous solution to this problem. (Part VI, Art. 76)

9. EXCLUSIVE ECONOMIC ZONE

In describing the evolution of the concept of the exclusive economic zone, reference should first be made to the impact of fishing disputes which had arisen frequently since the eighteenth century. Although local in nature, these disputes led to such a growth in tensions in the 1960's that it was obvious that discussion of a new concept would be essential at the Third UN Conference on the Law of the Sea in 1973-1982. When the 1958 and 1960 Conferences failed to extend the territorial sea beyond three nautical miles, many states sought "compensation" by establishing a fishery zone of twelve nautical miles or more. Between 1958 and 1973, more than forty states implemented such fishery zones. A further driving force in the development of the economic zone was the unanswered questions with respect to the limits of the continental shelf. Furthermore, there was a precedent of some Latin American states (Chile, Peru, Ecuador) which in the Santiago Declaration on the maritime zone of 1952 postulated that they possessed sole sovereignty and jurisdiction over an area of the sea of not less than two hundred nautical miles from the coast. Other Latin American states followed. At the beginning of the 1970's, many African states and several Asian states adopted a policy corresponding to the South American claims. For many important maritime nations, the survival of the freedom of navigation in general and in straits in particular was becoming a matter of serious concern.

This "exclusive two hundred miles" approach ultimately found general acceptance, with the exception of three principal restrictions:

1) Instead of sovereignty, the coastal state has only enumerated sovereign rights; (Art. 56)
2) With regard to living resources, the coastal state has only "preferential rights" instead of "exclusive rights"; (Art. 62, Para. 3)
3) The coastal state has to accept the principles of freedom of navigation and overflight. (Art. 87; Art. 58)

But in spite of these restrictions, the practical impact of the exclusive economic zone remains close to exclusive rights. The sovereign rights granted include all economic uses known today, including marine scientific research. The "preferential rights" in respect to living resources are based on provisions which make it nearly impossible for other states to exercise their rights to a surplus of the allowable catch (Art. 61; Art. 62, Para. 3) except through friendly co-operation. Commercial shipping in general, on which every coastal state economy relies to at least a certain extent, might be affected by many political, economic, ,or social matters, but will concern itself very little with particulars of rights from navigation regulations; there will be great interest, however, in seeing the same rules applied consistently on a global basis. Naval vessels, on the other hand, particularly those not simply passing through the zone, might find that traditional freedom of navigation does not apply fully in the exclusive economic zone.

The following states (list not exclusive) have benefited most from the establishment of the exclusive economic zone and archipelagic regime (approximated figures in million square nautical miles):

More than 2 million: Australia, Canada, Indonesia, New Zealand, USSR, USA

1-2 million:	Brazil, Chile, France (including overseas dependencies), India, Japan, Mexico, United Kingdom
0.5-1 million:	Argentina, China, Equador, Fiji, Kiribati, Madagascar, Mauritius, Norway, Papua New Guinea, Philippines, Portugal, Solomon Islands, South Africa

10. THE HIGH SEAS

Until recently, the high seas were almost identical with the ocean space. The new order of the oceans has reduced this space by more than one-third, and the sea-bed below the seas and its resources have been given a regime of their own, the Regime of the Area. (Part XI) The high seas are the ocean space beyond the jurisdiction of coastal states, the waters superjacent to the sea-bed, the ocean surface, and the atmosphere above (Art. 86; Art. 135; Art. 78, Para. 1) and cover almost half of the planet's surface.

The 1982 Convention bases the legal regime of the high seas on the principle of freedom of the sea, (Art. 87) a term which governed the law of the sea for a long time. It is not worthwhile to reconstruct the evolution of the term, but it can be pointed out that the principle was enforced by Great Britain's sea power from the nineteenth century onwards as essential for the administration of the far-flung colonial empire. Traditional freedom of the sea, in fact, meant only freedom of navigation and freedom of fishing. As far as other means of utilization were concerned, the doctrine was ineffectual. Freedom of navigation could easily find general assent, as the substance of the ocean was unaffected by a vessel using it for passage; an unlimited number of vessels could pass through the same space without "using up" the ocean. For a long time, the same was true of fishing, at least where the catch was small or where the stocks could renew themselves before that part of the ocean was fished again. The traditional regime worked only as long as, and in places where, this was the case, and wherever these conditions were not present, tensions inevitably resulted sooner or later. Invulnerability during use was sufficiently inherent in the traditional system.

The provisions of the 1982 Convention retain the concept of invulnerability. The following examples illustrate this:

(a) the high seas are reserved for peaceful purposes; (Art. 88)
(b) it is forbidden to make sovereignty claims on any part of the high seas; (Art. 89)
(c) co-operation is required among nations engaged in fishing, (Art. 118) and conservation measures may not discriminate against others; (Art. 119, Para. 3)
(d) due regard is to be given to the interests of other states and to activities in the Area; (Art. 87, Para. 2) and
(e) states have the obligation to protect and preserve the marine environment. (Art. 192)

The term "freedom" (Art. 87) is of less significance than would appear at first glance. The right of navigation is the logical consequence of the exclusion of sovereign rights to any part of the sea, (Art. 89) as is also the case for overflight, cables and pipelines, artificial islands, and scientific research. These and other theoretical uses can be "free" only if the invulnerability of the high seas is observed or accepted by the community of nations, e.g., in cases of lawful dumping. (Art. 210)

11. THE AREA - THE DEEP SEA-BED

The deep sea was completely unknown to man until recently, and even today it remains a mysterious part of the planet. Whereas the oceans cover roughly two-thirds of the earth's surface, the deep sea bed, designated by the 1982 Convention as the "Area", (Art. 1, Subpara. 1(1)) covers about half the globe. In general, the sea-bed of the Area starts where the oceans have a water depth of 2,500 meters, corresponding to the concept of the continental shelf. (Art. 76) The greatest depth of the ocean is over 10,000 meters. Based on present findings, the value of the sea-bed and its subsoil is in potato-sized nodules composed of metal ores. These nodules are scattered across large areas, especially at depths of three to four thousand meters. These deposits are estimated to be in excess of one trillion tons. Technology for deep sea mining will be "collection", "sweeping", or "vacuum cleaning". All mining techniques known today would have considerable effect on the ocean floor and the water at and around the place of operation. A price tag of one to three billion US dollars for one operation unit, the present state of the ore commodity market, open questions with respect to protection of the marine environment, and uncertainties about the general acceptance of the 1982 Convention by the community of nations make it unlikely that operational activities for mining of nodules will commence in the remaining years of this century.

Ten years ago, however, at the mid-point of the 1973-1982 Conference, prospects were brighter and the mood of the delegates was more optimistic; there was a willingness to come to a consensus of a new legal concept for the Area. The vast majority of delegates were finally able to agree on a comprehensive concept, (Part XI; Annexes III & IV) based on the principle that all rights in the resources of the Area (Art. 133, Subpara. (a)) are vested in mankind as a whole, on whose behalf an International Sea-Bed Authority is to act. (Art. 137, Para. 2) A law-making mechanism for almost every aspect concerning the Area, e.g., protection of human life, (Art. 146) installations, (Art. 147) and administrative procedures and mining operations, including environmental protection, transfer of technology, inspection, and so on. (Annex III, Art. 17) is to be established through the Sea-Bed Authority. The Convention, however, provides only the basic principles (Art. 136-149) and policy (Art. 150-153) which govern the Area.

As it was obvious toward the end of the 1973-1982 Conference that the setting up of a legal framework, as well as the ratification and entry into force of the Convention, would take time, a Preparatory Commission was conceived to act in the interim. (Final Act, Res. I, Annex I) The Commission has established special commissions, of which two deal with the legal framework with respect to rules and regulations for the Enterprise and the preparation of a sea-bed mining code. The Preparatory Commission also deals with claim applications of pioneer investors. (Final Act, Res. 1, Annex 1.)

C. ACTIVITIES ON THE OCEANS

1. SHIPS-VESSELS

Although the 1982 Convention uses in part the term "ship" (Part II-Part X) and in part the term "vessel", (Part I, Part XII-Part XV) the two words are identical in meaning. A definition for ships/vessels is not to be found in the Convention. The large range of topics covered by the Convention would have made a general definition inadequate, and it is completely acceptable to define the terms against the background of the aims and purposes of specific laws and regulations. For example, the Convention for Preventing Collisions at Sea, 1972 (COLREG), defines ships/vessels as follows:

> The word "vessel" includes every description of water craft, including non-displacement craft and seaplanes, used or capable of being used as a means of transportation on water.

At times the Convention refers to a type of ship, such as when it defines a warship, (Art. 29) and at other times to the function or activity of the ship, such as when it speaks of tankers, nuclear powered ships and ships carrying nuclear, dangerous, or noxious substances, (Art. 22-23) fishing vessels, (Art. 62, Para. 4) research vessels, (Art. 248, Subpara. (d)) or even pirate ships. (Art. 103) The Convention does not make further distinctions with regard to size, cargo, or other common criteria. All vessels must be registered by a state, thereby obtaining the nationality and the right to fly the flag of the registry state. (Art. 91)

2. NAVIGATION

Transportation and communication are the most important uses of the oceans. Vessels navigating from port to port in the conduct of regional and global economic activities carry more than 90% by weight of all international trade. Consequently, navigation is a very sensitive matter, and it comes as no surprise that this was one of the major concerns during the 1973-1982 Conference.

A significant objection to the retention of the principle of freedom of navigation involved jurisdiction with regard to pollution. In addition, coastal states in particular wanted more rights for security reasons. These two questions meshed into the parallel discussion of the coastal states' objectives of extending the territorial sea and establishing an economic zone, which in turn led to the question of the impact these zones would have on navigation. Some states feared that one or more states could generally or selectively hamper navigation through these zones. The Convention's solution is as follows:

(a) Beyond the territorial sea with its breadth of twelve nautical miles, (Art. 3) the traditional principle of the freedom of navigation remains effective (Art. 87) with the exception of these matters in which the coastal state has enumerated rights in the exclusive economic zone (Art. 58) or in the contiguous zone, (Art. 33) such as the implementation of safety zones around artificial islands, (Art. 60, Para. 4-7) regulations for clearly defined areas for the prevention of pollution, (Art. 211, Para. 5-7; Art. 234) enforcement of pollution .regulations, (Art. 220) and measures to avoid pollution from marine casualties; (Art. 221)

(b) An independent legal regime is established for straits used for international navigation (Part III) based on the right of transit passage. (Art. 38) Transit passage applies only if there is no acceptable route other than the traversal of the territorial sea of coastal states bordering the strait; (Art. 37; Art. 38, Para. 1)

(c) The concept of archipelagic sea lane passage through archipelagic waters was developed. (Art. 53, 54)

These three solutions settled the major questions involving navigation. The concept of "innocent passage", which was first codified at the 1958 Conference, was basically retained and applied in the territorial sea, but it was newly defined (Part II, Sec. 3) with the result that a coastal state can more easily deny that a vessel's passage is "innocent".

3. FISHERIES

The principle of freedom of fishing has a long historical tradition. However, the realization that the living resources of the ocean are in fact exhaustible, the needs of the rapidly growing world population, and the technological progress in the fishing industry have made a change unavoidable. Although the principle of the freedom of fishing continues to apply on the high seas,

(Art. 87, Subpara. 1(e)) there is very little substance to this freedom. More than 90% of the living resources of the oceans are concentrated in the zones subject to the sovereignty of coastal states, (Art. 56-57) and even within these zones the important part of the harvest comes from near the coast. The United States and other countries harvest about 60% of their total catch within twelve nautical miles of the coast, meaning that about one-third of the annual fish catch,

which has amounted in recent years to nearly 70 million tons, is harvested in the exclusive economic zones (but beyond the territorial sea). The Soviet Union and Japan each harvest annually more than 10% of the total world catch; the United States, Chile, Peru, China, Norway, and South Korea each harvest about 5%. These eight countries alone achieve more than half of the world total catch, whereby most of the catch is from fish stocks near the coast of these countries.

Ultimately, the greatest impact on fishing from the 1982 Convention is due to the extension of the territorial sea from three to twelve nautical miles. Within this zone, from which about half of the annual world fish harvest is obtained and which is subject to the full sovereign jurisdiction of the coastal state, the Convention does not have intervening jurisdiction.

The legal concept for fishing rights of the coastal state in its exclusive economic zone deviates from full sovereignty, although in practice this deviation might well prove insignificant. According to this concept, the coastal state has preferential fishing rights (Art. 62, Para. 2) and is responsible for conservation (Art. 61) and optimum'utilization. (Art. 62, Para. 1) Furthermore, the coastal state is obligated to allow other states to fish the surplus, (Art. 62, Para. 2) giving geographically disadvantaged and developing states preference, (Art. 69-70) and to co-operate with competent international organizations in conservation matters. (Art. 61) This legal concept will be successful only if the responsible states take all aspects, both rights and obligations, of the Convention seriously. If the Convention is to be of benefit for both coastal states and others, due regard must be paid to Convention requirements concerning marine scientific research, (Art. 56; Art. 239) protection of the marine environment, (Art. 56; Art. 194) cooperation, (Art. 61; Art. 62, Para. 2) acting in good faith when applying provisions of the Convention, (Art. 300) and a willingness to submit disputes to compulsory dispute settlement procedure (Part XV) rather than to compulsory conciliation. (Art. 297, Para. 3)

For the remaining ocean space, the high seas (Art. 86) (which cover about half of the planet's surface, but contain only 10% of the total living resources of the ocean), the principle of freedom of fishing survived, (Art. 87, Subpara. 1(e)) but only in its basic structure. The relative lack of resources in comparison with the efficiency of modern fishing technology and the pressing needs of the present and future world population permit fishing only on the basis of co-operation and sharing. (Art. 117; Art. 119, Para. 3) The essential measures for conservation (Art. 119-120) are beyond the capabilities of any single state engaged in high sea fishing.

4. OVERFLIGHT

Although the 1982 Convention has jurisdiction with respect to overflight of ocean space, it pays very little attention to the subject. In much the same way that shipping relies on regulations provided by the International Maritime Organization (IMO) for safety standards, aviation relies on international regulations and standards of the International Civil Aviation Organization (ICAO). Rights and obligations arising from these international regulations are not affected as long as they are compatible with the 1982 Convention. (Art. 311, Para. 2). The right of overflight is patterned on the right of navigation. The principle of freedom of overflight applies on the high seas; (Art. 87, Subpara. 1(b)) basically, the principle also applies in the exclusive economic zone, (Art. 58; Art. 87, Subpara. 1(b)) with the general restriction that overflights must be conducted with due regard for the rights and duties of the coastal state. (Art. 58, Para. 3) The coastal states are to enforce international pollution regulations and standards in the exclusive economic zone.

Over straits (Part III) and archipelagic waters, (Part IV) aircraft have the right of transit passage (Art. 38, Para. 1) or archipelagic sea lane passage. (Art. 53, Para. 2) They must observe the Rules of the Air and monitor at all. times the asigned radio frequency. (Art. 39; Art. 54)

The coastal state has full sovereignty in the air space over the territorial sea, and aircraft do not have a right of "innocent passage."

5. MARINE SCIENTIFIC RESEARCH

The safe and economic use of the oceans and the preservation of same are dependent in every respect on sufficient scientific research. The ocean is not only a source of exploitable resources; it is a very sensitive ecological system, which is often not obvious immediately only because the space is so huge and enormous quantities of water are involved.

Although there are today about 150 international non-governmental organizations and 100 governmental organizations as well as a large number of national institutions which are concerned to a greater or lesser degree with marine science, the exploration of the oceans has really barely begun, and thorough, efficient research will be possible only if all concerned work closely together. For the scientific community, the 1982 Convention was a setback, as marine scientific research in the exclusive economic zone (Art. 56, Subpara. 1(b)) and on the continental shelf (Art. 77, Para. 1) was delegated to the coastal states and cannot be conducted without their consent, (Art. 246, Para. 2) whereas only the high seas were declared open to research by all. (Art. 87, Subpara. 1(f)) These limitations on the space open for free research were caused by developing states who feared they might be excluded completely or not benefit sufficiently from research activities; they were also suspicious that such activities could be a cover for espionage. It remains to be seen whether global scientific research activities will be severely hampered by coastal states. Without a doubt, many coastal states will be forced to implement or improve their own research programmes, and this will in the long run enlarge considerably the scientific community and increase the amount of scientific data available.

The Convention provisions are designed to achieve this goal (Part XIII) as they require international co-operation (Art. 242-244) and development aid and the transfer of technology, (Part XIV) in particular demanding that research be conducted exclusively for peaceful purposes (Art. 242, Subpara. (a)) and that knowledge resulting from scientific research be made public. (Art. 244, Para. 1) Corresponding obligations apply for scientific research conducted in the Area (Art. 143) and are also designated as objectives of the Authority.

6. DEEP-SEA MINING

Deep-sea mining is without any historical precedents, and there are no activities being conducted even today, contrary to the belief of many of the participants of the 1973-1982 Conference that work would soon commence. The concept of the 1982 Convention for deep-sea mining (Part XI) is new and contains three basic aspects. First, the Convention contains a "Magna Carta" for ownership of the resources, (Art. 137, Para. 2) management, (Art. 156-185) and management policy. (Art. 136-155) Second, it provides administrative and technical provisions. (Art. 151-154; Annexes III and IV) Third, its provisions are designed to have an impact on the world market for minerals (Art. 133, Subpara (b)) recovered from the Area, (Art.

1, Subpara. 1(1)) whether with the goal of fostering healthy development of the world economy and balanced growth of international trade (Art. 150) or of protecting developing countries from adverse effects of such market policy (Art. 150, Subpara. (h)) in particular. The mining of deep-sea resources (Art. 153, Subpara. (a)) is to be carried out directly by the Enterprise of the Sea-Bed Authority (Art. 170) or, on specific authorization by and on the basis of a contract with the Authority, by operators. (Art. 151; Art. 153; Annex III) An operator is to designate in his application for exploitation an area (Annex III, Art. 8) large enough to allow two mining operations. The Authority then has the option of claiming either of the two sites for the Enterprise or a developing state. (Annex III, Art. 8-9) Under the present conditions, exploitation would be economically feasible only if three million metric tons were recovered annually over a period of twenty-five years, requiring initial investments of more than one billion US dollars. Deep-sea mining would consist of the following steps: prospecting, exploration, exploitation/collecting, transfer to the surface, transport to shore base, and processing. The Enterprise, which has title to all minerals and processed substances it produces, (Annex IV, Art. 12, Para. 4, Art. 1, Para. 1) may also carry out transportation and marketing. (Annex IV, Art. 1, Para. 1; Art. 170, Para. 1)

7. ARTIFICIAL ISLANDS AND STRUCTURES

The large-scale use of artificial structures has been common for quite some time, as the oil and gas industries began using them for off-shore operations. The Convention is silent on the precise meaning of an artificial structure, but refers only to artificial islands, installations, structures, and equipment, as well as the permanent means of warning of the presence of such structures, (e.g.. Art. 60, Para. 3; Art. 87, Para. 1; Art. 147; Art. 259) and establishes that in general artificial structures do not enjoy the legal status of islands. (Art. 121 (Art. 60, Para. 8; Art. 147, Subpara. 2(e); Art. 259)).

In terms of the theoretical possibilities for their uses for scientific research, military installations, power stations, industrial plants, fish farming, sea cities, and other operations, artificial islands are still very much mere prospects for the future. The first beneficiaries will be the coastal states having exclusive jurisdiction over such installations, (Art. 60, Para. 2) which are much more likely to be economically rewarding near the coast than anywhere else. Only on the high seas do all states enjoy the freedom to construct artificial islands and other installations; (Art. 87, Subpara. 1(d)) this includes the sea-bed area as long as the state is not engaged in activities controlled by the Sea-Bed Authority. (Art. 147) The use of artificial islands and installations can be governed by rules and regulations from three legal sources: regulations of the coastal state, (Art. 60; Art. 80) regulations of the Sea-Bed Authority with respect to activities in the Area, (Art. 147, Subpara. 2(a); Annex III, Art. 17) and, when such use is undertaken on the high seas, the national regulations of the state concerned or of the state of registry. (Art. 262) Regulations from any of these sources must be in accordance with the Convention. The principle that the high seas shall be reserved for peaceful purposes (Art. 88) and its counterparts for the Area (Art. 141; Art. 147, Subpara. 2(d)) are to be observed at all times. The Convention has specific regulations for artificial structures with regard to coastal state jurisdiction, (Art. 60) safety zones, impact on shipping, (Art. 60; Art. 147; Art. 260-261) identification marking and warning signals, (Art. 60, Para. 3; Art. 262) and their removal. (Art. 60, Para. 3; Art. 147, Subpara. 2(a))

One of the main concerns about artificial islands involves their impact on the marine environment. States are therefore required to take general measures to prevent damage to the environment (Art. 194, Para. 2) and, in particular, to regulate the design, construction, equipment, operation, and manning of such installations and devices; (Art. 194, Subpara. 3(c); Art. 60, Para. 2) coastal states are also required to implement damage prevention regulations (Art. 208, Para. 1) for sea-bed activities within their jurisdiction no less effective than international standards. (Ah. 208, Para. 3)

8. CABLES AND PIPELINES

The first technological utilization of the sea-bed was the laying of submarine cables. Although a cable was laid between France and England as early as 1851, the first transatlantic telephone cable (which could carry thirty-six conversations simultaneously) did not go into operation until 1956. But cables have been subject to international regulations for a long time. Sea-bed pipelines have only recently been employed, and then only for short-distance transportation purposes. The Convention does not break any new ground in this legal field. It confirms the right of states to use the sea-bed for cables and pipelines, (Art. 87, Subpara. 1(d); Art. 112) affirms this right (with only slight restrictions) for both the continental shelf and the exclusive economic zone, (Art. 79) and obliges states to adopt laws to regulate liability for breakage of cables and pipelines and cases of indemnity. (Art. 113-115)

9. DUMPING

Dumping is any deliberate disposal at sea which is not incidental to normal operations, excluding the case of matter placed in the sea for a purpose other than mere disposal (e.g., arising from transport operations). There are two methods of dumping: disposal of wastes in bulk, and disposal of wastes in containers from vessels, aircraft, platforms, or other man-made structures at sea. The 1982 Convention provides a detailed definition of dumping. (Art. 1, Subpara. 1(5))

Dumping early became a matter of public concern, as it is extremely difficult to predict long-term effects. Although not recognized in writing in the 1958 Convention on the Law of the Sea, dumping was regarded as one of the freedoms of the use of the sea. As such, the only restriction on its exercise was reasonable regard for the interests of other states in their exercise of the freedom of the seas. (1958 High Sea Convention, Art. 2) Under the 1982 Convention, dumping is the subject of pollution regulations (Art. 194, Subpara. 3(a), Art. 210; Art. 216) and may not be authorized by any state (Art. 210, Para. 3) if not permitted by global rules and standards (Art. 210, Para. 6). Dumping within areas of coastal state or Sea-Bed Authority jurisdiction is subject to their regulations, provisions, and enforcement. (Art. 210; Art. 216; Art. 209; Annex III, Art. 17, Subpara. 2(f), Art. 215) The flag state and the state of loading are also required to enforce applicable laws. (Art. 216, Subpara. 1(b)-(c))

Although dumping is the subject of codification under the 1982 Convention, it is still basically a non-written freedom of the high seas, as the Sea-Bed Authority's jurisdiction in dumping matters is restricted to activities in the Area. (Art. 1, Subpara. 1(3))

10. ARCHAEOLOGICAL AND HISTORICAL OBJECTS FOUND IN THE SEA

"Archaeological and historical objects found in the sea" conjures up images of ships, their holds full of gold and jewels, which sank during the time of the exploration (and exploitation) of the Americas; this can quickly be extended to include sunken cities and lost works of art, but these will generally be found only in waters near the coast in the territorial sea, and consequently subject to the sovereignty and jurisdiction of the coastal state. (Art. 2) In any case, the 1982 Convention obligates all states to protect such objects found at sea and to cooperate with this purpose. (Art. 303, Para. 1) The Convention neither defines which objects are archaeological or historical, nor does it state which "sea" is meant. As, however, the Convention deals expressly with finds in the Area, (Art. 149) "sea" can mean only the continental shelf (Art. 76) or the area inside the outer limits of the exclusive economic zone. (Art. 1, Subpara. 1(1); Art. 134; Art. 55) Since the Convention grants coastal states only limited rights for the control of traffic in such objects found in the contiguous zone, (Art. 303, Para. 2) it appears that coastal states do not enjoy any preferential rights with regard to objects found outside the contiguous zone. Objects found in the "sea" (outside coastal state sovereignty) are to be preserved or disposed of for the benefit of mankind as a whole, with due regard to states with preferential interests. (Art. 149) There remains the question as to what is of historical interest. In the North Sea and English Channel alone, there are about 10,000 wrecks (many from the fighting in two wars), and many of them must be quite old. The' solution to this problem will not be as difficult as it might appear. As the provisions apply to objects of "historical" nature, the interior of a ship which sank some decades ago and objects found in such a wreck could well fall under this classification today. But this solution as provided by the Convention does not prevail over the rights of identifiable owners and the law of salvage or other rules of admirality, nor does it prejudice international agreements. (Art. 303, Para. 3-4)

11. MILITARY USE

The basis for the work of the 1973-1982 Conference was the UN General Assembly Resolution 2749 (1970), which had declared that the area was to be open to use exclusively for peaceful purposes by all states. The 1982 Convention follows this directive to the letter, using exactly the same wording (Art. 141) as the resolution. Although of less weight, it is still significant that the Convention reserves the high seas for peaceful purposes (Art. 88; Art. 58, Para. 2) and, under the provision headlined "Peaceful Uses of the Sea", (Art. 301) requires States Parties to refrain from threat or use of force against the territorial integrity of any state or from acting in any manner inconsistent with the principles of international law embodied in the Charter of the United Nations.

Do these provisions have a general impact on the military use of the oceans? Of what importance is the Preamble to the 1982 Convention, which states that the codification of the law of the sea will contribute to the strengthening of peace and security? These principles show one face of the Convention's approach to military use of the oceans; the other is the direct application of Convention provisions and the impact thereof on naval forces. A quick review of the latter shows that naval forces are entitled to use the oceans just as commercial shipping is, and in some cases have a "better position", as naval ships enjoy immunity, (Art. 32; Art. 95) the regulations for the protection and preservation of the marine environment (Art. 192-236) do not apply to them, (Art. 236) and military activities can be excluded from compulsory dispute settlement. (Art. 298, Subpara. 1(b)) The naval superpowers pushed and prodded the 1973-1982 Conference to come to this result. But this summary does not reflect the many varied questions which have already arisen, much less the profusion of questions that will spring up if the 1982 Convention does not become the only legal authority within a reasonable period of time. Due to the vague and imprecise wording of many of the provisions, leaving considerable leeway for interpretation, the position of warships is not as unassailable as the summary could lead one to believe. It is questionable, for example, whether

(a) stricter regulations for prevention of pollution within a "clearly defined area" (Art. 211, Para. 5) apply to naval vessels; (Art. 236; Art. 58, Para. 3)

(b) the launching or taking on board of any military device is "innocent;" (Art. 19, Subpara. 2(a) and (f))

(c) military exercises, manoeuvres, or weapons tests in the exclusive economic zone of foreign coastal states are "associated with the operation of ships" and "compatible with the other provisions of this Convention." (Art. 58, Para. 1)

Only the future will show the impact of the 1982 Convention on the military use of the oceans. Any incident can quickly change the outlook. Personnel in navies operating internationally will have to have thorough knowledge of the legal regime of the oceans and be particularly sensitive to local and regional interpretations of the 1982 Convention or of the law of the sea. Their burden would be lessened by a global acknowledgement and acceptance of the 1982 Convention and an effective judicial system.

D. PREVENTION MEASURES

1. SAFETY OF SHIPPING

The term safety of shipping expresses the interest of shipowners, seafarers, passengers, cargo owners, and insurers as well as of the community at large that sea transportation by ship should be as safe as possible, especially for the protection of the marine environment. Regulations for the safety of shipping generally have to a greater or lesser degree an impact on the interests of the parties mentioned above. But as the Convention deals with public law and order rather than commercial aspects, its concerns are clearly related to safety of life at sea and pollution prevention matters on a scale represented principally by the work of the International Maritime Organization (IMO), especially as exemplified by the following list of Conventions:

(a) Convention on the Safety of Life at Sea (SOLAS), 1974;
(b) Convention on Loadlines, 1966;
(c) Convention for Preventing Collision at Sea (COLREG), 1972;
(d) Convention on Safety of Fishing Vessels, 1977;
(e) Convention on Standard of Training, Certification, and Watchkeeping for Seafarers, 1978;
(f) Convention on Maritime Search and Rescue, 1979;
(g) Convention for the Prevention of Pollution from Ships (MARPOL), 1973.

The central provision of the Convention in this respect requires flag states to exercise control in administrative, technical, and social matters to ensure the safety of ships at sea by taking various measures ranging from construction of the ship to the training of the crew, (Art. 94, Para. 1-4; Art. 194, Subpara. 3(b); Art. 211) while other provisions are related only to matters of navigation such as preventing collisions, (Art. 21, Para. 2; Art. 39, Para. 2; Art. 94, Subpara. 2(b)) the use of sea lanes and traffic separation schemes, (Art. 22; Art. 41; Art. 53, Para. 10) and safety measures in respect to artificial installations, (Art. 60; Art. 147; Art. 260-262) or when the Convention requires that ships render assistance to persons in danger at sea and that coastal states establish a search and rescue system. (Art. 98)

The Convention refers only to generally accepted international regulations, procedure, and practice (Art. 94, Para. 5) or uses similar wording, e.g., (Art. 211, Para. 2) but never specifically to any established conventions. There was a two-fold purpose to this method. On the one hand, it avoids a situation where states parties to the 1982 Convention would be bound to conventions which they have not ratified, and, on the other hand, opens several possibilities for interpretation as shown by the following example: when in regard to general safety of ships the 1982 Convention requires the flag state to "conform to...international regulations," (Art. 94, Para. 5) there is a certain leeway for freedom of interpretation, a deliberate measure to lessen the burden on developing countries trying to establish their own shipping industry. But it can easily be imagined that a precise determination would not be simple one way or the other.

2. PRESERVATION OF THE MARINE ENVIRONMENT

The part of the Convention dealing with the global regime for the prevention of pollution is one of the most detailed in the entire document, regulating the obligations, responsibilities, and powers of the states. (Part XII) There are two possible reasons for this. One is that pollution prevention law is a new legal field which is not burdened with older legal concepts; but of greater impact have undoubtedly been the shocks following disastrous tanker accidents and the growing concern that unless action is taken to stop the spread of pollution from vessels and other sources the marine environment will suffer serious and long-term damage. A major step towards the implementation of global and regional regulations and measures for the prevention of pollution and for the general protection and preservation of the marine environment was taken at the United Nations Conference on the Human Environment in 1972 in Stockholm. Following this conference, many regional agreements negotiated under the auspices of the UN Environment Programme (UNEP) were prepared.

The 1982 Convention defines pollution (Art. 1, Subpara. 1(4)) and establishes a general duty to protect the marine environment and the measures to be taken, (Art. 192; Art. 194) and outlines methods of co-operation, including monitoring and technical assistance. (Art. 197-206).

With respect to various sources of pollution, the Convention adheres closely to the policy of legislation, followed by enforcement. The pollution regulations can be divided into two parts: (a) pollution from the sources "land-based", (Art. 207; Art. 213) "seabed", (Art. 208; Art. 209) atmosphere, (Art. 212) and all kinds of dumping, (Art. 1, Subpara. 1(5); Art. 210; Art. 216; Art. 214; Art. 215) and (b) pollution from vessels, except warships and other governmental vessels in non-commercial service (Art. 236). Pollution matters in the second case are separate from the other sources in that provisions are implemented supplementary to the basic concept of legislation and enforcement in order to balance the interests between the flag state and the coastal state with respect to their jurisdiction.

The legislation provisions display the typical Convention approach in requiring the responsible states to adopt international regulations and standards, varying its requirements from "taking into account" (atmospheric (Art. 212, Para. 1) and land-based (Art. 207, Para. 1) sources) to "no less effective" (Art. 208, Para. 3; Art. 209, Para. 2; Art. 210, Para. 6) and "shall at least have the same effect" (for vessels) (Art. 211, Para. 2)). There are already conventions in force for the prevention of pollution by dumping and vessels, which can serve as guidelines for what is meant by "global rules and standards" to prevent dumping. (Art. 210, Para. 6) Where vessels are concerned, the provisions are quite precise, as reference is made to "generally accepted international rules and regulations established through the competent international organizations or general diplomatic conference." (Art. 211, Para. 2) The emphasis should be placed on "competent organization," in this case the International Maritime Organization (IMO), which adopted the

- Convention for the Prevention of Pollution from Ships (MARPOL), 1973, is also responsible for handling secretarial duties of the
- Convention on the Prevention of Marine Pollution by Dumping, 1972,
- and has issued many recommendations and codes directly or indirectly concerned with vessel pollution matters, e.g.,
- International Maritime Dangerous Goods Code (IMDG),
- Code for the Construction and Equipment of Mobile Offshore Drilling Units (MODU), and
- Code of Safety for Nuclear Merchant Ships.

There are no corresponding international agreements for prevention of pollution from land-based sources, aircraft, or sea-bed activities. Regulations to control pollution resulting from deep sea mining must be adopted by the Sea-Bed Authority. (Art. 145; Annex III, Art. 17; Art. 1, Subpara. 1(b)(xii)) In cases of pollution from other seabed activities, (Art. 208) from the atmosphere, or from land-based sources, the states are to establish global or regional regulations. (Art. 207, Para. 4; Art. 208, Para. 5; Art. 212, Para. 3)

Where vessels are concerned, responsibility for national legislation and enforcement depend on two states: the flag state and the coastal state. Whereas the coastal state has little manoeuvring room for enacting legislation, it can exercise a right to enforce anti-pollution laws to quite some degree. By and large, legislation by the coastal state has to reflect international rules. (Art. 21, Subpara. 1(f); Art. 211, Para.4-6; Art. 234) The right of a coastal state to enforce such laws by means of investigations, inspections, proceedings, and detention is dependent on the location of the incident and degree of pollution and the location of the vessel. (Art. 218-220; Art. 222) While in port, ships which are unseaworthy in respect to pollution can be detained. (Art. 219; Art. 226, Subpara. 1(c)) In order to avoid pollution resulting from "maritime casualties" (Art. 221, Para. 2) the coastal state can enforce measures beyond the territorial sea, pursuant to international customary or conventional law. (Art. 221, Para. 1) In this context, reference can be made to the

International Convention Relating to Intervention on the High Seas in Cases of Oil Pollution Casualties, Brussels 1969.

The coastal state may even institute investigations and proceedings against a vessel because of discharge beyond its general pollution jurisdiction. It may act on its own initiative if there are incidents on the high seas and in specific cases on request. (Art. 218)

In order to specify and limit the circumstances under which a coastal state may intervene, the Convention includes a set of safeguard regulations. (Art. 223-232). Coastal states bordering straits may not apply these regulations for ships in transit passage. (Art. 233)

They may implement laws in regard to discharge of oil and similar substances. (Art. 42, Subpara. 1(b)) Both user states and states bordering straits are to co-operate by means of agreements in pollution matters in straits. (Art. 43)

All states are to respect any obligatons assumed under special conventions, but these obligations are to be carried out in a manner consistent with the general provisions of the 1982 Convention, (Art. 237) and no agreements may be made which affect the basic principles of these provisions. (Art. 311, Para. 3) States are responsible for the fulfillment of their obligations and are liable according to international law (Art, 235; Art. 304) and are to ensure prompt compensation for any damage. (Art. 235, Para. 2)

3. INDEMNITY

The Convention rarely touches the question of damage compensation. This is largely a matter of other international conventions and sources of law, especially of private law; for example, in pollution matters, some important sources would be
- the Convention on Civil Liability for Oil Pollution Damage, 1969,
- the Convention on the Establishment of an International Fund for Compensation for Oil Pollution Damage, 1971,
- the Tanker Owners' Voluntary Agreement Concerning Liability for Oil Pollution (TOVALOP), and
- the Contract Regarding an Interim Supplement to Tanker Liability for Oil Pollution (CRISTAL);

or a more general convention on liability like the
- Convention Relating to the Limitation of the Liability of owners of Sea-Going Ships, Brussels, 1957,or one closely related to questions of liability, such as the
- Convention Relating to the Arrest of Sea-Going Ships, Brussels, 1952.

The Convention employs the principle that its provisions are without prejudice for the application of existing or newly developed international law. (Art. 304) Convention provisions having to do with this question concern the liability of the flag state for warships and other governmental vessels in non-commercial service, (Art, 31; Art. 42, Para. 5; Art. 54; Art. 42, Para. 5; Art. 236) activities in the Area, (Art. 139) marine scientific research, (Art. 263) hot pursuit, (Art. lll, Para. 8) pollution, and others. (Art. 106 (Piracy); Art. 110, Para. 3 (Right to visit)) In pollution matters, the Convention provides a general clause stating that states are responsible for the fulfillment of their international obligations and that they are liable in accordance with international law. (Art. 235) In addition, coastal states which take unlawful measures against foreign vessels are liable for damage or loss resulting from said measures. (Art. 232) International governmental organizations which accede to the Convention bear the same responsibility as states parties. (Art. 1, Subpara. 2(2); Annex IX, Art. 6) Where indemnity is called for, the Convention requires states to adopt laws providing procedures for compensation, (e.g., (Art. 235, Para. 2; Art. 232)) just as it does in the case of breakage of or damage to cables and pipelines. (Art. 112-115)

E. MEASURES FOR PEACE AND JUSTICE

1. ESTABLISHING PEACE

In compliance with the general obligations of all member states as laid down in the United Nations Charter to maintain peace and security and strengthen universal peace, (UN Charter, Art. 1) the 1982 Convention affirms these principles, (Preamble; Art. 138; Art. 301) but also goes further by reserving "the high seas for peaceful purposes", (Art. 88) opening the Area exclusively for peaceful purposes, (Art. 141; Art. 147, Subpara. 2(d)) and requiring that marine scientific research be conducted exclusively for peaceful purposes. (Art. 240, Subpara. (a); Art. 246, Para. 3) However, it is hard to see where these noble sentiments have a practical legal impact. In the third decade of the existence of the United Nations (1975-1985) alone, there were about fifteen fishing disputes, thirty major demarcation diputes, and a similar number of major military operations. The oceans are "packed" with military equipment and electronic devices. Some argue that this is necessary to maintain peace; others, of course, see it as a threat to peace. These contradictory viewpoints reflect the fact that the Convention is a compromise at the lowest common denominator, and as long as the phrase "for peaceful purposes" is not defined more precisely, its impact will depend on the politics of the moment and it will not develop any authority of its own. However, the mere fact that the phrase exists and is used in the Convention can lend weight to arguments and further demand for a definition of "peaceful purposes" in order to make the expression applicable.

2. MEASURES TO CLOSE THE ECONOMIC GAP

All in all, the Convention is a law which aims to establish and maintain justice for all, and as such will be of benefit for all. But as it is also a political document, there are some subjects more related to substantive goals rather than- simple regulation. Provisions of a regulatory nature can provide justice only when applied to relations among partners with equal footing in a social and economic system; the wider any existing gap between partners is, the less law will be able to provide justice. There is at the moment a considerable economic gap between the northern and southern hemispheres of our globe, and it is essential for the peace and security of the world that measures be provided to close this gap. The Convention incorporates to this end three substantive measures.

The first of these is, in particular, the dedication of the deep-sea area and its resources to all people (Art. 136-137) on the basis of "equal sharing" and, in general, the regime of the (Area. Part XI) Second, marine scientific research and marine technology are given a new dimension of importance, as almost 100 provisions, or one-third of the Convention, deal with various aspects and to varying degrees with these subjects. Finally, a complete Part of the Convention is dedicated to the development and transfer of marine technology (Part XIV) in order to encourage cooperation and the establishment of regional centres (Art. 275-277) by means of which research, training, and transfer of technology can be provided; this part is at all times to be read, interpreted, and practiced in accordance with the regime of marine scientific research and the regime of the Area.

These provisions aimed at reducing the economic differences between North and South are basically weak in spite of the impressiveness of the number, but they are nonetheless of significance because they have found their way into the charter of the oceans, require co-operation and transfer of technology, and impose considerable responsibility on international organizations.

3. THE UNIFICATION OF THE LAW OF THE SEA

The 1982 Convention is the Magna Carta of the law of the sea, and as such it provides only the general legal framework for all aspects of the use of the oceans. The framework contains considerable detail (which does not necessarily mean precision) with regard to some subjects, e.g., "innocent passage," (Art. 17-32) deep sea mining, (Part XI) and pollution from vessels. (Art. 211; Art. 217-234) In contrast, the Convention provides no more than a programme for some subjects, e.g., enclosed and semi-enclosed seas, (Part IX) and in some cases does no more than make a statement without further elaboration, e.g., the phrase "reserved for peaceful purposes." (Art. 88) But all provisions are intended to unify universal law and erect barriers against deviating national law, especially when it is less strict than international standards.

The Convention employs a number of methods - often only the results of compromises - to achieve this goal. The most direct method is the detailed regulation of a clearly defined subject, leaving little or no room for questions to arise. The right of navigation for all states, (Art. 90) the extent or establishment of zones, (Part II-VI) and piracy (Art. 101-107) are examples of this approach. The same level of quality of law is reached when states are obliged to apply codified international law or conventions. The Convention never uses the technique of referring directly to regulatory law, and only mentions the UNCITRAL Arbitration Rules, (Art. 108, Subpara. 2(c); Annex III, Art. 5, Para. 4) or the United Nations Charter. (Art. 19, Subpara. 2(a); Art. 39, Subpara. 1(b); Art. 138; Art. 279) When other law (conventions) is to be applied, the Convention uses instead terms such as "taking into account internationally agreed rules", e.g., (Art. 207) to conform to generally accepted international regulations, procedure, and practice, e.g., (Art. 94, Para. 5) "at least have the same effect as that of generally accepted international rules," e.g., (Art. 211, Para. 2) or "no less effective than international rules." e.g., (Art. 208, Para. 3) This technique allows varying degrees of flexibility of interpretation and enforcement of international regulations according to the interests and needs of each state, but still supports the intention of unification. With respect to pollution, the Convention uses the additional technique of requiring the states to establish international rules e.g., (Art. 43, Subpara. (b); Art. 208, Para. 5) and to re-examine them from time to time. (Art. 208, Para. 5; Art. 211, Para.1)

The following regulations are of a different nature:

(a) In order to avoid the undermining of the comprehensive application of the Convention, it is not permitted to make reservations and exceptions (Art. 309) or otherwise suspend or modify the objectives of the Convention. (Art. 311, Para. 3-6)
(b) The Convention requires the States Parties to fulfill their obligations in good faith, (Art. 300) which means that each state is to follow the "Golden Rule" and act as it would wish the other states to act in fulfilling their obligations
(c) One of the most significant instruments of unification is the compulsory dispute settlement system provided by the Convention. (Part XII) Decisions from these tribunals would in many respects be a great contribution to the law of the sea.
(d) Last but not least, reference should be made to the Preamble of the Convention, which calls for the achievement of justice and equal rights through the Convention, a goal which can only be reached by means of a highly unified law.

4. SETTLEMENT OF DISPUTES

The Convention system for settlement of disputes (Part XV) must be seen against the background of the international mechanism for resolving conflicts. Basically, all nations observe the principles of international law and fulfil their obligations on a kind of honour system and in good faith; if a nation refuses to observe these principles – and neither diplomacy nor political pressure can effect a change – military power may well be the only mechanism available to force this nation to meet its obligations, as the international legal system has virtually no means of enfolding judicial decisions or contractual obligations (such as treaties or international conventions). This century has seen many attempts to develop systems for the peaceful settlement of international disputes. One such attempt relevant for the 1982 Convention was the establishment of the International Court of Justice by the United Nations Charter of 1945. The Court of Justice is a principal organ of the United Nations, and all,members of the United Nations may apply to the Court; but there is no general obligation to submit disputes to the Court of Justice.

The importance of the dispute settlement system provided by the Convention is that states parties which disagree on the interpretation or application of the provisions of the Convention are, at least to some extent, (Art. 286; Art. 297-298) bound to settle the dispute through courts or tribunals as described in the Convention. (Art. 287) A special dispute settlement system is designed for the activities in the sea-bed Area. (Art. 287; Art. 186-190) Within the general system, states have the choice among four fora, which include the International Court of Justice; (Art. 287, Subpara. 1(b)) the other three are (a) the International Tribunal for the Law of the Sea, (b) an arbitral tribunal, and (c) a special arbitral tribunal. (Art. 287, Para. 1) To a large extent, this is the restdt of compromises which made it easier for the states to swallow the bitter pill of surrendering a part of their sovereignty in accepting a compulsory system by giving them a wider choice of the court or tribunal to which they might apply, depending on the trust they have in a particular judicial organ. The law of the sea dispute settlement system is urgently needed for the unification of the law of the sea. If one considers the complexity which has evolved in the law of the sea in only a few decades, the economic possibilities of the oceans, the importance of the seas for mankind, and the countless aspects which must be taken into account in achieving justice, one will be forced to the conclusion that a compulsory dispute settlement is essential.

Bernaerts' Guide to the Law of The Sea

The Text
of the
UN Convention and Agreement on Part XI

Table of Contents

UNITED NATIONS CONVENTION ON THE LAW OF THE SEA

	PREAMBLE		153
PART I.	INTRODUCTION		154
	Article 1. Use of terms and scope		154
PART II.	TERRITORIAL SEA AND CONTIGUOUS ZONE		155
	SECTION 1. GENERAL PROVISIONS		155
	Article 2. Legal status of territorial sea, of the air space over the territorial sea and of its bed and subsoil		155
	SECTION 2. LIMITS OF THE TERRITORIAL SEA		155
	Article 3.	Breadth of the territorial sea	155
	Article 4.	Outer limit of the territorial sea	155
	Article 5.	Normal baseline	155
	Article 6.	Reefs	155
	Article 7.	Straight baselines	156
	Article 8.	Internal waters	156
	Article 9.	Mouths of rivers	156
	Article 10.	Bays	156
	Article 11.	Ports	157
	Article 12.	Roadsteads	157
	Article 13.	Low-tide elevations	157
	Article 14.	Combination of methods for determining baselines	157
	Article 15.	Delimitation of the territorial sea between States with opposite or adjacent coasts	157
	Article 16.	Charts and lists of geographical co-ordinates	158
	SECTION 3. INNOCENT PASSAGE IN THE TERRITORIAL SEA		158
	SUBSECTION A. RULES APPLICABLE TO ALL SHIPS		
	Article 17.	Right of innocent passage	158
	Article 18.	Meaning of passage	158
	Article 19.	Meaning of innocent passage	158
	Article 20.	Submarines and other underwater vehicles	159
	Article 21.	Laws and regulations of the coastal State relating to innocent passage	159
	Article 22.	Sea lanes and traffic separation schemes in the territorial sea	160
	Article 23.	Foreign nuclear-powered ships and ships carrying nuclear or other inherently dangerous or noxious substances	160

Article 24.	Duties of the coastal State	160
Article 25.	Rights of protection of the coastal State	160
Article 26.	Charges which may be levied upon foreign ships	161

SUBSECTION B. RULES APPLICABLE TO MERCHANT SHIPS AND GOVERNMENT SHIPS OPERATED FOR COMMERCIAL PURPOSES

Article 27.	Criminal jurisdiction on board a foreign ship	161
Article 28.	Civil jurisdiction in relation to foreign ships	162

SUBSECTION C. RULES APPLICABLE TO WARSHIPS AND OTHER GOVERNMENT SHIPS OPERATED FOR NON-COMMERCIAL PURPOSES

Article 29.	Definition of warships	162
Article 30	Non-compliance by warships with the laws and regulations of the coastal State	162
Article 31.	Responsibility of the flag State for damage caused by a warship or other government ship operated for non-commercial purposes	162
Article 32.	Immunities of warships and other government ships operated for non-commercial purposes	162

SECTION 4. CONTIGUOUS ZONE

Article 33.	Contiguous zone	163

PART III. STRAITS USED FOR INTERNATIONAL NAVIGATION

SECTION 1. GENERAL PROVISIONS

Article 34.	Legal status of waters forming straits used for international navigation	163
Article 35.	Scope of this Part	163
Article 36.	High seas routes or routes through exclusive economic zones through straits used for international navigation	163

SECTION 2. TRANSIT PASSAGE

Article 37.	Scope of this section	164
Article 38.	Right of transit passage	164
Article 39.	Duties ships and aircraft during transit passage	164
Article 40.	Research and survey activities	165
Article 41.	Sea lanes and traffic separation schemes in straits used for international navigation	165
Article 42.	Laws and regulations of States bordering straits relating to transit passage	165
Article 43.	Navigational and safety aids and other improvements and the prevention, reduction and control of pollution	166
Article 44.	Duties of States bordering straits	166

SECTION 3. INNOCENT PASSAGE

	Article 45. Innocent passage	166
PART IV.	ARCHIPELAGIC STATES	
	Article 46. Use of terms	167
	Article 47. Archipelagic baselines	167
	Article 48. Measurement of the breadth of the territorial sea, the contiguous zone, the exclusive economic zone and the continental shelf	168
	Article 49. Legal status of archipelagic waters, of the air space over archipelagic waters and of their bed and subsoil	168
	Article 50. Delimitation of internal waters	168
	Article 51. Existing agreements, traditional fishing rights and existing submarine cables	168
	Article 52. Right of innocent passage	168
	Article 53. Right of archipelagic sea lanes passage	169
	Article 54. Duties of ships and aircraft during their passage, research and survey activities, duties of the archipelagic State and laws and regulations of the archipelagic State relating to archipelagic sea lanes passage	170
PART V.	EXCLUSIVE ECONOMIC ZONE	
	Article 55. Specific legal regime of the exclusive economic zone	170
	Article 56. Rights, jurisdiction and duties of the coastal State in the exclusive economic zone	170
	Article 57. Breadth of the exclusive economic zone	170
	Article 58. Rights and duties of other States in the exclusive economic zone	171
	Article 59. Basis for the resolution of conflicts regarding the attribution of rights and jurisdiction in the exclusive economic zone	171
	Article 60. Artificial islands, installations and structures in the exclusive economic zone	171
	Article 61. Conversation of the living resources	172
	Article 62. Utilization of the living resources	173
	Article 63. Stocks occurring within the exclusive economic zones of two or more costal States or both within the exclusive economic zone and in an area beyond and adjacent to it	174
	Article 64. Highly migratory species	174
	Article 65. Marine mammal	174
	Article 66. Anadromous stocks	174
	Article 67. Catadromous species	175
	Article 68. Sedentary species	175
	Article 69. Right of land-locked States	176
	Article 70. Right of geographically disadvantages States	176
	Article 71. Non –applicability of articles 69 and 70	177
	Article 72. Restrictions on transfer of rights	178

Article 73. Enforcement of laws and regulations of the coastal State	178
Article 74. Delimitation of the exclusive economic zone between States with opposite or adjacent coasts	178
Article 75. Charts and lists of geographical coordinates	178

PART VI. CONTINENTAL SHELF

Article 76. Definition of the continental shelf	179
Article 77. Rights of the coastal State over the continental shelf	180
Article 78. Legal status of the superjacent waters and airspace and the rights and freedoms of other States	180
Article 79. Submarine cables and pipelines on the continental shelf	180
Article 80. Artificial islands, installations and structures on the continental shelf	181
Article 81. Drilling on the continental shelf	181
Article 82. Payments and contributions with respect to the exploitation of the continental shelf beyond 200 nautical miles	181
Article 83. Delimitation of the continental shelf between States with opposite or adjacent coasts	181
Article 84. Charts and lists of geographical coordinates	182
Article 85. Tunneling	182

PART VII. HIGH SEAS

SECTION 1. GENERAL PROVISIONS

Article 86. Application of the provisions of this Part	182
Article 87. Freedom of the high seas	182
Article 88. Reservation of the high seas for peaceful purposes	183
Article 89. Invalidity of claims of sovereignty over the high seas	183
Article 90. Right of navigation	183
Article 91. Nationality of ships	183
Article 92. Status of ships	183
Article 93. Ships flying the flag of the United Nations, its specialized agencies and the International Atomic Energy Agency	183
Article 94. Duties of the flag State	184
Article 95. Immunity of warships on the high seas	184
Article 96. Immunity of ships used only on government non-commercial service	185
Article 97. Penal jurisdiction in matters of collision or any other incident of navigation	185
Article 98. Duty to render assistance	185
Article 99. Prohibition of the transport of slaves	185
Article 100. Duty to cooperate in the repression of piracy.	185
Article 101. Definition of piracy	186
Article 102. Piracy by warship, government ship or government	

	aircraft whose crew has mutinied	186
	Article 103. Definition of a pirate ship or aircraft	186
	Article 104. Retention or loss of the nationality of a pirate ship or aircraft	186
	Article 105. Seizure of a pirate ship or aircraft	186
	Article 106. Liability for seizure without adequate grounds	186
	Article 107. Ships and aircraft which are entitled to seize on account of piracy	187
	Article 108. Illicit traffic in narcotic drugs or psychotropic substances	187
	Article 109. Unauthorized broadcasting from the high seas	187
	Article 110. Right of visit	187
	Article 111. Right of hot pursuit	188
	Article 112. Right to lay submarine cables and pipelines	189
	Article 113. Breaking or injury of a submarine cable or Pipeline	189
	Article 114. Breaking or injury by owners of a submarine cable of pipeline of another submarine cable or pipeline	189
	Article 115. Indemnity for loss incurred in avoiding injury to a submarine cable or pipeline	189
	SECTION 2. CONSERVATION AND MANAGEMENT OF THE LIVING RESOURCES OF THE HIGH SEAS	
	Article 116. Right to fish on the high seas	189
	Article 117. Duty of States to adopt with respect to their nationals measures for the conservation of the living resources of the high seas	190
	Article 118. Co-operation of States in the conservation and management of living resources	190
	Article 119. Conservation of the living resources of the high seas	190
	Article 120. Marine mammals	190
PART VIII.	REGIME OF ISLANDS	
	Article 121. Regime of islands	191
PART IX.	ENCLOSED OR SEMI-ENCLOSED SEAS	
	Article 122. Definition	191
	Article 123.Cooperation of States bordering enclosed or semi-enclosed sea	191
PART X.	RIGHT OF ACCESS OF LAND-LOCKED STATES TO AND FROM THE SEA AND FREEDOM OF TRANSIT	
	Article 124. Use of terms	192
	Article 125. Right of access to and from the sea and freedom of transit	192
	Article 126. Exclusion of application of the most-favoured-nation Clause	192
	Article 127. Customs duties, taxes and other charges	193

Article 128. Free zones and other customs facilities	193
Article 129. Cooperation in the construction and improvement of means of transport	193
Article 130. Measures to avoid or eliminate delays or other difficulties of a technical nature in traffic in transit	193
Article 131. Equal treatment in maritime ports	193
Article 132. Grant of greater transit facilities	193

PART XI. THE AREA

SECTION 1. GENERAL PROVISIONS

Article 133. Use of terms	194
Article 134. Scope of this Part	194
Article 135. Legal status of the superjacent waters and air space	194

SECTION 2. PRINCIPLES GOVERNING THE AREA

Article 136. Common heritage of mankind	194
Article 137. Legal status of the Area and its resources	194
Article 138. General conduct of States in relation to the Area	195
Article 139. Responsibility to ensure compliance and liability for damage	195
Article 140. Benefit of mankind	195
Article 141. Use of the Area exclusively for peaceful purposes	195
Article 142. Rights and legitimate interests of coastal States	196
Article 143. Marine scientific research	196
Article 144. Transfer of technology	196
Article 145. Protection of the marine environment	197
Article 146. Protection of human life	197
Article 147. Accommodation of activities in the Area and in the marine environment	197
Article 148. Participation of developing States in activities in the Area	198
Article 149. Archaeological and historical objects	198

SECTION 3. DEVELOPMENT OF RESOURCES OF THE AREA

Article 150. Policies relating to activities in the Area	198
Article 151. Production policies	199
Article 152. Exercise of powers and functions by the Authority	202
Article 153. System of exploration and exploitation	202
Article 154. Periodic review	203
Article 155. The Review Conference	203

SECTION 4. THE AUTHORITY

SUBSECTION A. GENERAL PROVISIONS

Article 156. Establishment of the Authority — 204

Article 157. Nature and fundamental principles of the Authority — 204
Article 158. Organs of the Authority — 204

SUBSECTION B. THE ASSEMBLY

Article 159. Composition, procedure and voting — 205
Article 160. Powers and functions — 206

SUBSECTION C. THE COUNCIL

Article 161. Composition, procedure and voting — 207

Article 162. Powers and functions — 209
Article 163. Organs of the Council — 211
Article 164. The Economic Planning Commission — 212
Article 165. The Legal and Technical Commission — 213

SUBSECTION D. THE SECRETARIAT

Article 166. The Secretariat — 214
Article 167. The staff of the Authority — 214
Article 168. International character of the Secretariat — 215
Article 169. Consultation and cooperation with international and non-governmental organizations — 215

SUBSECTION E. THE ENTERPRISE

Article 170. The Enterprise — 216

SUBSECTION F. FINANCIAL ARRANGEMENTS OF THE AUTHORITY

Article 171. Funds of the Authority — 216
Article 172. Annual budget of the Authority — 216
Article 173. Expenses of the Authority — 217
Article 174. Borrowing power of the Authority — 217
Article 175. Annual audit — 217

SUBSECTION G. LEGAL STATUS, PRIVILEGES AND IMMUNITIES

Article 176. Legal status — 217
Article 177. Privileges and immunitie — 217
Article 178. Immunity from legal process — 218
Article 179. Immunity from search and any form of seizure — 218
Article 180. Exemption from restrictions, regulations, controls and moratoria — 218
Article 181. Archives and official communications of the

Authority	218
Article 182. Privileges and immunities of certain persons connected with the Authority	218
Article 183. Exemption from taxes and customs duties	218

SUBSECTION H. SUSPENSION OF THE EXERCISE OF RIGHTS AND PRIVILEGES OF MEMBERS

Article 184. Suspension of the exercise of voting rights	219
Article 185. Suspension of exercise of rights and privileges of membership	219

SECTION 5. SETTLEMENT OF DISPUTES AND ADVISORY OPINIONS

Article 186. Seabed Disputes Chamber of the International Tribunal for the Law of the Sea	219
Article 187. Jurisdiction of the Seabed Disputes Chamber	220
Article 188. Submission of disputes to a special chamber of the International Tribunal for the Law of the Sea or an ad hoc chamber of the Seabed Disputes Chamber or to binding commercial arbitration	220
Article 189. Limitation on jurisdiction with regard to decisions of the Authority	221
Article 190. Participation and appearance of sponsoring States Parties in proceedings	221
Article 191. Advisory opinions	221

PART XII. PROTECTION AND PRESERVATION OF THE MARINE ENVIRONMENT

SECTION 1. GENERAL PROVISIONS

Article 192. General obligation	222
Article 193. Sovereign right of States to exploit their natural resources	222
Article 194. Measures to prevent, reduce and control pollution of the marine environment	222
Article 195. Duty not to transfer damage or hazards or transform one type of pollution into another	223
Article 196. Use of technologies or introduction of alien or new species	223

SECTION 2. GLOBAL AND REGIONAL COOPERATION

Article 197. Cooperation on a global or regional basis	223
Article 198. Notification of imminent or actual damage	223
Article 199. Contingency plans against pollution	223
Article 200. Studies, research programmes and exchange of information and data	224
Article 201. Scientific criteria for regulations	224

SECTION 3. TECHNICAL ASSISTANCE

Article 202. Scientific and technical assistance to developing States — 224
Article 203. Preferential treatment for developing States — 224

SECTION 4. MONITORING AND ENVIRONMENTAL ASSESSMENT

Article 204. Monitoring of the risks or effects of pollution — 225
Article 205. Publication of reports — 225
Article 206. Assessment of potential effects of activities — 225

SECTION 5. INTERNATIONAL RULES AND NATIONAL LEGISLATION TO PREVENT, REDUCE AND CONTROL POLLUTION OF THE MARINE ENVIRONMENT

Article 207. Pollution from land-based sources — 225
Article 208. Pollution from seabed activities subject to national jurisdiction — 226
Article 209. Pollution from activities in the Area — 226
Article 210. Pollution by dumping — 226
Article 211. Pollution from vessels — 227
Article 212. Pollution from or through the atmosphere — 228

SECTION 6. ENFORCEMENT

Article 213. Enforcement with respect to pollution from land-based sources — 229
Article 214. Enforcement with respect to pollution from seabed activities — 229
Article 215. Enforcement with respect to pollution from activities in the Area — 229
Article 216. Enforcement with respect to pollution by dumping — 229
Article 217. Enforcement by flag States — 230
Article 218. Enforcement by port States — 230
Article 219. Measures relating to seaworthiness of vessels to avoid pollution — 231
Article 220. Enforcement by coastal States — 231
Article 221. Measures to avoid pollution arising from maritime casualties — 232
Article 222. Enforcement with respect to pollution from or through the atmosphere — 233

SECTION 7. SAFEGUARDS

Article 223. Measures to facilitate proceedings — 233

Article 224. Exercise of powers of enforcement 233
Article 225. Duty to avoid adverse consequences in the exercise of the powers of enforcement 233
Article 226. Investigation of foreign vessels 233
Article 227. Non-discrimination with respect to foreign vessels 234
Article 228. Suspension and restrictions on institution of proceedings 234
Article 229. Institution of civil proceedings 235
Article 230. Monetary penalties and the observance of recognized rights of the accused 235
Article 231. Notification to the flag State and other States concerned 235
Article 232. Liability of States arising from enforcement measures 235
Article 233. Safeguards with respect to straits used for international navigation 235

SECTION 8. ICE-COVERED AREAS
Article 234. Ice-covered areas 236

SECTION 9. RESPONSIBILITY AND LIABILITY
Article 235. Responsibility and liability 236

SECTION 10. SOVEREIGN IMMUNITY
Article 236. Sovereign immunity 236

SECTION 11. OBLIGATIONS UNDER OTHER CONVENTIONS ON THE PROTECTION AND PRESERVATION OF THE MARINE ENVIRONMENT
Article 237. Obligations under other conventions on the protection and preservation of the marine environment 237

PART XIII. MARINE SCIENTIFIC RESEARCH

SECTION 1. GENERAL PROVISIONS
Article 238. Right to conduct marine scientific research 237
Article 239. Promotion of marine scientific research 237
Article 240. General principles for the conduct of marine scientific research 237
Article 241. Non-recognition of marine scientific research activities as the legal basis for claims 238

SECTION 2. INTERNATIONAL COOPERATION
Article 242. Promotion of international cooperation 238
Article 243. Creation of favourable conditions 238
Article 244. Publication and dissemination of information and knowledge 238

SECTION 3. CONDUCT AND PROMOTION OF MARINE SCIENTIFIC RESEARCH
Article 245. Marine scientific research in the territorial sea 239
Article 246. Marine scientific research in the exclusive economic zone and on the continental shelf 239
Article 247. Marine scientific research projects undertaken by or under the auspices of international organizations 240

Article 248.	Duty to provide information to the coastal State	240
Article 249.	Duty to comply with certain conditions	240
Article 250.	Communications concerning marine scientific research projects	241
Article 251.	General criteria and guidelines	241
Article 252.	Implied consent	241
Article 253.	Suspension or cessation of marine scientific research activities	242
Article 254.	Rights of neighbouring land-locked and disadvantaged States	242
Article 255.	Measures to facilitate marine scientific research and assist research vessels	243
Article 256.	Marine scientific research in the Area	243
Article 257.	Marine scientific research in the water column beyond the exclusive economic zone	243

SECTION 4. SCIENTIFIC RESEARCH INSTALLATIONS OR EQUIPMENT IN THE MARINE ENVIRONMENT

Article 258.	Deployment and use	243
Article 259.	Legal status	243
Article 260.	Safety zones	244
Article 261.	Non-interference with shipping routes	244
Article 262.	Identification markings and warning signals	244

SECTION 5. RESPONSIBILITY AND LIABILITY

Article 263.	Responsibility and liability	244

SECTION 6. SETTLEMENT OF DISPUTES AND INTERIM MEASURES

Article 264.	Settlement of disputes	244
Article 265.	Interim measures	245

PART XIV. DEVELOPMENT AND TRANSFER OF MARINE TECHNOLOGY

SECTION 1. GENERAL PROVISIONS

Article 266.	Promotion of the development and transfer of marine technology	245
Article 267.	Protection of legitimate interests	245
Article 268.	Basic objectives	245
Article 269.	Measures to achieve the basic objectives	246

SECTION 2. INTERNATIONAL COOPERATION

Article 270.	Ways and means of international cooperation	246
Article 271.	Guidelines, criteria and standards	246
Article 272.	Coordination of international programmes	246
Article 273.	Cooperation with international organizations and the Authority	247
Article 274.	Objectives of the Authority	247

SECTION 3. NATIONAL AND REGIONAL MARINE SCIENTIFIC AND TECHNOLOGICAL CENTRES

Article 275.	Establishment of national centres	247
Article 276.	Establishment of regional centres	248

Article 277.	Functions of regional centres	248

SECTION 4. COOPERATION AMONG INTERNATIONAL ORGANIZATIONS

Article 278.	Cooperation among international organizations	248

PART XV. SETTLEMENT OF DISPUTES

SECTION 1. GENERAL PROVISIONS

Article 279.	Obligation to settle disputes by peaceful means	249
Article 280.	Settlement of disputes by any peaceful means chosen by the parties	249
Article 281.	Procedure where no settlement has been reached by the parties	249
Article 282.	Obligations under general, regional or bilateral agreements	249
Article 283.	Obligation to exchange views	249
Article 284.	Conciliation	250
Article 285.	Application of this section to disputes submitted pursuant to Part XI	250

SECTION 2. COMPULSORY PROCEDURES ENTAILING BINDING DECISIONS

Article 286.	Application of procedures under this section	250
Article 287.	Choice of procedure	250
Article 288.	Jurisdiction	251
Article 289.	Experts	251
Article 290.	Provisional measures	251
Article 291.	Access	252
Article 292.	Prompt release of vessels and crews	252
Article 293.	Applicable law	253
Article 294.	Preliminary proceedings	253
Article 295.	Exhaustion of local remedies	253
Article 296.	Finality and binding force of decisions	253

SECTION 3. LIMITATIONS AND EXCEPTIONS TO APPLICABILITY OF SECTION 2

Article 297.	Limitations on applicability of section 2	253
Article 298.	Optional exceptions to applicability of section 2	255
Article 299.	Right of the parties to agree upon a procedure	256

PART XVI. GENERAL PROVISIONS

Article 300.	Good faith and abuse of rights	256
Article 301.	Peaceful uses of the seas	256
Article 302.	Disclosure of information	256
Article 303.	Archaeological and historical objects found at sea	257
Article 304.	Responsibility and liability for damage	257

PART XVII. FINAL PROVISIONS

Article 305.	Signature	257
Article 306.	Ratification and formal confirmation	258

Article 307.	Accession	258
Article 308.	Entry into force	258
Article 309.	Reservations and exceptions	258
Article 310.	Declarations and statements	258
Article 311.	Relation to other conventions and international agreements	258
Article 312.	Amendment	259
Article 313.	Amendment by simplified procedure	259
Article 314.	Amendments to the provisions of this Convention relating to activities in the Area	260
Article 315.	Signature, ratification of, accession to and authentic texts of amendments	260
Article 316.	Entry into force of amendments	260
Article 317.	Denunciation	261
Article 318.	Status of Annexes	261
Article 319.	Depositary	261
Article 320.	Authentic texts	262

ANNEX I. HIGHLY MIGRATORY SPECIES   263

ANNEX II. COMMISSION ON THE LIMITS
OF THE CONTINENTAL SHELF   263

Article 1	263
Article 2	263
Article 3	264
Article 4	264
Article 5	264
Article 6	265
Article 7	265
Article 8	265
Article 9	265

ANNEX III. BASIC CONDITIONS OF PROSPECTING,
EXPLORATION AND EXPLOITATION   265

Article 1.	Title to minerals	265
Article 2.	Prospecting	265
Article 3.	Exploration and exploitation	266
Article 4.	Qualifications of applicants	266
Article 5.	Transfer of technology	267
Article 6.	Approval of plans of work	269

Article 7. Selection among applicants for production authorizations	270
Article 8. Reservation of areas	271
Article 9. Activities in reserved areas	271
Article 10. Preference and priority among applicants	272
Article 11. Joint arrangements	272
Article 12. Activities carried out by the Enterprise	272
Article 13. Financial terms of contracts	272
Article 14. Transfer of data	279
Article 15. Training programmes	279
Article 16. Exclusive right to explore and exploit	279
Article 17. Rules, regulations and procedures of the Authority	280
Article 18. Penalties	282
Article 19. Revision of contract	283
Article 20. Transfer of rights and obligations	283
Article 21. Applicable law	283
Article 22. Responsibility	283

ANNEX IV. STATUTE OF THE ENTERPRISE

Article 1. Purposes	284
Article 2. Relationship to the Authority	284
Article 3. Limitation of liability	284
Article 4. Structure	284
Article 5. Governing Board	284
Article 6. Powers and functions of the Governing Board	285
Article 7. Director-General and staff of the Enterprise	286
Article 8. Location	287
Article 9. Reports and financial statements	287
Article 10. Allocation of net income	287
Article 11. Finances	287
Article 12. Operations	289
Article 13. Legal status, privileges and immunities	290

ANNEX V. CONCILIATION

SECTION 1. CONCILIATION PROCEDURE PURSUANT TO SECTION 1 OF PART XV

Article 1. Institution of proceedings	292
Article 2. List of conciliators	292
Article 3. Constitution of conciliation commission	292
Article 4. Procedure	293
Article 5. Amicable settlement	293
Article 6. Functions of the commission	293
Article 7. Report	293
Article 8. Termination	294
Article 9. Fees and expenses	294
Article 10. Right of parties to modify procedure	294

SECTION 2. COMPULSORY SUBMISSION TO CONCILIATION PROCEDURE PURSUANT TO SECTION 3 OF PART XV

Article 11. Institution of proceedings 294
Article 12. Failure to reply or to submit to conciliation 294
Article 13. Competence 294
Article 14. Application of section 1 294

ANNEX VI. STATUTE OF THE INTERNATIONAL TRIBUNAL FOR THE LAW OF THE SEA
Article 1. General provisions 295
SECTION 1. ORGANIZATION OF THE TRIBUNAL
Article 2. Composition 295
Article 3. Membership 295
Article 4. Nominations and elections 295
Article 5. Term of office 296
Article 6. Vacancies 296
Article 7. Incompatible activities 297
Article 8. Conditions relating to participation of members in a particular case 297
Article 9. Consequence of ceasing to fulfil required conditions 297
Article 10. Privileges and immunities 297
Article 11. Solemn declaration by members 297
Article12. President, Vice-President and Registrar 298
Article 13. Quorum 298
Article 14. Seabed Disputes Chamber 298
Article 15. Special chambers 298
Article 16. Rules of the Tribunal 299
Article 17. Nationality of members 299
Article 18. Remuneration of members 299
Article 19. Expenses of the Tribunal 300
SECTION 2. COMPETENCE
Article 20. Access to the Tribunal 300
Article 21. Jurisdiction 300
Article 22. Reference of disputes subject to other agreements 300
Article 23. Applicable law 301
SECTION 3. PROCEDURE
Article 24. Institution of proceedings 301
Article 25. Provisional measures 301
Article 26. Hearing 301
Article 27. Conduct of case 301
Article 28. Default 302
Article 29. Majority for decision 302
Article 30. Judgment 302
Article 3l. Request to intervene 302
Article 32. Right to intervene in cases of interpretation or application 302
Article 33. Finality and binding force of decisions 303
Article 34. Costs 303
SECTION 4. SEABED DISPUTES CHAMBER

Article 35. Composition	303
Article 36. Ad hoc chambers	304
Article 37. Access	304
Article 38. Applicable law	304
Article 39. Enforcement of decisions of the Chamber	304
Article 40. Applicability of other sections of this Annex	304

SECTION 5. AMENDMENTS

Article 41. Amendments	305

ANNEX VII. ARBITRATION

Article 1.	Institution of proceedings	305
Article 2.	List of arbitrators	305
Article 3.	Constitution of arbitral tribunal	306
Article 4.	Functions of arbitral tribunal	307
Article 5.	Procedure	307
Article 6.	Duties of parties to a dispute	307
Article 7.	Expenses	307
Article 8.	Required majority for decisions	307
Article 9.	Default of appearance	307
Article 10.	Award	308
Article 11.	Finality of award	308
Article 12.	Interpretation or implementation of award	308
Article 13.	Application to entities other than States Parties	308

ANNEX VIII. SPECIAL ARBITRATION

Article 1.	Institution of proceedings	308
Article 2.	Lists of experts	309
Article 3.	Constitution of special arbitral tribunal	309
Article 4.	General provisions	310
Article 5.	Fact finding	310

ANNEX IX. PARTICIPATION BY INTERNATIONAL ORGANIZATIONS

Article 1. Use of terms	311
Article 2. Signature	311
Article 3. Formal confirmation and accession	311
Article 4. Extent of participation and rights and obligations	311
Article 5. Declarations, notifications and communications	312
Article 6. Responsibility and liability	312
Article 7. Settlement of disputes	313
Article 8. Applicability of Part XVII	313

AGREEMENT RELATING TO THE IMPLEMENTATION OF PART XI OF THE UNITED NATIONS CONVENTION ON THE LAW OF THE SEA OF 10 DECEMBER 1982; DONE AT NEW YORK, 28TH JULY 1994

Table of Contents	314
Article 1. Implementation of Part XI	315
Article 2. Relationship between this Agreement and Part XI	315
Article 3. Signature	315
Article 4. Consent to be bound	315
Article 5. Simplified procedure	316
Article 6. Entry into force	316
Article 7. Provisional application	316
Article 8. States Parties	317
Article 9. Depositary	317
Article 10. Authentic texts	317
Annex	318
SECTION 1. COSTS TO STATES PARTIES AND INSTITUTIONAL ARRANGEMENTS	318
SECTION 2. THE ENTERPRISE	322
SECTION 3. DECISION-MAKING	323

SECTION 4. REVIEW CONFERENCE	325
SECTION 5. TRANSFER OF TECHNOLOGY	325
SECTION 6. PRODUCTION POLICY	326
SECTION 7. ECONOMIC ASSISTANCE	327
SECTION 8. FINANCIAL TERMS OF CONTRACTS	327
SECTION 9. THE FINANCE COMMITTEE	328

Index 330

UNITED NATIONS CONVENTION ON THE LAW OF THE SEA

The States Parties to this Convention,

Prompted by the desire to settle, in a spirit of mutual understanding and co-operation, all issues relating to the law of the sea and aware of the historic significance of this Convention as an important contribution to the maintenance of peace, justice and progress for all peoples of the world,

Noting that developments since the United Nations Conferences on the Law of the Sea held at Geneva in 1958 and 1960 have accentuated the need for a new and generally acceptable Convention on the law of the sea,

Conscious that the problems of ocean space are closely interrelated and need to be considered as a whole,

Recognizing the desirability of establishing through this Convention, with due regard for the sovereignty of all States, a legal order for the seas and oceans which will facilitate international communication, and will promote the peaceful uses of the seas and oceans, the equitable and efficient utilization of their resources, the conservation of their living resources, and the study, protection and preservation of the marine environment,

Bearing in mind that the achievement of these goals will contribute to the realization of a just and equitable international economic order which takes into account the interests and needs of mankind as a whole and, in particular, the special interests and needs of developing countries, whether coastal or land-locked,

Desiring by this Convention to develop the principles embodied in resolution 2749 (XXV) of 17 December 1970 in which the General Assembly of the United Nations solemnly declared inter alia that the area of the sea-bed and ocean floor and the subsoil thereof, beyond the limits of national jurisdiction, as well as its resources, are the common heritage of mankind, the exploration and exploitation of which shall be carried out for the benefit of mankind as a whole, irrespective of the geographical location of States,

Believing that the codification and progressive development of the law of the sea achieved in this Convention will contribute to the strengthening of peace, security, co-operation and friendly relations among all nations in conformity with the principles of justice and equal rights and will promote the economic and social advancement of all peoples of the world, in accordance with the Purposes and Principles of the United Nations as set forth in the Charter,

Affirming that matters not regulated by this Convention continue to be governed by the rules and principles of general international law,

Have agreed as follows:

PART I
INTRODUCTION

Article 1
Use of terms and scope

1. For the purposes of this Convention:

(1) "Area" means the seabed and ocean floor and subsoil thereof, beyond the limits of national jurisdiction;

(2) "Authority" means the International Seabed Authority;

(3) "activities in the Area" means all activities of exploration for, and exploitation of, the resources of the Area;

(4) "pollution of the marine environment" means the introduction by man, directly or indirectly, of substances or energy into the marine environment, including estuaries, which results or is likely to result in such deleterious effects as harm to living resources and marine life, hazards to human health, hindrance to marine activities, including fishing and other legitimate uses of the sea, impairment of quality for use of sea water and reduction of amenities;

(5) (a) "dumping" means:
  (i) any deliberate disposal of wastes or other matter from vessels, aircraft, platforms or other man-made structures at sea;
  (ii) any deliberate disposal of vessels, aircraft, platforms or other man-made structures at sea;
 (b) "dumping" does not include:
  (i) the disposal of wastes or other matter incidental to, or derived from the normal operations of vessels, aircraft, platforms or other man-made structures at sea and their equipment, other than wastes or other matter transported by or to vessels, aircraft, platforms or other man-made structures at sea, operating for the purpose of disposal of such matter or derived from the treatment of such wastes or other matter on such vessels, aircraft, platformsor structures;
  (ii) placement of matter for a purpose other than the mere disposal thereof, provided that such placement is not contrary to the aims of this Convention.

2. (1) "States Parties" means States which have consented to be bound by this Convention and for which this Convention is in force.

(2) This Convention applies *mutatis mutandis* to the entities referred to in Article 305, paragraph 1 (b), (c), (d), (e) and (f), which become Parties to this Convention in accordance with the conditions relevant to each, and to that extent "States Parties" refers to those entities.

PART II
TERRITORIAL SEA AND CONTIGUOUS ZONE

SECTION 1. GENERAL PROVISIONS

Article 2
Legal status of the territorial sea, of the air space
over the territorial sea and of its bed and subsoil

1. The sovereignty of a coastal State extends, beyond its land territory and internal waters and, in the case of an archipelagic State, its archipelagic waters, to an adjacent belt of sea, described as the territorial sea.
2. This sovereignty extends to the air space over the territorial sea as well as to its bed and subsoil.
3. The sovereignty over the territorial sea is exercised subject to this Convention and to other rules of international law.

SECTION 2. LIMITS OF THE TERRITORIAL SEA

Article 3
Breadth of the territorial sea

Every State has the right to establish the breadth of its territorial sea up to a limit not exceeding 12 nautical miles, measured from baselines determined in accordance with this Convention.

Article 4
Outer limit of the territorial sea

The outer limit of the territorial sea is the line every point of which is at a distance from the nearest point of the baseline equal to the breadth of the territorial sea.

Article 5
Normal baseline

Except where otherwise provided in this Convention, the normal baseline for measuring the breadth of the territorial sea is the low-water line along the coast as marked on large-scale charts officially recognized by the coastal State.

Article 6
Reefs

In the case of islands situated on atolls or of islands having fringing reefs, the baseline for measuring the breadth of the territorial sea is the seaward low-water line of the reef, as shown by the appropriate symbol on charts officially recognized by the coastal State.

Article 7
Straight baselines

1. In localities where the coastline is deeply indented and cut into, or if there is a fringe of islands along the coast in its immediate vicinity, the method of straight baselines joining appropriate points may be employed in drawing the baseline from which the breadth of the territorial sea is measured.

2. Where because of the presence of a delta and other natural conditions the coastline is highly unstable, the appropriate points may be selected along the furthest seaward extent of the low-water line and, notwithstanding subsequent regression of the low-water line, the straight baselines shall remain effective until changed by the coastal State in accordance with this Convention.

3. The drawing of straight baselines must not depart to any appreciable extent from the general direction of the coast, and the sea areas lying within the lines must be sufficiently closely linked to the land domain to be subject to the regime of internal waters.

4. Straight baselines shall not be drawn to and from low-tide elevations, unless lighthouses or similar installations which are permanently above sea level have been built on them or except in instances where the drawing of baselines to and from such elevations has received general international recognition.

5. Where the method of straight baselines is applicable under paragraph 1, account may be taken, in determining particular baselines, of economic interests peculiar to the region concerned, the reality and the importance of which are clearly evidenced by long usage.

6. The system of straight baselines may not be applied by a State in such a manner as to cut off the territorial sea of another State from the high seas or an exclusive economic zone.

Article 8
Internal waters

1. Except as provided in Part IV, waters on the landward side of the baseline of the territorial sea form part of the internal waters of the State.

2. Where the establishment of a straight baseline in accordance with the method set forth in Article 7 has the effect of enclosing as internal waters areas which had not previously been considered as such, a right of innocent passage as provided in this Convention shall exist in those waters.

Article 9
Mouths of rivers

If a river flows directly into the sea, the baseline shall be a straight line across the mouth of the river between points on the low-water line of its banks.

Article 10
Bays

1. This Article relates only to bays the coasts of which belong to a single State.

2. For the purposes of this Convention, a bay is a well-marked indentation whose penetration is in such proportion to the width of its mouth as to contain land-locked waters and constitute more than a mere curvature of the coast. An indentation shall not, however, be regarded as a bay unless its area is as large as, or larger than, that of the semi-circle whose diameter is a line drawn across the mouth of that indentation.

3. For the purpose of measurement, the area of an indentation is that lying between the low-water mark around the shore of the indentation and a line joining the low-water mark of its natural entrance points. Where, because of the presence of islands, an indentation has more than one mouth, the semi-circle shall be drawn on a line as long as the sum total of the lengths of the lines across the different mouths. Islands within an indentation shall be included as if they were part of the water area of the indentation.

4. If the distance between the low-water marks of the natural entrance points of a bay does not exceed 24 nautical miles, a closing line may be drawn between these two low-water marks, and the waters enclosed thereby shall be considered as internal waters.

5. Where the distance between the low-water marks of the natural entrance points of a bay exceeds 24 nautical miles, a straight baseline of 24 nautical miles shall be drawn within the bay in such a manner as to enclose the maximum area of water that is possible with a line of that length.

6. The foregoing provisions do not apply to so-called "historic" bays, or in any case where the system of straight baselines provided for in Article 7 is applied.

Article 11
Ports

For the purpose of delimiting the territorial sea, the outermost permanent harbour works which form an integral part of the harbour system are regarded as forming part of the coast. Off-shore installations and artificial islands shall not be considered as permanent harbour works.

Article 12
Roadsteads

Roadsteads which are normally used for the loading, unloading and anchoring of ships, and which would otherwise be situated wholly or partly outside the outer limit of the territorial sea, are included in the territorial sea.

Article 13
Low-tide elevations

1. A low-tide elevation is a naturally formed area of land which is surrounded by and above water at low tide but submerged at high tide. Where a low-tide elevation is situated wholly or partly at a distance not exceeding the breadth of the territorial sea from the mainland or an island, the low-water line on that elevation may be used as the baseline for measuring the breadth of the territorial sea.

2. Where a low-tide elevation is wholly situated at a distance exceeding the breadth of the territorial sea from the mainland or an island, it has no territorial sea of its own.

Article 14
Combination of methods for determining baselines

The coastal State may determine baselines in turn by any of the methods provided for in the foregoing Article s to suit different conditions.

Article 15
Delimitation of the territorial sea between States with opposite or adjacent coasts

Where the coasts of two States are opposite or adjacent to each other, neither of the two States is entitled, failing agreement between them to the contrary, to extend its territorial sea beyond the median line every point of which is equidistant from the nearest points on the baselines from which the breadth of the territorial seas of each of the two States is measured.

The above provision does not apply, however, where it is necessary by reason of historic title or other special circumstances to delimit the territorial seas of the two States in a way which is at variance therewith.

Article 16
Charts and lists of geographical coordinates

1. The baselines for measuring the breadth of the territorial sea determined in accordance with Article s 7, 9 and 10, or the limits derived therefrom, and the lines of delimitation drawn in accordance with Article s 12 and 15 shall be shown on charts of a scale or scales adequate for ascertaining their position. Alternatively, a list of geographical coordinates of points, specifying the geodetic datum, may be substituted.

2. The coastal State shall give due publicity to such charts or lists of geographical coordinates and shall deposit a copy of each such chart or list with the Secretary-General of the United Nations.

SECTION 3. INNOCENT PASSAGE IN THE TERRITORIAL SEA

SUBSECTION A. RULES APPLICABLE TO ALL SHIPS

Article 17
Right of innocent passage

Subject to this Convention, ships of all States, whether coastal or land-locked, enjoy the right of innocent passage through the territorial sea.

Article 18
Meaning of passage

1. Passage means navigation through the territorial sea for the purpose of:
(a) traversing that sea without entering internal waters or calling at a roadstead or port facility outside internal waters; or
(b) proceeding to or from internal waters or a call at such roadstead or port facility.
2. Passage shall be continuous and expeditious. However, passage includes stopping and anchoring, but only in so far as the same are incidental to ordinary navigation or are rendered necessary by *force majeure* or distress or for the purpose of rendering assistance to persons, ships or aircraft in danger or distress.

Article 19
Meaning of innocent passage

1. Passage is innocent so long as it is not prejudicial to the peace, good order or security of the coastal State. Such passage shall take place in conformity with this Convention and with other rules of international law.
2. Passage of a foreign ship shall be considered to be prejudicial to the peace, good order or security of the coastal State if in the territorial sea it engages in any of the following activities:
(a) any threat or use of force against the sovereignty, territorial integrity or political independence of the coastal State, or in any other manner in violation of the principles of international law embodied in the Charter of the United Nations;

(b) any exercise or practice with weapons of any kind;
(c) any act aimed at collecting information to the prejudice of the defence or security of the coastal State;
(d) any act of propaganda aimed at affecting the defence or security of the coastal State;
(e) the launching, landing or taking on board of any aircraft;
(f) the launching, landing or taking on board of any military device;
(g) the loading or unloading of any commodity, currency or person contrary to the customs, fiscal, immigration or sanitary laws and regulations of the coastal State;
(h) any act of wilful and serious pollution contrary to this Convention;
(i) any fishing activities;
(j) the carrying out of research or survey activities;
(k) any act aimed at interfering with any systems of communication or any other facilities or installations of the coastal State;
(l) any other activity not having a direct bearing on passage.

Article 20
Submarines and other underwater vehicles

In the territorial sea, submarines and other underwater vehicles are required to navigate on the surface and to show their flag.

Article 21
Laws and regulations of the coastal State relating to innocent passage

1. The coastal State may adopt laws and regulations, in conformity with the provisions of this Convention and other rules of international law, relating to innocent passage through the territorial sea, in respect of all or any of the following:
(a) the safety of navigation and the regulation of maritime traffic;
(b) the protection of navigational aids and facilities and other facilities or installations;
(c) the protection of cables and pipelines;
(d) the conservation of the living resources of the sea;
(e) the prevention of infringement of the fisheries laws and regulations of the coastal State;
(f) the preservation of the environment of the coastal State and the prevention, reduction and control of pollution thereof;
(g) marine scientific research and hydro- graphic surveys;
(h) the prevention of infringement of the customs, fiscal, immigration or sanitary laws and regulations of the coastal State.

2. Such laws and regulations shall not apply to the design, construction, manning or equipment of foreign ships unless they are giving effect to generally accepted international rules or standards.
3. The coastal State shall give due publicity to all such laws and regulations.
4. Foreign ships exercising the right of innocent passage through the territorial sea shall comply with all such laws and regulations and all generally accepted international regulations relating to the prevention of collisions at sea.

Article 22
Sea lanes and traffic separation schemes in the territorial sea

1. The coastal State may, where necessary having regard to the safety of navigation, require foreign ships exercising the right of innocent passage through its territorial sea to use such sea lanes and traffic separation schemes as it may designate or prescribe for the regulation of the passage of ships.

2. In particular, tankers, nuclear-powered ships and ships carrying nuclear or other inherently dangerous or noxious substances or materials may be required to confine their passage to such sea lanes.

3. In the designation of sea lanes and the prescription of traffic separation schemes under this Article, the coastal State shall take into account:
   (a) the recommendations of the competent international organization;
   (b) any channels customarily used for international navigation;
   (c) the special characteristics of particular ships and channels; and
   (d) the density of traffic.

4. The coastal State shall clearly indicate such sea lanes and traffic separation schemes on charts to which due publicity shall be given.

Article 23
Foreign nuclear-powered ships and ships carrying nuclear or other inherently dangerous or noxious substances

Foreign nuclear-powered ships and ships carrying nuclear or other inherently dangerous or noxious substances shall, when exercising the right of innocent passage through the territorial sea, carry documents and observe special precautionary measures established for such ships by international agreements.

Article 24
Duties of the coastal State

1. The coastal State shall not hamper the innocent passage of foreign ships through the territorial sea except in accordance with this Convention. In particular, in the application of this Convention or of any laws or regulations adopted in conformity with this Convention, the coastal State shall not:
   (a) impose requirements on foreign ships which have the practical effect of denying or impairing the right of innocent passage; or
   (b) discriminate in form or in fact against the ships of any State or against ships carrying cargoes to, from or on behalf of any State.

2. The coastal State shall give appropriate publicity to any danger to navigation, of which it has knowledge, within its territorial sea.

Article 25
Rights of protection of the coastal State

1. The coastal State may take the necessary steps in its territorial sea to prevent passage which is not innocent.

2. In the case of ships proceeding to internal waters or a call at a port facility outside internal waters, the coastal State also has the right to take the necessary steps to prevent any breach of the conditions to which admission of those ships to internal waters or such a call is subject.

3. The coastal State may, without discrimination in form or in fact among foreign ships, suspend temporarily in specified areas of its territorial sea the innocent passage of foreign

ships if such suspension is essential for the protection of its security, including weapons exercises. Such suspension shall take effect only after having been duly published.

Article 26
Charges which may be levied upon foreign ships

1. No charge may be levied upon foreign ships by reason only of their passage through the territorial sea.
2. Charges may be levied upon a foreign ship passing through the territorial sea as payment only for specific services rendered to the ship. These charges shall be levied without discrimination.

SUBSECTION B. RULES APPLICABLE TO MERCHANT SHIPS AND GOVERNMENT SHIPS OPERATED FOR COMMERCIAL PURPOSES

Article 27
Criminal jurisdiction on board a foreign ship

1. The criminal jurisdiction of the coastal State should not be exercised on board a foreign ship passing through the territorial sea to arrest any person or to conduct any investigation in connection with any crime committed on board the ship during its passage, save only in the following cases:
 (a) if the consequences of the crime extend to the coastal State;
 (b) if the crime is of a kind to disturb the peace of the country or the good order of the territorial sea;
 (c) if the assistance of the local authorities has been requested by the master of the ship or by a diplomatic agent or consular officer of the flag State; or
 (d) if such measures are necessary for the suppression of illicit traffic in narcotic drugs or psychotropic substances.
2. The above provisions do not affect the right of the coastal State to take any steps authorized by its laws for the purpose of an arrest or investigation on board a foreign ship passing through the territorial sea after leaving internal waters.
3. In the cases provided for in paragraphs 1 and 2, the coastal State shall, if the master so requests, notify a diplomatic agent or consular officer of the flag State before taking any steps, and shall facilitate contact between such agent or officer and the ship's crew. In cases of emergency this notification may be communicated while the measures are being taken.
4. In considering whether or in what manner an arrest should be made, the local authorities shall have due regard to the interests of navigation.
5. Except as provided in Part XII or with respect to violations of laws and regulations adopted in accordance with Part V, the coastal State may not take any steps on board a foreign ship passing through the territorial sea to arrest any person or to conduct any investigation in connection with any crime committed before the ship entered the territorial sea, if the ship, proceeding from a foreign port, is only passing through the territorial sea without entering internal waters.

Article 28
Civil jurisdiction in relation to foreign ships

1. The coastal State should not stop or divert a foreign ship passing through the territorial sea for the purpose of exercising civil jurisdiction in relation to a person on board the ship.

2. The coastal State may not levy execution against or arrest the ship for the purpose of any civil proceedings, save only in respect of obligations or liabilities assumed or incurred by the ship itself in the course or for the purpose of its voyage through the waters of the coastal State.

3. Paragraph 2 is without prejudice to the right of the coastal State, in accordance with its laws, to levy execution against or to arrest, for the purpose of any civil proceedings, a foreign ship lying in the territorial sea, or passing through the territorial sea after leaving internal waters.

SUBSECTION C. RULES APPLICABLE TO WARSHIPS AND OTHER GOVERNMENT SHIPS OPERATED FOR NON-COMMERCIAL PURPOSES

Article 29
Definition of warships

For the purposes of this Convention, "warship" means a ship belonging to the armed forces of a State bearing the external marks distinguishing such ships of its nationality, under the command of an officer duly commissioned by the government of the State and whose name appears in the appropriate service list or its equivalent, and manned by a crew which is under regular armed forces discipline.

Article 30
Non-compliance by warships with the laws and regulations of the coastal State

If any warship does not comply with the laws and regulations of the coastal State concerning passage through the territorial sea and disregards any request for compliance therewith which is made to it, the coastal State may require it to leave the territorial sea immediately.

Article 31
Responsibility of the flag State for damage caused by a warship or other government ship operated for non-commercial purposes

The flag State shall bear international responsibility for any loss or damage to the coastal State resulting from the non-compliance by a warship or other government ship operated for non-commercial purposes with the laws and regulations of the coastal State concerning passage through the territorial sea or with the provisions of this Convention or other rules of international law.

Article 32
Immunities of warships and other government ships operated for non-commercial purposes

With such exceptions as are contained in subsection A and in Articles 30 and 31, nothing in this Convention affects the immunities of warships and other government ships operated for non-commercial purposes.

SECTION 4. CONTIGUOUS ZONE

Article 33
Contiguous zone

1. In a zone contiguous to its territorial sea, described as the contiguous zone, the coastal State may exercise the control necessary to:
   (a) prevent infringement of its customs, fiscal, immigration or sanitary laws and regulations within its territory or territorial sea;
   (b) punish infringement of the above laws and regulations committed within its territory or territorial sea.
2. The contiguous zone may not extend beyond 24 nautical miles from the baselines from which the breadth of the territorial sea is measured.

PART III
STRAITS USED FOR INTERNATIONAL NAVIGATION

SECTION 1. GENERAL PROVISIONS

Article 34
Legal status of waters forming straits used for international navigation

1. The regime of passage through straits used for international navigation established in this Part shall not in other respects affect the legal status of the waters forming such straits or the exercise by the States bordering the straits of their sovereignty or jurisdiction over such waters and their air space, bed and subsoil.
2. The sovereignty or jurisdiction of the States bordering the straits is exercised subject to this Part and to other rules of international law.

Article 35
Scope of this Part

Nothing in this Part affects:
(a) any areas of internal waters within a strait, except where the establishment of a straight baseline in accordance with the method set forth in Article 7 has the effect of enclosing as internal waters areas which had not previously been considered as such;
(b) the legal status of the waters beyond the territorial seas of States bordering straits as exclusive economic zones or high seas; or
(c) the legal regime in straits in which passage is regulated in whole or in part by long-standing international conventions in force specifically relating to such straits.

Article 36
High seas routes or routes through exclusive economic zones through straits used for international navigation

This Part does not apply to a strait used for international navigation if there exists through the strait a route through the high seas or through an exclusive economic zone of similar convenience with respect to navigational and hydrographical characteristics; in such routes, the other relevant Parts of this Convention, including the provisions regarding the freedoms of navigation and overflight, apply.

SECTION 2. TRANSIT PASSAGE

Article 37
Scope of this section

This section applies to straits which are used for international navigation between one part of the high seas or an exclusive economic zone and another part of the high seas or an exclusive economic zone.

Article 38
Right of transit passage

1. In straits referred to in Article 37, all ships and aircraft enjoy the right of transit passage, which shall not be impeded; except that, if the strait is formed by an island of a State bordering the strait and its mainland, transit passage shall not apply if there exists seaward of the island a route through the high seas or through an exclusive economic zone of similar convenience with respect to navigational and hydrographical characteristics.
2. Transit passage means the exercise in accordance with this Part of the freedom of navigation and overflight solely for the purpose of continuous and expeditious transit of the strait between one part of the high seas or an exclusive economic zone and another part of the high seas or an exclusive economic zone. However, the requirement of continuous and expeditious transit does not preclude passage through the strait for the purpose of entering, leaving or returning from a State bordering the strait, subject to the conditions of entry to that State.
3. Any activity which is not an exercise of the right of transit passage through a strait remains subject to the other applicable provisions of this Convention.

Article 39
Duties of ships and aircraft during transit passage

1. Ships and aircraft, while exercising the right of transit passage, shall:
   (a) proceed without delay through or over the strait;
   (b) refrain from any threat or use of force against the sovereignty, territorial integrity or political independence of States bordering the strait, or in any other manner in violation of the principles of international law embodied in the Charter of the United Nations;
   (c) refrain from any activities other than those incident to their normal modes of continuous and expeditious transit unless rendered necessary by *force majeure* or by distress;
   (d) comply with other relevant provisions of this Part.
2. Ships in transit passage shall:
   (a) comply with generally accepted international regulations, procedures and practices for safety at sea, including the International Regulations for Preventing Collisions at Sea;
   (b) comply with generally accepted

international regulations, procedures and practices for the prevention, reduction and control of pollution from ships.
3. Aircraft in transit passage shall:
   (a) observe the Rules of the Air established by the International Civil Aviation Organization as they apply to civil aircraft; state aircraft will normally comply with such safety measures and will at all times operate with due regard for the safety of navigation;
   (b) at all times monitor the radio frequency assigned by the competent internationally designated air traffic control authority or the appropriate international distress radio frequency.

Article 40
Research and survey activities

During transit passage, foreign ships, including marine scientific research and hydrographic survey ships, may not carry out any research or survey activities without the prior authorization of the States bordering straits.

Article 41
Sea lanes and traffic separation schemes in straits used for international navigation

1. In conformity with this Part, States bordering straits may designate sea lanes and prescribe traffic separation schemes for navigation in straits where necessary to promote the safe passage of ships.
2. Such States may, when circumstances require, and after giving due publicity thereto, substitute other sea lanes or traffic separation schemes for any sea lanes or traffic separation schemes previously designated or prescribed by them.
3. Such sea lanes and traffic separation schemes shall conform to generally accepted international regulations.
4. Before designating or substituting sea lanes or prescribing or substituting traffic separation schemes, States bordering straits shall refer proposals to the competent international organization with a view to their adoption. The organization may adopt only such sea lanes and traffic separation schemes as may be agreed with the States bordering the straits, after which the States may designate, prescribe or substitute them.
5. In respect of a strait where sea lanes or traffic separation schemes through the waters of two or more States bordering the strait are being proposed, the States concerned shall cooperate in formulating proposals in consultation with the competent international organization.
6. States bordering straits shall clearly indicate all sea lanes and traffic separation schemes designated or prescribed by them on charts to which due publicity shall be given.
7. Ships in transit passage shall respect applicable sea lanes and traffic separation schemes established in accordance with this Article .

Article 42
Laws and regulations of States bordering straits relating to transit passage

1. Subject to the provisions of this section, States bordering straits may adopt laws and regulations relating to transit passage through straits, in respect of all or any of the following:

(a) the safety of navigation and the regulation of maritime traffic, as provided in Article 41;
(b) the prevention, reduction and control of pollution, by giving effect to applicable international regulations regarding the discharge of oil, oily wastes and other noxious substances in the strait;
(c) with respect to fishing vessels, the prevention of fishing, including the stowage of fishing gear;
(d) the loading or unloading of any commodity, currency or person in contravention of the customs, fiscal, immigration or sanitary laws and regulations of States bordering straits.

2. Such laws and regulations shall not discriminate in form or in fact among foreign ships or in their application have the practical effect of denying, hampering or impairing the right of transit passage as defined in this section.

3. States bordering straits shall give due publicity to all such laws and regulations.

4. Foreign ships exercising the right of transit passage shall comply with such laws and regulations.

5. The flag State of a ship or the State of registry of an aircraft entitled to sovereign immunity which acts in a manner contrary to such laws and regulations or other provisions of this Part shall bear international responsibility for any loss or damage which results to States bordering straits.

Article 43
Navigational and safety aids and other improvements and the prevention, reduction and control of pollution

User States and States bordering a strait should by agreement cooperate:
(a) in the establishment and maintenance in a strait of necessary navigational and safety aids or other improvements in aid of international navigation; and
(b) for the prevention, reduction and control of pollution from ships.

Article 44
Duties of States bordering straits

States bordering straits shall not hamper transit passage and shall give appropriate publicity to any danger to navigation or overflight within or over the strait of which they have knowledge. There shall be no suspension of transit passage.

SECTION 3. INNOCENT PASSAGE

Article 45
Innocent passage

1. The regime of innocent passage, in accordance with Part II, section 3, shall apply in straits used for international navigation:
   a) excluded from the application of the regime of transit passage under Article 38, paragraph 1; or
   b) between a part of the high seas or an exclusive economic zone and the territorial sea of a foreign State.

2. There shall be no suspension of innocent passage through such straits.

PART IV
ARCHIPELAGIC STATES

Article 46
Use of terms

For the purposes of this Convention:
(a) "archipelagic State" means a State constituted wholly by one or more archipelagos and may include other islands;
(b) "archipelago" means a group of islands, including parts of islands, interconnecting waters and other natural features which are so closely interrelated that such islands, waters and other natural features form an intrinsic geographical, economic and political entity, or which historically have been regarded as such.

Article 47
Archipelagic baselines

1. An archipelagic State may draw straight archipelagic baselines joining the outermost points of the outermost islands and drying reefs of the archipelago provided that within such baselines are included the main islands and an area in which the ratio of the area of the water to the area of the land, including atolls, is between 1 to 1 and 9 to 1.
2. The length of such baselines shall not exceed 100 nautical miles, except that up to 3 per cent of the total number of baselines enclosing any archipelago may exceed that length, up to a maximum length of 125 nautical miles.
3. The drawing of such baselines shall not depart to any appreciable extent from the general configuration of the archipelago.
4. Such baselines shall not be drawn to and from low-tide elevations, unless lighthouses or similar installations which are permanently above sea level have been built on them or where a low-tide elevation is situated wholly or partly at a distance not exceeding the breadth of the territorial sea from the nearest island.
5. The system of such baselines shall not be applied by an archipelagic State in such a manner as to cut off from the high seas or the exclusive economic zone the territorial sea of another State.
6. If a part of the archipelagic waters of an archipelagic State lies between two parts of an immediately adjacent neighbouring State, existing rights and all other legitimate interests which the latter State has traditionally exercised in such waters and all rights stipulated by agreement between those States shall continue and be respected.
7. For the purpose of computing the ratio of water to land under paragraph 1, land areas may include waters lying within the fringing reefs of islands and atolls, including that part of a steep-sided oceanic plateau which is enclosed or nearly enclosed by a chain of limestone islands and drying reefs lying on the perimeter of the plateau.
8. The baselines drawn in accordance with this Article shall be shown on charts of a scale or scales adequate for ascertaining their position. Alternatively, lists of geographical coordinates of points, specifying the geodetic datum, may be substituted.
9. The archipelagic State shall give due publicity to such charts or lists of geographical coordinates and shall deposit a copy of each such chart or list with the Secretary-General of the United Nations.

Article 48
Measurement of the breadth of the territorial sea, the contiguous zone, the exclusive economic zone and the continental shelf

The breadth of the territorial sea, the contiguous zone, the exclusive economic zone and the continental shelf shall be measured from archipelagic baselines drawn in accordance with Article 47.

Article 49
Legal status of archipelagic waters, of the air space over archipelagic waters and of their bed and subsoil

1. The sovereignty of an archipelagic State extends to the waters enclosed by the archipelagic baselines drawn in accordance with Article 47, described as archipelagic waters, regardless of their depth or distance from the coast.
2. This sovereignty extends to the air space over the archipelagic waters, as well as to their bed and subsoil, and the resources contained therein.
3. This sovereignty is exercised subject to this Part.
4. The regime of archipelagic sea lanes passage established in this Part shall not in other respects affect the status of the archipelagic waters, including the sea lanes, or the exercise by the archipelagic State of its sovereignty over such waters and their air space, bed and subsoil, and the resources contained therein.

Article 50
Delimitation of internal waters

Within its archipelagic waters, the archipelagic State may draw closing lines for the delimitation of internal waters, in accordance with Article s 9, 10 and 11.

Article 51
Existing agreements, traditional fishing rights and existing submarine cables

1. Without prejudice to Article 49, an archipelagic State shall respect existing agreements with other States and shall recognize traditional fishing rights and other legitimate activities of the immediately adjacent neighbouring States in certain areas falling within archipelagic waters. The terms and conditions for the exercise of such rights and activities, including the nature, the extent and the areas to which they apply, shall, at the request of any of the States concerned, be regulated by bilateral agreements between them. Such rights shall not be transferred to or shared with third States or their nationals.
2. An archipelagic State shall respect existing submarine cables laid by other States and passing through its waters without making a landfall. An archipelagic State shall permit the maintenance and replacement of such cables upon receiving due notice of their location and the intention to repair or replace them.

Article 52
Right of innocent passage

1. Subject to Article 53 and without prejudice to Article 50, ships of all States enjoy the right of innocent passage through archipelagic waters, in accordance with Part II, section 3.
2. The archipelagic State may, without discrimination in form or in fact among foreign ships, suspend temporarily in specified areas of its archipelagic waters the innocent passage of foreign ships if such suspension is essential for the protection of its security. Such suspension shall take effect only after having been duly published.

Article 53
Right of archipelagic sea lanes passage

1. An archipelagic State may designate sea lanes and air routes thereabove, suitable for the continuous and expeditious passage of foreign ships and aircraft through or over its archipelagic waters and the adjacent territorial sea.

2. All ships and aircraft enjoy the right of archipelagic sea lanes passage in such sea lanes and air routes.

3. Archipelagic sea lanes passage means the exercise in accordance with this Convention of the rights of navigation and overflight in the normal mode solely for the purpose of continuous, expeditious and unobstructed transit between one part of the high seas or an exclusive economic zone and another part of the high seas or an exclusive economic zone.

4. Such sea lanes and air routes shall traverse the archipelagic waters and the adjacent territorial sea and shall include all normal passage routes used as routes for international navigation or overflight through or over archipelagic waters and, within such routes, so far as ships are concerned, all normal navigational channels, provided that duplication of routes of similar convenience between the same entry and exit points shall not be necessary.

5. Such sea lanes and air routes shall be defined by a series of continuous axis lines from the entry points of passage routes to the exit points. Ships and aircraft in archipelagic sea lanes passage shall not deviate more than 25 nautical miles to either side of such axis lines during passage, provided that such ships and aircraft shall not navigate closer to the coasts than 10 per cent of the distance between the nearest points on islands bordering the sea lane.

6. An archipelagic State which designates sea lanes under this Article may also prescribe traffic separation schemes for the safe passage of ships through narrow channels in such sea lanes.

7. An archipelagic State may, when circumstances require, after giving due publicity thereto, substitute other sea lanes or traffic separation schemes for any sea lanes or traffic separation schemes previously designated or prescribed by it.

8. Such sea lanes and traffic separation schemes shall conform to generally accepted international regulations.

9. In designating or substituting sea lanes or prescribing or substituting traffic separation schemes, an archipelagic State shall refer proposals to the competent international organization with a view to their adoption. The organization may adopt only such sea lanes and traffic separation schemes as may be agreed with the archipelagic State, after which the archipelagic State may designate, prescribe or substitute them.

10. The archipelagic State shall clearly indicate the axis of the sea lanes and the traffic separation schemes designated or prescribed by it on charts to which due publicity shall be given.

11. Ships in archipelagic sea lanes passage shall respect applicable sea lanes and traffic separation schemes established in accordance with this Article .

12. If an archipelagic State does not designate sea lanes or air routes, the right of archipelagic sea lanes passage may be exercised through the routes normally used for international navigation.

Article 54
Duties of ships and aircraft during their passage, research and survey activities, duties of the archipelagic State and laws and regulations of the archipelagic State relating to archipelagic sea lanes passage

Article s 39, 40, 42 and 44 apply *mutatis mutandis* to archipelagic sea lanes passage.

PART V
EXCLUSIVE ECONOMIC ZONE

Article 55
Specific legal regime of the exclusive economic zone

The exclusive economic zone is an area beyond and adjacent to the territorial sea, subject to the specific legal regime established in this Part, under which the rights and jurisdiction of the coastal State and the rights and freedoms of other States are governed by the relevant provisions of this Convention.

Article 56
Rights, jurisdiction and duties of the coastal State in the exclusive economic zone

1. In the exclusive economic zone, the coastal State has:
(a) sovereign rights for the purpose of exploring and exploiting, conserving and managing the natural resources, whether living or non-living, of the waters superjacent to the seabed and of the seabed and its subsoil, and with regard to other activities for the economic exploitation and exploration of the zone, such as the production of energy from the water, currents and winds;
(b) jurisdiction as provided for in the relevant provisions of this Convention with regard to:
   (i) the establishment and use of artificial islands, installations and structures;
   (ii) marine scientific research;
   (iii) the protection and preservation of
       the marine environment;
(c) other rights and duties provided for in this Convention.

2. In exercising its rights and performing its duties under this Convention in the exclusive economic zone, the coastal State shall have due regard to the rights and duties of other States and shall act in a manner compatible with the provisions of this Convention.

3. The rights set out in this Article with respect to the seabed and subsoil shall be exercised in accordance with Part VI.

Article 57
Breadth of the exclusive economic zone

The exclusive economic zone shall not extend beyond 200 nautical miles from the baselines from which the breadth of the territorial sea is measured.

Article 58
Rights and duties of other States in the exclusive economic zone

1. In the exclusive economic zone, all States, whether coastal or land-locked, enjoy, subject to the relevant provisions of this Convention, the freedoms referred to in Article 87 of navigation and overflight and of the laying of submarine cables and pipelines, and other internationally lawful uses of the sea related to these freedoms, such as those associated with the operation of ships, aircraft and submarine cables and pipelines, and compatible with the other provisions of this Convention.
2. Article s 88 to 115 and other pertinent rules of international law apply to the exclusive economic zone in so far as they are not incompatible with this Part.
3. In exercising their rights and performing their duties under this Convention in the exclusive economic zone, States shall have due regard to the rights and duties of the coastal State and shall comply with the laws and regulations adopted by the coastal State in accordance with the provisions of this Convention and other rules of international law in so far as they are not incompatible with this Part.

Article 59
Basis for the resolution of conflicts regarding the attribution of rights and jurisdiction in the exclusive economic zone

In cases where this Convention does not attribute rights or jurisdiction to the coastal State or to other States within the exclusive economic zone, and a conflict arises between the interests of the coastal State and any other State or States, the conflict should be resolved on the basis of equity and in the light of all the relevant circumstances, taking into account the respective importance of the interests involved to the parties as well as to the international community as a whole.

Article 60
Artificial islands, installations and structures in the exclusive economic zone

1. In the exclusive economic zone, the coastal State shall have the exclusive right to construct and to authorize and regulate the construction, operation and use of:
   (a) artificial islands;
   (b) installations and structures for the purposes provided for in Article 56 and other economic purposes;
   (c) installations and structures which may interfere with the exercise of the rights of the coastal State in the zone.
2. The coastal State shall have exclusive jurisdiction over such artificial islands, installations and structures, including jurisdiction with regard to customs, fiscal, health, safety and immigration laws and regulations.
3. Due notice must be given of the construction of such artificial islands, installations or structures, and permanent means for giving warning of their presence must be maintained. Any installations or structures which are abandoned or disused shall be removed to ensure safety of navigation, taking into account any generally accepted international standards established in this regard by the competent international organization. Such removal shall also have due regard to fishing, the protection of the marine environment and the rights and

duties of other States. Appropriate publicity shall be given to the depth, position and dimensions of any installations or structures not entirely removed.

4. The coastal State may, where necessary, establish reasonable safety zones around such artificial islands, installations and structures in which it may take appropriate measures to ensure the safety both of navigation and of the artificial islands, installations and structures.

5. The breadth of the safety zones shall be determined by the coastal State, taking into account applicable international standards. Such zones shall be designed to ensure that they are reasonably related to the nature and function of the artificial islands, installations or structures, and shall not exceed a distance of 500 metres around them, measured from each point of their outer edge, except as authorized by generally accepted international standards or as recommended by the competent international organization. Due notice shall be given of the extent of safety zones.

6. All ships must respect these safety zones and shall comply with generally accepted international standards regarding navigation in the vicinity of artificial islands, installations, structures and safety zones.

7. Artificial islands, installations and structures and the safety zones around them may not be established where interference may be caused to the use of recognized sea lanes essential to international navigation.

8. Artificial islands, installations and structures do not possess the status of islands. They have no territorial sea of their own, and their presence does not affect the delimitation of the territorial sea, the exclusive economic zone or the continental shelf.

Article 61
Conservation of the living resources

1. The coastal State shall determine the allowable catch of the living resources in its exclusive economic zone.

2. The coastal State, taking into account the best scientific evidence available to it, shall ensure through proper conservation and management measures that the maintenance of the living resources in the exclusive economic zone is not endangered by over-exploitation. As appropriate, the coastal State and competent international organizations, whether subregional, regional or global, shall cooperate to this end.

3. Such measures shall also be designed to maintain or restore populations of harvested species at levels which can produce the maximum sustainable yield, as qualified by relevant environmental and economic factors, including the economic needs of coastal fishing communities and the special requirements of developing States, and taking into account fishing patterns, the interdependence of stocks and any generally recommended international minimum standards, whether subregional, regional or global.

4. In taking such measures the coastal State shall take into consideration the effects on species associated with or dependent upon harvested species with a view to maintaining or restoring populations of such associated or dependent species above levels at which their reproduction may become seriously threatened.

5. Available scientific information, catch and fishing effort statistics, and other data relevant to the conservation of fish stocks shall be contributed and exchanged on a regular basis through competent international organizations, whether subregional, regional or global, where appropriate and with participation by all States concerned, including States whose nationals are allowed to fish in the exclusive economic zone.

Article 62
Utilization of the living resources

1. The coastal State shall promote the objective of optimum utilization of the living resources in the exclusive economic zone without prejudice to Article 61.
2. The coastal State shall determine its capacity to harvest the living resources of the exclusive economic zone. Where the coastal State does not have the capacity to harvest the entire allowable catch, it shall, through agreements or other arrangements and pursuant to the terms, conditions, laws and regulations referred to in paragraph 4, give other States access to the surplus of the allowable catch, having particular regard to the provisions of Article s 69 and 70, especially in relation to the developing States mentioned therein.
3. In giving access to other States to its exclusive economic zone under this Article, the coastal State shall take into account all relevant factors, including, *inter alia*, the significance of the living resources of the area to the economy of the coastal State concerned and its other national interests, the provisions of Article s 69 and 70, the requirements of developing States in the subregion or region in harvesting part of the surplus and the need to minimize economic dislocation in States whose nationals have habitually fished in the zone or which have made substantial efforts in research and identification of stocks.
4. Nationals of other States fishing in the exclusive economic zone shall comply with the conservation measures and with the other terms and conditions established in the laws and regulations of the coastal State. These laws and regulations shall be consistent with this Convention and may relate, *inter alia*, to the following:
    (a) licensing of fishermen, fishing vessels and equipment, including payment of fees and other forms of remuneration, which, in the case of developing coastal States, may consist of adequate compensation in the field of financing, equipment and technology relating to the fishing industry;
    (b) determining the species which may be caught, and fixing quotas of catch, whether in relation to particular stocks or groups of stocks or catch per vessel over a period of time or to the catch by nationals of any State during a specified period;
    (c) regulating seasons and areas of fishing, the types, sizes and amount of gear, and the types, sizes and number of fishing vessels that may be used;
    (d) fixing the age and size of fish and other species that may be caught;
    (e) specifying information required of fishing vessels, including catch and effort statistics and vessel position reports;
    (f) requiring, under the authorization and control of the coastal State, the conduct of specified fisheries research programmes and regulating the conduct of such research, including the sampling of catches, disposition of samples and reporting of associated scientific data;
    (g) the placing of observers or trainees on board such vessels by the coastal State;
    (h) the landing of all or any part of the catch by such vessels in the ports of the coastal State;
    (i) terms and conditions relating to joint ventures or other cooperative arrangements;
    (j) requirements for the training of personnel and the transfer of fisheries technology, including enhancement of the coastal State's capability of undertaking fisheries research;
    (k) enforcement procedures.
5. Coastal States shall give due notice of conservation and management laws and regulations.

Article 63
Stocks occurring within the exclusive economic zones of two or more coastal States or both within the exclusive economic zone and in an area beyond and adjacent to it

1. Where the same stock or stocks of associated species occur within the exclusive economic zones of two or more coastal States, these States shall seek, either directly or through appropriate subregional or regional organizations, to agree upon the measures necessary to coordinate and ensure the conservation and development of such stocks without prejudice to the other provisions of this Part.

2. Where the same stock or stocks of associated species occur both within the exclusive economic zone and in an area beyond and adjacent to the zone, the coastal State and the States fishing for such stocks in the adjacent area shall seek, either directly or through appropriate subregional or regional organizations, to agree upon the measures necessary for the conservation of these stocks in the adjacent area.

Article 64
Highly migratory species

1. The coastal State and other States whose nationals fish in the region for the highly migratory species listed in Annex I shall cooperate directly or through appropriate international organizations with a view to ensuring conservation and promoting the objective of optimum utilization of such species throughout the region, both within and beyond the exclusive economic zone. In regions for which no appropriate international organization exists, the coastal State and other States whose nationals harvest these species in the region shall cooperate to establish such an organization and participate in its work.

2. The provisions of paragraph 1 apply in addition to the other provisions of this Part.

Article 65
Marine mammals

Nothing in this Part restricts the right of a coastal State or the competence of an international organization, as appropriate, to prohibit, limit or regulate the exploitation of marine mammals more strictly than provided for in this Part. States shall cooperate with a view to the conservation of marine mammals and in the case of cetaceans shall in particular work through the appropriate international organizations for their conservation, management and study.

Article 66
Anadromous stocks

1. States in whose rivers anadromous stocks originate shall have the primary interest in and responsibility for such stocks.

2. The State of origin of anadromous stocks shall ensure their conservation by the establishment of appropriate regulatory measures for fishing in all waters landward of the outer limits of its exclusive economic zone and for fishing provided for in paragraph 3(b). The State of origin may, after consultations with the other States referred to in paragraphs 3 and 4 fishing these stocks, establish total allowable catches for stocks originating in its rivers.

3. (a) Fisheries for anadromous stocks shall be conducted only in waters landward of the outer limits of exclusive economic zones, except in cases where this provision would

result in economic dislocation for a State other than the State of origin. With respect to such fishing beyond the outer limits of the exclusive economic zone, States concerned shall maintain consultations with a view to achieving agreement on terms and conditions of such fishing giving due regard to the conservation requirements and the needs of the State of origin in respect of these stocks.
(b) The State of origin shall cooperate in minimizing economic dislocation in such other States fishing these stocks, taking into account the normal catch and the mode of operations of such States, and all the areas in which such fishing has occurred.
(c) States referred to in subparagraph (b), participating by agreement with the State of origin in measures to renew anadromous stocks, particularly by expenditures for that purpose, shall be given special consideration by the State of origin in the harvesting of stocks originating in its rivers.
(d) Enforcement of regulations regarding anadromous stocks beyond the exclusive economic zone shall be by agreement between the State of origin and the other States concerned.
4. In cases where anadromous stocks migrate into or through the waters landward of the outer limits of the exclusive economic zone of a State other than the State of origin, such State shall cooperate with the State of origin with regard to the conservation and management of such stocks.
5. The State of origin of anadromous stocks and other States fishing these stocks shall make arrangements for the implementation of the provisions of this Article , where appropriate, through regional organizations.

Article 67
Catadromous species

1. A coastal State in whose waters catadromous species spend the greater part of their life cycle shall have responsibility for the management of these species and shall ensure the ingress and egress of migrating fish.
2. Harvesting of catadromous species shall be conducted only in waters landward of the outer limits of exclusive economic zones. When conducted in exclusive economic zones, harvesting shall be subject to this Article and the other provisions of this Convention concerning fishing in these zones.
3. In cases where catadromous fish migrate through the exclusive economic zone of another State, whether as juvenile or maturing fish, the management, including harvesting, of such fish shall be regulated by agreement between the State mentioned in paragraph 1 and the other State concerned. Such agreement shall ensure the rational management of the species and take into account the responsibilities of the State mentioned in paragraph 1 for the maintenance of these species.

Article 68
Sedentary species

This Part does not apply to sedentary species as defined in Article 77, paragraph 4.

Article 69
Right of land-locked States

1. Land-locked States shall have the right to participate, on an equitable basis, in the exploitation of an appropriate part of the surplus of the living resources of the exclusive economic zones of coastal States of the same subregion or region, taking into account the relevant economic and geographical circumstances of all the States concerned and in conformity with the provisions of this Article and of Article s 61 and 62.

2. The terms and modalities of such participation shall be established by the States concerned through bilateral, subregional or regional agreements taking into account, *inter alia*:
   (a) the need to avoid effects detrimental to fishing communities or fishing industries of the coastal State;
   (b) the extent to which the land-locked State, in accordance with the provisions of this Article, is participating or is entitled to participate under existing bilateral, subregional or regional agreements in the exploitation of living resources of the exclusive economic zones of other coastal States;
   (c) the extent to which other land-locked States and geographically disadvantaged States are participating in the exploitation of the living resources of the exclusive economic zone of the coastal State and the consequent need to avoid a particular burden for any single coastal State or a part of it;
   (d) the nutritional needs of the populations of the respective States.

3. When the harvesting capacity of a coastal State approaches a point which would enable it to harvest the entire allowable catch of the living resources in its exclusive economic zone, the coastal State and other States concerned shall cooperate in the establishment of equitable arrangements on a bilateral, subregional or regional basis to allow for participation of developing land-locked States of the same subregion or region in the exploitation of the living resources of the exclusive economic zones of coastal States of the subregion or region, as may be appropriate in the circumstances and on terms satisfactory to all parties. In the implementation of this provision the factors mentioned in paragraph 2 shall also be taken into account.

4. Developed land-locked States shall, under the provisions of this Article, be entitled to participate in the exploitation of living resources only in the exclusive economic zones of developed coastal States of the same subregion or region having regard to the extent to which the coastal State, in giving access to other States to the living resources of its exclusive economic zone, has taken into account the need to minimize detrimental effects on fishing communities and economic dislocation in States whose nationals have habitually fished in the zone.

5. The above provisions are without prejudice to arrangements agreed upon in subregions or regions where the coastal States may grant to land-locked States of the same subregion or region equal or preferential rights for the exploitation of the living resources in the exclusive economic zones.

Article 70
Right of geographically disadvantaged States

1. Geographically disadvantaged States shall have the right to participate, on an equitable basis, in the exploitation of an appropriate part of the surplus of the living resources of the exclusive economic zones of coastal States of the same subregion or region, taking into account the relevant economic and geographical circumstances of all the States concerned and in conformity with the provisions of this Article and of Article s 61 and 62.

2. For the purposes of this Part, "geographically disadvantaged States" means coastal States, including States bordering enclosed or semi-enclosed seas, whose geographical situation makes them dependent upon the exploitation of the living resources of the exclusive economic zones of other States in the subregion or region for adequate supplies of fish for the nutritional purposes of their populations or parts thereof, and coastal States which can claim no exclusive economic zones of their own.

3. The terms and modalities of such participation shall be established by the States concerned through bilateral, subregional or regional agreements taking into account, *inter alia*:
- (a) the need to avoid effects detrimental to fishing communities or fishing industries of the coastal State;
- (b) the extent to which the geographically disadvantaged State, in accordance with the provisions of this Article , is participating or is entitled to participate under existing bilateral, subregional or regional agreements in the exploitation of living resources of the exclusive economic zones of other coastal States;
- (c) the extent to which other geographically disadvantaged States and land-locked States are participating in the exploitation of the living resources of the exclusive economic zone of the coastal State and the consequent need to avoid a particular burden for any single coastal State or a part of it;
- (d) the nutritional needs of the populations of the respective States.

4. When the harvesting capacity of a coastal State approaches a point which would enable it to harvest the entire allowable catch of the living resources in its exclusive economic zone, the coastal State and other States concerned shall cooperate in the establishment of equitable arrangements on a bilateral, subregional or regional basis to allow for participation of developing geographically disadvantaged States of the same subregion or region in the exploitation of the living resources of the exclusive economic zones of coastal States of the subregion or region, as may be appropriate in the circumstances and on terms satisfactory to all parties. In the implementation of this provision the factors mentioned in paragraph 3 shall also be taken into account.

5. Developed geographically disadvantaged States shall, under the provisions of this Article , be entitled to participate in the exploitation of living resources only in the exclusive economic zones of developed coastal States of the same subregion or region having regard to the extent to which the coastal State, in giving access to other States to the living resources of its exclusive economic zone, has taken into account the need to minimize detrimental effects on fishing communities and economic dislocation in States whose nationals have habitually fished in the zone.

6. The above provisions are without prejudice to arrangements agreed upon in subregions or regions where the coastal States may grant to geographically disadvantaged States of the same subregion or region equal or preferential rights for the exploitation of the living resources in the exclusive economic zones.

Article 71
Non-applicability of Article s 69 and 70.

The provisions of Article s 69 and 70 do not apply in the case of a coastal State whose economy is overwhelmingly dependent on the exploitation of the living resources of its exclusive economic zone.

Article 72
Restrictions on transfer of rights

1. Rights provided under Article s 69 and 70 to exploit living resources shall not be directly or indirectly transferred to third States or their nationals by lease or licence, by establishing joint ventures or in any other manner which has the effect of such transfer unless otherwise agreed by the States concerned.
2. The foregoing provision does not preclude the States concerned from obtaining technical or financial assistance from third States or international organizations in order to facilitate the exercise of the rights pursuant to Article s 69 and 70, provided that it does not have the effect referred to in paragraph 1.

Article 73
Enforcement of laws and regulations of the coastal State

1. The coastal State may, in the exercise of its sovereign rights to explore, exploit, conserve and manage the living resources in the exclusive economic zone, take such measures, including boarding, inspection, arrest and judicial proceedings, as may be necessary to ensure compliance with the laws and regulations adopted by it in conformity with this Convention.
2. Arrested vessels and their crews shall be promptly released upon the posting of reasonable bond or other security.
3. Coastal State penalties for violations of fisheries laws and regulations in the exclusive economic zone may not include imprisonment, in the absence of agreements to the contrary by the States concerned, or any other form of corporal punishment.
4. In cases of arrest or detention of foreign vessels the coastal State shall promptly notify the flag State, through appropriate channels, of the action taken and of any penalties subsequently imposed.

Article 74
Delimitation of the exclusive economic zone between States with opposite or adjacent coasts

1. The delimitation of the exclusive economic zone between States with opposite or adjacent coasts shall be effected by agreement on the basis of international law, as referred to in Article 38 of the Statute of the International Court of Justice, in order to achieve an equitable solution.
2. If no agreement can be reached within a reasonable period of time, the States concerned shall resort to the procedures provided for in Part XV.
3. Pending agreement as provided for in paragraph 1, the States concerned, in a spirit of understanding and cooperation, shall make every effort to enter into provisional arrangements of a practical nature and, during this transitional period, not to jeopardize or hamper the reaching of the final agreement. Such arrangements shall be without prejudice to the final delimitation.
4. Where there is an agreement in force between the States concerned, questions relating to the delimitation of the exclusive economic zone shall be determined in accordance with the provisions of that agreement.

Article 75
Charts and lists of geographical coordinates

1. Subject to this Part, the outer limit lines of the exclusive economic zone and the lines of delimitation drawn in accordance with Article 74 shall be shown on charts of a scale or scales adequate for ascertaining their position. Where appropriate, lists of geographical

coordinates of points, specifying the geodetic datum, may be substituted for such outer limit lines or lines of delimitation.

2. The coastal State shall give due publicity to such charts or lists of geographical coordinates and shall deposit a copy of each such chart or list with the Secretary-General of the United Nations.

PART VI
CONTINENTAL SHELF

Article 76
Definition of the continental shelf

1. The continental shelf of a coastal State comprises the seabed and subsoil of the submarine areas that extend beyond its territorial sea throughout the natural prolongation of its land territory to the outer edge of the continental margin, or to a distance of 200 nautical miles from the baselines from which the breadth of the territorial sea is measured where the outer edge of the continental margin does not extend up to that distance.

2. The continental shelf of a coastal State shall not extend beyond the limits provided for in paragraphs 4 to 6.

3. The continental margin comprises the submerged prolongation of the land mass of the coastal State, and consists of the seabed and subsoil of the shelf, the slope and the rise. It does not include the deep ocean floor with its oceanic ridges or the subsoil thereof.

4. (a) For the purposes of this Convention, the coastal State shall establish the outer edge of the continental margin wherever the margin extends beyond 200 nautical miles from the baselines from which the breadth of the territorial sea is measured, by either:

(i) a line delineated in accordance with paragraph 7 by reference to the outermost fixed points at each of which the thickness of sedimentary rocks is at least 1 per cent of the shortest distance from such point to the foot of the continental slope; or

(ii) a line delineated in accordance with paragraph 7 by reference to fixed points not more than 60 nautical miles from the foot of the continental slope.

(b) In the absence of evidence to the contrary, the foot of the continental slope shall be determined as the point of maximum change in the gradient at its base.

5. The fixed points comprising the line of the outer limits of the continental shelf on the seabed, drawn in accordance with paragraph 4 (a)(i) and (ii), either shall not exceed 350 nautical miles from the baselines from which the breadth of the territorial sea is measured or shall not exceed 100 nautical miles from the 2,500 metre isobath, which is a line connecting the depth of 2,500 metres.

6. Notwithstanding the provisions of paragraph 5, on submarine ridges, the outer limit of the continental shelf shall not exceed 350 nautical miles from the baselines from which the breadth of the territorial sea is measured. This paragraph does not apply to submarine elevations that are natural components of the continental margin, such as its plateaux, rises, caps, banks and spurs.

7. The coastal State shall delineate the outer limits of its continental shelf, where that shelf extends beyond 200 nautical miles from the baselines from which the breadth of the territorial sea is measured, by straight lines not exceeding 60 nautical miles in length, connecting fixed points, defined by coordinates of latitude and longitude.

8. Information on the limits of the continental shelf beyond 200 nautical miles from the baselines from which the breadth of the territorial sea is measured shall be submitted by

the coastal State to the Commission on the Limits of the Continental Shelf set up under Annex II on the basis of equitable geographical representation. The Commission shall make recommendations to coastal States on matters related to the establishment of the outer limits of their continental shelf. The limits of the shelf established by a coastal State on the basis of these recommendations shall be final and binding.

9. The coastal State shall deposit with the Secretary-General of the United Nations charts and relevant information, including geodetic data, permanently describing the outer limits of its continental shelf. The Secretary-General shall give due publicity thereto.

10. The provisions of this Article are without prejudice to the question of delimitation of the continental shelf between States with opposite or adjacent coasts.

Article 77
Rights of the coastal State over the continental shelf

1. The coastal State exercises over the continental shelf sovereign rights for the purpose of exploring it and exploiting its natural resources.

2. The rights referred to in paragraph 1 are exclusive in the sense that if the coastal State does not explore the continental shelf or exploit its natural resources, no one may undertake these activities without the express consent of the coastal State.

3. The rights of the coastal State over the continental shelf do not depend on occupation, effective or notional, or on any express proclamation.

4. The natural resources referred to in this Part consist of the mineral and other non-living resources of the seabed and subsoil together with living organisms belonging to sedentary species, that is to say, organisms which, at the harvestable stage, either are immobile on or under the seabed or are unable to move except in constant physical contact with the seabed or the subsoil.

Article 78
Legal status of the superjacent waters and air space and the rights and freedoms of other States

1. The rights of the coastal State over the continental shelf do not affect the legal status of the superjacent waters or of the air space above those waters.

2. The exercise of the rights of the coastal State over the continental shelf must not infringe or result in any unjustifiable interference with navigation and other rights and freedoms of other States as provided for in this Convention.

Article 79
Submarine cables and pipelines on the continental shelf

1. All States are entitled to lay submarine cables and pipelines on the continental shelf, in accordance with the provisions of this Article .

2. Subject to its right to take reasonable measures for the exploration of the continental shelf, the exploitation of its natural resources and the prevention, reduction and control of pollution from pipelines, the coastal State may not impede the laying or maintenance of such cables or pipelines.

3. The delineation of the course for the laying of such pipelines on the continental shelf is subject to the consent of the coastal State.

4. Nothing in this Part affects the right of the coastal State to establish conditions for cables or pipelines entering its territory or territorial sea, or its jurisdiction over cables and pipelines constructed or used in connection with the exploration of its continental shelf or

exploitation of its resources or the operations of artificial islands, installations and structures under its jurisdiction.

5. When laying submarine cables or pipelines, States shall have due regard to cables or pipelines already in position. In particular, possibilities of repairing existing cables or pipelines shall not be prejudiced.

Article 80
Artificial islands, installations and structures on the continental shelf

Article 60 applies *mutatis mutandis* to artificial islands, installations and structures on the continental shelf.

Article 81
Drilling on the continental shelf

The coastal State shall have the exclusive right to authorize and regulate drilling on the continental shelf for all purposes.

Article 82
Payments and contributions with respect to the exploitation of the continental shelf beyond 200 nautical miles

1. The coastal State shall make payments or contributions in kind in respect of the exploitation of the non-living resources of the continental shelf beyond 200 nautical miles from the baselines from which the breadth of the territorial sea is measured.

2. The payments and contributions shall be made annually with respect to all production at a site after the first five years of production at that site. For the sixth year, the rate of payment or contribution shall be 1 per cent of the value or volume of production at the site. The rate shall increase by 1 per cent for each subsequent year until the twelfth year and shall remain at 7 per cent thereafter. Production does not include resources used in connection with exploitation.

3. A developing State which is a net importer of a mineral resource produced from its continental shelf is exempt from making such payments or contributions in respect of that mineral resource.

4. The payments or contributions shall be made through the Authority, which shall distribute them to States Parties to this Convention, on the basis of equitable sharing criteria, taking into account the interests and needs of developing States, particularly the least developed and the land-locked among them.

Article 83
Delimitation of the continental shelf between States with opposite or adjacent coasts

1. The delimitation of the continental shelf between States with opposite or adjacent coasts shall be effected by agreement on the basis of international law, as referred to in Article 38 of the Statute of the International Court of Justice, in order to achieve an equitable solution.

2. If no agreement can be reached within a reasonable period of time, the States concerned shall resort to the procedures provided for in Part XV.

3. Pending agreement as provided for in paragraph 1, the States concerned, in a spirit of understanding and cooperation, shall make every effort to enter into provisional

arrangements of a practical nature and, during this transitional period, not to jeopardize or hamper the reaching of the final agreement. Such arrangements shall be without prejudice to the final delimitation.

4. Where there is an agreement in force between the States concerned, questions relating to the delimitation of the continental shelf shall be determined in accordance with the provisions of that agreement.

Article 84
Charts and lists of geographical coordinates

1. Subject to this Part, the outer limit lines of the continental shelf and the lines of delimitation drawn in accordance with Article 83 shall be shown on charts of a scale or scales adequate for ascertaining their position. Where appropriate, lists of geographical coordinates of points, specifying the geodetic datum, may be substituted for such outer limit lines or lines of delimitation.

2. The coastal State shall give due publicity to such charts or lists of geographical coordinates and shall deposit a copy of each such chart or list with the Secretary-General of the United Nations and, in the case of those showing the outer limit lines of the continental shelf, with the Secretary-General of the Authority.

Article 85
Tunnelling

This Part does not prejudice the right of the coastal State to exploit the subsoil by means of tunnelling, irrespective of the depth of water above the subsoil.

PART VII
HIGH SEAS

SECTION 1. GENERAL PROVISIONS

Article 86
Application of the provisions of this Part

The provisions of this Part apply to all parts of the sea that are not included in the exclusive economic zone, in the territorial sea or in the internal waters of a State, or in the archipelagic waters of an archipelagic State. This Article does not entail any abridgement of the freedoms enjoyed by all States in the exclusive economic zone in accordance with Article 58.

Article 87
Freedom of the high seas

1. The high seas are open to all States, whether coastal or land-locked. Freedom of the high seas is exercised under the conditions laid down by this Convention and by other rules of international law. It comprises, *inter alia*, both for coastal and land-locked States:

(a) freedom of navigation;
(b) freedom of overflight;
(c) freedom to lay submarine cables and pipelines, subject to Part VI;
(d) freedom to construct artificial islands and other installations permitted under international law, subject to Part VI;

(e) freedom of fishing, subject to the conditions laid down in section 2;
(f) freedom of scientific research, subject to Parts VI and XIII.

2. These freedoms shall be exercised by all States with due regard for the interests of other States in their exercise of the freedom of the high seas, and also with due regard for the rights under this Convention with respect to activities in the Area.

Article 88
Reservation of the high seas for peaceful purposes

The high seas shall be reserved for peaceful purposes.

Article 89
Invalidity of claims of sovereignty over the high seas

No State may validly purport to subject any part of the high seas to its sovereignty.

Article 90
Right of navigation

Every State, whether coastal or land-locked, has the right to sail ships flying its flag on the high seas.

Article 91
Nationality of ships

1. Every State shall fix the conditions for the grant of its nationality to ships, for the registration of ships in its territory, and for the right to fly its flag. Ships have the nationality of the State whose flag they are entitled to fly. There must exist a genuine link between the State and the ship.

2. Every State shall issue to ships to which it has granted the right to fly its flag documents to that effect.

Article 92

Status of ships

1. Ships shall sail under the flag of one State only and, save in exceptional cases expressly provided for in international treaties or in this Convention, shall be subject to its exclusive jurisdiction on the high seas. A ship may not change its flag during a voyage or while in a port of call, save in the case of a real transfer of ownership or change of registry.

2. A ship which sails under the flags of two or more States, using them according to convenience, may not claim any of the nationalities in question with respect to any other State, and may be assimilated to a ship without nationality.

Article 93
Ships flying the flag of the United Nations, its specialized agencies and the International Atomic Energy Agency

The preceding Article s do not prejudice the question of ships employed on the official service of the United Nations, its specialized agencies or the International Atomic Energy Agency, flying the flag of the organization.

Article 94
Duties of the flag State

1. Every State shall effectively exercise its jurisdiction and control in administrative, technical and social matters over ships flying its flag.
2. In particular every State shall:
(a) maintain a register of ships containing the names and particulars of ships flying its flag, except those which are excluded from generally accepted international regulations on account of their small size; and
(b) assume jurisdiction under its internal law over each ship flying its flag and its master, officers and crew in respect of administrative, technical and social matters concerning the ship.
3. Every State shall take such measures for ships flying its flag as are necessary to ensure safety at sea with regard, *inter alia*, to:
(a) the construction, equipment and seaworthiness of ships;
(b) the manning of ships, labour conditions and the training of crews, taking into account the applicable international instruments;
(c) the use of signals, the maintenance of communications and the prevention of collisions.
4. Such measures shall include those necessary to ensure:
(a) that each ship, before registration and thereafter at appropriate intervals, is surveyed by a qualified surveyor of ships, and has on board such charts, nautical publications and navigational equipment and instruments as are appropriate for the safe navigation of the ship;
(b) that each ship is in the charge of a master and officers who possess appropriate qualifications, in particular in seamanship, navigation, communications and marine engineering, and that the crew is appropriate in qualification and numbers for the type, size, machinery and equipment of the ship;
(c) that the master, officers and, to the extent appropriate, the crew are fully conversant with and required to observe the applicable international regulations concerning the safety of life at sea, the prevention of collisions, the prevention, reduction and control of marine pollution, and the maintenance of communications by radio.
5. In taking the measures called for in paragraphs 3 and 4 each State is required to conform to generally accepted international regulations, procedures and practices and to take any steps which may be necessary to secure their observance.
6. A State which has clear grounds to believe that proper jurisdiction and control with respect to a ship have not been exercised may report the facts to the flag State. Upon receiving such a report, the flag State shall investigate the matter and, if appropriate, take any action necessary to remedy the situation.
7. Each State shall cause an inquiry to be held by or before a suitably qualified person or persons into every marine casualty or incident of navigation on the high seas involving a ship flying its flag and causing loss of life or serious injury to nationals of another State or serious damage to ships or installations of another State or to the marine environment. The flag State and the other State shall cooperate in the conduct of any inquiry held by that other State into any such marine casualty or incident of navigation.

Article 95
Immunity of warships on the high seas

Warships on the high seas have complete immunity from the jurisdiction of any State other than the flag State.

Article 96
Immunity of ships used only on government non-commercial service

Ships owned or operated by a State and used only on government non-commercial service shall, on the high seas, have complete immunity from the jurisdiction of any State other than the flag State.

Article 97
Penal jurisdiction in matters of collision or any other incident of navigation

1. In the event of a collision or any other incident of navigation concerning a ship on the high seas, involving the penal or disciplinary responsibility of the master or of any other person in the service of the ship, no penal or disciplinary proceedings may be instituted against such person except before the judicial or administrative authorities either of the flag State or of the State of which such person is a national.
2. In disciplinary matters, the State which has issued a master's certificate or a certificate of competence or licence shall alone be competent, after due legal process, to pronounce the withdrawal of such certificates, even if the holder is not a national of the State which issued them.
3. No arrest or detention of the ship, even as a measure of investigation, shall be ordered by any authorities other than those of the flag State.

Article 98
Duty to render assistance

1. Every State shall require the master of a ship flying its flag, in so far as he can do so without serious danger to the ship, the crew or the passengers:
    (a) to render assistance to any person found at sea in danger of being lost;
    (b) to proceed with all possible speed to the rescue of persons in distress, if informed of their need of assistance, in so far as such action may reasonably be expected of him;
    (c) after a collision, to render assistance to the other ship, its crew and its passengers and, where possible, to inform the other ship of the name of his own ship, its port of registry and the nearest port at which it will call.
2. Every coastal State shall promote the establishment, operation and maintenance of an adequate and effective search and rescue service regarding safety on and over the sea and, where circumstances so require, by way of mutual regional arrangements cooperate with neighbouring States for this purpose.

Article 99
Prohibition of the transport of slaves

Every State shall take effective measures to prevent and punish the transport of slaves in ships authorized to fly its flag and to prevent the unlawful use of its flag for that purpose. Any slave taking refuge on board any ship, whatever its flag, shall *ipso facto* be free.

Article 100
Duty to cooperate in the repression of piracy

All States shall cooperate to the fullest possible extent in the repression of piracy on the high seas or in any other place outside the jurisdiction of any State.

Article 101
Definition of piracy

Piracy consists of any of the following acts:
(a) any illegal acts of violence or detention, or any act of depredation, committed for private ends by the crew or the passengers of a private ship or a private aircraft, and directed:
   (i) on the high seas, against another ship or aircraft, or against persons or property on board such ship or aircraft;
   (ii) against a ship, aircraft, persons or property in a place outside the jurisdiction of any State;
(b) any act of voluntary participation in the operation of a ship or of an aircraft with knowledge of facts making it a pirate ship or aircraft;
(c) any act of inciting or of intentionally facilitating an act described in subparagraph (a) or (b).

Article 102
Piracy by a warship, government ship or government aircraft whose crew has mutinied

The acts of piracy, as defined in Article 101, committed by a warship, government ship or government aircraft whose crew has mutinied and taken control of the ship or aircraft are assimilated to acts committed by a private ship or aircraft.

Article 103
Definition of a pirate ship or aircraft

A ship or aircraft is considered a pirate ship or aircraft if it is intended by the persons in dominant control to be used for the purpose of committing one of the acts referred to in Article 101. The same applies if the ship or aircraft has been used to commit any such act, so long as it remains under the control of the persons guilty of that act.

Article 104
Retention or loss of the nationality of a pirate ship or aircraft

A ship or aircraft may retain its nationality although it has become a pirate ship or aircraft. The retention or loss of nationality is determined by the law of the State from which such nationality was derived.

Article 105
Seizure of a pirate ship or aircraft

On the high seas, or in any other place outside the jurisdiction of any State, every State may seize a pirate ship or aircraft, or a ship or aircraft taken by piracy and under the control of pirates, and arrest the persons and seize the property on board. The courts of the State which carried out the seizure may decide upon the penalties to be imposed, and may also determine the action to be taken with regard to the ships, aircraft or property, subject to the rights of third parties acting in good faith.

Article 106
Liability for seizure without adequate grounds

Where the seizure of a ship or aircraft on suspicion of piracy has been effected without adequate grounds, the State making the seizure shall be liable to the State the nationality of which is possessed by the ship or aircraft for any loss or damage caused by the seizure.

Article 107
Ships and aircraft which are entitled to seize on account of piracy

A seizure on account of piracy may be carried out only by warships or military aircraft, or other ships or aircraft clearly marked and identifiable as being on government service and authorized to that effect.

Article 108
Illicit traffic in narcotic drugs or psychotropic substances

1. All States shall cooperate in the suppression of illicit traffic in narcotic drugs and psychotropic substances engaged in by ships on the high seas contrary to international conventions.
2. Any State which has reasonable grounds for believing that a ship flying its flag is engaged in illicit traffic in narcotic drugs or psychotropic substances may request the cooperation of other States to suppress such traffic.

Article 109
Unauthorized broadcasting from the high seas

1. All States shall cooperate in the suppression of unauthorized broadcasting from the high seas.
2. For the purposes of this Convention, "unauthorized broadcasting" means the transmission of sound radio or television broadcasts from a ship or installation on the high seas intended for reception by the general public contrary to international regulations, but excluding the transmission of distress calls.
3. Any person engaged in unauthorized broadcasting may be prosecuted before the court of:
   (a) the flag State of the ship;
   (b) the State of registry of the installation;
   (c) the State of which the person is a national;
   (d) any State where the transmissions can be received; or
   (e) any State where authorized radio communication is suffering interference.
4. On the high seas, a State having jurisdiction in accordance with paragraph 3 may, in conformity with Article 110, arrest any person or ship engaged in unauthorized broadcasting and seize the broadcasting apparatus.

Article 110
Right of visit

1. Except where acts of interference derive from powers conferred by treaty, a warship which encounters on the high seas a foreign ship, other than a ship entitled to complete immunity in accordance with Article s 95 and 96, is not justified in boarding it unless there is reasonable ground for suspecting that:
   (a) the ship is engaged in piracy;
   (b) the ship is engaged in the slave trade;
   (c) the ship is engaged in unauthorized broadcasting and the flag State of the warship has jurisdiction under Article 109;
   (d) the ship is without nationality; or
   (e) though flying a foreign flag or refusing to show its flag, the ship is, in reality, of the same nationality as the warship.
2. In the cases provided for in paragraph 1, the warship may proceed to verify the ship's right to fly its flag. To this end, it may send a boat under the command of an officer to the

suspected ship. If suspicion remains after the documents have been checked, it may proceed to a further examination on board the ship, which must be carried out with all possible consideration.

3. If the suspicions prove to be unfounded, and provided that the ship boarded has not committed any act justifying them, it shall be compensated for any loss or damage that may have been sustained.

4. These provisions apply *mutatis mutandis* to military aircraft.

5. These provisions also apply to any other duly authorized ships or aircraft clearly marked and identifiable as being on government service.

Article 111
Right of hot pursuit

1. The hot pursuit of a foreign ship may be undertaken when the competent authorities of the coastal State have good reason to believe that the ship has violated the laws and regulations of that State. Such pursuit must be commenced when the foreign ship or one of its boats is within the internal waters, the archipelagic waters, the territorial sea or the contiguous zone of the pursuing State, and may only be continued outside the territorial sea or the contiguous zone if the pursuit has not been interrupted. It is not necessary that, at the time when the foreign ship within the territorial sea or the contiguous zone receives the order to stop, the ship giving the order should likewise be within the territorial sea or the contiguous zone. If the foreign ship is within a contiguous zone, as defined in Article 33, the pursuit may only be undertaken if there has been a violation of the rights for the protection of which the zone was established.

2. The right of hot pursuit shall apply *mutatis mutandis* to violations in the exclusive economic zone or on the continental shelf, including safety zones around continental shelf installations, of the laws and regulations of the coastal State applicable in accordance with this Convention to the exclusive economic zone or the continental shelf, including such safety zones.

3. The right of hot pursuit ceases as soon as the ship pursued enters the territorial sea of its own State or of a third State.

4. Hot pursuit is not deemed to have begun unless the pursuing ship has satisfied itself by such practicable means as may be available that the ship pursued or one of its boats or other craft working as a team and using the ship pursued as a mother ship is within the limits of the territorial sea, or, as the case may be, within the contiguous zone or the exclusive economic zone or above the continental shelf. The pursuit may only be commenced after a visual or auditory signal to stop has been given at a distance which enables it to be seen or heard by the foreign ship.

5. The right of hot pursuit may be exercised only by warships or military aircraft, or other ships or aircraft clearly marked and identifiable as being on government service and authorized to that effect.

6. Where hot pursuit is effected by an aircraft:

   (a) the provisions of paragraphs 1 to 4 shall apply *mutatis mutandis*;
   (b) the aircraft giving the order to stop must itself actively pursue the ship until a ship or another aircraft of the coastal State, summoned by the aircraft, arrives to take over the pursuit, unless the aircraft is itself able to arrest the ship. It does not suffice to justify an arrest outside the territorial sea that the ship was merely sighted by the aircraft as an offender or suspected offender, if it was not both ordered to stop and pursued by the aircraft itself or other aircraft or ships which continue the pursuit without interruption.

7. The release of a ship arrested within the jurisdiction of a State and escorted to a port of that State for the purposes of an inquiry before the competent authorities may not be claimed

solely on the ground that the ship, in the course of its voyage, was escorted across a portion of the exclusive economic zone or the high seas, if the circumstances rendered this necessary.

8. Where a ship has been stopped or arrested outside the territorial sea in circumstances which do not justify the exercise of the right of hot pursuit, it shall be compensated for any loss or damage that may have been thereby sustained.

Article 112
Right to lay submarine cables and pipelines

1. All States are entitled to lay submarine cables and pipelines on the bed of the high seas beyond the continental shelf.
2. Article 79, paragraph 5, applies to such cables and pipelines.

Article 113
Breaking or injury of a submarine cable or pipeline

Every State shall adopt the laws and regulations necessary to provide that the breaking or injury by a ship flying its flag or by a person subject to its jurisdiction of a submarine cable beneath the high seas done wilfully or through culpable negligence, in such a manner as to be liable to interrupt or obstruct telegraphic or telephonic communications, and similarly the breaking or injury of a submarine pipeline or high-voltage power cable, shall be a punishable offence. This provision shall apply also to conduct calculated or likely to result in such breaking or injury. However, it shall not apply to any break or injury caused by persons who acted merely with the legitimate object of saving their lives or their ships, after having taken all necessary precautions to avoid such break or injury.

Article 114
Breaking or injury by owners of a submarine cable or pipeline of another submarine cable or pipeline

Every State shall adopt the laws and regulations necessary to provide that, if persons subject to its jurisdiction who are the owners of a submarine cable or pipeline beneath the high seas, in laying or repairing that cable or pipeline, cause a break in or injury to another cable or pipeline, they shall bear the cost of the repairs.

Article 115
Indemnity for loss incurred in avoiding injury
to a submarine cable or pipeline

Every State shall adopt the laws and regulations necessary to ensure that the owners of ships who can prove that they have sacrificed an anchor, a net or any other fishing gear, in order to avoid injuring a submarine cable or pipeline, shall be indemnified by the owner of the cable or pipeline, provided that the owner of the ship has taken all reasonable precautionary measures beforehand.

SECTION 2. CONSERVATION AND MANAGEMENT OF THE LIVING RESOURCES OF THE HIGH SEAS

Article 116
Right to fish on the high seas

All States have the right for their nationals to engage in fishing on the high seas subject to:
(a) their treaty obligations;

(b) the rights and duties as well as the interests of coastal States provided for, *inter alia*, in Article 63, paragraph 2, and Article s 64 to 67; and

(c) the provisions of this section.

Article 117
Duty of States to adopt with respect to their nationals measures for the conservation of the living resources of the high seas

All States have the duty to take, or to cooperate with other States in taking, such measures for their respective nationals as may be necessary for the conservation of the living resources of the high seas.

Article 118
Cooperation of States in the conservation and management of living resources

States shall cooperate with each other in the conservation and management of living resources in the areas of the high seas. States whose nationals exploit identical living resources, or different living resources in the same area, shall enter into negotiations with a view to taking the measures necessary for the conservation of the living resources concerned. They shall, as appropriate, cooperate to establish subregional or regional fisheries organizations to this end.

Article 119
Conservation of the living resources of the high seas

1. In determining the allowable catch and establishing other conservation measures for the living resources in the high seas, States shall:
    (a) take measures which are designed, on the best scientific evidence available to the States concerned, to maintain or restore populations of harvested species at levels which can produce the maximum sustainable yield, as qualified by relevant environmental and economic factors, including the special requirements of developing States, and taking into account fishing patterns, the interdependence of stocks and any generally recommended international minimum standards, whether subregional, regional or global;
    (b) take into consideration the effects on species associated with or dependent upon harvested species with a view to maintaining or restoring populations of such associated or dependent species above levels at which their reproduction may become seriously threatened.
2. Available scientific information, catch and fishing effort statistics, and other data relevant to the conservation of fish stocks shall be contributed and exchanged on a regular basis through competent international organizations, whether subregional, regional or global, where appropriate and with participation by all States concerned.
3. States concerned shall ensure that conservation measures and their implementation do not discriminate in form or in fact against the fishermen of any State.

Article 120
Marine mammals

Article 65 also applies to the conservation and management of marine mammals in the high seas.

PART VIII
REGIME OF ISLANDS

Article 121
Regime of islands

1. An island is a naturally formed area of land, surrounded by water, which is above water at high tide.
2. Except as provided for in paragraph 3, the territorial sea, the contiguous zone, the exclusive economic zone and the continental shelf of an island are determined in accordance with the provisions of this Convention applicable to other land territory.
3. Rocks which cannot sustain human habitation or economic life of their own shall have no exclusive economic zone or continental shelf.

PART IX
ENCLOSED OR SEMI-ENCLOSED SEAS

Article 122
Definition

For the purposes of this Convention, "enclosed or semi-enclosed sea" means a gulf, basin or sea surrounded by two or more States and connected to another sea or the ocean by a narrow outlet or consisting entirely or primarily of the territorial seas and exclusive economic zones of two or more coastal States.

Article 123
Cooperation of States bordering
enclosed or semi-enclosed seas

States bordering an enclosed or semi-enclosed sea should cooperate with each other in the exercise of their rights and in the performance of their duties under this Convention. To this end they shall endeavour, directly or through an appropriate regional organization:
  (a) to coordinate the management, conservation, exploration and exploitation of the living resources of the sea;
  (b) to coordinate the implementation of their rights and duties with respect to the protection and preservation of the marine environment;
  (c) to coordinate their scientific research policies and undertake where appropriate joint programmes of scientific research in the area;
  (d) to invite, as appropriate, other interested States or international organizations to cooperate with them in furtherance of the provisions of this Article .

PART X

RIGHT OF ACCESS OF LAND-LOCKED STATES TO AND FROM THE SEA AND FREEDOM OF TRANSIT

Article 124
Use of terms

1. For the purposes of this Convention:
   (a) "land-locked State" means a State which has no sea-coast;
   (b) "transit State" means a State, with or without a sea-coast, situated between a land-locked State and the sea, through whose territory traffic in transit passes;
   (c) "traffic in transit" means transit of persons, baggage, goods and means of transport across the territory of one or more transit States, when the passage across such territory, with or without trans-shipment, warehousing, breaking bulk or change in the mode of transport, is only a portion of a complete journey which begins or terminates within the territory of the land-locked State;
   (d) "means of transport" means:
      (i) railway rolling stock, sea, lake and river craft and road vehicles;
      (ii) where local conditions so require, porters and pack animals.

2. Land-locked States and transit States may, by agreement between them, include as means of transport pipelines and gas lines and means of transport other than those included in paragraph 1.

Article 125
Right of access to and from the sea and freedom of transit

1. Land-locked States shall have the right of access to and from the sea for the purpose of exercising the rights provided for in this Convention including those relating to the freedom of the high seas and the common heritage of mankind. To this end, land-locked States shall enjoy freedom of transit through the territory of transit States by all means of transport.

2. The terms and modalities for exercising freedom of transit shall be agreed between the land-locked States and transit States concerned through bilateral, subregional or regional agreements.

3. Transit States, in the exercise of their full sovereignty over their territory, shall have the right to take all measures necessary to ensure that the rights and facilities provided for in this Part for land-locked States shall in no way infringe their legitimate interests.

Article 126
Exclusion of application of the most-favoured-nation clause

The provisions of this Convention, as well as special agreements relating to the exercise of the right of access to and from the sea, establishing rights and facilities on account of the special geographical position of land-locked States, are excluded from the application of the most-favoured-nation clause.

Article 127
Customs duties, taxes and other charges

1. Traffic in transit shall not be subject to any customs duties, taxes or other charges except charges levied for specific services rendered in connection with such traffic.
2. Means of transport in transit and other facilities provided for and used by land-locked States shall not be subject to taxes or charges higher than those levied for the use of means of transport of the transit State.

Article 128
Free zones and other customs facilities

For the convenience of traffic in transit, free zones or other customs facilities may be provided at the ports of entry and exit in the transit States, by agreement between those States and the land-locked States.

Article 129
Cooperation in the construction and improvement of means of transport

Where there are no means of transport in transit States to give effect to the freedom of transit or where the existing means, including the port installations and equipment, are inadequate in any respect, the transit States and land-locked States concerned may cooperate in constructing or improving them.

Article 130
Measures to avoid or eliminate delays or other difficulties of a technical nature in traffic in transit

1. Transit States shall take all appropriate measures to avoid delays or other difficulties of a technical nature in traffic in transit.
2. Should such delays or difficulties occur, the competent authorities of the transit States and land-locked States concerned shall cooperate towards their expeditious elimination.

Article 131
Equal treatment in maritime ports

Ships flying the flag of land-locked States shall enjoy treatment equal to that accorded to other foreign ships in maritime ports.

Article 132
Grant of greater transit facilities

This Convention does not entail in any way the withdrawal of transit facilities which are greater than those provided for in this Convention and which are agreed between States Parties to this Convention or granted by a State Party. This Convention also does not preclude such grant of greater facilities in the future.

PART XI

THE AREA

SECTION 1. GENERAL PROVISIONS

Article 133
Use of terms

For the purposes of this Part:

(a) "resources" means all solid, liquid or gaseous mineral resources *in situ* in the Area at or beneath the seabed, including polymetallic nodules;
(b) resources, when recovered from the Area, are referred to as "minerals".

Article 134
Scope of this Part

1. This Part applies to the Area.
2. Activities in the Area shall be governed by the provisions of this Part.
3. The requirements concerning deposit of, and publicity to be given to, the charts or lists of geographical coordinates showing the limits referred to in Article 1, paragraph 1(1), are set forth in Part VI.
4. Nothing in this Article affects the establishment of the outer limits of the continental shelf in accordance with Part VI or the validity of agreements relating to delimitation between States with opposite or adjacent coasts.

Article 135
Legal status of the superjacent waters and air space

Neither this Part nor any rights granted or exercised pursuant thereto shall affect the legal status of the waters superjacent to the Area or that of the air space above those waters.

SECTION 2. PRINCIPLES GOVERNING THE AREA

Article 136
Common heritage of mankind

The Area and its resources are the common heritage of mankind.

Article 137
Legal status of the Area and its resources

1. No State shall claim or exercise sovereignty or sovereign rights over any part of the Area or its resources, nor shall any State or natural or juridical person appropriate any part thereof. No such claim or exercise of sovereignty or sovereign rights nor such appropriation shall be recognized.
2. All rights in the resources of the Area are vested in mankind as a whole, on whose behalf the Authority shall act. These resources are not subject to alienation. The minerals recovered from the Area, however, may only be alienated in accordance with this Part and the rules, regulations and procedures of the Authority.

3. No State or natural or juridical person shall claim, acquire or exercise rights with respect to the minerals recovered from the Area except in accordance with this Part. Otherwise, no such claim, acquisition or exercise of such rights shall be recognized.

Article 138
General conduct of States in relation to the Area

The general conduct of States in relation to the Area shall be in accordance with the provisions of this Part, the principles embodied in the Charter of the United Nations and other rules of international law in the interests of maintaining peace and security and promoting international cooperation and mutual understanding.

Article 139
Responsibility to ensure compliance and liability for damage

1. States Parties shall have the responsibility to ensure that activities in the Area, whether carried out by States Parties, or state enterprises or natural or juridical persons which possess the nationality of States Parties or are effectively controlled by them or their nationals, shall be carried out in conformity with this Part. The same responsibility applies to international organizations for activities in the Area carried out by such organizations.
2. Without prejudice to the rules of international law and Annex III, Article 22, damage caused by the failure of a State Party or international organization to carry out its responsibilities under this Part shall entail liability; States Parties or international organizations acting together shall bear joint and several liability. A State Party shall not however be liable for damage caused by any failure to comply with this Part by a person whom it has sponsored under Article 153, paragraph 2(b), if the State Party has taken all necessary and appropriate measures to secure effective compliance under Article 153, paragraph 4, and Annex III, Article 4, paragraph 4.
3. States Parties that are members of international organizations shall take appropriate measures to ensure the implementation of this Article with respect to such organizations.

Article 140
Benefit of mankind

1. Activities in the Area shall, as specifically provided for in this Part, be carried out for the benefit of mankind as a whole, irrespective of the geographical location of States, whether coastal or land-locked, and taking into particular consideration the interests and needs of developing States and of peoples who have not attained full independence or other self-governing status recognized by the United Nations in accordance with General Assembly resolution 1514 (XV) and other relevant General Assembly resolutions.
2. The Authority shall provide for the equitable sharing of financial and other economic benefits derived from activities in the Area through any appropriate mechanism, on a non-discriminatory basis, in accordance with Article 160, paragraph 2 (f)(i).

Article 141
Use of the Area exclusively for peaceful purposes

The Area shall be open to use exclusively for peaceful purposes by all States, whether coastal or land-locked, without discrimination and without prejudice to the other provisions of this Part.

Article 142
Rights and legitimate interests of coastal States

1. Activities in the Area, with respect to resource deposits in the Area which lie across limits of national jurisdiction, shall be conducted with due regard to the rights and legitimate interests of any coastal State across whose jurisdiction such deposits lie.

2. Consultations, including a system of prior notification, shall be maintained with the State concerned, with a view to avoiding infringement of such rights and interests. In cases where activities in the Area may result in the exploitation of resources lying within national jurisdiction, the prior consent of the coastal State concerned shall be required.

3. Neither this Part nor any rights granted or exercised pursuant thereto shall affect the rights of coastal States to take such measures consistent with the relevant provisions of Part XII as may be necessary to prevent, mitigate or eliminate grave and imminent danger to their coastline, or related interests from pollution or threat thereof or from other hazardous occurrences resulting from or caused by any activities in the Area.

Article 143
Marine scientific research

1. Marine scientific research in the Area shall be carried out exclusively for peaceful purposes and for the benefit of mankind as a whole, in accordance with Part XIII.

2. The Authority may carry out marine scientific research concerning the Area and its resources, and may enter into contracts for that purpose. The Authority shall promote and encourage the conduct of marine scientific research in the Area, and shall coordinate and disseminate the results of such research and analysis when available.

3. States Parties may carry out marine scientific research in the Area. States Parties shall promote international cooperation in marine scientific research in the Area by:
- (a) participating in international programmes and encouraging cooperation in marine scientific research by personnel of different countries and of the Authority;
- (b) ensuring that programmes are developed through the Authority or other international organizations as appropriate for the benefit of developing States and technologically less developed States with a view to:
  - (i) strengthening their research capabilities;
  - (ii) training their personnel and the personnel of the Authority in the techniques and applications of research;
  - (iii) fostering the employment of their qualified personnel in research in the Area;
- (c) effectively disseminating the results of research and analysis when available, through the Authority or other international channels when appropriate.

Article 144
Transfer of technology

1. The Authority shall take measures in accordance with this Convention:
- (a) to acquire technology and scientific knowledge relating to activities in the Area; and
- (b) to promote and encourage the transfer to developing States of such technology and scientific knowledge so that all States Parties benefit therefrom.

2. To this end the Authority and States Parties shall cooperate in promoting the transfer of technology and scientific knowledge relating to activities in the Area so that the

Enterprise and all States Parties may benefit therefrom. In particular they shall initiate and promote:
  (a) programmes for the transfer of technology to the Enterprise and to developing States with regard to activities in the Area, including, *inter alia*, facilitating the access of the Enterprise and of developing States to the relevant technology, under fair and reasonable terms and conditions;
  (b) measures directed towards the advancement of the technology of the Enterprise and the domestic technology of developing States, particularly by providing opportunities to personnel from the Enterprise and from developing States for training in marine science and technology and for their full participation in activities in the Area.

Article 145
Protection of the marine environment

Necessary measures shall be taken in accordance with this Convention with respect to activities in the Area to ensure effective protection for the marine environment from harmful effects which may arise from such activities. To this end the Authority shall adopt appropriate rules, regulations and procedures for *inter alia*:
  (a) the prevention, reduction and control of pollution and other hazards to the marine environment, including the coastline, and of interference with the ecological balance of the marine environment, particular attention being paid to the need for protection from harmful effects of such activities as drilling, dredging, excavation, disposal of waste, construction and operation or maintenance of installations, pipelines and other devices related to such activities;
  (b) the protection and conservation of the natural resources of the Area and the prevention of damage to the flora and fauna of the marine environment.

Article 146
Protection of human life

With respect to activities in the Area, necessary measures shall be taken to ensure effective protection of human life. To this end the Authority shall adopt appropriate rules, regulations and procedures to supplement existing international law as embodied in relevant treaties.

Article 147
Accommodation of activities in the Area and in the marine environment

1. Activities in the Area shall be carried out with reasonable regard for other activities in the marine environment.
2. Installations used for carrying out activities in the Area shall be subject to the following conditions:
  (a) such installations shall be erected, emplaced and removed solely in accordance with this Part and subject to the rules, regulations and procedures of the Authority. Due notice must be given of the erection, emplacement and removal of such installations, and permanent means for giving warning of their presence must be maintained;

(b) such installations may not be established where interference may be caused to the use of recognized sea lanes essential to international navigation or in areas of intense fishing activity;
(c) safety zones shall be established around such installations with appropriate markings to ensure the safety of both navigation and the installations. The configuration and location of such safety zones shall not be such as to form a belt impeding the lawful access of shipping to particular maritime zones or navigation along international sea lanes;
(d) such installations shall be used exclusively for peaceful purposes;
(e) such installations do not possess the status of islands. They have no territorial sea of their own, and their presence does not affect the delimitation of the territorial sea, the exclusive economic zone or the continental shelf.

3. Other activities in the marine environment shall be conducted with reasonable regard for activities in the Area.

Article 148
Participation of developing States in activities in the Area

The effective participation of developing States in activities in the Area shall be promoted as specifically provided for in this Part, having due regard to their special interests and needs, and in particular to the special need of the land-locked and geographically disadvantaged among them to overcome obstacles arising from their disadvantaged location, including remoteness from the Area and difficulty of access to and from it.

Article 149
Archaeological and historical objects

All objects of an archaeological and historical nature found in the Area shall be preserved or disposed of for the benefit of mankind as a whole, particular regard being paid to the preferential rights of the State or country of origin, or the State of cultural origin, or the State of historical and archaeological origin.

SECTION 3. DEVELOPMENT OF RESOURCES OF THE AREA

Article 150
Policies relating to activities in the Area

Activities in the Area shall, as specifically provided for in this Part, be carried out in such a manner as to foster healthy development of the world economy and balanced growth of international trade, and to promote international cooperation for the over-all development of all countries, especially developing States, and with a view to ensuring:
(a) the development of the resources of the Area;
(b) orderly, safe and rational management of the resources of the Area, including the efficient conduct of activities in the Area and, in accordance with sound principles of conservation, the avoidance of unnecessary waste;

(c) the expansion of opportunities for participation in such activities consistent in particular with Article s 144 and 148;
(d) participation in revenues by the Authority and the transfer of technology to the Enterprise and developing States as provided for in this Convention;
(e) increased availability of the minerals derived from the Area as needed in conjunction with minerals derived from other sources, to ensure supplies to consumers of such minerals;
(f) the promotion of just and stable prices remunerative to producers and fair to consumers for minerals derived both from the Area and from other sources, and the promotion of long-term equilibrium between supply and demand;
(g) the enhancement of opportunities for all States Parties, irrespective of their social and economic systems or geographical location, to participate in the development of the resources of the Area and the prevention of monopolization of activities in the Area;
(h) the protection of developing countries from adverse effects on their economies or on their export earnings resulting from a reduction in the price of an affected mineral, or in the volume of exports of that mineral, to the extent that such reduction is caused by activities in the Area, as provided in Article 151;
(i) the development of the common heritage for the benefit of mankind as a whole; and
(j) conditions of access to markets for the imports of minerals produced from the resources of the Area and for imports of commodities produced from such minerals shall not be more favourable than the most favourable applied to imports from other sources.

Article 151
Production policies

1.(a) Without prejudice to the objectives set forth in Article 150 and for the purpose of implementing subparagraph (h) of that Article, the Authority, acting through existing forums or such new arrangements or agreements as may be appropriate, in which all interested parties, including both producers and consumers, participate, shall take measures necessary to promote the growth, efficiency and stability of markets for those commodities produced from the minerals derived from the Area, at prices remunerative to producers and fair to consumers. All States Parties shall cooperate to this end.
(b) The Authority shall have the right to participate in any commodity conference dealing with those commodities and in which all interested parties including both producers and consumers participate. The Authority shall have the right to become a party to any arrangement or agreement resulting from such conferences. Participation of the Authority in any organs established under those arrangements or agreements shall be in respect of production in the Area and in accordance with the relevant rules of those organs.
(c) The Authority shall carry out its obligations under the arrangements or agreements referred to in this paragraph in a manner which assures a uniform and non-discriminatory implementation in respect of all production in the Area of the minerals concerned. In doing so, the Authority shall act in a manner consistent with the terms of existing contracts and approved plans of work of the Enterprise.
2. (a) During the interim period specified in paragraph 3, commercial production shall not be undertaken pursuant to an approved plan of work until the operator has applied for and has been issued a production authorization by the Authority. Such production authorizations may not be applied for or issued more than five years

prior to the planned commencement of commercial production under the plan of work unless, having regard to the nature and timing of project development, the rules, regulations and procedures of the Authority prescribe another period.

(b) In the application for the production authorization, the operator shall specify the annual quantity of nickel expected to be recovered under the approved plan of work. The application shall include a schedule of expenditures to be made by the operator after he has received the authorization which are reasonably calculated to allow him to begin commercial production on the date planned.

(c) For the purposes of subparagraphs (a) and (b), the Authority shall establish appropriate performance requirements in accordance with Annex III, Article 17.

(d) The Authority shall issue a production authorization for the level of production applied for unless the sum of that level and the levels already authorized exceeds the nickel production ceiling, as calculated pursuant to paragraph 4 in the year of issuance of the authorization, during any year of planned production falling within the interim period.

(e) When issued, the production authorization and approved application shall become a part of the approved plan of work.

(f) If the operator's application for a production authorization is denied pursuant to subparagraph (d), the operator may apply again to the Authority at any time.

3. The interim period shall begin five years prior to 1 January of the year in which the earliest commercial production is planned to commence under an approved plan of work. If the earliest commercial production is delayed beyond the year originally planned, the beginning of the interim period and the production ceiling originally calculated shall be adjusted accordingly. The interim period shall last 25 years or until the end of the Review Conference referred to in Article 155 or until the day when such new arrangements or agreements as are referred to in paragraph 1 enter into force, whichever is earliest. The Authority shall resume the power provided in this Article for the remainder of the interim period if the said arrangements or agreements should lapse or become ineffective for any reason whatsoever.

4. (a) The production ceiling for any year of the interim period shall be the sum of:
(i) the difference between the trend line values for nickel consumption, as calculated pursuant to subparagraph (b), for the year immediately prior to the year of the earliest commercial production and the year immediately prior to the commencement of the interim period; and
(ii) sixty per cent of the difference between the trend line values for nickel consumption, as calculated pursuant to subparagraph (b), for the year for which the production authorization is being applied for and the year immediately prior to the year of the earliest commercial production.

(b) For the purposes of subparagraph (a):
(i) trend line values used for computing the nickel production ceiling shall be those annual nickel consumption values on a trend line computed during the year in which a production authorization is issued. The trend line shall be derived from a linear regression of the logarithms of actual nickel consumption for the most recent 15-year period for which such data are available, time being the independent variable. This trend line shall be referred to as the original trend line;
(ii) if the annual rate of increase of the original trend line is less than 3 per cent, then the trend line used to determine the quantities referred to in subparagraph (a) shall instead be one passing through the original trend line at the value for the first year of the relevant 15-year period, and increasing at 3 per cent annually; provided however that the production ceiling established for any year of the interim period

may not in any case exceed the difference between the original trend line value for that year and the original trend line value for the year immediately prior to the commencement of the interim period.

5. The Authority shall reserve to the Enterprise for its initial production a quantity of 38,000 metric tonnes of nickel from the available production ceiling calculated pursuant to paragraph 4.

6. (a) An operator may in any year produce less than or up to 8 per cent more than the level of annual production of minerals from polymetallic nodules specified in his production authorization, provided that the over-all amount of production shall not exceed that specified in the authorization. Any excess over 8 per cent and up to 20 per cent in any year, or any excess in the first and subsequent years following two consecutive years in which excesses occur, shall be negotiated with the Authority, which may require the operator to obtain a supplementary production authorization to cover additional production.

(b) Applications for such supplementary production authorizations shall be considered by the Authority only after all pending applications by operators who have not yet received production authorizations have been acted upon and due account has been taken of other likely applicants. The Authority shall be guided by the principle of not exceeding the total production allowed under the production ceiling in any year of the interim period. It shall not authorize the production under any plan of work of a quantity in excess of 46,500 metric tonnes of nickel per year.

7. The levels of production of other metals such as copper, cobalt and manganese extracted from the polymetallic nodules that are recovered pursuant to a production authorization should not be higher than those which would have been produced had the operator produced the maximum level of nickel from those nodules pursuant to this Article. The Authority shall establish rules, regulations and procedures pursuant to Annex III, Article 17, to implement this paragraph.

8. Rights and obligations relating to unfair economic practices under relevant multilateral trade agreements shall apply to the exploration for and exploitation of minerals from the Area. In the settlement of disputes arising under this provision, States Parties which are Parties to such multilateral trade agreements shall have recourse to the dispute settlement procedures of such agreements.

9. The Authority shall have the power to limit the level of production of minerals from the Area, other than minerals from polymetallic nodules, under such conditions and applying such methods as may be appropriate by adopting regulations in accordance with Article 161, paragraph 8.

10. Upon the recommendation of the Council on the basis of advice from the Economic Planning Commission, the Assembly shall establish a system of compensation or take other measures of economic adjustment assistance including cooperation with specialized agencies and other international organizations to assist developing countries which suffer serious adverse effects on their export earnings or economies resulting from a reduction in the price of an affected mineral or in the volume of exports of that mineral, to the extent that such reduction is caused by activities in the Area. The Authority on request shall initiate studies on the problems of those States which are likely to be most seriously affected with a view to minimizing their difficulties and assisting them in their economic adjustment.

Article 152
Exercise of powers and functions by the Authority

1. The Authority shall avoid discrimination in the exercise of its powers and functions, including the granting of opportunities for activities in the Area.

2. Nevertheless, special consideration for developing States, including particular consideration for the land-locked and geographically disadvantaged among them, specifically provided for in this Part shall be permitted.

Article 153
System of exploration and exploitation

1. Activities in the Area shall be organized, carried out and controlled by the Authority on behalf of mankind as a whole in accordance with this Article as well as other relevant provisions of this Part and the relevant Annexes, and the rules, regulations and procedures of the Authority.

2. Activities in the Area shall be carried out as prescribed in paragraph 3:
   (a) by the Enterprise, and
   (b) in association with the Authority by States Parties, or state enterprises or natural or juridical persons which possess the nationality of States Parties or are effectively controlled by them or their nationals, when sponsored by such States, or any group of the foregoing which meets the requirements provided in this Part and in Annex III.

3. Activities in the Area shall be carried out in accordance with a formal written plan of work drawn up in accordance with Annex III and approved by the Council after review by the Legal and Technical Commission. In the case of activities in the Area carried out as authorized by the Authority by the entities specified in paragraph 2(b), the plan of work shall, in accordance with Annex III, Article 3, be in the form of a contract. Such contracts may provide for joint arrangements in accordance with Annex III, Article 11.

4. The Authority shall exercise such control over activities in the Area as is necessary for the purpose of securing compliance with the relevant provisions of this Part and the Annexes relating thereto, and the rules, regulations and procedures of the Authority, and the plans of work approved in accordance with paragraph 3. States Parties shall assist the Authority by taking all measures necessary to ensure such compliance in accordance with Article 139.

5. The Authority shall have the right to take at any time any measures provided for under this Part to ensure compliance with its provisions and the exercise of the functions of control and regulation assigned to it thereunder or under any contract. The Authority shall have the right to inspect all installations in the Area used in connection with activities in the Area.

6. A contract under paragraph 3 shall provide for security of tenure. Accordingly, the contract shall not be revised, suspended or terminated except in accordance with Annex III, Article s 18 and 19.

Article 154
Periodic review

Every five years from the entry into force of this Convention, the Assembly shall undertake a general and systematic review of the manner in which the international regime of the Area established in this Convention has operated in practice. In the light of this review the Assembly may take, or recommend that other organs take, measures in accordance with the provisions and procedures of this Part and the Annexes relating thereto which will lead to the improvement of the operation of the regime.

Article 155
The Review Conference

1. Fifteen years from 1 January of the year in which the earliest commercial production commences under an approved plan of work, the Assembly shall convene a conference for the review of those provisions of this Part and the relevant Annexes which govern the system of exploration and exploitation of the resources of the Area. The Review Conference shall consider in detail, in the light of the experience acquired during that period:
   a) whether the provisions of this Part which govern the system of exploration and exploitation of the resources of the Area have achieved their aims in all respects, including whether they have benefited mankind as a whole;
   b) whether, during the 15-year period, reserved areas have been exploited in an effective and balanced manner in comparison with non-reserved areas;
   c) whether the development and use of the Area and its resources have been undertaken in such a manner as to foster healthy development of the world economy and balanced growth of international trade;
   d) whether monopolization of activities in the Area has been prevented;
   e) whether the policies set forth in Article s 150 and 151 have been fulfilled; and
   f) whether the system has resulted in the equitable sharing of benefits derived from activities in the Area, taking into particular consideration the interests and needs of the developing States.

2. The Review Conference shall ensure the maintenance of the principle of the common heritage of mankind, the international regime designed to ensure equitable exploitation of the resources of the Area for the benefit of all countries, especially the developing States, and an Authority to organize, conduct and control activities in the Area. It shall also ensure the maintenance of the principles laid down in this Part with regard to the exclusion of claims or exercise of sovereignty over any part of the Area, the rights of States and their general conduct in relation to the Area, and their participation in activities in the Area in conformity with this Convention, the prevention of monopolization of activities in the Area, the use of the Area exclusively for peaceful purposes, economic aspects of activities in the Area, marine scientific research, transfer of technology, protection of the marine environment, protection of human life, rights of coastal States, the legal status of the waters superjacent to the Area and that of the air space above those waters and accommodation between activities in the Area and other activities in the marine environment.

3. The decision-making procedure applicable at the Review Conference shall be the same as that applicable at the Third United Nations Conference on the Law of the Sea. The Conference shall make every effort to reach agreement on any amendments by way of consensus and there

should be no voting on such matters until all efforts at achieving consensus have been exhausted.

4. If, five years after its commencement, the Review Conference has not reached agreement on the system of exploration and exploitation of the resources of the Area, it may decide during the ensuing 12 months, by a three-fourths majority of the States Parties, to adopt and submit to the States Parties for ratification or accession such amendments changing or modifying the system as it determines necessary and appropriate. Such amendments shall enter into force for all States Parties 12 months after the deposit of instruments of ratification or accession by three fourths of the States Parties.

5. Amendments adopted by the Review Conference pursuant to this Article shall not affect rights acquired under existing contracts.

SECTION 4. THE AUTHORITY

SUBSECTION A. GENERAL PROVISIONS

Article 156
Establishment of the Authority

1. There is hereby established the International Seabed Authority, which shall function in accordance with this Part.

2. All States Parties are *ipso facto* members of the Authority.

3. Observers at the Third United Nations Conference on the Law of the Sea who have signed the Final Act and who are not referred to in Article 305, paragraph 1(c), (d), (e) or (f), shall have the right to participate in the Authority as observers, in accordance with its rules, regulations and procedures.

4. The seat of the Authority shall be in Jamaica.

5. The Authority may establish such regional centres or offices as it deems necessary for the exercise of its functions.

Article 157
Nature and fundamental principles of the Authority

1. The Authority is the organization through which States Parties shall, in accordance with this Part, organize and control activities in the Area, particularly with a view to administering the resources of the Area.

2. The powers and functions of the Authority shall be those expressly conferred upon it by this Convention. The Authority shall have such incidental powers, consistent with this Convention, as are implicit in and necessary for the exercise of those powers and functions with respect to activities in the Area.

3. The Authority is based on the principle of the sovereign equality of all its members.

4. All members of the Authority shall fulfil in good faith the obligations assumed by them in accordance with this Part in order to ensure to all of them the rights and benefits resulting from membership.

Article 158
Organs of the Authority

1. There are hereby established, as the principal organs of the Authority, an Assembly, a Council and a Secretariat.

2. There is hereby established the Enterprise, the organ through which the Authority shall carry out the functions referred to in Article 170, paragraph 1.

3. Such subsidiary organs as may be found necessary may be established in accordance with this Part.

4. Each principal organ of the Authority and the Enterprise shall be responsible for exercising those powers and functions which are conferred upon it. In exercising such powers and functions each organ shall avoid taking any action which may derogate from or impede the exercise of specific powers and functions conferred upon another organ.

SUBSECTION B. THE ASSEMBLY

Article 159
Composition, procedure and voting

1. The Assembly shall consist of all the members of the Authority. Each member shall have one representative in the Assembly, who may be accompanied by alternates and advisers.

2. The Assembly shall meet in regular annual sessions and in such special sessions as may be decided by the Assembly, or convened by the Secretary-General at the request of the Council or of a majority of the members of the Authority.

3. Sessions shall take place at the seat of the Authority unless otherwise decided by the Assembly.

4. The Assembly shall adopt its rules of procedure. At the beginning of each regular session, it shall elect its President and such other officers as may be required. They shall hold office until a new President and other officers are elected at the next regular session.

5. A majority of the members of the Assembly shall constitute a quorum.

6. Each member of the Assembly shall have one vote.

7. Decisions on questions of procedure, including decisions to convene special sessions of the Assembly, shall be taken by a majority of the members present and voting.

8. Decisions on questions of substance shall be taken by a two-thirds majority of the members present and voting, provided that such majority includes a majority of the members participating in the session. When the issue arises as to whether a question is one of substance or not, that question shall be treated as one of substance unless otherwise decided by the Assembly by the majority required for decisions on questions of substance.

9. When a question of substance comes up for voting for the first time, the President may, and shall, if requested by at least one fifth of the members of the Assembly, defer the issue of taking a vote on that question for a period not exceeding five calendar days. This rule may be applied only once to any question, and shall not be applied so as to defer the question beyond the end of the session.

10. Upon a written request addressed to the President and sponsored by at least one fourth of the members of the Authority for an advisory opinion on the conformity with this Convention of a proposal before the Assembly on any matter, the Assembly shall request the Seabed Disputes Chamber of the International Tribunal for the Law of the Sea to give an advisory opinion thereon and shall defer voting on that proposal pending receipt of the advisory opinion by the Chamber. If the advisory opinion is not received

before the final week of the session in which it is requested, the Assembly shall decide when it will meet to vote upon the deferred proposal.

Article 160
Powers and functions

1. The Assembly, as the sole organ of the Authority consisting of all the members, shall be considered the supreme organ of the Authority to which the other principal organs shall be accountable as specifically provided for in this Convention. The Assembly shall have the power to establish general policies in conformity with the relevant provisions of this Convention on any question or matter within the competence of the Authority.

2. In addition, the powers and functions of the Assembly shall be:

(a) to elect the members of the Council in accordance with Article 161;

(b) to elect the Secretary-General from among the candidates proposed by the Council;

(c) to elect, upon the recommendation of the Council, the members of the Governing Board of the Enterprise and the Director-General of the Enterprise;

(d) to establish such subsidiary organs as it finds necessary for the exercise of its functions in accordance with this Part. In the composition of these subsidiary organs due account shall be taken of the principle of equitable geographical distribution and of special interests and the need for members qualified and competent in the relevant technical questions dealt with by such organs;

(e) to assess the contributions of members to the administrative budget of the Authority in accordance with an agreed scale of assessment based upon the scale used for the regular budget of the United Nations until the Authority shall have sufficient income from other sources to meet its administrative expenses;

(f) (i) to consider and approve, upon the recommendation of the Council, the rules, regulations and procedures on the equitable sharing of financial and other economic benefits derived from activities in the Area and the payments and contributions made pursuant to Article 82, taking into particular consideration the interests and needs of developing States and peoples who have not attained full independence or other self-governing status. If the Assembly does not approve the recommendations of the Council, the Assembly shall return them to the Council for reconsideration in the light of the views expressed by the Assembly;

(ii) to consider and approve the rules, regulations and procedures of the Authority, and any amendments thereto, provisionally adopted by the Council pursuant to Article 162, paragraph 2 (o)(ii). These rules, regulations and procedures shall relate to prospecting, exploration and exploitation in the Area, the financial management and internal administration of the Authority, and, upon the recommendation of the Governing Board of the Enterprise, to the transfer of funds from the Enterprise to the Authority;

(g) to decide upon the equitable sharing of financial and other economic benefits derived from activities in the Area, consistent with this Convention and the rules, regulations and procedures of the Authority;

(h) to consider and approve the proposed annual budget of the Authority submitted by the Council;

(i) to examine periodic reports from the Council and from the Enterprise and special reports requested from the Council or any other organ of the Authority;

(j) to initiate studies and make recommendations for the purpose of promoting international cooperation concerning activities in the Area and encouraging the progressive development of international law relating thereto and its codification;

(k) to consider problems of a general nature in connection with activities in the Area arising in particular for developing States, as well as those problems for States in connection with activities in the Area that are due to their geographical location, particularly for land-locked and geographically disadvantaged States;

(l) to establish, upon the recommendation of the Council, on the basis of advice from the Economic Planning Commission, a system of compensation or other measures of economic adjustment assistance as provided in Article 151, paragraph 10;

(m) to suspend the exercise of rights and privileges of membership pursuant to Article 185;

(n) to discuss any question or matter within the competence of the Authority and to decide as to which organ of the Authority shall deal with any such question or matter not specifically entrusted to a particular organ, consistent with the distribution of powers and functions among the organs of the Authority.

SUBSECTION C. THE COUNCIL

Article 161
Composition, procedure and voting

1. The Council shall consist of 36 members of the Authority elected by the Assembly in the following order:

(a) four members from among those States Parties which, during the last five years for which statistics are available, have either consumed more than 2 per cent of total world consumption or have had net imports of more than 2 per cent of total world imports of the commodities produced from the categories of minerals to be derived from the Area, and in any case one State from the Eastern European (Socialist) region, as well as the largest consumer;

(b) four members from among the eight States Parties which have the largest investments in preparation for and in the conduct of activities in the Area, either directly or through their nationals, including at least one State from the Eastern European (Socialist) region;

(c) four members from among States Parties which on the basis of production in areas under their jurisdiction are major net exporters of the categories of minerals to be derived from the Area, including at least two developing States whose exports of such minerals have a substantial bearing upon their economies;

(d) six members from among developing States Parties, representing special interests. The special interests to be represented shall include those of States with large populations, States which are land-locked or geographically disadvantaged, States which are major importers of the categories of minerals to be derived from the Area, States which are potential producers of such minerals, and least developed States;

(e) eighteen members elected according to the principle of ensuring an equitable geographical distribution of seats in the Council as a whole, provided that each geographical region shall have at least one member elected under this subparagraph.

For this purpose, the geographical regions shall be Africa, Asia, Eastern European (Socialist), Latin America and Western European and Others.

2. In electing the members of the Council in accordance with paragraph 1, the Assembly shall ensure that:
- (a) land-locked and geographically disadvantaged States are represented to a degree which is reasonably proportionate to their representation in the Assembly;
- (b) coastal States, especially developing States, which do not qualify under paragraph 1(a), (b), (c) or (d) are represented to a degree which is reasonably proportionate to their representation in the Assembly;
- (c) each group of States Parties to be represented on the Council is represented by those members, if any, which are nominated by that group.

3. Elections shall take place at regular sessions of the Assembly. Each member of the Council shall be elected for four years. At the first election, however, the term of one half of the members of each group referred to in paragraph 1 shall be two years.

4. Members of the Council shall be eligible for re-election, but due regard should be paid to the desirability of rotation of membership.

5. The Council shall function at the seat of the Authority, and shall meet as often as the business of the Authority may require, but not less than three times a year.

6. A majority of the members of the Council shall constitute a quorum.

7. Each member of the Council shall have one vote.

8. (a) Decisions on questions of procedure shall be taken by a majority of the members present and voting.
- (b) Decisions on questions of substance arising under the following provisions shall be taken by a two-thirds majority of the members present and voting, provided that such majority includes a majority of the members of the Council: Article 162, paragraph 2, subparagraphs (f); (g); (h); (i); (n); (p); (v); Article 191.
- (c) Decisions on questions of substance arising under the following provisions shall be taken by a three-fourths majority of the members present and voting, provided that such majority includes a majority of the members of the Council: Article 162, paragraph 1; Article 162, paragraph 2, subparagraphs (a); (b); (c); (d); (e); (l); (q); (r); (s); (t); (u) in cases of non-compliance by a contractor or a sponsor; (w) provided that orders issued thereunder may be binding for not more than 30 days unless confirmed by a decision taken in accordance with subparagraph (d); Article 162, paragraph 2, subparagraphs (x); (y); (z); Article 163, paragraph 2; Article 174, paragraph 3; Annex IV, Article 11.
- (d) Decisions on questions of substance arising under the following provisions shall be taken by consensus: Article 162, paragraph 2(m) and (o); adoption of amendments to Part XI.
- (e) For the purposes of subparagraphs (d), (f) and (g), "consensus" means the absence of any formal objection. Within 14 days of the submission of a proposal to the Council, the President of the Council shall determine whether there would be a formal objection to the adoption of the proposal. If the President determines that there would be such an objection, the President shall establish and convene, within three days following such determination, a conciliation committee consisting of not more than nine members of the Council, with the President as chairman, for the purpose of reconciling the differences and producing a proposal which can be adopted by consensus. The committee shall work expeditiously and report to the Council within 14 days following its establishment. If the committee is unable to recommend a proposal which can be adopted by consensus, it shall set out in its report the grounds on which the proposal is being opposed.

(f) Decisions on questions not listed above which the Council is authorized to take by the rules, regulations and procedures of the Authority or otherwise shall be taken pursuant to the subparagraphs of this paragraph specified in the rules, regulations and procedures or, if not specified therein, then pursuant to the subparagraph determined by the Council if possible in advance, by consensus.

(g) When the issue arises as to whether a question is within subparagraph (a), (b), (c) or (d), the question shall be treated as being within the subparagraph requiring the higher or highest majority or consensus as the case may be, unless otherwise decided by the Council by the said majority or by consensus.

9. The Council shall establish a procedure whereby a member of the Authority not represented on the Council may send a representative to attend a meeting of the Council when a request is made by such member, or a matter particularly affecting it is under consideration. Such a representative shall be entitled to participate in the deliberations but not to vote.

Article 162
Powers and functions

1. The Council is the executive organ of the Authority. The Council shall have the power to establish, in conformity with this Convention and the general policies established by the Assembly, the specific policies to be pursued by the Authority on any question or matter within the competence of the Authority.

2. In addition, the Council shall:

(a) supervise and coordinate the implementation of the provisions of this Part on all questions and matters within the competence of the Authority and invite the attention of the Assembly to cases of non-compliance;

(b) propose to the Assembly a list of candidates for the election of the Secretary - General;

(c) recommend to the Assembly candidates for the election of the members of the Governing Board of the Enterprise and the Director-General of the Enterprise;

(d) establish, as appropriate, and with due regard to economy and efficiency, such subsidiary organs as it finds necessary for the exercise of its functions in accordance with this Part. In the composition of subsidiary organs, emphasis shall be placed on the need for members qualified and competent in relevant technical matters dealt with by those organs provided that due account shall be taken of the principle of equitable geographical distribution and of special interests;

(e) adopt its rules of procedure including the method of selecting its president;

(f) enter into agreements with the United Nations or other international organizations on behalf of the Authority and within its competence, subject to approval by the Assembly;

(g) consider the reports of the Enterprise and transmit them to the Assembly with its recommendations;

(h) present to the Assembly annual reports and such special reports as the Assembly may request;

(i) issue directives to the Enterprise in accordance with Article 170;

(j) approve plans of work in accordance with Annex III, Article 6. The Council shall act upon each plan of work within 60 days of its submission by the Legal and Technical

Commission at a session of the Council in accordance with the following procedures:

(i) if the Commission recommends the approval of a plan of work, it shall be deemed to have been approved by the Council if no member of the Council submits in writing to the President within 14 days a specific objection alleging non-compliance with the requirements of Annex III, Article 6. If there is an objection, the conciliation procedure set forth in Article 161, paragraph 8(e), shall apply. If, at the end of the conciliation procedure, the objection is still maintained, the plan of work shall be deemed to have been approved by the Council unless the Council disapproves it by consensus among its members excluding any State or States making the application or sponsoring the applicant;

(ii) if the Commission recommends the disapproval of a plan of work or does not make a recommendation, the Council may approve the plan of work by a three-fourths majority of the members present and voting, provided that such majority includes a majority of the members participating in the session;

(k) approve plans of work submitted by the Enterprise in accordance with Annex IV, Article 12, applying, *mutatis mutandis*, the procedures set forth in subparagraph (j);

(l) exercise control over activities in the Area in accordance with Article 153, paragraph 4, and the rules, regulations and procedures of the Authority;

(m) take, upon the recommendation of the Economic Planning Commission, necessary and appropriate measures in accordance with Article 150, subparagraph (h), to provide protection from the adverse economic effects specified therein;

(n) make recommendations to the Assembly, on the basis of advice from the Economic Planning Commission, for a system of compensation or other measures of economic adjustment assistance as provided in Article 151, paragraph 10;

(o) (i) recommend to the Assembly rules, regulations and procedures on the equitable sharing of financial and other economic benefits derived from activities in the Area and the payments and contributions made pursuant to Article 82, taking into particular consideration the interests and needs of the developing States and peoples who have not attained full independence or other self-governing status;

(ii) adopt and apply provisionally, pending approval by the Assembly, the rules, regulations and procedures of the Authority, and any amendments thereto, taking into account the recommendations of the Legal and Technical Commission or other subordinate organ concerned. These rules, regulations and procedures shall relate to prospecting, exploration and exploitation in the Area and the financial management and internal administration of the Authority. Priority shall be given to the adoption of rules, regulations and procedures for the exploration for and exploitation of polymetallic nodules. Rules, regulations and procedures for the exploration for and exploitation of any resource other than polymetallic nodules shall be adopted within three years from the date of a request to the Authority by any of its members to adopt such rules, regulations and procedures in respect of such resource. All rules, regulations and procedures shall remain in effect on a provisional basis until approved by the Assembly or until amended by the Council in the light of any views expressed by the Assembly;

(p) review the collection of all payments to be made by or to the Authority in connection with operations pursuant to this Part;
(q) make the selection from among applicants for production authorizations pursuant to Annex III, Article 7, where such selection is required by that provision;
(r) submit the proposed annual budget of the Authority to the Assembly for its approval;
(s) make recommendations to the Assembly concerning policies on any question or matter within the competence of the Authority;
(t) make recommendations to the Assembly concerning suspension of the exercise of the rights and privileges of membership pursuant to Article 185;
(u) institute proceedings on behalf of the Authority before the Seabed Disputes Chamber in cases of non-compliance;
(v) notify the Assembly upon a decision by the Seabed Disputes Chamber in proceedings instituted under subparagraph (u), and make any recommendations which it may find appropriate with respect to measures to be taken;
(w) issue emergency orders, which may include orders for the suspension or adjustment of operations, to prevent serious harm to the marine environment arising out of activities in the Area;
(x) disapprove areas for exploitation by contractors or the Enterprise in cases where substantial evidence indicates the risk of serious harm to the marine environment;
(y) establish a subsidiary organ for the elaboration of draft financial rules, regulations and procedures relating to:
 (i) financial management in accordance with Article s 171 to 175; and
 (ii) financial arrangements in accordance with Annex III, Article 13 and Article 17, paragraph 1(c);
(z) establish appropriate mechanisms for directing and supervising a staff of inspectors who shall inspect activities in the Area to determine whether this Part, the rules, regulations and procedures of the Authority, and the terms and conditions of any contract with the Authority are being complied with.

Article 163
Organs of the Council

1. There are hereby established the following organs of the Council:
(a) an Economic Planning Commission;
(b) a Legal and Technical Commission.

2. Each Commission shall be composed of 15 members, elected by the Council from among the candidates nominated by the States Parties. However, if necessary, the Council may decide to increase the size of either Commission having due regard to economy and efficiency.

3. Members of a Commission shall have appropriate qualifications in the area of competence of that Commission. States Parties shall nominate candidates of the highest standards of competence and integrity with qualifications in relevant fields so as to ensure the effective exercise of the functions of the Commissions.

4. In the election of members of the Commissions, due account shall be taken of the need for equitable geographical distribution and the representation of special interests.

5. No State Party may nominate more than one candidate for the same Commission. No person shall be elected to serve on more than one Commission.

6. Members of the Commissions shall hold office for a term of five years. They shall be eligible for re-election for a further term.

7. In the event of the death, incapacity or resignation of a member of a Commission prior to the expiration of the term of office, the Council shall elect for the remainder of the term, a member from the same geographical region or area of interest.

8. Members of Commissions shall have no financial interest in any activity relating to exploration and exploitation in the Area. Subject to their responsibilities to the Commissions upon which they serve, they shall not disclose, even after the termination of their functions, any industrial secret, proprietary data which are transferred to the Authority in accordance with Annex III, Article 14, or any other confidential information coming to their knowledge by reason of their duties for the Authority.

9. Each Commission shall exercise its functions in accordance with such guidelines and directives as the Council may adopt.

10. Each Commission shall formulate and submit to the Council for approval such rules and regulations as may be necessary for the efficient conduct of the Commission's functions.

11. The decision-making procedures of the Commissions shall be established by the rules, regulations and procedures of the Authority. Recommendations to the Council shall, where necessary, be accompanied by a summary on the divergencies of opinion in the Commission.

12. Each Commission shall normally function at the seat of the Authority and shall meet as often as is required for the efficient exercise of its functions.

13. In the exercise of its functions, each Commission may, where appropriate, consult another commission, any competent organ of the United Nations or of its specialized agencies or any international organizations with competence in the subject-matter of such consultation.

Article 164
The Economic Planning Commission

1. Members of the Economic Planning Commission shall have appropriate qualifications such as those relevant to mining, management of mineral resource activities, international trade or international economics. The Council shall endeavour to ensure that the membership of the Commission reflects all appropriate qualifications. The Commission shall include at least two members from developing States whose exports of the categories of minerals to be derived from the Area have a substantial bearing upon their economies.

2. The Commission shall:
(a) propose, upon the request of the Council, measures to implement decisions relating to activities in the Area taken in accordance with this Convention;

(b) review the trends of and the factors affecting supply, demand and prices of minerals which may be derived from the Area, bearing in mind the interests of both importing and exporting countries, and in particular of the developing States among them;
(c) examine any situation likely to lead to the adverse effects referred to in Article 150, subparagraph (h), brought to its attention by the State Party or States Parties concerned, and make appropriate recommendations to the Council;
(d) propose to the Council for submission to the Assembly, as provided in Article 151, paragraph 10, a system of compensation or other measures of economic adjustment assistance for developing States which suffer adverse effects caused by activities in the Area. The Commission shall make the recommendations to the Council that are necessary for the application of the system or other measures adopted by the Assembly in specific cases.

Article 165
The Legal and Technical Commission

1. Members of the Legal and Technical Commission shall have appropriate qualifications such as those relevant to exploration for and exploitation and processing of mineral resources, oceanology, protection of the marine environment, or economic or legal matters relating to ocean mining and related fields of expertise. The Council shall endeavour to ensure that the membership of the Commission reflects all appropriate qualifications.
2. The Commission shall:
   (a) make recommendations with regard to the exercise of the Authority's functions upon the request of the Council;
   (b) review formal written plans of work for activities in the Area in accordance with Article 153, paragraph 3, and submit appropriate recommendations to the Council. The Commission shall base its recommendations solely on the grounds stated in Annex III and shall report fully thereon to the Council;
   (c) supervise, upon the request of the Council, activities in the Area, where appropriate, in consultation and collaboration with any entity carrying out such activities or State or States concerned and report to the Council;
   (d) prepare assessments of the environmental implications of activities in the Area;
   (e) make recommendations to the Council on the protection of the marine environment, taking into account the views of recognized experts in that field;
   (f) formulate and submit to the Council the rules, regulations and procedures referred to in Article 162, paragraph 2(o), taking into account all relevant factors including assessments of the environmental implications of activities in the Area;
   (g) keep such rules, regulations and procedures under review and recommend to the Council from time to time such amendments thereto as it may deem necessary or desirable;
   (h) make recommendations to the Council regarding the establishment of a monitoring programme to observe, measure, evaluate and analyse, by recognized scientific methods, on a regular basis, the risks or effects of pollution of the marine environment resulting from activities in the Area, ensure that existing regulations are adequate and are complied with and coordinate the implementation of the monitoring programme approved by the Council;

(i) recommend to the Council that proceedings be instituted on behalf of the Authority before the Seabed Disputes Chamber, in accordance with this Part and the relevant Annexes taking into account particularly Article 187;

(j) make recommendations to the Council with respect to measures to be taken, upon a decision by the Seabed Disputes Chamber in proceedings instituted in accordance with subparagraph (i);

(k) make recommendations to the Council to issue emergency orders, which may include orders for the suspension or adjustment of operations, to prevent serious harm to the marine environment arising out of activities in the Area. Such recommendations shall be taken up by the Council on a priority basis;

(l) make recommendations to the Council to disapprove areas for exploitation by contractors or the Enterprise in cases where substantial evidence indicates the risk of serious harm to the marine environment;

(m) make recommendations to the Council regarding the direction and supervision of a staff of inspectors who shall inspect activities in the Area to determine whether the provisions of this Part, the rules, regulations and procedures of the Authority, and the terms and conditions of any contract with the Authority are being complied with;

(n) calculate the production ceiling and issue production authorizations on behalf of the Authority pursuant to Article 151, paragraphs 2 to 7, following any necessary selection among applicants for production authorizations by the Council in accordance with Annex III, Article 7.

3. The members of the Commission shall, upon request by any State Party or other party concerned, be accompanied by a representative of such State or other party concerned when carrying out their function of supervision and inspection.

SUBSECTION D. THE SECRETARIAT

Article 166
The Secretariat

1. The Secretariat of the Authority shall comprise a Secretary-General and such staff as the Authority may require.

2. The Secretary-General shall be elected for four years by the Assembly from among the candidates proposed by the Council and may be re-elected.

3. The Secretary-General shall be the chief administrative officer of the Authority, and shall act in that capacity in all meetings of the Assembly, of the Council and of any subsidiary organ, and shall perform such other administrative functions as are entrusted to the Secretary-General by these organs.

4. The Secretary-General shall make an annual report to the Assembly on the work of the Authority.

Article 167
The staff of the Authority

1. The staff of the Authority shall consist of such qualified scientific and technical and other personnel as may be required to fulfil the administrative functions of the Authority.

2. The paramount consideration in the recruitment and employment of the staff and in the determination of their conditions of service shall be the necessity of securing the highest standards of efficiency, competence and integrity. Subject to this consideration, due regard shall be paid to the importance of recruiting the staff on as wide a geographical basis as possible.

3. The staff shall be appointed by the Secretary-General. The terms and conditions on which they shall be appointed, remunerated and dismissed shall be in accordance with the rules, regulations and procedures of the Authority.

Article 168
International character of the Secretariat

1. In the performance of their duties the Secretary-General and the staff shall not seek or receive instructions from any government or from any other source external to the Authority. They shall refrain from any action which might reflect on their position as international officials responsible only to the Authority. Each State Party undertakes to respect the exclusively international character of the responsibilities of the Secretary-General and the staff and not to seek to influence them in the discharge of their responsibilities. Any violation of responsibilities by a staff member shall be submitted to the appropriate administrative tribunal as provided in the rules, regulations and procedures of the Authority.

2. The Secretary-General and the staff shall have no financial interest in any activity relating to exploration and exploitation in the Area. Subject to their responsibilities to the Authority, they shall not disclose, even after the termination of their functions, any industrial secret, proprietary data which are transferred to the Authority in accordance with Annex III, Article 14, or any other confidential information coming to their knowledge by reason of their employment with the Authority.

3. Violations of the obligations of a staff member of the Authority set forth in paragraph 2 shall, on the request of a State Party affected by such violation, or a natural or juridical person, sponsored by a State Party as provided in Article 153, paragraph 2(b), and affected by such violation, be submitted by the Authority against the staff member concerned to a tribunal designated by the rules, regulations and procedures of the Authority. The Party affected shall have the right to take part in the proceedings. If the tribunal so recommends, the Secretary-General shall dismiss the staff member concerned.

4. The rules, regulations and procedures of the Authority shall contain such provisions as are necessary to implement this Article .

Article 169
Consultation and cooperation with international
and non-governmental organizations

1. The Secretary-General shall, on matters within the competence of the Authority, make suitable arrangements, with the approval of the Council, for consultation and cooperation with international and non-governmental organizations recognized by the Economic and Social Council of the United Nations.

2. Any organization with which the Secretary-General has entered into an arrangement under paragraph 1 may designate representatives to attend meetings of the organs of the Authority as observers in accordance with the rules of procedure of these organs. Procedures shall be established for obtaining the views of such organizations in appropriate cases.

3. The Secretary-General may distribute to States Parties written reports submitted by the non-governmental organizations referred to in paragraph 1 on subjects in which they have special competence and which are related to the work of the Authority.

SUBSECTION E. THE ENTERPRISE

Article 170
The Enterprise

1. The Enterprise shall be the organ of the Authority which shall carry out activities in the Area directly, pursuant to Article 153, paragraph 2(a), as well as the transporting, processing and marketing of minerals recovered from the Area.

2. The Enterprise shall, within the framework of the international legal personality of the Authority, have such legal capacity as is provided for in the Statute set forth in Annex IV. The Enterprise shall act in accordance with this Convention and the rules, regulations and procedures of the Authority, as well as the general policies established by the Assembly, and shall be subject to the directives and control of the Council.

3. The Enterprise shall have its principal place of business at the seat of the Authority.

4. The Enterprise shall, in accordance with Article 173, paragraph 2, and Annex IV, Article 11, be provided with such funds as it may require to carry out its functions, and shall receive technology as provided in Article 144 and other relevant provisions of this Convention.

SUBSECTION F. FINANCIAL ARRANGEMENTS OF THE AUTHORITY

Article 171
Funds of the Authority

The funds of the Authority shall include:
 (a) assessed contributions made by members of the Authority in accordance with Article 160, paragraph 2(e);
 (b) funds received by the Authority pursuant to Annex III, Article 13, in connection with activities in the Area;
 (c) funds transferred from the Enterprise in accordance with Annex IV, Article 10;
 (d) funds borrowed pursuant to Article 174;
 (e) voluntary contributions made by members or other entities; and
 (f) payments to a compensation fund, in accordance with Article 151, paragraph 10, whose sources are to be recommended by the Economic Planning Commission.

Article 172
Annual budget of the Authority

The Secretary-General shall draft the proposed annual budget of the Authority and submit it to the Council. The Council shall consider the proposed annual budget and submit it to the Assembly, together with any recommendations thereon. The Assembly shall consider and approve the proposed annual budget in accordance with Article 160, paragraph 2(h).

Article 173
Expenses of the Authority

1. The contributions referred to in Article 171, subparagraph (a), shall be paid into a special account to meet the administrative expenses of the Authority until the Authority has sufficient funds from other sources to meet those expenses.

2. The administrative expenses of the Authority shall be a first call upon the funds of the Authority. Except for the assessed contributions referred to in Article 171, subparagraph (a), the funds which remain after payment of administrative expenses may, *inter alia*:
   (a) be shared in accordance with Article 140 and Article 160, paragraph 2(g);
   (b) be used to provide the Enterprise with funds in accordance with Article 170, paragraph 4;
   (c) be used to compensate developing States in accordance with Article 151, paragraph 10, and Article 160, paragraph 2(l).

Article 174
Borrowing power of the Authority

1. The Authority shall have the power to borrow funds.
2. The Assembly shall prescribe the limits on the borrowing power of the Authority in the financial regulations adopted pursuant to Article 160, paragraph 2(f).
3. The Council shall exercise the borrowing power of the Authority.
4. States Parties shall not be liable for the debts of the Authority.

Article 175
Annual audit

The records, books and accounts of the Authority, including its annual financial statements, shall be audited annually by an independent auditor appointed by the Assembly.

SUBSECTION G. LEGAL STATUS, PRIVILEGES AND IMMUNITIES

Article 176
Legal status

The Authority shall have international legal personality and such legal capacity as may be necessary for the exercise of its functions and the fulfilment of its purposes.

Article 177
Privileges and immunities

To enable the Authority to exercise its functions, it shall enjoy in the territory of each State Party the privileges and immunities set forth in this subsection. The privileges and immunities relating to the Enterprise shall be those set forth in Annex IV, Article 13.

Article 178
Immunity from legal process

The Authority, its property and assets, shall enjoy immunity from legal process except to the extent that the Authority expressly waives this immunity in a particular case.

Article 179
Immunity from search and any form of seizure

The property and assets of the Authority, wherever located and by whomsoever held, shall be immune from search, requisition, confiscation, expropriation or any other form of seizure by executive or legislative action.

Article 180
Exemption from restrictions, regulations, controls and moratoria

The property and assets of the Authority shall be exempt from restrictions, regulations, controls and moratoria of any nature.

Article 181
Archives and official communications of the Authority

1. The archives of the Authority, wherever located, shall be inviolable.
2. Proprietary data, industrial secrets or similar information and personnel records shall not be placed in archives which are open to public inspection.
3. With regard to its official communi-cations, the Authority shall be accorded by each State Party treatment no less favourable than that accorded by that State to other international organizations.

Article 182
Privileges and immunities of certain persons connected with the Authority

Representatives of States Parties attending meetings of the Assembly, the Council or organs of the Assembly or the Council, and the Secretary-General and staff of the Authority, shall enjoy in the territory of each State Party:
  (a) immunity from legal process with respect to acts performed by them in the exercise of their functions, except to the extent that the State which they represent or the Authority, as appropriate, expressly waives this immunity in a particular case;
  (b) if they are not nationals of that State Party, the same exemptions from immigration restrictions, alien registration requirements and national service obligations, the same facilities as regards exchange restrictions and the same treatment in respect of travelling facilities as are accorded by that State to the representatives, officials and employees of comparable rank of other States Parties.

Article 183
Exemption from taxes and customs duties

1. Within the scope of its official activities, the Authority, its assets and property, its income, and its operations and transactions, authorized by this Convention, shall be exempt from all direct taxation and goods imported or exported for its official use shall be exempt from all customs duties. The Authority shall not claim exemption from taxes which are no more than charges for services rendered.

2. When purchases of goods or services of substantial value necessary for the official activities of the Authority are made by or on behalf of the Authority, and when the price of such goods or services includes taxes or duties, appropriate measures shall, to the extent practicable, be taken by States Parties to grant exemption from such taxes or duties or provide for their reimbursement. Goods imported or purchased under an exemption provided for in this Article shall not be sold or otherwise disposed of in the territory of the State Party which granted the exemption, except under conditions agreed with that State Party.

3. No tax shall be levied by States Parties on or in respect of salaries and emoluments paid or any other form of payment made by the Authority to the Secretary-General and staff of the Authority, as well as experts performing missions for the Authority, who are not their nationals.

SUBSECTION H. SUSPENSION OF THE EXERCISE OF RIGHTS AND PRIVILEGES OF MEMBERS

Article 184
Suspension of the exercise of voting rights

A State Party which is in arrears in the payment of its financial contributions to the Authority shall have no vote if the amount of its arrears equals or exceeds the amount of the contributions due from it for the preceding two full years. The Assembly may, nevertheless, permit such a member to vote if it is satisfied that the failure to pay is due to conditions beyond the control of the member.

Article 185
Suspension of exercise of rights and privileges of membership

1. A State Party which has grossly and persistently violated the provisions of this Part may be suspended from the exercise of the rights and privileges of membership by the Assembly upon the recommendation of the Council.

2. No action may be taken under paragraph 1 until the Seabed Disputes Chamber has found that a State Party has grossly and persistently violated the provisions of this Part.

SECTION 5. SETTLEMENT OF DISPUTES AND ADVISORY OPINIONS

Article 186
Seabed Disputes Chamber of the International Tribunal for the Law of the Sea

The establishment of the Seabed Disputes Chamber and the manner in which it shall exercise its jurisdiction shall be governed by the provisions of this section, of Part XV and of Annex VI.

Article 187
Jurisdiction of the Seabed Disputes Chamber

The Seabed Disputes Chamber shall have jurisdiction under this Part and the Annexes relating thereto in disputes with respect to activities in the Area falling within the following categories:
  (a) disputes between States Parties concerning the interpretation or application of this Part and the Annexes relating thereto;
  (b) disputes between a State Party and the Authority concerning:
     (i) acts or omissions of the Authority or of a State Party alleged to be in violation of this Part or the Annexes relating thereto or of rules, regulations and procedures of the Authority adopted in accordance therewith; or
     (ii) acts of the Authority alleged to be in excess of jurisdiction or a misuse of power;
  (c) disputes between parties to a contract,
     being States Parties, the Authority or the Enterprise, state enterprises and natural or juridical persons referred to in Article 153, paragraph 2(b), concerning:
     (i) the interpretation or application of a relevant contract or a plan of work; or
     (ii) acts or omissions of a party to the contract relating to activities in the Area and directed to the other party or directly affecting its legitimate interests;
  (d) disputes between the Authority and a prospective contractor who has been sponsored by a State as provided in Article 153, paragraph 2(b), and has duly fulfilled the conditions referred to in Annex III, Article 4, paragraph 6, and Article 13, paragraph 2, concerning the refusal of a contract or a legal issue arising in the negotiation of the contract;
  (e) disputes between the Authority and a State Party, a state enterprise or a natural or juridical person sponsored by a State Party as provided for in Article 153, paragraph 2(b), where it is alleged that the Authority has incurred liability as provided in Annex III, Article 22;
  (f) any other disputes for which the jurisdiction of the Chamber is specifically provided in this Convention.

Article 188
Submission of disputes to a special chamber of the International Tribunal for the Law of the Sea or an ad hoc chamber of the Seabed Disputes Chamber or to binding commercial arbitration

1. Disputes between States Parties referred to in Article 187, subparagraph (a), may be submitted:
  (a) at the request of the parties to the dispute, to a special chamber of the International Tribunal for the Law of the Sea to be formed in accordance with Annex VI, Article s 15 and 17; or
  (b) at the request of any party to the dispute, to an *ad hoc* chamber of the Seabed Disputes Chamber to be formed in accordance with Annex VI, Article 36.
2. (a) Disputes concerning the interpretation or application of a contract referred to in Article 187, subparagraph (c)(i), shall be submitted, at the request of any party to the dispute, to binding commercial arbitration, unless the parties otherwise agree. A commercial arbitral tribunal to which the dispute is submitted shall have no jurisdiction to decide any question of interpretation of this Convention. When the dispute also involves a question of the interpretation of Part XI and the Annexes relating thereto, with respect to activities in the Area, that question shall be referred to the Seabed Disputes Chamber for a ruling.

(b) If, at the commencement of or in the course of such arbitration, the arbitral tribunal determines, either at the request of any party to the dispute or *proprio motu*, that its decision depends upon a ruling of the Seabed Disputes Chamber, the arbitral tribunal shall refer such question to the Seabed Disputes Chamber for such ruling. The arbitral tribunal shall then proceed to render its award in conformity with the ruling of the Seabed Disputes Chamber.

(c) In the absence of a provision in the contract on the arbitration procedure to be applied in the dispute, the arbitration shall be conducted in accordance with the UNCITRAL Arbitration Rules or such other arbitration rules as may be prescribed in the rules, regulations and procedures of the Authority, unless the parties to the dispute otherwise agree.

Article 189
Limitation on jurisdiction with regard to decisions of the Authority

The Seabed Disputes Chamber shall have no jurisdiction with regard to the exercise by the Authority of its discretionary powers in accordance with this Part; in no case shall it substitute its discretion for that of the Authority. Without prejudice to Article 191, in exercising its jurisdiction pursuant to Article 187, the Seabed Disputes Chamber shall not pronounce itself on the question of whether any rules, regulations and procedures of the Authority are in conformity with this Convention, nor declare invalid any such rules, regulations and procedures. Its jurisdiction in this regard shall be confined to deciding claims that the application of any rules, regulations and procedures of the Authority in individual cases would be in conflict with the contractual obligations of the parties to the dispute or their obligations under this Convention, claims concerning excess of jurisdiction or misuse of power, and to claims for damages to be paid or other remedy to be given to the party concerned for the failure of the other party to comply with its contractual obligations or its obligations under this Convention.

Article 190
Participation and appearance of sponsoring States Parties in proceedings

1. If a natural or juridical person is a party to a dispute referred to in Article 187, the sponsoring State shall be given notice thereof and shall have the right to participate in the proceedings by submitting written or oral statements.

2. If an action is brought against a State Party by a natural or juridical person sponsored by another State Party in a dispute referred to in Article 187, subparagraph (c), the respondent State may request the State sponsoring that person to appear in the proceedings on behalf of that person. Failing such appearance, the respondent State may arrange to be represented by a juridical person of its nationality.

Article 191
Advisory opinions

The Seabed Disputes Chamber shall give advisory opinions at the request of the Assembly or the Council on legal questions arising within the scope of their activities. Such opinions shall be given as a matter of urgency.

PART XII
PROTECTION AND PRESERVATION OF THE MARINE ENVIRONMENT

SECTION 1. GENERAL PROVISIONS

Article 192
General obligation

States have the obligation to protect and preserve the marine environment.

Article 193
Sovereign right of States to exploit their natural resources

States have the sovereign right to exploit their natural resources pursuant to their environmental policies and in accordance with their duty to protect and preserve the marine environment.

Article 194
Measures to prevent, reduce and control
pollution of the marine environment

1. States shall take, individually or jointly as appropriate, all measures consistent with this Convention that are necessary to prevent, reduce and control pollution of the marine environment from any source, using for this purpose the best practicable means at their disposal and in accordance with their capabilities, and they shall endeavour to harmonize their policies in this connection.
2. States shall take all measures necessary to ensure that activities under their jurisdiction or control are so conducted as not to cause damage by pollution to other States and their environment, and that pollution arising from incidents or activities under their jurisdiction or control does not spread beyond the areas where they exercise sovereign rights in accordance with this Convention.
3. The measures taken pursuant to this Part shall deal with all sources of pollution of the marine environment. These measures shall include, *inter alia*, those designed to minimize to the fullest possible extent:
    (a) the release of toxic, harmful or noxious substances, especially those which are persistent, from land-based sources, from or through the atmosphere or by dumping;
    (b) pollution from vessels, in particular measures for preventing accidents and dealing with emergencies, ensuring the safety of operations at sea, preventing intentional and unintentional discharges, and regulating the design, construction, equipment, operation and manning of vessels;
    (c) pollution from installations and devices used in exploration or exploitation of the natural resources of the seabed and subsoil, in particular measures for preventing accidents and dealing with emergencies, ensuring the safety of operations at sea, and regulating the design, construction, equipment, operation and manning of such installations or devices;
    (d) pollution from other installations and devices operating in the marine environment, in particular measures for preventing accidents and dealing with emergencies, ensuring

the safety of operations at sea, and regulating the design, construction, equipment, operation and manning of such installations or devices.

4. In taking measures to prevent, reduce or control pollution of the marine environment, States shall refrain from unjustifiable interference with activities carried out by other States in the exercise of their rights and in pursuance of their duties in conformity with this Convention.

5. The measures taken in accordance with this Part shall include those necessary to protect and preserve rare or fragile ecosystems as well as the habitat of depleted, threatened or endangered species and other forms of marine life.

Article 195
Duty not to transfer damage or hazards
or transform one type of pollution into another

In taking measures to prevent, reduce and control pollution of the marine environment, States shall act so as not to transfer, directly or indirectly, damage or hazards from one area to another or transform one type of pollution into another.

Article 196
Use of technologies or introduction of alien or new species

1. States shall take all measures necessary to prevent, reduce and control pollution of the marine environment resulting from the use of technologies under their jurisdiction or control, or the intentional or accidental introduction of species, alien or new, to a particular part of the marine environment, which may cause significant and harmful changes thereto.

2. This Article does not affect the application of this Convention regarding the prevention, reduction and control of pollution of the marine environment.

SECTION 2. GLOBAL AND REGIONAL COOPERATION

Article 197
Cooperation on a global or regional basis

States shall cooperate on a global basis and, as appropriate, on a regional basis, directly or through competent international organizations, in formulating and elaborating international rules, standards and recommended practices and procedures consistent with this Convention, for the protection and preservation of the marine environment, taking into account characteristic regional features.

Article 198
Notification of imminent or actual damage

When a State becomes aware of cases in which the marine environment is in imminent danger of being damaged or has been damaged by pollution, it shall immediately notify other States it deems likely to be affected by such damage, as well as the competent international organizations.

Article 199
Contingency plans against pollution

In the cases referred to in Article 198, States in the area affected, in accordance with their capabilities, and the competent international organizations shall cooperate, to the extent possible, in eliminating the effects of pollution and preventing or minimizing the damage. To this end, States shall jointly develop and promote contingency plans for responding to pollution incidents in the marine environment.

Article 200
Studies, research programmes and exchange of information and data

States shall cooperate, directly or through competent international organizations, for the purpose of promoting studies, undertaking programmes of scientific research and encouraging the exchange of information and data acquired about pollution of the marine environment. They shall endeavour to participate actively in regional and global programmes to acquire knowledge for the assessment of the nature and extent of pollution, exposure to it, and its pathways, risks and remedies.

Article 201
Scientific criteria for regulations

In the light of the information and data acquired pursuant to Article 200, States shall cooperate, directly or through competent international organizations, in establishing appropriate scientific criteria for the formulation and elaboration of rules, standards and recommended practices and procedures for the prevention, reduction and control of pollution of the marine environment.

SECTION 3. TECHNICAL ASSISTANCE

Article 202
Scientific and technical assistance to developing States

States shall, directly or through competent international organizations:
 (a) promote programmes of scientific, educational, technical and other assistance to developing States for the protection and preservation of the marine environment and the prevention, reduction and control of marine pollution. Such assistance shall include, *inter alia*:
   (i) training of their scientific and technical personnel;
   (ii) facilitating their participation in relevant international programmes;
   (iii) supplying them with necessary equipment and facilities;
   (iv) enhancing their capacity to manufacture such equipment;
   (v) advice on and developing facilities for research, monitoring, educational and other programmes;
 (b) provide appropriate assistance, especially to developing States, for the minimization of the effects of major incidents which may cause serious pollution of the marine environment;
 (c) provide appropriate assistance, especially to developing States, concerning the preparation of environmental assessments.

Article 203
Preferential treatment for developing States

Developing States shall, for the purposes of prevention, reduction and control of pollution of the marine environment or minimization of its effects, be granted preference by international organizations in:
 (a) the allocation of appropriate funds and technical assistance; and

(b) the utilization of their specialized services.

SECTION 4. MONITORING AND ENVIRONMENTAL ASSESSMENT

Article 204
Monitoring of the risks or effects of pollution

1. States shall, consistent with the rights of other States, endeavour, as far as practicable, directly or through the competent international organizations, to observe, measure, evaluate and analyse, by recognized scientific methods, the risks or effects of pollution of the marine environment.
2. In particular, States shall keep under surveillance the effects of any activities which they permit or in which they engage in order to determine whether these activities are likely to pollute the marine environment.

Article 205
Publication of reports

States shall publish reports of the results obtained pursuant to Article 204 or provide such reports at appropriate intervals to the competent international organizations, which should make them available to all States.

Article 206
Assessment of potential effects of activities

When States have reasonable grounds for believing that planned activities under their jurisdiction or control may cause substantial pollution of or significant and harmful changes to the marine environment, they shall, as far as practicable, assess the potential effects of such activities on the marine environment and shall communicate reports of the results of such assessments in the manner provided in Article 205.

SECTION 5. INTERNATIONAL RULES AND NATIONAL LEGISLATION TO PREVENT, REDUCE AND CONTROL POLLUTION OF THE MARINE ENVIRONMENT

Article 207
Pollution from land-based sources

1. States shall adopt laws and regulations to prevent, reduce and control pollution of the marine environment from land-based sources, including rivers, estuaries, pipelines and outfall structures, taking into account internationally agreed rules, standards and recommended practices and procedures.
2. States shall take other measures as may be necessary to prevent, reduce and control such pollution.
3. States shall endeavour to harmonize their policies in this connection at the appropriate regional level.
4. States, acting especially through competent international organizations or diplomatic conference, shall endeavour to establish global and regional rules, standards and recommended

practices and procedures to prevent, reduce and control pollution of the marine environment from land-based sources, taking into account characteristic regional features, the economic capacity of developing States and their need for economic development. Such rules, standards and recommended practices and procedures shall be re-examined from time to time as necessary.

5. Laws, regulations, measures, rules, standards and recommended practices and procedures referred to in paragraphs 1, 2 and 4 shall include those designed to minimize, to the fullest extent possible, the release of toxic, harmful or noxious substances, especially those which are persistent, into the marine environment.

Article 208
Pollution from seabed activities subject to national jurisdiction

1 Coastal States shall adopt laws and regulations to prevent, reduce and control pollution of the marine environment arising from or in connection with seabed activities subject to their jurisdiction and from artificial islands, installations and structures under their jurisdiction, pursuant to Article s 60 and 80.

2. States shall take other measures as may be necessary to prevent, reduce and control such pollution.

3. Such laws, regulations and measures shall be no less effective than international rules, standards and recommended practices and procedures.

4. States shall endeavour to harmonize their policies in this connection at the appropriate regional level.

5. States, acting especially through competent international organizations or diplomatic conference, shall establish global and regional rules, standards and recommended practices and procedures to prevent, reduce and control pollution of the marine environment referred to in paragraph l. Such rules, standards and recommended practices and procedures shall be re-examined from time to time as necessary.

Article 209
Pollution from activities in the Area

1. International rules, regulations and procedures shall be established in accordance with Part XI to prevent, reduce and control pollution of the marine environment from activities in the Area. Such rules, regulations and procedures shall be re-examined from time to time as necessary.

2. Subject to the relevant provisions of this section, States shall adopt laws and regulations to prevent, reduce and control pollution of the marine environment from activities in the Area undertaken by vessels, installations, structures and other devices flying their flag or of their registry or operating under their authority, as the case may be. The requirements of such laws and regulations shall be no less effective than the international rules, regulations and procedures referred to in paragraph 1.

Article 210
Pollution by dumping

1. States shall adopt laws and regulations to prevent, reduce and control pollution of the marine environment by dumping.

2. States shall take other measures as may be necessary to prevent, reduce and control such pollution.

3. Such laws, regulations and measures shall ensure that dumping is not carried out without the permission of the competent authorities of States.

4. States, acting especially through competent international organizations or diplomatic conference, shall endeavour to establish global and regional rules, standards and

recommended practices and procedures to prevent, reduce and control such pollution. Such rules, standards and recommended practices and procedures shall be re-examined from time to time as necessary.

5. Dumping within the territorial sea and the exclusive economic zone or onto the continental shelf shall not be carried out without the express prior approval of the coastal State, which has the right to permit, regulate and control such dumping after due consideration of the matter with other States which by reason of their geographical situation may be adversely affected thereby.

6. National laws, regulations and measures shall be no less effective in preventing, reducing and controlling such pollution than the global rules and standards.

Article 211
Pollution from vessels

1. States, acting through the competent international organization or general diplomatic conference, shall establish international rules and standards to prevent, reduce and control pollution of the marine environment from vessels and promote the adoption, in the same manner, wherever appropriate, of routeing systems designed to minimize the threat of accidents which might cause pollution of the marine environment, including the coastline, and pollution damage to the related interests of coastal States. Such rules and standards shall, in the same manner, be re-examined from time to time as necessary.

2. States shall adopt laws and regulations for the prevention, reduction and control of pollution of the marine environment from vessels flying their flag or of their registry. Such laws and regulations shall at least have the same effect as that of generally accepted international rules and standards established through the competent international organization or general diplomatic conference.

3. States which establish particular requirements for the prevention, reduction and control of pollution of the marine environment as a condition for the entry of foreign vessels into their ports or internal waters or for a call at their off-shore terminals shall give due publicity to such requirements and shall communicate them to the competent international organization. Whenever such requirements are established in identical form by two or more coastal States in an endeavour to harmonize policy, the communication shall indicate which States are participating in such cooperative arrangements. Every State shall require the master of a vessel flying its flag or of its registry, when navigating within the territorial sea of a State participating in such cooperative arrangements, to furnish, upon the request of that State, information as to whether it is proceeding to a State of the same region participating in such cooperative arrangements and, if so, to indicate whether it complies with the port entry requirements of that State. This Article is without prejudice to the continued exercise by a vessel of its right of innocent passage or to the application of Article 25, paragraph 2.

4. Coastal States may, in the exercise of their sovereignty within their territorial sea, adopt laws and regulations for the prevention, reduction and control of marine pollution from foreign vessels, including vessels exercising the right of innocent passage. Such laws and regulations shall, in accordance with Part II, section 3, not hamper innocent passage of foreign vessels.

5. Coastal States, for the purpose of enforcement as provided for in section 6, may in respect of their exclusive economic zones adopt laws and regulations for the prevention, reduction and control of pollution from vessels conforming to and giving effect to generally accepted international rules and standards established through the competent international organization or general diplomatic conference.

6. (a) Where the international rules and standards referred to in paragraph 1 are inadequate to meet special circumstances and coastal States have reasonable grounds for believing that a particular, clearly defined area of their respective exclusive economic zones is an area where the adoption of special mandatory measures for the prevention of pollution from vessels is required for recognized technical reasons in relation to its oceanographical and ecological conditions, as well as its utilization or the protection of its resources and the particular character of its traffic, the coastal States, after appropriate consultations through the competent international organization with any other States concerned, may, for that area, direct a communication to that organization, submitting scientific and technical evidence in support and information on necessary reception facilities. Within 12 months after receiving such a communication, the organization shall determine whether the conditions in that area correspond to the requirements set out above. If the organization so determines, the coastal States may, for that area, adopt laws and regulations for the prevention, reduction and control of pollution from vessels implementing such international rules and standards or navigational practices as are made applicable, through the organization, for special areas. These laws and regulations shall not become applicable to foreign vessels until 15 months after the submission of the communication to the organization.

(b) The coastal States shall publish the limits of any such particular, clearly defined area.

(c) If the coastal States intend to adopt additional laws and regulations for the same area for the prevention, reduction and control of pollution from vessels, they shall, when submitting the aforesaid communication, at the same time notify the organization thereof. Such additional laws and regulations may relate to discharges or navigational practices but shall not require foreign vessels to observe design, construction, manning or equipment standards other than generally accepted international rules and standards; they shall become applicable to foreign vessels 15 months after the submission of the communication to the organization, provided that the organization agrees within 12 months after the submission of the communication.

7. The international rules and standards referred to in this Article should include *inter alia* those relating to prompt notification to coastal States, whose coastline or related interests may be affected by incidents, including maritime casualties, which involve discharges or probability of discharges.

Article 212
Pollution from or through the atmosphere

1. States shall adopt laws and regulations to prevent, reduce and control pollution of the marine environment from or through the atmosphere, applicable to the air space under their sovereignty and to vessels flying their flag or vessels or aircraft of their registry, taking into account internationally agreed rules, standards and recommended practices and procedures and the safety of air navigation.

2. States shall take other measures as may be necessary to prevent, reduce and control such pollution.

3. States, acting especially through competent international organizations or diplomatic conference, shall endeavour to establish global and regional rules, standards and recommended practices and procedures to prevent, reduce and control such pollution.

SECTION 6. ENFORCEMENT

Article 213
Enforcement with respect to pollution from land-based sources

States shall enforce their laws and regulations adopted in accordance with Article 207 and shall adopt laws and regulations and take other measures necessary to implement applicable international rules and standards established through competent international organizations or diplomatic conference to prevent, reduce and control pollution of the marine environment from land-based sources.

Article 214
Enforcement with respect to pollution from seabed activities

States shall enforce their laws and regulations adopted in accordance with Article 208 and shall adopt laws and regulations and take other measures necessary to implement applicable international rules and standards established through competent international organizations or diplomatic conference to prevent, reduce and control pollution of the marine environment arising from or in connection with seabed activities subject to their jurisdiction and from artificial islands, installations and structures under their jurisdiction, pursuant to Article s 60 and 80.

Article 215
Enforcement with respect to pollution from activities in the Area

Enforcement of international rules, regulations and procedures established in accordance with Part XI to prevent, reduce and control pollution of the marine environment from activities in the Area shall be governed by that Part.

Article 216
Enforcement with respect to pollution by dumping

1. Laws and regulations adopted in accordance with this Convention and applicable international rules and standards established through competent international organizations or diplomatic conference for the prevention, reduction and control of pollution of the marine environment by dumping shall be enforced:
    (a) by the coastal State with regard to dumping within its territorial sea or its exclusive economic zone or onto its continental shelf;
    (b) by the flag State with regard to vessels flying its flag or vessels or aircraft of its registry;
    (c) by any State with regard to acts of loading of wastes or other matter occurring within its territory or at its off-shore terminals.
2. No State shall be obliged by virtue of this Article to institute proceedings when another State has already instituted proceedings in accordance with this Article .

Article 217
Enforcement by flag States

1. States shall ensure compliance by vessels flying their flag or of their registry with applicable international rules and standards, established through the competent international organization or general diplomatic conference, and with their laws and

regulations adopted in accordance with this Convention for the prevention, reduction and control of pollution of the marine environment from vessels and shall accordingly adopt laws and regulations and take other measures necessary for their implementation. Flag States shall provide for the effective enforcement of such rules, standards, laws and regulations, irrespective of where a violation occurs.

2. States shall, in particular, take appropriate measures in order to ensure that vessels flying their flag or of their registry are prohibited from sailing, until they can proceed to sea in compliance with the requirements of the international rules and standards referred to in paragraph 1, including requirements in respect of design, construction, equipment and manning of vessels.

3. States shall ensure that vessels flying their flag or of their registry carry on board certificates required by and issued pursuant to international rules and standards referred to in paragraph 1. States shall ensure that vessels flying their flag are periodically inspected in order to verify that such certificates are in conformity with the actual condition of the vessels. These certificates shall be accepted by other States as evidence of the condition of the vessels and shall be regarded as having the same force as certificates issued by them, unless there are clear grounds for believing that the condition of the vessel does not correspond substantially with the particulars of the certificates.

4. If a vessel commits a violation of rules and standards established through the competent international organization or general diplomatic conference, the flag State, without prejudice to Article s 218, 220 and 228, shall provide for immediate investigation and where appropriate institute proceedings in respect of the alleged violation irrespective of where the violation occurred or where the pollution caused by such violation has occurred or has been spotted.

5. Flag States conducting an investigation of the violation may request the assistance of any other State whose cooperation could be useful in clarifying the circumstances of the case. States shall endeavour to meet appropriate requests of flag States.

6. States shall, at the written request of any State, investigate any violation alleged to have been committed by vessels flying their flag. If satisfied that sufficient evidence is available to enable proceedings to be brought in respect of the alleged violation, flag States shall without delay institute such proceedings in accordance with their laws.

7. Flag States shall promptly inform the requesting State and the competent international organization of the action taken and its outcome. Such information shall be available to all States.

8. Penalties provided for by the laws and regulations of States for vessels flying their flag shall be adequate in severity to discourage violations wherever they occur.

Article 218
Enforcement by port States

1. When a vessel is voluntarily within a port or at an off-shore terminal of a State, that State may undertake investigations and, where the evidence so warrants, institute proceedings in respect of any discharge from that vessel outside the internal waters, territorial sea or exclusive economic zone of that State in violation of applicable international rules and standards established through the competent international organization or general diplomatic conference.

2. No proceedings pursuant to paragraph 1 shall be instituted in respect of a discharge violation in the internal waters, territorial sea or exclusive economic zone of another State unless requested by that State, the flag State, or a State damaged or threatened by the discharge violation, or unless the violation has caused or is likely to cause pollution in the

internal waters, territorial sea or exclusive economic zone of the State instituting the proceedings.

3. When a vessel is voluntarily within a port or at an off-shore terminal of a State, that State shall, as far as practicable, comply with requests from any State for investigation of a discharge violation referred to in paragraph 1, believed to have occurred in, caused, or threatened damage to the internal waters, territorial sea or exclusive economic zone of the requesting State. It shall likewise, as far as practicable, comply with requests from the flag State for investigation of such a violation, irrespective of where the violation occurred.

4. The records of the investigation carried out by a port State pursuant to this Article shall be transmitted upon request to the flag State or to the coastal State. Any proceedings instituted by the port State on the basis of such an investigation may, subject to section 7, be suspended at the request of the coastal State when the violation has occurred within its internal waters, territorial sea or exclusive economic zone. The evidence and records of the case, together with any bond or other financial security posted with the authorities of the port State, shall in that event be transmitted to the coastal State. Such transmittal shall preclude the continuation of proceedings in the port State.

Article 219
Measures relating to seaworthiness of vessels to avoid pollution

Subject to section 7, States which, upon request or on their own initiative, have ascertained that a vessel within one of their ports or at one of their off-shore terminals is in violation of applicable international rules and standards relating to seaworthiness of vessels and thereby threatens damage to the marine environment shall, as far as practicable, take administrative measures to prevent the vessel from sailing. Such States may permit the vessel to proceed only to the nearest appropriate repair yard and, upon removal of the causes of the violation, shall permit the vessel to continue immediately.

Article 220
Enforcement by coastal States

1. When a vessel is voluntarily within a port or at an off-shore terminal of a State, that State may, subject to section 7, institute proceedings in respect of any violation of its laws and regulations adopted in accordance with this Convention or applicable international rules and standards for the prevention, reduction and control of pollution from vessels when the violation has occurred within the territorial sea or the exclusive economic zone of that State.

2. Where there are clear grounds for believing that a vessel navigating in the territorial sea of a State has, during its passage therein, violated laws and regulations of that State adopted in accordance with this Convention or applicable international rules and standards for the prevention, reduction and control of pollution from vessels, that State, without prejudice to the application of the relevant provisions of Part II, section 3, may undertake physical inspection of the vessel relating to the violation and may, where the evidence so warrants, institute proceedings, including detention of the vessel, in accordance with its laws, subject to the provisions of section 7.

3. Where there are clear grounds for believing that a vessel navigating in the exclusive economic zone or the territorial sea of a State has, in the exclusive economic zone, committed a violation of applicable international rules and standards for the prevention, reduction and control of pollution from vessels or laws and regulations of that State conforming and giving effect to such rules and standards, that State may require the vessel

to give information regarding its identity and port of registry, its last and its next port of call and other relevant information required to establish whether a violation has occurred.

4. States shall adopt laws and regulations and take other measures so that vessels flying their flag comply with requests for information pursuant to paragraph 3.

5. Where there are clear grounds for believing that a vessel navigating in the exclusive economic zone or the territorial sea of a State has, in the exclusive economic zone, committed a violation referred to in paragraph 3 resulting in a substantial discharge causing or threatening significant pollution of the marine environment, that State may undertake physical inspection of the vessel for matters relating to the violation if the vessel has refused to give information or if the information supplied by the vessel is manifestly at variance with the evident factual situation and if the circumstances of the case justify such inspection.

6. Where there is clear objective evidence that a vessel navigating in the exclusive economic zone or the territorial sea of a State has, in the exclusive economic zone, committed a violation referred to in paragraph 3 resulting in a discharge causing major damage or threat of major damage to the coastline or related interests of the coastal State, or to any resources of its territorial sea or exclusive economic zone, that State may, subject to section 7, provided that the evidence so warrants, institute proceedings, including detention of the vessel, in accordance with its laws.

7. Notwithstanding the provisions of paragraph 6, whenever appropriate procedures have been established, either through the competent international organization or as otherwise agreed, whereby compliance with requirements for bonding or other appropriate financial security has been assured, the coastal State if bound by such procedures shall allow the vessel to proceed.

8. The provisions of paragraphs 3, 4, 5, 6and 7 also apply in respect of national laws and regulations adopted pursuant to Article 211, paragraph 6.

Article 221
Measures to avoid pollution arising from maritime casualties

1. Nothing in this Part shall prejudice the right of States, pursuant to international law, both customary and conventional, to take and enforce measures beyond the territorial sea proportionate to the actual or threatened damage to protect their coastline or related interests, including fishing, from pollution or threat of pollution following upon a maritime casualty or acts relating to such a casualty, which may reasonably be expected to result in major harmful consequences.

2. For the purposes of this Article , "maritime casualty" means a collision of vessels, stranding or other incident of navigation, or other occurrence on board a vessel or external to it resulting in material damage or imminent threat of material damage to a vessel or cargo.

Article 222
Enforcement with respect to pollution from or through the atmosphere

States shall enforce, within the air space under their sovereignty or with regard to vessels flying their flag or vessels or aircraft of their registry, their laws and regulations adopted in accordance with Article 212, paragraph 1, and with other provisions of this Convention and shall adopt laws and regulations and take other measures necessary to implement applicable international rules and standards established through competent international organizations or diplomatic conference to prevent, reduce and control pollution of the marine environment from or through the atmosphere, in conformity with all relevant international rules and standards concerning the safety of air navigation.

SECTION 7. SAFEGUARDS

Article 223
Measures to facilitate proceedings

In proceedings instituted pursuant to this Part, States shall take measures to facilitate the hearing of witnesses and the admission of evidence submitted by authorities of another State, or by the competent international organization, and shall facilitate the attendance at such proceedings of official representatives of the competent international organization, the flag State and any State affected by pollution arising out of any violation. The official representatives attending such proceedings shall have such rights and duties as may be provided under national laws and regulations or international law.

Article 224
Exercise of powers of enforcement

The powers of enforcement against foreign vessels under this Part may only be exercised by officials or by warships, military aircraft, or other ships or aircraft clearly marked and identifiable as being on government service and authorized to that effect.

Article 225
*Duty to avoid adverse consequences
in the exercise of the powers of enforcement*

In the exercise under this Convention of their powers of enforcement against foreign vessels, States shall not endanger the safety of navigation or otherwise create any hazard to a vessel, or bring it to an unsafe port or anchorage, or expose the marine environment to an unreasonable risk.

Article 226
Investigation of foreign vessels

1. (a) States shall not delay a foreign vessel longer than is essential for purposes of the investigations provided for in Article s 216, 218 and 220. Any physical inspection of a foreign vessel shall be limited to an examination of such certificates, records or other documents as the vessel is required to carry by generally accepted international rules and standards or of any similar documents which it is carrying; further physical inspection of the vessel may be undertaken only after such an examination and only when:
    (i) there are clear grounds for believing that the condition of the vessel or its equipment does not correspond substantially with the particulars of those documents;
    (ii) the contents of such documents are not sufficient to confirm or verify a suspected violation; or
    (iii) the vessel is not carrying valid certificates and records.
  (b) If the investigation indicates a violation of applicable laws and regulations or international rules and standards for the protection and preservation of the marine environment,

release shall be made promptly subject to reasonable procedures such as bonding or other appropriate financial security.

(c) Without prejudice to applicable international rules and standards relating to the seaworthiness of vessels, the release of a vessel may, whenever it would present an unreasonable threat of damage to the marine environment, be refused or made conditional upon proceeding to the nearest appropriate repair yard. Where release has been refused or made conditional, the flag State of the vessel must be promptly notified, and may seek release of the vessel in accordance with Part XV.

2. States shall cooperate to develop procedures for the avoidance of unnecessary physical inspection of vessels at sea.

Article 227
Non-discrimination with respect to foreign vessels

In exercising their rights and performing their duties under this Part, States shall not discriminate in form or in fact against vessels of any other State.

Article 228
Suspension and restrictions on institution of proceedings

1. Proceedings to impose penalties in respect of any violation of applicable laws and regulations or international rules and standards relating to the prevention, reduction and control of pollution from vessels committed by a foreign vessel beyond the territorial sea of the State instituting proceedings shall be suspended upon the taking of proceedings to impose penalties in respect of corresponding charges by the flag State within six months of the date on which proceedings were first instituted, unless those proceedings relate to a case of major damage to the coastal State or the flag State in question has repeatedly disregarded its obligation to enforce effectively the applicable international rules and standards in respect of violations committed by its vessels. The flag State shall in due course make available to the State previously instituting proceedings a full dossier of the case and the records of the proceedings, whenever the flag State has requested the suspension of proceedings in accordance with this Article . When proceedings instituted by the flag State have been brought to a conclusion, the suspended proceedings shall be terminated. Upon payment of costs incurred in respect of such proceedings, any bond posted or other financial security provided in connection with the suspended proceedings shall be released by the coastal State.

2. Proceedings to impose penalties on foreign vessels shall not be instituted after the expiry of three years from the date on which the violation was committed, and shall not be taken by any State in the event of proceedings having been instituted by another State subject to the provisions set out in paragraph 1.

3. The provisions of this Article are without prejudice to the right of the flag State to take any measures, including proceedings to impose penalties, according to its laws irrespective of prior proceedings by another State.

Article 229
Institution of civil proceedings

Nothing in this Convention affects the institution of civil proceedings in respect of any claim for loss or damage resulting from pollution of the marine environment.

Article 230
Monetary penalties and the observance of recognized rights of the accused

1. Monetary penalties only may be imposed with respect to violations of national laws and regulations or applicable international rules and standards for the prevention, reduction and control of pollution of the marine environment, committed by foreign vessels beyond the territorial sea.
2. Monetary penalties only may be imposed with respect to violations of national laws and regulations or applicable international rules and standards for the prevention, reduction and control of pollution of the marine environment, committed by foreign vessels in the territorial sea, except in the case of a wilful and serious act of pollution in the territorial sea.
3. In the conduct of proceedings in respect of such violations committed by a foreign vessel which may result in the imposition of penalties, recognized rights of the accused shall be observed.

Article 231
Notification to the flag State and other States concerned

States shall promptly notify the flag State and any other State concerned of any measures taken pursuant to section 6 against foreign vessels, and shall submit to the flag State all official reports concerning such measures. However, with respect to violations committed in the territorial sea, the foregoing obligations of the coastal State apply only to such measures as are taken in proceedings. The diplomatic agents or consular officers and where possible the maritime authority of the flag State, shall be immediately informed of any such measures taken pursuant to section 6 against foreign vessels.

Article 232
Liability of States arising from enforcement measures

States shall be liable for damage or loss attributable to them arising from measures taken pursuant to section 6 when such measures are unlawful or exceed those reasonably required in the light of available information. States shall provide for recourse in their courts for actions in respect of such damage or loss.

Article 233
Safeguards with respect to straits used for international navigation

Nothing in sections 5, 6 and 7 affects the legal regime of straits used for international navigation. However, if a foreign ship other than those referred to in section 10 has committed a violation of the laws and regulations referred to in Article 42, paragraph 1(a) and (b), causing or threatening major damage to the marine environment of the straits, the States bordering the straits may take appropriate enforcement measures and if so shall respect *mutatis mutandis* the provisions of this section.

SECTION 8. ICE-COVERED AREAS

Article 234
Ice-covered areas

Coastal States have the right to adopt and enforce non-discriminatory laws and regulations for the prevention, reduction and control of marine pollution from vessels in ice-covered areas within the limits of the exclusive economic zone, where particularly severe climatic conditions and the presence of ice covering such areas for most of the year create obstructions or exceptional hazards to navigation, and pollution of the marine environment could cause major harm to or irreversible disturbance of the ecological balance. Such laws and regulations shall have due regard to navigation and the protection and preservation of the marine environment based on the best available scientific evidence.

SECTION 9. RESPONSIBILITY AND LIABILITY

Article 235
Responsibility and liability

1. States are responsible for the fulfillment of their international obligations concerning the protection and preservation of the marine environment. They shall be liable in accordance with international law.
2. States shall ensure that recourse is available in accordance with their legal systems for prompt and adequate compensation or other relief in respect of damage caused by pollution of the marine environment by natural or juridical persons under their jurisdiction.
3. With the objective of assuring prompt and adequate compensation in respect of all damage caused by pollution of the marine environment, States shall cooperate in the implementation of existing international law and the further development of international law relating to responsibility and liability for the assessment of and compensation for damage and the settlement of related disputes, as well as, where appropriate, development of criteria and procedures for payment of adequate compensation, such as compulsory insurance or compensation funds.

SECTION 10. SOVEREIGN IMMUNITY

Article 236
Sovereign immunity

The provisions of this Convention regarding the protection and preservation of the marine environment do not apply to any warship, naval auxiliary, other vessels or aircraft owned or operated by a State and used, for the time being, only on government non-commercial service. However, each State shall ensure, by the adoption of appropriate measures not impairing operations or operational capabilities of such vessels or aircraft owned or operated by it, that such vessels or aircraft act in a manner consistent, so far as is reasonable and practicable, with this Convention.

SECTION 11. OBLIGATIONS UNDER OTHER CONVENTIONS ON THE PROTECTION AND PRESERVATION OF THE MARINE ENVIRONMENT

Article 237
Obligations under other conventions on the protection and preservation of the marine environment

1. The provisions of this Part are without prejudice to the specific obligations assumed by States under special conventions and agreements concluded previously which relate to the protection and preservation of the marine environment and to agreements which may be concluded in furtherance of the general principles set forth in this Convention.
2. Specific obligations assumed by States under special conventions, with respect to the protection and preservation of the marine environment, should be carried out in a manner consistent with the general principles and objectives of this Convention.

PART XIII
MARINE SCIENTIFIC RESEARCH

SECTION 1. GENERAL PROVISIONS

Article 238
Right to conduct marine scientific research

All States, irrespective of their geographical location, and competent international organizations have the right to conduct marine scientific research subject to the rights and duties of other States as provided for in this Convention.

Article 239
Promotion of marine scientific research

States and competent international organizations shall promote and facilitate the development and conduct of marine scientific research in accordance with this Convention.

Article 240
General principles for the conduct of marine scientific research

In the conduct of marine scientific research the following principles shall apply:
(a) marine scientific research shall be conducted exclusively for peaceful purposes;
(b) marine scientific research shall be conducted with appropriate scientific methods and means compatible with this Convention;
(c) marine scientific research shall not unjustifiably interfere with other legitimate uses of the sea compatible with this Convention and shall be duly respected in the course of such uses;
(d) marine scientific research shall be conducted in compliance with all relevant regulations adopted in conformity with this Convention including those for the protection and preservation of the marine environment.

Article 241
Non-recognition of marine scientific research activities as the legal basis for claims

Marine scientific research activities shall not constitute the legal basis for any claim to any part of the marine environment or its resources.

SECTION 2. INTERNATIONAL COOPERATION

Article 242
Promotion of international cooperation

1. States and competent international organizations shall, in accordance with the principle of respect for sovereignty and jurisdiction and on the basis of mutual benefit, promote international cooperation in marine scientific research for peaceful purposes.
2. In this context, without prejudice to the rights and duties of States under this Convention, a State, in the application of this Part, shall provide, as appropriate, other States with a reasonable opportunity to obtain from it, or with its cooperation, information necessary to prevent and control damage to the health and safety of persons and to the marine environment.

Article 243
Creation of favourable conditions

States and competent international organizations shall cooperate, through the conclusion of bilateral and multilateral agreements, to create favourable conditions for the conduct of marine scientific research in the marine environment and to integrate the efforts of scientists in studying the essence of phenomena and processes occurring in the marine environment and the interrelations between them.

Article 244
Publication and dissemination of information and knowledge

1. States and competent international organizations shall, in accordance with this Convention, make available by publication and dissemination through appropriate channels information on proposed major programmes and their objectives as well as knowledge resulting from marine scientific research.
2. For this purpose, States, both individually and in cooperation with other States and with competent international organizations, shall actively promote the flow of scientific data and information and the transfer of knowledge resulting from marine scientific research, especially to developing States, as well as the strengthening of the autonomous marine scientific research capabilities of developing States through, *inter alia*, programmes to provide adequate education and training of their technical and scientific personnel.

SECTION 3. CONDUCT AND PROMOTION OF MARINE SCIENTIFIC RESEARCH

Article 245
Marine scientific research in the territorial sea

Coastal States, in the exercise of their sovereignty, have the exclusive right to regulate, authorize and conduct marine scientific research in their territorial sea. Marine scientific research therein shall be conducted only with the express consent of and under the conditions set forth by the coastal State.

Article 246
Marine scientific research in the exclusive economic zone and on the continental shelf

1. Coastal States, in the exercise of their jurisdiction, have the right to regulate, authorize and conduct marine scientific research in their exclusive economic zone and on their continental shelf in accordance with the relevant provisions of this Convention.
2. Marine scientific research in the exclusive economic zone and on the continental shelf shall be conducted with the consent of the coastal State.
3. Coastal States shall, in normal circumstances, grant their consent for marine scientific research projects by other States or competent international organizations in their exclusive economic zone or on their continental shelf to be carried out in accordance with this Convention exclusively for peaceful purposes and in order to increase scientific knowledge of the marine environment for the benefit of all mankind. To this end, coastal States shall establish rules and procedures ensuring that such consent will not be delayed or denied unreasonably.
4. For the purposes of applying paragraph 3, normal circumstances may exist in spite of the absence of diplomatic relations between the coastal State and the researching State.
5. Coastal States may however in their discretion withhold their consent to the conduct of a marine scientific research project of another State or competent international organization in the exclusive economic zone or on the continental shelf of the coastal State if that project:
(a) is of direct significance for the exploration and exploitation of natural resources, whether living or non-living;
(b) involves drilling into the continental shelf, the use of explosives or the introduction of harmful substances into the marine environment;
(c) involves the construction, operation or use of artificial islands, installations and structures referred to in Article s 60 and 80;
(d) contains information communicated pursuant to Article 248 regarding the nature and objectives of the project which is inaccurate or if the researching State or competent international organization has outstanding obligations to the coastal State from a prior research project.
6. Notwithstanding the provisions of paragraph 5, coastal States may not exercise their discretion to withhold consent under subparagraph (a) of that paragraph in respect of marine scientific research projects to be undertaken in accordance with the provisions of this Part on the continental shelf, beyond 200 nautical miles from the baselines from which the breadth of the territorial sea is measured, outside those specific areas which coastal States may at any time publicly designate as areas in which exploitation or detailed exploratory operations focused on those areas are occurring or will occur within a reasonable period of time. Coastal States shall give reasonable notice of the designation of

such areas, as well as any modifications thereto, but shall not be obliged to give details of the operations therein.

7. The provisions of paragraph 6 are without prejudice to the rights of coastal States over the continental shelf as established in Article 77.

8. Marine scientific research activities referred to in this Article shall not unjustifiably interfere with activities undertaken by coastal States in the exercise of their sovereign rights and jurisdiction provided for in this Convention.

Article 247
Marine scientific research projects undertakenby or under the auspices of international organizations

A coastal State which is a member of or has a bilateral agreement with an international organization, and in whose exclusive economic zone or on whose continental shelf that organization wants to carry out a marine scientific research project, directly or under its auspices, shall be deemed to have authorized the project to be carried out in conformity with the agreed specifications if that State approved the detailed project when the decision was made by the organization for the undertaking of the project, or is willing to participate in it, and has not expressed any objection within four months of notification of the project by the organization to the coastal State.

Article 248
Duty to provide information to the coastal State

States and competent international organizations which intend to undertake marine scientific research in the exclusive economic zone or on the continental shelf of a coastal State shall, not less than six months in advance of the expected starting date of the marine scientific research project, provide that State with a full description of:

(a) the nature and objectives of the project;

(b) the method and means to be used, including name, tonnage, type and class of vessels and a description of scientific equipment;

(c) the precise geographical areas in which the project is to be conducted;

(d) the expected date of first appearance and final departure of the research vessels, or deployment of the equipment and its removal, as appropriate;

(e) the name of the sponsoring institution, its director, and the person in charge of the project; and

(f) the extent to which it is considered that the coastal State should be able to participate or to be represented in the project.

Article 249
Duty to comply with certain conditions

1. States and competent international organizations when undertaking marine scientific research in the exclusive economic zone or on the continental shelf of a coastal State shall comply with the following conditions:

(a) ensure the right of the coastal State, if it so desires, to participate or be represented in the marine scientific research project, especially on board research vessels and other craft or scientific research installations, when practicable, without payment of any remuneration to the scientists of the coastal State and without obligation to contribute towards the costs of the project;

(b) provide the coastal State, at its request, with preliminary reports, as soon as practicable, and with the final results and conclusions after the completion of the research;

(c) undertake to provide access for the coastal State, at its request, to all data and samples derived from the marine scientific research project and likewise to furnish it with data which may be copied and samples which may be divided without detriment to their scientific value;

(d) if requested, provide the coastal State with an assessment of such data, samples and research results or provide assistance in their assessment or interpretation;

(e) ensure, subject to paragraph 2, that the research results are made internationally available through appropriate national or international channels, as soon as practicable;

(f) inform the coastal State immediately of any major change in the research programme;

(g) unless otherwise agreed, remove the scientific research installations or equipment once the research is completed.

2. This Article is without prejudice to the conditions established by the laws and regulations of the coastal State for the exercise of its discretion to grant or withhold consent pursuant to Article 246, paragraph 5, including requiring prior agreement for making internationally available the research results of a project of direct significance for the exploration and exploitation of natural resources.

Article 250
Communications concerning marine scientific research projects

Communications concerning the marine scientific research projects shall be made through appropriate official channels, unless otherwise agreed.

Article 251
General criteria and guidelines

States shall seek to promote through competent international organizations the establishment of general criteria and guidelines to assist States in ascertaining the nature and implications of marine scientific research.

Article 252
Implied consent

States or competent international organizations may proceed with a marine scientific research project six months after the date upon which the information required pursuant to Article 248 was provided to the coastal State unless within four months of the receipt of the communication containing such information the coastal State has informed the State or organization conducting the research that:

(a) it has withheld its consent under the provisions of Article 246; or

(b) the information given by that State or competent international organization regarding the nature or objectives of the project does not conform to the manifestly evident facts; or

(c) it requires supplementary information relevant to conditions and the information provided for under Article s 248 and 249; or

(d) outstanding obligations exist with respect to a previous marine scientific research project carried out by that State or organization, with regard to conditions established in Article 249.

Article 253
Suspension or cessation of marine scientific research activities

1. A coastal State shall have the right to require the suspension of any marine scientific research activities in progress within its exclusive economic zone or on its continental shelf if:

(a) the research activities are not being conducted in accordance with the information communicated as provided under Article 248 upon which the consent of the coastal State was based; or

(b) the State or competent international organization conducting the research activities fails to comply with the provisions of Article 249 concerning the rights of the coastal State with respect to the marine scientific research project.

2. A coastal State shall have the right to require the cessation of any marine scientific research activities in case of any non-compliance with the provisions of Article 248 which amounts to a major change in the research project or the research activities.

3. A coastal State may also require cessation of marine scientific research activities if any of the situations contemplated in paragraph 1 are not rectified within a reasonable period of time.

4. Following notification by the coastal State of its decision to order suspension or cessation, States or competent international organizations authorized to conduct marine scientific research activities shall terminate the research activities that are the subject of such a notification.

5. An order of suspension under paragraph 1 shall be lifted by the coastal State and the marine scientific research activities allowed to continue once the researching State or competent international organization has complied with the conditions required under Article s 248 and 249.

Article 254
Rights of neighbouring land-locked and geographically disadvantaged States

1. States and competent international organizations which have submitted to a coastal State a project to undertake marine scientific research referred to in Article 246, paragraph 3, shall give notice to the neighbouring land-locked and geographically disadvantaged States of the proposed research project, and shall notify the coastal State thereof.

2. After the consent has been given for the proposed marine scientific research project by the coastal State concerned, in accordance with Article 246 and other relevant provisions of this Convention, States and competent international organizations undertaking such a project shall provide to the neighbouring land-locked and geographically disadvantaged States, at their request and when appropriate, relevant information as specified in Article 248 and Article 249, paragraph 1(f).

3. The neighbouring land-locked and geographically disadvantaged States referred to above shall, at their request, be given the opportunity to participate, whenever feasible, in the proposed marine scientific research project through qualified experts appointed by them and not objected to by the coastal State, in accordance with the conditions agreed for the project, in conformity with the provisions of this Convention, between the coastal State concerned and the State or competent international organizations conducting the marine scientific research.

4. States and competent international organizations referred to in paragraph 1 shall provide to the above-mentioned land-locked and geographically disadvantaged States, at

their request, the information and assistance specified in Article 249, paragraph 1(d), subject to the provisions of Article 249, paragraph 2.

Article 255
Measures to facilitate marine scientific research and assist research vessels

States shall endeavour to adopt reasonable rules, regulations and procedures to promote and facilitate marine scientific research conducted in accordance with this Convention beyond their territorial sea and, as appropriate, to facilitate, subject to the provisions of their laws and regulations, access to their harbours and promote assistance for marine scientific research vessels which comply with the relevant provisions of this Part.

Article 256
Marine scientific research in the Area

All States, irrespective of their geographical location, and competent international organizations have the right, in conformity with the provisions of Part XI, to conduct marine scientific research in the Area.

Article 257
Marine scientific research in the water column beyond the exclusive economic zone

All States, irrespective of their geographical location, and competent international organizations have the right, in conformity with this Convention, to conduct marine scientific research in the water column beyond the limits of the exclusive economic zone.

SECTION 4. SCIENTIFIC RESEARCH INSTALLATIONS OR EQUIPMENT IN THE MARINE ENVIRONMENT

Article 258
Deployment and use

The deployment and use of any type of scientific research installations or equipment in any area of the marine environment shall be subject to the same conditions as are prescribed in this Convention for the conduct of marine scientific research in any such area.

Article 259
Legal status

The installations or equipment referred to in this section do not possess the status of islands. They have no territorial sea of their own, and their presence does not affect the delimitation of the territorial sea, the exclusive economic zone or the continental shelf.

Article 260
Safety zones

Safety zones of a reasonable breadth not exceeding a distance of 500 metres may be created around scientific research installations in accordance with the relevant provisions of this Convention. All States shall ensure that such safety zones are respected by their vessels.

Article 261
Non-interference with shipping routes

The deployment and use of any type of scientific research installations or equipment shall not constitute an obstacle to established international shipping routes.

Article 262
Identification markings and warning signals

Installations or equipment referred to in this section shall bear identification markings indicating the State of registry or the international organization to which they belong and shall have adequate internationally agreed warning signals to ensure safety at sea and the safety of air navigation, taking into account rules and standards established by competent international organizations.

SECTION 5. RESPONSIBILITY AND LIABILITY

Article 263
Responsibility and liability

1. States and competent international organizations shall be responsible for ensuring that marine scientific research, whether undertaken by them or on their behalf, is conducted in accordance with this Convention.
2. States and competent international organizations shall be responsible and liable for the measures they take in contravention of this Convention in respect of marine scientific research conducted by other States, their natural or juridical persons or by competent international organizations, and shall provide compensation for damage resulting from such measures.
3. States and competent international organizations shall be responsible and liable pursuant to Article 235 for damage caused by pollution of the marine environment arising out of marine scientific research undertaken by them or on their behalf.

SECTION 6. SETTLEMENT OF DISPUTES AND INTERIM MEASURES

Article 264
Settlement of disputes

Disputes concerning the interpretation or application of the provisions of this Convention with regard to marine scientific research shall be settled in accordance with Part XV, sections 2 and 3.

Article 265
Interim measures

Pending settlement of a dispute in accordance with Part XV, sections 2 and 3, the State or competent international organization authorized to conduct a marine scientific research project shall not allow research activities to commence or continue without the express consent of the coastal State concerned.

PART XIV
DEVELOPMENT AND TRANSFER OF MARINE TECHNOLOGY

SECTION 1. GENERAL PROVISIONS

Article 266
Promotion of the development and transfer of marine technology

1. States, directly or through competent international organizations, shall cooperate in accordance with their capabilities to promote actively the development and transfer of marine science and marine technology on fair and reasonable terms and conditions.
2. States shall promote the development of the marine scientific and technological capacity of States which may need and request technical assistance in this field, particularly developing States, including land-locked and geographically disadvantaged States, with regard to the exploration, exploitation, conservation and management of marine resources, the protection and preservation of the marine environment, marine scientific research and other activities in the marine environment compatible with this Convention, with a view to accelerating the social and economic development of the developing States.
3. States shall endeavour to foster favourable economic and legal conditions for the transfer of marine technology for the benefit of all parties concerned on an equitable basis.

Article 267
Protection of legitimate interests

States, in promoting cooperation pursuant to Article 266, shall have due regard for all legitimate interests including, *inter alia*, the rights and duties of holders, suppliers and recipients of marine technology.

Article 268
Basic objectives

States, directly or through competent international organizations, shall promote:
(a) the acquisition, evaluation and dissemination of marine technological knowledge and facilitate access to such information and data;
(b) the development of appropriate marine technology;
(c) the development of the necessary technological infrastructure to facilitate the transfer of marine technology;

(d) the development of human resources through training and education of nationals of developing States and countries and especially the nationals of the least developed among them;

(e) international cooperation at all levels, particularly at the regional, subregional and bilateral levels.

Article 269
Measures to achieve the basic objectives

In order to achieve the objectives referred to in Article 268, States, directly or through competent international organizations, shall endeavour, *inter alia*, to:

(a) establish programmes of technical cooperation for the effective transfer of all kinds of marine technology to States which may need and request technical assistance in this field, particularly the developing land-locked and geographically disadvantaged States, as well as other developing States which have not been able either to establish or develop their own technological capacity in marine science and in the exploration and exploitation of marine resources or to develop the infrastructure of such technology;

(b) promote favourable conditions for the conclusion of agreements, contracts and other similar arrangements, under equitable and reasonable conditions;

(c) hold conferences, seminars and symposia on scientific and technological subjects, in particular on policies and methods for the transfer of marine technology;

(d) promote the exchange of scientists and of technological and other experts;

(e) undertake projects and promote joint ventures and other forms of bilateral and multilateral cooperation.

SECTION 2. INTERNATIONAL COOPERATION

Article 270
Ways and means of international cooperation

International cooperation for the development and transfer of marine technology shall be carried out, where feasible and appropriate, through existing bilateral, regional or multilateral programmes, and also through expanded and new programmes in order to facilitate marine scientific research, the transfer of marine technology, particularly in new fields, and appropriate international funding for ocean research and development.

Article 271
Guidelines, criteria and standards

States, directly or through competent international organizations, shall promote the establishment of generally accepted guidelines, criteria and standards for the transfer of marine technology on a bilateral basis or within the framework of international organizations and other fora, taking into account, in particular, the interests and needs of developing States.

Article 272
Coordination of international programmes

In the field of transfer of marine technology, States shall endeavour to ensure that competent international organizations coordinate their activities, including any regional or global programmes, taking into account the interests and needs of developing States, particularly land-locked and geographically disadvantaged States.

Article 273
Cooperation with international organizations and the Authority

States shall cooperate actively with competent international organizations and the Authority to encourage and facilitate the transfer to developing States, their nationals and the Enterprise of skills and marine technology with regard to activities in the Area.

Article 274
Objectives of the Authority

Subject to all legitimate interests including, *inter alia*, the rights and duties of holders, suppliers and recipients of technology, the Authority, with regard to activities in the Area, shall ensure that:

(a) on the basis of the principle of equitable geographical distribution, nationals of developing States, whether coastal, land-locked or geographically disadvantaged, shall be taken on for the purposes of training as members of the managerial, research and technical staff constituted for its undertakings;

(b) the technical documentation on the relevant equipment, machinery, devices and processes is made available to all States, in particular developing States which may need and request technical assistance in this field;

(c) adequate provision is made by the Authority to facilitate the acquisition of technical assistance in the field of marine technology by States which may need and request it, in particular developing States, and the acquisition by their nationals of the necessary skills and know-how, including professional training;

(d) States which may need and request technical assistance in this field, in particular developing States, are assisted in the acquisition of necessary equipment, processes, plant and other technical know-how through any financial arrangements provided for in this Convention.

SECTION 3. NATIONAL AND REGIONAL MARINE SCIENTIFIC AND TECHNOLOGICAL CENTRES

Article 275
Establishment of national centres

1. States, directly or through competent international organizations and the Authority, shall promote the establishment, particularly in developing coastal States, of national marine scientific and technological research centres and the strengthening of existing national centres, in order to stimulate and advance the conduct of marine scientific research by developing coastal States and to enhance their national capabilities to utilize and preserve their marine resources for their economic benefit.

2. States, through competent international organizations and the Authority, shall give adequate support to facilitate the establishment and strengthening of such national centres so as to provide for advanced training facilities and necessary equipment, skills and know-

how as well as technical experts to such States which may need and request such assistance.

Article 276
Establishment of regional centres

1. States, in coordination with the competent international organizations, the Authority and national marine scientific and technological research institutions, shall promote the establishment of regional marine scientific and technological research centres, particularly in developing States, in order to stimulate and advance the conduct of marine scientific research by developing States and foster the transfer of marine technology.

2. All States of a region shall cooperate with the regional centres therein to ensure the more effective achievement of their objectives.

Article 277
Functions of regional centres

The functions of such regional centres shall include, *inter alia*:

(a) training and educational programmes at all levels on various aspects of marine scientific and technological research, particularly marine biology, including conservation and management of living resources, oceanography, hydrography, engineering, geological exploration of the seabed, mining and desalination technologies;

(b) management studies;

(c) study programmes related to the protection and preservation of the marine environment and the prevention, reduction and control of pollution;

(d) organization of regional conferences, seminars and symposia;

(e) acquisition and processing of marine scientific and technological data and information;

(f) prompt dissemination of results of marine scientific and technological research in readily available publications;

(g) publicizing national policies with regard to the transfer of marine technology and systematic comparative study of those policies;

(h) compilation and systematization of information on the marketing of technology and on contracts and other arrangements concerning patents;

(i) technical cooperation with other States of the region.

SECTION 4. COOPERATION AMONG INTERNATIONAL ORGANIZATIONS

Article 278
Cooperation among international organizations

The competent international organizations referred to in this Part and in Part XIII shall take all appropriate measures to ensure, either directly or in close cooperation among themselves, the effective discharge of their functions and responsibilities under this Part.

PART XV
SETTLEMENT OF DISPUTES

SECTION 1. GENERAL PROVISIONS

Article 279
Obligation to settle disputes by peaceful means

States Parties shall settle any dispute between them concerning the interpretation or application of this Convention by peaceful means in accordance with Article 2, paragraph 3, of the Charter of the United Nations and, to this end, shall seek a solution by the means indicated in Article 33, paragraph 1, of the Charter.

Article 280
Settlement of disputes by any peaceful means chosen by the parties

Nothing in this Part impairs the right of any States Parties to agree at any time to settle a dispute between them concerning the interpretation or application of this Convention by any peaceful means of their own choice.

Article 281
Procedure where no settlement has been reached by the parties

1. If the States Parties which are parties to a dispute concerning the interpretation or application of this Convention have agreed to seek settlement of the dispute by a peaceful means of their own choice, the procedures provided for in this Part apply only where no settlement has been reached by recourse to such means and the agreement between the parties does not exclude any further procedure.
2. If the parties have also agreed on a time-limit, paragraph 1 applies only upon the expiration of that time-limit.

Article 282
Obligations under general, regional or bilateral agreements

If the States Parties which are parties to a dispute concerning the interpretation or application of this Convention have agreed, through a general, regional or bilateral agreement or otherwise, that such dispute shall, at the request of any party to the dispute, be submitted to a procedure that entails a binding decision, that procedure shall apply in lieu of the procedures provided for in this Part, unless the parties to the dispute otherwise agree.

Article 283
Obligation to exchange views

1. When a dispute arises between States Parties concerning the interpretation or application of this Convention, the parties to the dispute shall proceed expeditiously to an exchange of views regarding its settlement by negotiation or other peaceful means.
2. The parties shall also proceed expeditiously to an exchange of views where a procedure for the settlement of such a dispute has been terminated without a settlement or where a settlement has been reached and the circumstances require consultation regarding the manner of implementing the settlement.

Article 284
Conciliation

1. A State Party which is a party to a dispute concerning the interpretation or application of this Convention may invite the other party or parties to submit the dispute to conciliation in accordance with the procedure under Annex V, section 1, or another conciliation procedure.

2. If the invitation is accepted and if the parties agree upon the conciliation procedure to be applied, any party may submit the dispute to that procedure.

3. If the invitation is not accepted or the parties do not agree upon the procedure, the conciliation proceedings shall be deemed to be terminated.

4. Unless the parties otherwise agree, when a dispute has been submitted to conciliation, the proceedings may be terminated only in accordance with the agreed conciliation procedure.

Article 285
Application of this section to disputes submitted pursuant to Part XI

This section applies to any dispute which pursuant to Part XI, section 5, is to be settled in accordance with procedures provided for in this Part. If an entity other than a State Party is a party to such a dispute, this section applies *mutatis mutandis*.

SECTION 2. COMPULSORY PROCEDURES ENTAILING BINDING DECISIONS

Article 286
Application of procedures under this section

Subject to section 3, any dispute concerning the interpretation or application of this Convention shall, where no settlement has been reached by recourse to section 1, be submitted at the request of any party to the dispute to the court or tribunal having jurisdiction under this section.

Article 287
Choice of procedure

1. When signing, ratifying or acceding to this Convention or at any time thereafter, a State shall be free to choose, by means of a written declaration, one or more of the following means for the settlement of disputes concerning the interpretation or application of this Convention:

(a) the International Tribunal for the Law of the Sea established in accordance with Annex VI;

(b) the International Court of Justice;

(c) an arbitral tribunal constituted in accordance with Annex VII;

(d) a special arbitral tribunal constituted in accordance with Annex VIII for one or more of the categories of disputes specified therein.

2. A declaration made under paragraph 1 shall not affect or be affected by the obligation of a State Party to accept the jurisdiction of the Seabed Disputes Chamber of the International Tribunal for the Law of the Sea to the extent and in the manner provided for in Part XI, section 5.

3. A State Party, which is a party to a dispute not covered by a declaration in force, shall be deemed to have accepted arbitration in accordance with Annex VII.

4. If the parties to a dispute have accepted the same procedure for the settlement of the dispute, it may be submitted only to that procedure, unless the parties otherwise agree.

5. If the parties to a dispute have not accepted the same procedure for the settlement of the dispute, it may be submitted only to arbitration in accordance with Annex VII, unless the parties otherwise agree.

6. A declaration made under paragraph 1 shall remain in force until three months after notice of revocation has been deposited with the Secretary-General of the United Nations.

7. A new declaration, a notice of revocation or the expiry of a declaration does not in any way affect proceedings pending before a court or tribunal having jurisdiction under this Article , unless the parties otherwise agree.

8. Declarations and notices referred to in this Article shall be deposited with the Secretary-General of the United Nations, who shall transmit copies thereof to the States Parties.

Article 288
Jurisdiction

1. A court or tribunal referred to in Article 287 shall have jurisdiction over any dispute concerning the interpretation or application of this Convention which is submitted to it in accordance with this Part.

2. A court or tribunal referred to in Article 287 shall also have jurisdiction over any dispute concerning the interpretation or application of an international agreement related to the purposes of this Convention, which is submitted to it in accordance with the agreement.

3. The Seabed Disputes Chamber of the International Tribunal for the Law of the Sea established in accordance with Annex VI, and any other chamber or arbitral tribunal referred to in Part XI, section 5, shall have jurisdiction in any matter which is submitted to it in accordance therewith.

4. In the event of a dispute as to whether a court or tribunal has jurisdiction, the matter shall be settled by decision of that court or tribunal.

Article 289
Experts

In any dispute involving scientific or technical matters, a court or tribunal exercising jurisdiction under this section may, at the request of a party or *proprio motu*, select in consultation with the parties no fewer than two scientific or technical experts chosen preferably from the relevant list prepared in accordance with Annex VIII, Article 2, to sit with the court or tribunal but without the right to vote.

Article 290
Provisional measures

1. If a dispute has been duly submitted to a court or tribunal which considers that *prima facie* it has jurisdiction under this Part or Part XI, section 5, the court or tribunal may prescribe any provisional measures which it considers appropriate under the circumstances to preserve the respective rights of the parties to the dispute or to prevent serious harm to the marine environment, pending the final decision.

2. Provisional measures may be modified or revoked as soon as the circumstances justifying them have changed or ceased to exist.

3. Provisional measures may be prescribed, modified or revoked under this Article only at the request of a party to the dispute and after the parties have been given an opportunity to be heard.

4. The court or tribunal shall forthwith give notice to the parties to the dispute, and to such other States Parties as it considers appropriate, of the prescription, modification or revocation of provisional measures.

5. Pending the constitution of an arbitral tribunal to which a dispute is being submitted under this section, any court or tribunal agreed upon by the parties or, failing such agreement within two weeks from the date of the request for provisional measures, the International Tribunal for the Law of the Sea or, with respect to activities in the Area, the Seabed Disputes Chamber, may prescribe, modify or revoke provisional measures in accordance with this Article if it considers that *prima facie* the tribunal which is to be constituted would have jurisdiction and that the urgency of the situation so requires. Once constituted, the tribunal to which the dispute has been submitted may modify, revoke or affirm those provisional measures, acting in conformity with paragraphs 1 to 4.

6. The parties to the dispute shall comply promptly with any provisional measures prescribed under this Article .

Article 291
Access

1. All the dispute settlement procedures specified in this Part shall be open to States Parties.

2. The dispute settlement procedures specified in this Part shall be open to entities other than States Parties only as specifically provided for in this Convention.

Article 292
Prompt release of vessels and crews

1. Where the authorities of a State Party have detained a vessel flying the flag of another State Party and it is alleged that the detaining State has not complied with the provisions of this Convention for the prompt release of the vessel or its crew upon the posting of a reasonable bond or other financial security, the question of release from detention may be submitted to any court or tribunal agreed upon by the parties or, failing such agreement within 10 days from the time of detention, to a court or tribunal accepted by the detaining State under Article 287 or to the International Tribunal for the Law of the Sea, unless the parties otherwise agree.

2. The application for release may be made only by or on behalf of the flag State of the vessel.

3. The court or tribunal shall deal without delay with the application for release and shall deal only with the question of release, without prejudice to the merits of any case before the appropriate domestic forum against the vessel, its owner or its crew. The authorities of the detaining State remain competent to release the vessel or its crew at any time.

4. Upon the posting of the bond or other financial security determined by the court or tribunal, the authorities of the detaining State shall comply promptly with the decision of the court or tribunal concerning the release of the vessel or its crew.

Article 293
Applicable law

1. A court or tribunal having jurisdiction under this section shall apply this Convention and other rules of international law not incompatible with this Convention.
2. Paragraph 1 does not prejudice the power of the court or tribunal having jurisdiction under this section to decide a case *ex aequo et bono*, if the parties so agree.

Article 294
Preliminary proceedings

1. A court or tribunal provided for in Article 287 to which an application is made in respect of a dispute referred to in Article 297 shall determine at the request of a party, or may determine *proprio motu*, whether the claim constitutes an abuse of legal process or whether *prima facie* it is well founded. If the court or tribunal determines that the claim constitutes an abuse of legal process or is *prima facie* unfounded, it shall take no further action in the case.
2. Upon receipt of the application, the court or tribunal shall immediately notify the other party or parties of the application, and shall fix a reasonable time-limit within which they may request it to make a determination in accordance with paragraph 1.
3. Nothing in this Article affects the right of any party to a dispute to make preliminary objections in accordance with the applicable rules of procedure.

Article 295
Exhaustion of local remedies

Any dispute between States Parties concerning the interpretation or application of this Convention may be submitted to the procedures provided for in this section only after local remedies have been exhausted where this is required by international law.

Article 296
Finality and binding force of decisions

1. Any decision rendered by a court or tribunal having jurisdiction under this section shall be final and shall be complied with by all the parties to the dispute.
2. Any such decision shall have no binding force except between the parties and in respect of that particular dispute.

SECTION 3. LIMITATIONS AND EXCEPTIONS TO APPLICABILITY OF SECTION 2

Article 297
Limitations on applicability of section 2

1. Disputes concerning the interpretation or application of this Convention with regard to the exercise by a coastal State of its sovereign rights or jurisdiction provided for in this Convention shall be subject to the procedures provided for in section 2 in the following cases:

(a) when it is alleged that a coastal State has acted in contravention of the provisions of this Convention in regard to the freedoms and rights of navigation, overflight or the laying of submarine cables and pipelines, or in regard to other internationally lawful uses of the sea specified in Article 58;

(b) when it is alleged that a State in exercising the aforementioned freedoms, rights or uses has acted in contravention of this Convention or of laws or regulations adopted by the coastal State in conformity with this Convention and other rules of international law not incompatible with this Convention; or

(c) when it is alleged that a coastal State has acted in contravention of specified international rules and standards for the protection and preservation of the marine environment which are applicable to the coastal State and which have been established by this Convention or through a competent international organization or diplomatic conference in accordance with this Convention.

2. (a) Disputes concerning the interpretation or application of the provisions of this Convention with regard to marine scientific research shall be settled in accordance with section 2, except that the coastal State shall not be obliged to accept the submission to such settlement of any dispute arising out of:

(i) the exercise by the coastal State of a right or discretion in accordance with Article 246; or

(ii) a decision by the coastal State to order suspension or cessation of a research project in accordance with Article 253.

(b) A dispute arising from an allegation by the researching State that with respect to a specific project the coastal State is not exercising its rights under Article s 246 and 253 in a manner compatible with this Convention shall be submitted, at the request of either party, to conciliation under Annex V, section 2, provided that the conciliation commission shall not call in question the exercise by the coastal State of its discretion to designate specific areas as referred to in Article 246, paragraph 6, or of its discretion to withhold consent in accordance with Article 246, paragraph 5.

3. (a) Disputes concerning the interpretation or application of the provisions of this Convention with regard to fisheries shall be settled in accordance with section 2, except that the coastal State shall not be obliged to accept the submission to such settlement of any dispute relating to its sovereign rights with respect to the living resources in the exclusive economic zone or their exercise, including its discretionary powers for determining the allowable catch, its harvesting capacity, the allocation of surpluses to other States and the terms and conditions established in its conservation and management laws and regulations.

(b) Where no settlement has been reached by recourse to section 1 of this Part, a dispute shall be submitted to conciliation under Annex V, section 2, at the request of any party to the dispute, when it is alleged that:

(i) a coastal State has manifestly failed to comply with its obligations to ensure through proper conservation and management measures that the maintenance of the living resources in the exclusive economic zone is not seriously endangered;

(ii) a coastal State has arbitrarily refused to determine, at the request of another State, the allowable catch and its capacity to harvest living resources with respect to stocks which that other State is interested in fishing; or

(iii) a coastal State has arbitrarily refused to allocate to any State, under Article s 62, 69 and 70 and under the terms and conditions established by the coastal State consistent with this Convention, the whole or part of the surplus it has declared to exist.

(c) In no case shall the conciliation commission substitute its discretion for that of the coastal State.

(d) The report of the conciliation commission shall be communicated to the appropriate international organizations.

(e) In negotiating agreements pursuant to Article s 69 and 70, States Parties, unless they otherwise agree, shall include a clause on measures which they shall take in order to minimize the possibility of a disagreement concerning the interpretation or application of the agreement, and on how they should proceed if a disagreement nevertheless arises.

Article 298
Optional exceptions to applicability of section 2

1. When signing, ratifying or acceding to this Convention or at any time thereafter, a State may, without prejudice to the obligations arising under section 1, declare in writing that it does not accept any one or more of the procedures provided for in section 2 with respect to one or more of the following categories of disputes:

(a) (i) disputes concerning the interpretation or application of Article s 15, 74 and 83 relating to sea boundary delimitations, or those involving historic bays or titles, provided that a State having made such a declaration shall, when such a dispute arises subsequent to the entry into force of this Convention and where no agreement within a reasonable period of time is reached in negotiations between the parties, at the request of any party to the dispute, accept submission of the matter to conciliation under Annex V, section 2; and provided further that any dispute that necessarily involves the concurrent consideration of any unsettled dispute concerning sovereignty or other rights over continental or insular land territory shall be excluded from such submission;

(ii) after the conciliation commission has presented its report, which shall state the reasons on which it is based, the parties shall negotiate an agreement on the basis of that report; if these negotiations do not result in an agreement, the parties shall, by mutual consent, submit the question to one of the procedures provided for in section 2, unless the parties otherwise agree;

(iii) this subparagraph does not apply to any sea boundary dispute finally settled by an arrangement between the parties, or to any such dispute which is to be settled in accordance with a bilateral or multilateral agreement binding upon those parties;

(b) disputes concerning military activities, including military activities by government vessels and aircraft engaged in non-commercial service, and disputes concerning law enforcement activities in regard to the exercise of sovereign rights or jurisdiction excluded from the jurisdiction of a court or tribunal under Article 297, paragraph 2 or 3;

(c) disputes in respect of which the Security Council of the United Nations is exercising the functions assigned to it by the Charter of the United Nations, unless the Security Council decides to remove the matter from its agenda or calls upon the parties to settle it by the means provided for in this Convention.

2. A State Party which has made a declaration under paragraph 1 may at any time withdraw it, or agree to submit a dispute excluded by such declaration to any procedure specified in this Convention.

3. A State Party which has made a declaration under paragraph 1 shall not be entitled to submit any dispute falling within the excepted category of disputes to any procedure in this Convention as against another State Party, without the consent of that party.

4. If one of the States Parties has made a declaration under paragraph 1(a), any other State Party may submit any dispute falling within an excepted category against the declarant party to the procedure specified in such declaration.

5. A new declaration, or the withdrawal of a declaration, does not in any way affect proceedings pending before a court or tribunal in accordance with this Article, unless the parties otherwise agree.

6. Declarations and notices of withdrawal of declarations under this Article shall be deposited with the Secretary-General of the United Nations, who shall transmit copies thereof to the States Parties.

Article 299
Right of the parties to agree upon a procedure

1. A dispute excluded under Article 297 or excepted by a declaration made under Article 298 from the dispute settlement procedures provided for in section 2 may be submitted to such procedures only by agreement of the parties to the dispute.

2. Nothing in this section impairs the right of the parties to the dispute to agree to some other procedure for the settlement of such dispute or to reach an amicable settlement.

PART XVI
GENERAL PROVISIONS

Article 300
Good faith and abuse of rights

States Parties shall fulfil in good faith the obligations assumed under this Convention and shall exercise the rights, jurisdiction and freedoms recognized in this Convention in a manner which would not constitute an abuse of right.

Article 301
Peaceful uses of the seas

In exercising their rights and performing their duties under this Convention, States Parties shall refrain from any threat or use of force against the territorial integrity or political independence of any State, or in any other manner inconsistent with the principles of international law embodied in the Charter of the United Nations.

Article 302
Disclosure of information

Without prejudice to the right of a State Party to resort to the procedures for the settlement of disputes provided for in this Convention, nothing in this Convention shall be deemed to require a State Party, in the fulfilment of its obligations under this Convention, to supply information the disclosure of which is contrary to the essential interests of its security.

Article 303
Archaeological and historical objects found at sea

1. States have the duty to protect objects of an archaeological and historical nature found at sea and shall cooperate for this purpose.
2. In order to control traffic in such objects, the coastal State may, in applying Article 33, presume that their removal from the seabed in the zone referred to in that Article without its approval would result in an infringement within its territory or territorial sea of the laws and regulations referred to in that Article .
3. Nothing in this Article affects the rights of identifiable owners, the law of salvage or other rules of admiralty, or laws and practices with respect to cultural exchanges.
4. This Article is without prejudice to other international agreements and rules of international law regarding the protection of objects of an archaeological and historical nature.

Article 304
Responsibility and liability for damage

The provisions of this Convention regarding responsibility and liability for damage are without prejudice to the application of existing rules and the development of further rules regarding responsibility and liability under international law.

PART XVII
FINAL PROVISIONS

Article 305
Signature

1. This Convention shall be open for signature by:
 (a) all States;
 (b) Namibia, represented by the United Nations Council for Namibia;
 (c) all self-governing associated States which have chosen that status in an act of self-determination supervised and approved by the United Nations in accordance with General Assembly resolution 1514 (XV) and which have competence over the matters governed by this Convention, including the competence to enter into treaties in respect of those matters;
 (d) all self-governing associated States which, in accordance with their respective instruments of association, have competence over the matters governed by this Convention, including the competence to enter into treaties in respect of those matters;
 (e) all territories which enjoy full internal self-government, recognized as such by the United Nations, but have not attained full independence in accordance with General Assembly resolution 1514 (XV) and which have competence over the matters governed by this Convention, including the competence to enter into treaties in respect of those matters;
 (f) international organizations, in accordance with Annex IX.
2. This Convention shall remain open for signature until 9 December 1984 at the Ministry of Foreign Affairs of Jamaica and also, from 1 July 1983 until 9 December 1984, at United Nations Headquarters in New York.

Article 306
Ratification and formal confirmation

This Convention is subject to ratification by States and the other entities referred to in Article 305, paragraph l(b), (c), (d) and (e), and to formal confirmation, in accordance with Annex IX, by the entities referred to in Article 305, paragraph l(f). The instruments of ratification and of formal confirmation shall be deposited with the Secretary-General of the United Nations.

Article 307
Accession

This Convention shall remain open for accession by States and the other entities referred to in Article 305. Accession by the entities referred to in Article 305, paragraph l(f), shall be in accordance with Annex IX. The instruments of accession shall be deposited with the Secretary-General of the United Nations.

Article 308
Entry into force

1. This Convention shall enter into force 12 months after the date of deposit of the sixtieth instrument of ratification or accession.
2. For each State ratifying or acceding to this Convention after the deposit of the sixtieth instrument of ratification or accession, the Convention shall enter into force on the thirtieth day following the deposit of its instrument of ratification or accession, subject to paragraph 1.
3. The Assembly of the Authority shall meet on the date of entry into force of this Convention and shall elect the Council of the Authority. The first Council shall be constituted in a manner consistent with the purpose of Article 161 if the provisions of that Article cannot be strictly applied.
4. The rules, regulations and procedures drafted by the Preparatory Commission shall apply provisionally pending their formal adoption by the Authority in accordance with Part XI.
5. The Authority and its organs shall act in accordance with resolution II of the Third United Nations Conference on the Law of the Sea relating to preparatory investment and with decisions of the Preparatory Commission taken pursuant to that resolution.

Article 309
Reservations and exceptions

No reservations or exceptions may be made to this Convention unless expressly permitted by other Article s of this Convention.

Article 310
Declarations and statements

Article 309 does not preclude a State, when signing, ratifying or acceding to this Convention, from making declarations or statements, however phrased or named, with a view, *inter alia*, to the harmonization of its laws and regulations with the provisions of this Convention, provided that such declarations or statements do not purport to exclude or to modify the legal effect of the provisions of this Convention in their application to that State.

Article 311
Relation to other conventions and international agreements

1. This Convention shall prevail, as between States Parties, over the Geneva Conventions on the Law of the Sea of 29 April 1958.

2. This Convention shall not alter the rights and obligations of States Parties which arise from other agreements compatible with this Convention and which do not affect the enjoyment by other States Parties of their rights or the performance of their obligations under this Convention.

3. Two or more States Parties may conclude agreements modifying or suspending the operation of provisions of this Convention, applicable solely to the relations between them, provided that such agreements do not relate to a provision derogation from which is incompatible with the effective execution of the object and purpose of this Convention, and provided further that such agreements shall not affect the application of the basic principles embodied herein, and that the provisions of such agreements do not affect the enjoyment by other States Parties of their rights or the performance of their obligations under this Convention.

4. States Parties intending to conclude an agreement referred to in paragraph 3 shall notify the other States Parties through the depositary of this Convention of their intention to conclude the agreement and of the modification or suspension for which it provides.

5. This Article does not affect international agreements expressly permitted or preserved by other Article s of this Convention.

6. States Parties agree that there shall be no amendments to the basic principle relating to the common heritage of mankind set forth in Article 136 and that they shall not be party to any agreement in derogation thereof.

Article 312
Amendment

1. After the expiry of a period of 10 years from the date of entry into force of this Convention, a State Party may, by written communication addressed to the Secretary-General of the United Nations, propose specific amendments to this Convention, other than those relating to activities in the Area, and request the convening of a conference to consider such proposed amendments. The Secretary-General shall circulate such communication to all States Parties. If, within 12 months from the date of the circulation of the communication, not less than one half of the States Parties reply favourably to the request, the Secretary-General shall convene the conference.

2. The decision-making procedure applicable at the amendment conference shall be the same as that applicable at the Third United Nations Conference on the Law of the Sea unless otherwise decided by the conference. The conference should make every effort to reach agreement on any amendments by way of consensus and there should be no voting on them until all efforts at consensus have been exhausted.

Article 313
Amendment by simplified procedure

1. A State Party may, by written communication addressed to the Secretary-General of the United Nations, propose an amendment to this Convention, other than an amendment relating to activities in the Area, to be adopted by the simplified procedure set forth in this Article without convening a conference. The Secretary-General shall circulate the communication to all States Parties.

2. If, within a period of 12 months from the date of the circulation of the communication, a State Party objects to the proposed amendment or to the proposal for its adoption by the simplified procedure, the amendment shall be considered rejected. The Secretary-General shall immediately notify all States Parties accordingly.

3. If, 12 months from the date of the circulation of the communication, no State Party has objected to the proposed amendment or to the proposal for its adoption by the simplified procedure, the proposed amendment shall be considered adopted. The Secretary-General shall notify all States Parties that the proposed amendment has been adopted.

Article 314
Amendments to the provisions of this Convention relating exclusively to activities in the Area

1. A State Party may, by written communication addressed to the Secretary-General of the Authority, propose an amendment to the provisions of this Convention relating exclusively to activities in the Area, including Annex VI, section 4. The Secretary-General shall circulate such communication to all States Parties. The proposed amendment shall be subject to approval by the Assembly following its approval by the Council. Representatives of States Parties in those organs shall have full powers to consider and approve the proposed amendment. The proposed amendment as approved by the Council and the Assembly shall be considered adopted.
2. Before approving any amendment under paragraph 1, the Council and the Assembly shall ensure that it does not prejudice the system of exploration for and exploitation of the resources of the Area, pending the Review Conference in accordance with Article 155.

Article 315
Signature, ratification of, accession to and authentic texts of amendments

1. Once adopted, amendments to this Convention shall be open for signature by States Parties for 12 months from the date of adoption, at United Nations Headquarters in New York, unless otherwise provided in the amendment itself.
2. Article s 306, 307 and 320 apply to all amendments to this Convention.

Article 316
Entry into force of amendments

1. Amendments to this Convention, other than those referred to in paragraph 5, shall enter into force for the States Parties ratifying or acceding to them on the thirtieth day following the deposit of instruments of ratification or accession by two thirds of the States Parties or by 60 States Parties, whichever is greater. Such amendments shall not affect the enjoyment by other States Parties of their rights or the performance of their obligations under this Convention.
2. An amendment may provide that a larger number of ratifications or accessions shall be required for its entry into force than are required by this Article.
3. For each State Party ratifying or acceding to an amendment referred to in paragraph 1 after the deposit of the required number of instruments of ratification or accession, the amendment shall enter into force on the thirtieth day following the deposit of its instrument of ratification or accession.
4. A State which becomes a Party to this Convention after the entry into force of an amendment in accordance with paragraph 1 shall, failing an expression of a different intention by that State:
(a) be considered as a Party to this Convention as so amended; and

(b) be considered as a Party to the unamended Convention in relation to any State Party not bound by the amendment.

5. Any amendment relating exclusively to activities in the Area and any amendment to Annex VI shall enter into force for all States Parties one year following the deposit of instruments of ratification or accession by three fourths of the States Parties.

6. A State which becomes a Party to this Convention after the entry into force of amendments in accordance with paragraph 5 shall be considered as a Party to this Convention as so amended.

Article 317
Denunciation

1. A State Party may, by written notification addressed to the Secretary-General of the United Nations, denounce this Convention and may indicate its reasons. Failure to indicate reasons shall not affect the validity of the denunciation. The denunciation shall take effect one year after the date of receipt of the notification, unless the notification specifies a later date.

2. A State shall not be discharged by reason of the denunciation from the financial and contractual obligations which accrued while it was a Party to this Convention, nor shall the denunciation affect any right, obligation or legal situation of that State created through the execution of this Convention prior to its termination for that State.

3. The denunciation shall not in any way affect the duty of any State Party to fulfil any obligation embodied in this Convention to which it would be subject under international law independently of this Convention.

Article 318
Status of Annexes

The Annexes form an integral part of this Convention and, unless expressly provided otherwise, a reference to this Convention or to one of its Parts includes a reference to the Annexes relating thereto.

Article 319
Depositary

1. The Secretary-General of the United Nations shall be the depositary of this Convention and amendments thereto.

2. In addition to his functions as depositary, the Secretary-General shall:

(a) report to all States Parties, the Authority and competent international organizations on issues of a general nature that have arisen with respect to this Convention;

(b) notify the Authority of ratifications and formal confirmations of and accessions to this Convention and amendments thereto, as well as of denunciations of this Convention;

(c) notify States Parties of agreements in accordance with Article 311, paragraph 4;

(d) circulate amendments adopted in accordance with this Convention to States Parties for ratification or accession;

(e) convene necessary meetings of States Parties in accordance with this Convention.

3. (a) The Secretary-General shall also transmit to the observers referred to in Article 156:

(i) reports referred to in paragraph 2(a);

(ii) notifications referred to in paragraph 2(b) and (c); and

(iii) texts of amendments referred to in paragraph 2(d), for their information.

(b) The Secretary-General shall also invite those observers to participate as observers at meetings of States Parties referred to in paragraph 2(e).

Article 320
Authentic texts

The original of this Convention, of which the Arabic, Chinese, English, French, Russian and Spanish texts are equally authentic, shall, subject to Article 305, paragraph 2, be deposited with the Secretary-General of the United Nations.

IN WITNESS WHEREOF, the undersigned Plenipotentiaries, being duly authorized thereto, have signed this Convention.

DONE AT MONTEGO BAY, this tenth day of December, one thousand nine hundred and eighty-two.

ANNEX I. HIGHLY MIGRATORY SPECIES

1. Albacore tuna: *Thunnus alalunga*.
2. Bluefin tuna: *Thunnus thynnus*.
3. Bigeye tuna: *Thunnus obesus*.
4. Skipjack tuna: *Katsuwonus pelamis*.
5. Yellowfin tuna: *Thunnus albacares*.
6. Blackfin tuna: *Thunnus atlanticus*.
7. Little tuna: *Euthynnus alletteratus*; *Euthynnus affinis*.
8. Southern bluefin tuna: *Thunnus maccoyii*.
9. Frigate mackerel: *Auxis thazard*; *Auxis rochei*.
10. Pomfrets: Family *Bramidae*.
11. Marlins: *Tetrapturus angustirostris*; *Tetrapturus belone*; *Tetrapturus pfluegeri*; *Tetrapturus albidus*; *Tetrapturus audax*; *Tetrapturus georgei*; *Makaira mazara*; *Makaira indica*; *Makaira nigricans*.
12. Sail-fishes: *Istiophorus platypterus*; *Istiophorus albicans*.
13. Swordfish: *Xiphias gladius*.
14. Sauries: *Scomberesox saurus*; *Cololabis saira*; *Cololabis adocetus*; *Scomberesox saurus scombroides*.
15. Dolphin: *Coryphaena hippurus*; *Coryphaena equiselis*.
16. Oceanic sharks: *Hexanchus griseus*; *Cetorhinus maximus*; Family *Alopiidae*; *Rhincodon typus*; Family *Carcharhinidae*; Family *Sphyrnidae*; Family *Isurida*.
17. Cetaceans: Family *Physeteridae*; Family *Balaenopteridae*; Family *Balaenidae*; Family *Eschrichtiidae*; Family *Monodontidae*; Family *Ziphiidae*; Family *Delphinidae*.

ANNEX II. COMMISSION ON THE LIMITS OF THE CONTINENTAL SHELF

Article 1

In accordance with the provisions of article 76, a Commission on the Limits of the Continental Shelf beyond 200 nautical miles shall be established in conformity with the following articles.

Article 2

1. The Commission shall consist of 21 members who shall be experts in the field of geology, geophysics or hydrography, elected by States Parties to this Convention from among their nationals, having due regard to the need to ensure equitable geographical representation, who shall serve in their personal capacities.

2. The initial election shall be held as soon as possible but in any case within 18 months after the date of entry into force of this Convention. At least three months before the date of each election, the Secretary-General of the United Nations shall address a letter to the States Parties, inviting the submission of nominations, after appropriate regional consultations, within three months. The

Secretary-General shall prepare a list in alphabetical order of all persons thus nominated and shall submit it to all the States Parties.

3. Elections of the members of the Commission shall be held at a meeting of States Parties convened by the Secretary-General at United Nations Headquarters. At that meeting, for which two thirds of the States Parties shall constitute a quorum, the persons elected to the Commission shall be those nominees who obtain a two-thirds majority of the votes of the representatives of States Parties present and voting. Not less than three members shall be elected from each geographical region.

4. The members of the Commission shall be elected for a term of five years. They shall be eligible for re-election.

5. The State Party which submitted the nomination of a member of the Commission shall defray the expenses of that member while in performance of Commission duties. The coastal State concerned shall defray the expenses incurred in respect of the advice referred to in article 3, paragraph 1(b), of this Annex. The secretariat of the Commission shall be provided by the Secretary-General of the United Nations.

Article 3

1. The functions of the Commission shall be:

(a) to consider the data and other material submitted by coastal States concerning the outer limits of the continental shelf in areas where those limits extend beyond 200 nautical miles, and to make recommendations in accordance with article 76 and the Statement of Understanding adopted on 29 August 1980 by the Third United Nations Conference on the Law of the Sea;

(b) to provide scientific and technical advice, if requested by the coastal State concerned during the preparation of the data referred to in subparagraph (a).

2. The Commission may cooperate, to the extent considered necessary and useful, with the Intergovernmental Oceanographic Commission of UNESCO, the International Hydrographic Organization and other competent international organizations with a view to exchanging scientific and technical information which might be of assistance in discharging the Commission's responsibilities.

Article 4

Where a coastal State intends to establish, in accordance with article 76, the outer limits of its continental shelf beyond 200 nautical miles, it shall submit particulars of such limits to the Commission along with supporting scientific and technical data as soon as possible but in any case within 10 years of the entry into force of this Convention for that State. The coastal State shall at the same time give the names of any Commission members who have provided it with scientific and technical advice.

Article 5

Unless the Commission decides otherwise, the Commission shall function by way of sub-commissions composed of seven members, appointed in a balanced manner taking into account the specific elements of each submission by a coastal State. Nationals of the coastal State making the submission who are members of the Commission and any Commission member who has assisted a coastal State by providing scientific and technical advice with respect to the delineation shall not be a member of the sub-commission dealing with that submission but has the right to participate as a member in the proceedings of the Commission concerning the said submission. The coastal State which has made a submission to the Commission may send its representatives to participate in the relevant proceedings without the right to vote.

Article 6

1. The sub-commission shall submit its recommendations to the Commission.
2. Approval by the Commission of the recommendations of the sub-commission shall be by a majority of two thirds of Commission members present and voting.
3. The recommendations of the Commission shall be submitted in writing to the coastal State which made the submission and to the Secretary-General of the United Nations.

Article 7

Coastal States shall establish the outer limits of the continental shelf in conformity with the provisions of article 76, paragraph 8, and in accordance with the appropriate national procedures.

Article 8

In the case of disagreement by the coastal State with the recommendations of the Commission, the coastal State shall, within a reasonable time, make a revised or new submission to the Commission.

Article 9

The actions of the Commission shall not prejudice matters relating to delimitation of boundaries between States with opposite or adjacent coasts.

ANNEX III. BASIC CONDITIONS OF PROSPECTING, EXPLORATION AND EXPLOITATION

Article 1
Title to minerals

Title to minerals shall pass upon recovery in accordance with this Convention.

Article 2
Prospecting

1.(a) The Authority shall encourage prospecting in the Area.

(b) Prospecting shall be conducted only after the Authority has received a satisfactory written undertaking that the proposed prospector will comply with this Convention and the relevant rules, regulations and procedures of the Authority concerning cooperation in the training programmes referred to in articles 143 and 144 and the protection of the marine environment, and will accept verification by the Authority of compliance therewith. The proposed prospector shall, at the same time, notify the Authority of the approximate area or areas in which prospecting is to be conducted.

(c) Prospecting may be conducted simultaneously by more than one prospector in the same area or areas.

2. Prospecting shall not confer on the prospector any rights with respect to resources. A prospector may, however, recover a reasonable quantity of minerals to be used for testing.

Article 3
Exploration and exploitation

1. The Enterprise, States Parties, and the other entities referred to in article 153, paragraph 2(b), may apply to the Authority for approval of plans of work for activities in the Area.

2. The Enterprise may apply with respect to any part of the Area, but applications by others with respect to reserved areas are subject to the additional requirements of article 9 of this Annex.

3. Exploration and exploitation shall be carried out only in areas specified in plans of work referred to in article 153, paragraph 3, and approved by the Authority in accordance with this Convention and the relevant rules, regulations and procedures of the Authority.

4. Every approved plan of work shall:

(a) be in conformity with this Convention and the rules, regulations and procedures of the Authority;
(b) provide for control by the Authority of activities in the Area in accordance with article 153, paragraph 4
(c) confer on the operator, in accordance with the rules, regulations and procedures of the Authority, the exclusive right to explore for and exploit the specified categories of resources in the area covered by the plan of work. If, however, the applicant presents for approval a plan of work covering only the stage of exploration or the stage of exploitation, the approved plan of work shall confer such exclusive right with respect to that stage only.

5. Upon its approval by the Authority, every plan of work, except those presented by the Enterprise, shall be in the form of a contract concluded between the Authority and the applicant or applicants.

Article 4
Qualifications of applicants

1. Applicants, other than the Enterprise, shall be qualified if they have the nationality or control and sponsorship required by article 153, paragraph 2(b), and if they follow the procedures and meet the qualification standards set forth in the rules, regulations and procedures of the Authority.

2. Except as provided in paragraph 6, such qualification standards shall relate to the financial and technical capabilities of the applicant and his performance under any previous contracts with the Authority.

3. Each applicant shall be sponsored by the State Party of which it is a national unless the applicant has more than one nationality, as in the case of a partnership or consortium of entities from several States, in which event all States Parties involved shall sponsor the application, or unless the applicant is effectively controlled by another State Party or its nationals, in which event both States Parties shall sponsor the application. The criteria and procedures for implementation of the sponsorship requirements shall be set forth in the rules, regulations and procedures of the Authority.

4. The sponsoring State or States shall, pursuant to article 139, have the responsibility to ensure, within their legal systems, that a contractor so sponsored shall carry out activities in the Area in conformity with the terms of its contract and its obligations under this Convention. A sponsoring State shall not, however, be liable for damage caused by any failure of a contractor sponsored by it to comply with its obligations if that State Party has adopted laws and regulations and taken administrative measures which are, within the framework of its legal system, reasonably appropriate for securing compliance by persons under its jurisdiction.

5. The procedures for assessing the qualifications of States Parties which are applicants shall take into account their character as States.

6. The qualification standards shall require that every applicant, without exception, shall as part of his application undertake:

(a) to accept as enforceable and comply with the applicable obligations created by the provisions of Part XI, the rules, regulations and procedures of the Authority, the decisions of the organs of the Authority and terms of his contracts with the Authority;

(b) to accept control by the Authority of activities in the Area, as authorized by this Convention;

(c) to provide the Authority with a written assurance that his obligations under the contract will be fulfilled in good faith;

(d) to comply with the provisions on the transfer of technology set forth in article 5 of this Annex.

Article 5
Transfer of technology

1. When submitting a plan of work, every applicant shall make available to the Authority a general description of the equipment and methods to be used in carrying out activities in the Area, and other relevant non-proprietary information about the characteristics of such technology and information as to where such technology is available.

2. Every operator shall inform the Authority of revisions in the description and information made available pursuant to paragraph 1 whenever a substantial technological change or innovation is introduced.

3. Every contract for carrying out activities in the Area shall contain the following undertakings by the contractor:

(a) to make available to the Enterprise on fair and reasonable commercial terms and conditions, whenever the Authority so requests, the technology which he uses in carrying out activities in the Area under the contract, which the contractor is legally entitled to transfer. This shall be done by means of licences or other appropriate arrangements which the contractor shall negotiate with the Enterprise and which shall be set forth in a specific agreement supplementary to the contract. This undertaking may be invoked only if the Enterprise finds that it is unable to obtain the same or equally efficient and useful technology on the open market on fair and reasonable commercial terms and conditions;

(b) to obtain a written assurance from the owner of any technology used in carrying out activities in the Area under the contract, which is not generally available on the open market and which is not covered by subparagraph (a), that the owner will, whenever the Authority so requests, make that technology available to the Enterprise under licence or other appropriate arrangements and on fair and reasonable commercial terms and conditions, to the same extent as made available to the contractor. If this assurance is not obtained, the technology in question shall not be used by the contractor in carrying out activities in the Area;

(c) to acquire from the owner by means of an enforceable contract, upon the request of the Enterprise and if it is possible to do so without substantial cost to the contractor, the legal right to transfer to the Enterprise any technology used by the contractor, in carrying out activities in the Area under the contract, which the contractor is otherwise not legally entitled to transfer and which is not generally available on the open market. In cases where there is a substantial corporate relationship between the contractor and the owner of the technology, the closeness of this relationship and the degree of control or influence shall be relevant to the determination whether all feasible measures have been taken to acquire such a right. In cases where the contractor exercises effective control over the owner, failure to acquire from the owner the legal right shall be considered relevant to the contractor's qualification for any subsequent application for approval of a plan of work;

(d) to facilitate, upon the request of the Enterprise, the acquisition by the Enterprise of any technology covered by subparagraph (b), under licence or other appropriate arrangements and on fair and reasonable commercial terms and conditions, if the Enterprise decides to negotiate directly with the owner of the technology;

(e) to take the same measures as are prescribed in subparagraphs (a), (b), (c) and (d) for the benefit of a developing State or group of developing States which has applied for a contract under article 9 of this Annex, provided that these measures shall be limited to the exploitation of the part of the area proposed by the contractor which has been reserved pursuant to article 8 of this Annex and provided that activities under the contract sought by the developing State or group of developing States would not involve transfer of technology to a third State or the nationals of a third State. The obligation under this provision shall only apply with respect to any given contractor where technology has not been requested by the Enterprise or transferred by that contractor to the Enterprise.

4. Disputes concerning undertakings required by paragraph 3, like other provisions of the contracts, shall be subject to compulsory settlement in accordance with Part XI and, in cases of violation of these undertakings, suspension or termination of the contract or monetary penalties may be ordered in accordance with article 18 of this Annex. Disputes as to whether offers made by the contractor are within the range of fair and reasonable commercial terms and conditions may be submitted by either party to binding commercial arbitration in accordance with the UNCITRAL Arbitration Rules or such other arbitration rules as may be prescribed in the rules, regulations and procedures of the Authority. If the finding is that the offer made by the contractor is not within the range of fair and reasonable commercial terms and conditions, the contractor shall be given 45 days to revise his offer to bring it within that range before the Authority takes any action in accordance with article 18 of this Annex.

5. If the Enterprise is unable to obtain on fair and reasonable commercial terms and conditions appropriate technology to enable it to commence in a timely manner the recovery and processing of minerals from the Area, either the Council or the Assembly may convene a group of States Parties composed of those which are engaged in activities in the Area, those which have sponsored entities which are engaged in activities in the Area and other States Parties having access to such technology. This group shall consult together and shall take effective measures to ensure that such technology is made available to the Enterprise on fair and reasonable commercial terms and conditions. Each such State Party shall take all feasible measures to this end within its own legal system.

6. In the case of joint ventures with the Enterprise, transfer of technology will be in accordance with the terms of the joint venture agreement.

7. The undertakings required by paragraph 3 shall be included in each contract for the carrying out of activities in the Area until 10 years after the commencement of commercial production by the Enterprise, and may be invoked during that period.

8. For the purposes of this article, "technology" means the specialized equipment and technical know-how, including manuals, designs, operating instructions, training and technical advice and assistance, necessary to assemble, maintain and operate a viable system and the legal right to use these items for that purpose on a non-exclusive basis.

Article 6
Approval of plans of work

1. Six months after the entry into force of this Convention, and thereafter each fourth month, the Authority shall take up for consideration proposed plans of work.

2. When considering an application for approval of a plan of work in the form of a contract, the Authority shall first ascertain whether:

(a) the applicant has complied with the procedures established for applications in accordance with article 4 of this Annex and has given the Authority the undertakings and assurances required by that article. In cases of non-compliance with these procedures or in the absence of any of these undertakings and assurances, the applicant shall be given 45 days to remedy these defects;

(b) the applicant possesses the requisite qualifications provided for in article 4 of this Annex.

3. All proposed plans of work shall be taken up in the order in which they are received. The proposed plans of work shall comply with and be governed by the relevant provisions of this Convention and the rules, regulations and procedures of the Authority, including those on operational requirements, financial contributions and the undertakings concerning the transfer of technology. If the proposed plans of work conform to these requirements, the Authority shall approve them provided that they are in accordance with the uniform and non-discriminatory requirements set forth in the rules, regulations and procedures of the Authority, unless:

(a) part or all of the area covered by the proposed plan of work is included in an approved plan of work or a previously submitted proposed plan of work which has not yet been finally acted on by the Authority;

(b) part or all of the area covered by the proposed plan of work is disapproved by the Authority pursuant to article 162, paragraph 2(x); or

(c) the proposed plan of work has been submitted or sponsored by a State Party which already holds:

(i) plans of work for exploration and exploitation of polymetallic nodules in non-reserved areas that, together with either part of the area covered by the application for a plan of work, exceed in size 30 per cent of a circular area of 400,000 square kilometres surrounding the centre of either part of the area covered by the proposed plan of work;

(ii) plans of work for the exploration and exploitation of polymetallic nodules in non-reserved areas which, taken together, constitute 2 per cent of the total seabed area which is not reserved or disapproved for exploitation pursuant to article 162, paragraph (2)(x).

4. For the purpose of the standard set forth in paragraph 3(c), a plan of work submitted by a partnership or consortium shall be counted on a *pro rata* basis among the sponsoring States Parties involved in accordance with article 4, paragraph 3, of this Annex. The Authority may approve plans of work covered by paragraph 3(c) if it determines that such approval would not permit a State Party or entities sponsored by it to monopolize the conduct of activities in the Area or to preclude other States Parties from activities in the Area.

5. Notwithstanding paragraph 3(a), after the end of the interim period specified in article 151, paragraph 3, the Authority may adopt by means of rules, regulations and procedures other procedures and criteria consistent with this Convention for deciding which applicants shall have plans of work approved in cases of selection among applicants for a proposed area. These procedures and criteria shall ensure approval of plans of work on an equitable and non-discriminatory basis.

Article 7
Selection among applicants for production authorizations

1. Six months after the entry into force of this Convention, and thereafter each fourth month, the Authority shall take up for consideration applications for production authorizations submitted during the immediately preceding period. The Authority shall issue the authorizations applied for if all such applications can be approved without exceeding the production limitation or contravening the obligations of the Authority under a commodity agreement or arrangement to which it has become a party, as provided in article 151.

2. When a selection must be made among applicants for production authorizations because of the production limitation set forth in article 151, paragraphs 2 to 7, or because of the obligations of the Authority under a commodity agreement or arrangement to which it has become a party, as provided for in article 151, paragraph 1, the Authority shall make the selection on the basis of objective and non-discriminatory standards set forth in its rules, regulations and procedures.

3. In the application of paragraph 2, the Authority shall give priority to those applicants which:

(a) give better assurance of performance, taking into account their financial and technical qualifications and their performance, if any, under previously approved plans of work;

(b) provide earlier prospective financial benefits to the Authority, taking into account when commercial production is scheduled to begin;

(c) have already invested the most resources and effort in prospecting or exploration.

4. Applicants which are not selected in any period shall have priority in subsequent periods until they receive a production authorization.

5. Selection shall be made taking into account the need to enhance opportunities for all States Parties, irrespective of their social and economic systems or geographical locations so as to avoid discrimination against any State or system, to participate in activities in the Area and to prevent monopolization of those activities.

6. Whenever fewer reserved areas than non-reserved areas are under exploitation, applications for production authorizations with respect to reserved areas shall have priority.

7. The decisions referred to in this article shall be taken as soon as possible after the close of each period.

Article 8
Reservation of areas

Each application, other than those submitted by the Enterprise or by any other entities for reserved areas, shall cover a total area, which need not be a single continuous area, sufficiently large and of sufficient estimated commercial value to allow two mining operations. The applicant shall indicate the coordinates dividing the area into two parts of equal estimated commercial value and submit all the data obtained by him with respect to both parts. Without prejudice to the powers of the Authority pursuant to article 17 of this Annex, the data to be submitted concerning polymetallic nodules shall relate to mapping, sampling, the abundance of nodules, and their metal content. Within 45 days of receiving such data, the Authority shall designate which part is to be reserved solely for the conduct of activities by the Authority through the Enterprise or in association with developing States. This designation may be deferred for a further period of 45 days if the Authority requests an independent expert to assess whether all data required by this article has been submitted. The area designated shall become a reserved area as soon as the plan of work for the non-reserved area is approved and the contract is signed.

Article 9
Activities in reserved areas

1. The Enterprise shall be given an opportunity to decide whether it intends to carry out activities in each reserved area. This decision may be taken at any time, unless a notification pursuant to paragraph 4 is received by the Authority, in which event the Enterprise shall take its decision within a reasonable time. The Enterprise may decide to exploit such areas in joint ventures with the interested State or entity.

2. The Enterprise may conclude contracts for the execution of part of its activities in accordance with Annex IV, article 12. It may also enter into joint ventures for the conduct of such activities with any entities which are eligible to carry out activities in the Area pursuant to article 153, paragraph 2(b). When considering such joint ventures, the Enterprise shall offer to States Parties which are developing States and their nationals the opportunity of effective participation.

3. The Authority may prescribe, in its rules, regulations and procedures, substantive and procedural requirements and conditions with respect to such contracts and joint ventures.

4. Any State Party which is a developing State or any natural or juridical person sponsored by it and effectively controlled by it or by other developing State which is a qualified applicant, or any group of the foregoing, may notify the Authority that it wishes to submit a plan of work pursuant to article 6 of this Annex with respect to a reserved area. The plan of work shall be considered if the Enterprise decides, pursuant to paragraph 1, that it does not intend to carry out activities in that area.

Article 10
Preference and priority among applicants

An operator who has an approved plan of work for exploration only, as provided in article 3, paragraph 4(c), of this Annex shall have a preference and a priority among applicants for a plan of work covering exploitation of the same area and resources. However, such preference or priority may be withdrawn if the operator's performance has not been satisfactory.

Article 11
Joint arrangements

1. Contracts may provide for joint arrangements between the contractor and the Authority through the Enterprise, in the form of joint ventures or production sharing, as well as any other form of joint arrangement, which shall have the same protection against revision, suspension or termination as contracts with the Authority.

2. Contractors entering into such joint arrangements with the Enterprise may receive financial incentives as provided for in article 13 of this Annex.

3. Partners in joint ventures with the Enterprise shall be liable for the payments required by article 13 of this Annex to the extent of their share in the joint ventures, subject to financial incentives as provided for in that article.

Article 12
Activities carried out by the Enterprise

1. Activities in the Area carried out by the Enterprise pursuant to article 153, paragraph 2(a), shall be governed by Part XI, the rules, regulations and procedures of the Authority and its relevant decisions.

2. Any plan of work submitted by the Enterprise shall be accompanied by evidence supporting its financial and technical capabilities.

Article 13
Financial terms of contracts

1. In adopting rules, regulations and procedures concerning the financial terms of a contract between the Authority and the entities referred to in article 153, paragraph 2(b), and in negotiating those financial terms in accordance with Part XI and those rules, regulations and procedures, the Authority shall be guided by the following objectives:

(a) to ensure optimum revenues for the Authority from the proceeds of commercial production;

(b) to attract investments and technology to the exploration and exploitation of the Area;

(c) to ensure equality of financial treatment and comparable financial obligations for contractors;

(d) to provide incentives on a uniform and non-discriminatory basis for contractors to undertake joint arrangements with the Enterprise and developing States or their nationals, to stimulate the transfer of technology thereto, and to train the personnel of the Authority and of developing States;

(e) to enable the Enterprise to engage in seabed mining effectively at the same time as the entities referred to in article 153, paragraph 2(b); and

(f) to ensure that, as a result of the financial incentives provided to contractors under paragraph 14, under the terms of contracts reviewed in accordance with article 19 of this Annex or under the provisions of article 11 of this Annex with respect to joint ventures, contractors are not subsidized so as to be given an artificial competitive advantage with respect to land-based miners.

2. A fee shall be levied for the administrative cost of processing an application for approval of a plan of work in the form of a contract and shall be fixed at an amount of $US 500,000 per application. The amount of the fee shall be reviewed from time to time by the Council in order to ensure that it covers the administrative cost incurred. If such administrative cost incurred by the Authority in processing an application is less than the fixed amount, the Authority shall refund the difference to the applicant.

3. A contractor shall pay an annual fixed fee of $US 1 million from the date of entry into force of the contract. If the approved date of commencement of commercial production is postponed because of a delay in issuing the production authorization, in accordance with article 151, the annual fixed fee shall be waived for the period of postponement. From the date of commencement of commercial production, the contractor shall pay either the production charge or the annual fixed fee, whichever is greater.

4. Within a year of the date of commencement of commercial production, in conformity with paragraph 3, a contractor shall choose to make his financial contribution to the Authority by either:
    (a) paying a production charge only; or
    (b) paying a combination of a production charge and a share of net proceeds.

5. (a) If a contractor chooses to make his financial contribution to the Authority by paying a production charge only, it shall be fixed at a percentage of the market value of the processed metals produced from the polymetallic nodules recovered from the area covered by the contract. This percentage shall be fixed as follows:

(i) years 1-10 of commercial production 5 per cent

(ii) years 11 to the end of commercial production 12 per cent

(b) The said market value shall be the product of the quantity of the processed metals produced from the polymetallic nodules extracted from the area covered by the contract and the average price for those metals during the relevant accounting year, as defined in paragraphs 7 and 8.

6. If a contractor chooses to make his financial contribution to the Authority by paying a combination of a production charge and a share of net proceeds, such payments shall be determined as follows:

(a) The production charge shall be fixed at a percentage of the market value, determined in accordance with subpara-graph (b), of the processed metals produced from the polymetallic nodules recovered from the area covered by the contract. This percentage shall be fixed as follows:

(i) first period of commercial production   2 per cent

(ii) second period of commercial production 4 per cent

If, in the second period of commercial production, as defined in subparagraph (d), the return on investment in any accounting year as defined in subparagraph (m) falls below 15 per cent as a result of the payment of the production charge at 4 per cent, the production charge shall be 2 per cent instead of 4 per cent in that accounting year.

(b) The said market value shall be the product of the quantity of the processed metals produced from the polymetallic nodules recovered from the area covered by the contract and the average price for those metals during the relevant accounting year as defined in paragraphs 7 and 8.

(c) (i) The Authority's share of net proceeds shall be taken out of that portion of the contractor's net proceeds which is attributable to the mining of the resources of the area covered by the contract, referred to hereinafter as attributable net proceeds.

(ii) The Authority's share of attributable net proceeds shall be determined in accordance with the following incremental schedule:

Portion of attributable net proceeds	Share of the Authority	
	First period of commercial production	Second period of commercial production
That portion representing a return on investment which is greater than 0 per cent, but less than 10 per cent	35 per cent	40 per cent
That portion representing a return on investment which is 10 per cent or greater, but less than 20 per cent	42.5 per cent	50 per cent
That portion representing a return on investment which is 20 per cent or greater	50 per cent	70 per cent

(d) (i) The first period of commercial production referred to in subparagraphs (a) and (c) shall commence in the first accounting year of commercial production and terminate in the accounting year in which the contractor's development costs with interest on the unrecovered portion thereof are fully recovered by his cash surplus, as follows:
In the first accounting year during which development costs are incurred, unrecovered development costs shall equal the development costs less cash surplus in that year. In each subsequent accounting year, unrecovered development costs shall equal the unrecovered development costs at the end of the preceding accounting year, plus interest thereon at the rate of 10 per cent per annum, plus development costs incurred in the current accounting year and less contractor's cash surplus in the current accounting year. The accounting year in which unrecovered development costs become zero for the first time shall be the accounting year in which the contractor's development costs with interest on the unrecovered portion thereof are fully recovered by his cash surplus. The contractor's cash surplus in any accounting year shall be his gross proceeds less his operating costs and less his payments to the Authority under subparagraph (c).

(ii) The second period of commercial production shall commence in the accounting year following the termination of the first period of commercial production and shall continue until the end of the contract.

(e) "Attributable net proceeds" means the product of the contractor's net proceeds and the ratio of the development costs in the mining sector to the contractor's development costs. If the contractor engages in mining, transporting polymetallic nodules and production primarily of three processed metals, namely, cobalt, copper and nickel, the amount of attributable net proceeds shall not be less than 25 per cent of the contractor's net proceeds. Subject to subparagraph (n), in all other cases, including those where the contractor engages in mining, transporting polymetallic nodules, and production primarily of four processed metals, namely, cobalt, copper, manganese and nickel, the Authority may, in its rules, regulations and procedures, prescribe appropriate floors which shall bear the same relationship to each case as the 25 per cent floor does to the three-metal case.

(f) "Contractor's net proceeds" means the contractor's gross proceeds less his operating costs and less the recovery of his development costs as set out in subparagraph (j).

(g) (i) If the contractor engages in mining, transporting polymetallic nodules and production of processed metals, "contractor's gross proceeds" means the gross revenues from the sale of the processed metals and any other monies deemed reasonably attributable to operations under the contract in accordance with the financial rules, regulations and procedures of the Authority.

(ii) In all cases other than those specified in subparagraphs (g)(i) and (n)(iii), "contractor's gross proceeds" means the gross revenues from the sale of the semi-processed metals from the polymetallic nodules recovered from the area covered by the contract, and any other monies deemed reasonably attributable to operations under the contract in accordance with the financial rules, regulations and procedures of the Authority.

(h) "Contractor's development costs" means:

(i) all expenditures incurred prior to the commencement of commercial production which are directly related to the development of the productive capacity of the area covered by the contract and the activities related thereto for operations under the contract in all cases other than that specified in subparagraph (n), in conformity with generally recognized accounting principles, including, *inter alia*, costs of machinery, equipment, ships, processing plant, construction, buildings, land, roads, prospecting and exploration of the area covered by the contract, research and development, interest, required leases, licences and fees; and

(ii) expenditures similar to those set forth in (i) above incurred subsequent to the commencement of commercial production and necessary to carry out the plan of work, except those chargeable to operating costs.

(i) The proceeds from the disposal of capital assets and the market value of those capital assets which are no longer required for operations under the contract and which are not sold shall be deducted from the contractor's development costs during the relevant accounting year. When these deductions exceed the contractor's development costs the excess shall be added to the contractor's gross proceeds.

(j) The contractor's development costs incurred prior to the commencement of commercial production referred to in subparagraphs (h)(i) and (n)(iv) shall be recovered in 10 equal annual instalments from the date of commencement of commercial production. The contractor's development costs incurred subsequent to the commencement of commercial production referred to in subparagraphs (h)(ii) and (n)(iv) shall be recovered in 10 or fewer equal annual instalments so as to ensure their complete recovery by the end of the contract.

(k) "Contractor's operating costs" means all expenditures incurred after the commencement of commercial production in the operation of the productive capacity of the area covered by the contract and the activities related thereto for operations under the contract, in conformity with generally recognized accounting principles, including, *inter alia*, the annual fixed fee or the production charge, whichever is greater, expenditures for wages, salaries, employee benefits, materials, services, transporting, processing and marketing costs, interest, utilities, preservation of the marine environment, overhead and administrative costs specifically related to operations under the contract, and any net operating losses carried forward or backward as specified herein. Net operating losses may be carried forward for two consecutive years except in the last two years of the contract in which case they may be carried backward to the two preceding years.

(l) If the contractor engages in mining, transporting of polymetallic nodules, and production of processed and semi-processed metals, "development costs of the mining sector" means the portion of the contractor's development costs which is directly related to the mining of the resources of the area covered by the contract, in conformity with generally recognized accounting principles, and the financial rules, regulations and procedures of the Authority, including, *inter alia*, application fee, annual fixed fee and, where applicable, costs of prospecting and exploration of the area covered by the contract, and a portion of research and development costs.

(m) "Return on investment" in any accounting year means the ratio of attributable net proceeds in that year to the development costs of the mining sector. For the purpose of computing this ratio the development costs of the mining sector shall include expenditures on new or replacement equipment in the mining sector less the original cost of the equipment replaced.

(n) If the contractor engages in mining only:

(i) "attributable net proceeds" means the whole of the contractor's net proceeds;

(ii) "contractor's net proceeds" shall be as defined in subparagraph (f);

(iii) "contractor's gross proceeds" means the gross revenues from the sale of the polymetallic nodules, and any other monies deemed reasonably attributable to operations under the contract in accordance with the financial rules, regulations and procedures of the Authority;

(iv) "contractor's development costs" means all expenditures incurred prior to the commencement of commercial production as set forth in subparagraph (h)(i), and all expenditures incurred subsequent to the commencement of commercial production as set forth in subparagraph (h)(ii), which are directly related to the mining of the resources of the area covered by the contract, in conformity with generally recognized accounting principles;

(v) "contractor's operating costs" means the contractor's operating costs as in subparagraph (k) which are directly related to the mining of the resources of the area covered by the contract in conformity with generally recognized accounting principles;

(vi) "return on investment" in any accounting year means the ratio of the contractor's net proceeds in that year to the contractor's development costs. For the purpose of computing this ratio, the contractor's development costs shall include expenditures on new or replacement equipment less the original cost of the equipment replaced.

(o) The costs referred to in subparagraphs (h), (k), (l) and (n) in respect of interest paid by the contractor shall be allowed to the extent that, in all the circumstances, the Authority approves, pursuant to article 4, paragraph 1, of this Annex, the debt-equity ratio and the rates of interest as reasonable, having regard to existing commercial practice.

(p) The costs referred to in this paragraph shall not be interpreted as including payments of corporate income taxes or similar charges levied by States in respect of the operations of the contractor.

7. (a) "Processed metals", referred to in paragraphs 5 and 6, means the metals in the most basic form in which they are customarily traded on international terminal markets. For this purpose, the Authority shall specify, in its financial rules, regulations and procedures, the relevant international

terminal market. For the metals which are not traded on such markets, "processed metals" means the metals in the most basic form in which they are customarily traded in representative arm's length transactions.

(b) If the Authority cannot otherwise determine the quantity of the processed metals produced from the polymetallic nodules recovered from the area covered by the contract referred to in paragraphs 5(b) and 6(b), the quantity shall be determined on the basis of the metal content of the nodules, processing recovery efficiency and other relevant factors, in accordance with the rules, regulations and procedures of the Authority and in conformity with generally recognized accounting principles.

8. If an international terminal market provides a representative pricing mechanism for processed metals, polymetallic nodules and semi-processed metals from the nodules, the average price on that market shall be used. In all other cases, the Authority shall, after consulting the contractor, determine a fair price for the said products in accordance with paragraph 9.

9. (a) All costs, expenditures, proceeds and revenues and all determinations of price and value referred to in this article shall be the result of free market or arm's length transactions. In the absence thereof, they shall be determined by the Authority, after consulting the contractor, as though they were the result of free market or arm's length transactions, taking into account relevant transactions in other markets.

(b) In order to ensure compliance with and enforcement of the provisions of this paragraph, the Authority shall be guided by the principles adopted for, and the interpretation given to, arm's length transactions by the Commission on Transnational Corporations of the United Nations, the Group of Experts on Tax Treaties between Developing and Developed Countries and other international organizations, and shall, in its rules, regulations and procedures, specify uniform and internationally acceptable accounting rules and procedures, and the means of selection by the contractor of certified independent accountants acceptable to the Authority for the purpose of carrying out auditing in compliance with those rules, regulations and procedures.

10. The contractor shall make available to the accountants, in accordance with the financial rules, regulations and procedures of the Authority, such financial data as are required to determine compliance with this article.

11. All costs, expenditures, proceeds and revenues, and all prices and values referred to in this article, shall be determined in accordance with generally recognized accounting principles and the financial rules, regulations and procedures of the Authority.

12. Payments to the Authority under paragraphs 5 and 6 shall be made in freely usable currencies or currencies which are freely available and effectively usable on the major foreign exchange markets or, at the contractor's option, in the equivalents of processed metals at market value. The market value shall be determined in accordance with paragraph 5(b). The freely usable currencies and currencies which are freely available and effectively usable on the major foreign exchange markets shall be defined in the rules, regulations and procedures of the Authority in accordance with prevailing international monetary practice.

13. All financial obligations of the contractor to the Authority, as well as all his fees, costs, expenditures, proceeds and revenues referred to in this article, shall be adjusted by expressing them in constant terms relative to a base year.

14. The Authority may, taking into account any recommendations of the Economic Planning Commission and the Legal and Technical Commission, adopt rules, regulations and procedures that

provide for incentives, on a uniform and non-discriminatory basis, to contractors to further the objectives set out in paragraph 1.

15. In the event of a dispute between the Authority and a contractor over the interpretation or application of the financial terms of a contract, either party may submit the dispute to binding commercial arbitration, unless both parties agree to settle the dispute by other means, in accordance with article 188, paragraph 2.

Article 14
Transfer of data

1. The operator shall transfer to the Authority, in accordance with its rules, regulations and procedures and the terms and conditions of the plan of work, at time intervals determined by the Authority all data which are both necessary for and relevant to the effective exercise of the powers and functions of the principal organs of the Authority in respect of the area covered by the plan of work.

2. Transferred data in respect of the area covered by the plan of work, deemed proprietary, may only be used for the purposes set forth in this article. Data necessary for the formulation by the Authority of rules, regulations and procedures concerning protection of the marine environment and safety, other than equipment design data, shall not be deemed proprietary.

3. Data transferred to the Authority by prospectors, applicants for contracts or contractors, deemed proprietary, shall not be disclosed by the Authority to the Enterprise or to anyone external to the Authority, but data on the reserved areas may be disclosed to the Enterprise. Such data transferred by such persons to the Enterprise shall not be disclosed by the Enterprise to the Authority or to anyone external to the Authority.

Article 15
Training programmes

The contractor shall draw up practical programmes for the training of personnel of the Authority and developing States, including the participation of such personnel in all activities in the Area which are covered by the contract, in accordance with article 144, paragraph 2.

Article 16
Exclusive right to explore and exploit

The Authority shall, pursuant to Part XI and its rules, regulations and procedures, accord the operator the exclusive right to explore and exploit the area covered by the plan of work in respect of a specified category of resources and shall ensure that no other entity operates in the same area for a different category of resources in a manner which might interfere with the operations of the operator. The operator shall have security of tenure in accordance with article 153, paragraph 6.

Article 17
Rules, regulations and procedures of the Authority

1. The Authority shall adopt and uniformly apply rules, regulations and procedures in accordance with article 160, paragraph 2(f)(ii), and article 162, paragraph 2(o)(ii), for the exercise of its functions as set forth in Part XI on, *inter alia*, the following matters:

(a) administrative procedures relating to prospecting, exploration and exploitation in the Area;

(b) operations:
 (i) size of area;
 (ii) duration of operations;

 (iii) performance requirements including assurances pursuant to article 4, paragraph 6(c), of this Annex;

 (iv) categories of resources;
 (v) renunciation of areas;
 (vi) progress reports;
 (vii) submission of data;
 (viii) inspection and supervision of operations;
 (ix) prevention of interference with other activities in the marine environment;
 (x) transfer of rights and obligations by a contractor;
 (xi) procedures for transfer of technology to developing States in accordance with article 144 and for their direct participation;
 (xii) mining standards and practices, including those relating to operational safety, conservation of the resources and the protection of the marine environment;
 (xiii) definition of commercial production;
 (xiv) qualification standards for applicants;

(c) financial matters:

 (i) establishment of uniform and non-dis criminatory costing and accounting rules and the method of selection of auditors;

 (ii) apportionment of proceeds of operations;

 (iii) the incentives referred to in article 13 of this Annex;

(d) implementation of decisions taken pursuant to article 151, paragraph 10, and article 164, paragraph 2(d).

2. Rules, regulations and procedures on the following items shall fully reflect the objective criteria set out below:

(a) Size of areas:

The Authority shall determine the appropriate size of areas for exploration which may be up to twice as large as those for exploitation in order to permit intensive exploration operations. The size of area shall be calculated to satisfy the requirements of article 8 of this Annex on reservation of areas as well as stated production requirements consistent with article 151 in accordance with the terms of the contract taking into account the state of the art of technology then available for seabed mining and the relevant physical characteristics of the areas. Areas shall be neither smaller nor larger than are necessary to satisfy this objective.

(b) Duration of operations:
(i) Prospecting shall be without time-limit;

(ii) Exploration should be of sufficient duration to permit a thorough survey of the specific area, the design and construction of mining equipment for the area and the design and construction of small and medium-size processing plants for the purpose of testing mining and processing systems;

(iii) The duration of exploitation should be related to the economic life of the mining project, taking into consideration such factors as the depletion of the ore, the useful life of mining equipment and processing facilities and commercial viability. Exploitation should be of sufficient duration to permit commercial extraction of minerals of the area and should include a reasonable time period for construction of commercial-scale mining and processing systems, during which period commercial production should not be required. The total duration of exploitation, however, should also be short enough to give the Authority an opportunity to amend the terms and conditions of the plan of work at the time it considers renewal in accordance with rules, regulations and procedures which it has adopted subsequent to approving the plan of work.

(c) Performance requirements:

The Authority shall require that during the exploration stage periodic expenditures be made by the operator which are reasonably related to the size of the area covered by the plan of work and the expenditures which would be expected of a *bona fide* operator who intended to bring the area into commercial production within the time-limits established by the Authority. The required expenditures should not be established at a level which would discourage prospective operators with less costly technology than is prevalently in use. The Authority shall establish a maximum time interval, after the exploration stage is completed and the exploitation stage begins, to achieve commercial production. To determine this interval, the Authority should take into consideration that construction of large-scale mining and processing systems cannot be initiated until after the termination of the exploration stage and the commencement of the exploitation stage. Accordingly, the interval to bring an area into commercial production should take into account the time necessary for this construction after the completion of the exploration stage and reasonable allowance should be made for unavoidable delays in the construction schedule. Once commercial production is achieved, the Authority shall within reasonable limits and taking into consideration all relevant factors require the operator to maintain commercial production throughout the period of the plan of work.

(d) Categories of resources:

In determining the category of resources in respect of which a plan of work may be approved, the Authority shall give emphasis *inter alia* to the following characteristics:

(i) that certain resources require the use of similar mining methods; and

(ii) that some resources can be developed simultaneously without undue interference between operators developing different resources in the same area.

Nothing in this subparagraph shall preclude the Authority from approving a plan of work with respect to more than one category of resources in the same area to the same applicant.

(e) Renunciation of areas:

The operator shall have the right at any time to renounce without penalty the whole or part of his rights in the area covered by a plan of work.

(f) Protection of the marine environment:

Rules, regulations and procedures shall be drawn up in order to secure effective protection of the marine environment from harmful effects directly resulting from activities in the Area or from shipboard processing immediately above a mine site of minerals derived from that mine site, taking into account the extent to which such harmful effects may directly result from drilling, dredging, coring and excavation and from disposal, dumping and discharge into the marine environment of sediment, wastes or other effluents.

(g) Commercial production:

Commercial production shall be deemed to have begun if an operator engages in sustained large-scale recovery operations which yield a quantity of materials sufficient to indicate clearly that the principal purpose is large-scale production rather than production intended for information gathering, analysis or the testing of equipment or plant.

Article 18
Penalties

1. A contractor's rights under the contract may be suspended or terminated only in the following cases:

(a) if, in spite of warnings by the Authority, the contractor has conducted his activities in such a way as to result in serious, persistent and wilful violations of the fundamental terms of the contract, Part XI and the rules, regulations and procedures of the Authority; or

(b) if the contractor has failed to comply with a final binding decision of the dispute settlement body applicable to him.

2. In the case of any violation of the contract not covered by paragraph 1(a), or in lieu of suspension or termination under paragraph 1(a), the Authority may impose upon the contractor monetary penalties proportionate to the seriousness of the violation.

3. Except for emergency orders under article 162, paragraph 2(w), the Authority may not execute a decision involving monetary penalties, suspension or termination until the contractor has been accorded a reasonable opportunity to exhaust the judicial remedies available to him pursuant to Part XI, section 5.

Article 19
Revision of contract

1. When circumstances have arisen or are likely to arise which, in the opinion of either party, would render the contract inequitable or make it impracticable or impossible to achieve the objectives set out in the contract or in Part XI, the parties shall enter into negotiations to revise it accordingly.

2. Any contract entered into in accordance with article 153, paragraph 3, may be revised only with the consent of the parties.

Article 20
Transfer of rights and obligations

The rights and obligations arising under a contract may be transferred only with the consent of the Authority, and in accordance with its rules, regulations and procedures. The Authority shall not unreasonably withhold consent to the transfer if the proposed transferee is in all respects a qualified applicant and assumes all of the obligations of the transferor and if the transfer does not confer to the transferee a plan of work, the approval of which would be forbidden by article 6, paragraph 3(c), of this Annex.

Article 21
Applicable law

1. The contract shall be governed by the terms of the contract, the rules, regulations and procedures of the Authority, Part XI and other rules of international law not incompatible with this Convention.

2. Any final decision rendered by a court or tribunal having jurisdiction under this Convention relating to the rights and obligations of the Authority and of the contractor shall be enforceable in the territory of each State Party.

3. No State Party may impose conditions on a contractor that are inconsistent with Part XI. However, the application by a State Party to contractors sponsored by it, or to ships flying its flag, of environmental or other laws and regulations more stringent than those in the rules, regulations and procedures of the Authority adopted pursuant to article 17, paragraph 2(f), of this Annex shall not be deemed inconsistent with Part XI.

Article 22
Responsibility

The contractor shall have responsibility or liability for any damage arising out of wrongful acts in the conduct of its operations, account being taken of contributory acts or omissions by the Authority. Similarly, the Authority shall have responsibility or liability for any damage arising out of wrongful acts in the exercise of its powers and functions, including violations under article 168, paragraph 2, account being taken of contributory acts or omissions by the contractor. Liability in every case shall be for the actual amount of damage.

ANNEX IV. STATUTE OF THE ENTERPRISE

Article 1
Purposes

1. The Enterprise is the organ of the Authority which shall carry out activities in the Area directly, pursuant to article 153, paragraph 2 (a), as well as the transporting, processing and marketing of minerals recovered from the Area.

2. In carrying out its purposes and in the exercise of its functions, the Enterprise shall act in accordance with this Convention and the rules, regulations and procedures of the Authority.

3. In developing the resources of the Area pursuant to paragraph 1, the Enterprise shall, subject to this Convention, operate in accordance with sound commercial principles.

Article 2
Relationship to the Authority

1. Pursuant to article 170, the Enterprise shall act in accordance with the general policies of the Assembly and the directives of the Council.

2. Subject to paragraph l, the Enterprise shall enjoy autonomy in the conduct of its operations.

3. Nothing in this Convention shall make the Enterprise liable for the acts or obligations of the Authority, or make the Authority liable for the acts or obligations of the Enterprise.

Article 3
Limitation of liability

Without prejudice to article 11, paragraph 3, of this Annex, no member of the Authority shall be liable by reason only of its membership for the acts or obligations of the Enterprise.

Article 4
Structure

The Enterprise shall have a Governing Board, a Director-General and the staff necessary for the exercise of its functions.

Article 5
Governing Board

1. The Governing Board shall be composed of 15 members elected by the Assembly in accordance with article 160, paragraph 2(c). In the election of the members of the Board, due regard shall be paid to the principle of equitable geographical distribution. In submitting nominations of candidates for election to the Board, members of the Authority shall bear in mind the need to nominate candidates of the highest standard of competence, with qualifications in relevant fields, so as to ensure the viability and success of the Enterprise.

2. Members of the Board shall be elected for four years and may be re-elected; and due regard shall be paid to the principle of rotation of membership.

3. Members of the Board shall continue in office until their successors are elected. If the office of a member of the Board becomes vacant, the Assembly shall, in accordance with article 160, paragraph 2(c), elect a new member for the remainder of his predecessor's term.

4. Members of the Board shall act in their personal capacity. In the performance of their duties they shall not seek or receive instructions from any government or from any other source. Each member of the Authority shall respect the independent character of the members of the Board and shall refrain from all attempts to influence any of them in the discharge of their duties.

5. Each member of the Board shall receive remuneration to be paid out of the funds of the Enterprise. The amount of remuneration shall be fixed by the Assembly, upon the recommendation of the Council.

6. The Board shall normally function at the principal office of the Enterprise and shall meet as often as the business of the Enterprise may require.

7. Two thirds of the members of the Board shall constitute a quorum.

8. Each member of the Board shall have one vote. All matters before the Board shall be decided by a majority of its members. If a member has a conflict of interest on a matter before the Board he shall refrain from voting on that matter.

9. Any member of the Authority may ask the Board for information in respect of its operations which particularly affect that member. The Board shall endeavour to provide such information.

Article 6
Powers and functions of the Governing Board

The Governing Board shall direct the operations of the Enterprise. Subject to this Convention, the Governing Board shall exercise the powers necessary to fulfil the purposes of the Enterprise, including powers:

(a) to elect a Chairman from among its members;

(b) to adopt its rules of procedure;

(c) to draw up and submit formal written plans of work to the Council in accordance with article 153, paragraph 3, and article 162, paragraph 2(j);

(d) to develop plans of work and programmes for carrying out the activities specified in article 170;

(e) to prepare and submit to the Council applications for production authorizations in accordance with article 151, paragraphs 2 to 7;

(f) to authorize negotiations concerning the acquisition of technology, including those provided for in Annex III, article 5, paragraph 3(a), (c) and (d), and to approve the results of those negotiations;

(g) to establish terms and conditions, and to authorize negotiations, concerning joint ventures and other forms of joint arrangements referred to in Annex III, articles 9 and 11, and to approve the results of such negotiations;

(h) to recommend to the Assembly what portion of the net income of the Enterprise should be retained as its reserves in accordance with article 160, paragraph 2(f), and article 10 of this Annex;

(i) to approve the annual budget of the Enterprise;

(j) to authorize the procurement of goods and services in accordance with article 12, paragraph 3, of this Annex;

(k) to submit an annual report to the Council in accordance with article 9 of this Annex;

(l) to submit to the Council for the approval of the Assembly draft rules in respect of the organization, management, appointment and dismissal of the staff of the Enterprise and to adopt regulations to give effect to such rules;

(m) to borrow funds and to furnish such collateral or other security as it may determine in accordance with article 11, paragraph 2, of this Annex;

(n) to enter into any legal proceedings, agreements and transactions and to take any other actions in accordance with article 13 of this Annex;

(o) to delegate, subject to the approval of the Council, any non-discretionary powers to the Director-General and to its committees.

Article 7
Director-General and staff of the Enterprise

1. The Assembly shall, upon the recommendation of the Council and the nomination of the Governing Board, elect the Director-General of the Enterprise who shall not be a member of the Board. The Director-General shall hold office for a fixed term, not exceeding five years, and may be re-elected for further terms.

2. The Director-General shall be the legal representative and chief executive of the Enterprise and shall be directly responsible to the Board for the conduct of the operations of the Enterprise. He shall be responsible for the organization, management, appointment and dismissal of the staff of the Enterprise in accordance with the rules and regulations referred to in article 6, subparagraph (l), of this Annex. He shall participate, without the right to vote, in the meetings of the Board and may participate, without the right to vote, in the meetings of the Assembly and the Council when these organs are dealing with matters concerning the Enterprise.

3. The paramount consideration in the recruitment and employment of the staff and in the determination of their conditions of service shall be the necessity of securing the highest standards of efficiency and of technical competence. Subject to this consideration, due regard shall be paid to the importance of recruiting the staff on an equitable geographical basis.

4. In the performance of their duties the Director-General and the staff shall not seek or receive instructions from any government or from any other source external to the Enterprise. They shall refrain from any action which might reflect on their position as international officials of the

Enterprise responsible only to the Enterprise. Each State Party undertakes to respect the exclusively international character of the responsibilities of the Director-General and the staff and not to seek to influence them in the discharge of their responsibilities.

5. The responsibilities set forth in article 168, paragraph 2, are equally applicable to the staff of the Enterprise.

Article 8
Location

The Enterprise shall have its principal office at the seat of the Authority. The Enterprise may establish other offices and facilities in the territory of any State Party with the consent of that State Party.

Article 9
Reports and financial statements

1. The Enterprise shall, not later than three months after the end of each financial year, submit to the Council for its consideration an annual report containing an audited statement of its accounts and shall transmit to the Council at appropriate intervals a summary statement of its financial position and a profit and loss statement showing the results of its operations.

2. The Enterprise shall publish its annual report and such other reports as it finds appropriate.

3. All reports and financial statements referred to in this article shall be distributed to the members of the Authority.

Article 10
Allocation of net income

1. Subject to paragraph 3, the Enterprise shall make payments to the Authority under Annex III, article 13, or their equivalent.

2. The Assembly shall, upon the recommendation of the Governing Board, determine what portion of the net income of the Enterprise shall be retained as reserves of the Enterprise. The remainder shall be transferred to the Authority.

3. During an initial period required for the Enterprise to become self-supporting, which shall not exceed 10 years from the commencement of commercial production by it, the Assembly shall exempt the Enterprise from the payments referred to in paragraph 1, and shall leave all of the net income of the Enterprise in its reserves.

Article 11
Finances

1. The funds of the Enterprise shall include:

(a) amounts received from the Authority in accordance with article 173, paragraph 2(b);

(b) voluntary contributions made by States Parties for the purpose of financing activities of the Enterprise;

(c) amounts borrowed by the Enterprise in accordance with paragraphs 2 and 3;

(d) income of the Enterprise from its operations;

(e) other funds made available to the Enterprise to enable it to commence operations as soon as possible and to carry out its functions.

2. (a) The Enterprise shall have the power to borrow funds and to furnish such collateral or other security as it may determine. Before making a public sale of its obligations in the financial markets or currency of a State Party, the Enterprise shall obtain the approval of that State Party. The total amount of borrowings shall be approved by the Council upon the recommendation of the Governing Board.

(b) States Parties shall make every reasonable effort to support applications by the Enterprise for loans on capital markets and from international financial institutions.

3. (a) The Enterprise shall be provided with the funds necessary to explore and exploit one mine site, and to transport, process and market the minerals recovered therefrom and the nickel, copper, cobalt and manganese obtained, and to meet its initial administrative expenses. The amount of the said funds, and the criteria and factors for its adjustment, shall be included by the Preparatory Commission in the draft rules, regulations and procedures of the Authority.

(b) All States Parties shall make available to the Enterprise an amount equivalent to one half of the funds referred to in subparagraph (a) by way of long-term interest-free loans in accordance with the scale of assessments for the United Nations regular budget in force at the time when the assessments are made, adjusted to take into account the States which are not members of the United Nations. Debts incurred by the Enterprise in raising the other half of the funds shall be guaranteed by all States Parties in accordance with the same scale.

(c) If the sum of the financial contributions of States Parties is less than the funds to be provided to the Enterprise under subparagraph (a), the Assembly shall, at its first session, consider the extent of the shortfall and adopt by consensus measures for dealing with this shortfall, taking into account the obligation of States Parties under subparagraphs (a) and (b) and any recommendations of the Preparatory Commission.

(d) (i) Each State Party shall, within 60 days after the entry into force of this Convention, or within 30 days after the deposit of its instrument of ratification or accession, whichever is later, deposit with the Enterprise irrevocable, non-negotiable, non-interest-bearing promissory notes in the amount of the share of such State Party of interest-free loans pursuant to subparagraph (b).

(ii) The Board shall prepare, at the earliest practicable date after this Convention enters into force, and thereafter at annual or other appropriate intervals, a schedule of the magnitude and timing of its requirements for the funding of its administrative expenses and for activities carried out by the Enterprise in accordance with article 170 and article 12 of this Annex.

(iii) The States Parties shall, thereupon, be notified by the Enterprise, through the Authority, of their respective shares of the funds in accordance with subparagraph (b), required for such expenses. The Enterprise shall encash such amounts of the promissory notes as may be required to meet the expenditure referred to in the schedule with respect to interest-free loans.

(iv) States Parties shall, upon receipt of the notification, make available their respective shares of debt guarantees for the Enterprise in accordance with subparagraph (b).

(e) (i) If the Enterprise so requests, State Parties may provide debt guarantees in addition to those provided in accordance with the scale referred to in subparagraph (b).

(ii) In lieu of debt guarantees, a State Party may make a voluntary contribution to the Enterprise in an amount equivalent to that portion of the debts which it would otherwise be liable to guarantee.

(f) Repayment of the interest-bearing loans shall have priority over the repayment of the interest-free loans. Repayment of interest-free loans shall be in accordance with a schedule adopted by the Assembly, upon the recommendation of the Council and the advice of the Board. In the exercise of this function the Board shall be guided by the relevant provisions of the rules, regulations and procedures of the Authority, which shall take into account the paramount importance of ensuring the effective functioning of the Enterprise and, in particular, ensuring its financial independence.

(g) Funds made available to the Enterprise shall be in freely usable currencies or currencies which are freely available and effectively usable in the major foreign exchange markets. These currencies shall be defined in the rules, regulations and procedures of the Authority in accordance with prevailing international monetary practice. Except as provided in paragraph 2, no State Party shall maintain or impose restrictions on the holding, use or exchange by the Enterprise of these funds.

(h) "Debt guarantee" means a promise of a State Party to creditors of the Enterprise to pay, *pro rata* in accordance with the appropriate scale, the financial obligations of the Enterprise covered by the guarantee following notice by the creditors to the State Party of a default by the Enterprise. Procedures for the payment of those obligations shall be in conformity with the rules, regulations and procedures of the Authority.

4. The funds, assets and expenses of the Enterprise shall be kept separate from those of the Authority. This article shall not prevent the Enterprise from making arrangements with the Authority regarding facilities, personnel and services and arrangements for reimbursement of administrative expenses paid by either on behalf of the other.

5. The records, books and accounts of the Enterprise, including its annual financial statements, shall be audited annually by an independent auditor appointed by the Council.

Article 12
Operations

1. The Enterprise shall propose to the Council projects for carrying out activities in accordance with article 170. Such proposals shall include a formal written plan of work for activities in the Area in accordance with article 153, paragraph 3, and all such other information and data as may be required from time to time for its appraisal by the Legal and Technical Commission and approval by the Council.

2. Upon approval by the Council, the Enterprise shall execute the project on the basis of the formal written plan of work referred to in paragraph 1.

3. (a) If the Enterprise does not possess the goods and services required for its operations it may procure them. For that purpose, it shall issue invitations to tender and award contracts to bidders offering the best combination of quality, price and delivery time.

(b) If there is more than one bid offering such a combination, the contract shall be awarded in accordance with:

(i) the principle of non-discrimination on the basis of political or other considerations not relevant to the carrying out of operations with due diligence and efficiency; and

(ii) guidelines approved by the Council with regard to the preferences to be accorded to goods and services originating in developing States, including the land-locked and geographically disadvantaged among them.

(c) The Governing Board may adopt rules determining the special circumstances in which the requirement of invitations to bid may, in the best interests of the Enterprise, be dispensed with.

4. The Enterprise shall have title to all minerals and processed substances produced by it.

5. The Enterprise shall sell its products on a non-discriminatory basis. It shall not give non-commercial discounts.

6. Without prejudice to any general or special power conferred on the Enterprise under any other provision of this Convention, the Enterprise shall exercise such powers incidental to its business as shall be necessary.

7. The Enterprise shall not interfere in the political affairs of any State Party; nor shall it be influenced in its decisions by the political character of the State Party concerned. Only commercial considerations shall be relevant to its decisions, and these considerations shall be weighed impartially in order to carry out the purposes specified in article 1 of this Annex.

Article 13
Legal status, privileges and immunities

1. To enable the Enterprise to exercise its functions, the status, privileges and immunities set forth in this article shall be accorded to the Enterprise in the territories of States Parties. To give effect to this principle the Enterprise and States Parties may, where necessary, enter into special agreements.

2. The Enterprise shall have such legal capacity as is necessary for the exercise of its functions and the fulfilment of its purposes and, in particular, the capacity:

(a) to enter into contracts, joint arrangements or other arrangements, including agreements with States and international organizations;

(b) to acquire, lease, hold and dispose of immovable and movable property;

(c) to be a party to legal proceedings.

3. (a) Actions may be brought against the Enterprise only in a court of competent jurisdiction in the territory of a State Party in which the Enterprise:

(i) has an office or facility;

(ii) has appointed an agent for the purpose of accepting service or notice of process;

(iii) has entered into a contract for goods or services;

(iv) has issued securities; or

(v) is otherwise engaged in commercial activity.

(b) The property and assets of the Enterprise, wherever located and by whomsoever held, shall be immune from all forms of seizure, attachment or execution before the delivery of final judgment against the Enterprise.

4. (a) The property and assets of the Enterprise, wherever located and by whomsoever held, shall be immune from requisition, confiscation, expropriation or any other form of seizure by executive or legislative action.

(b) The property and assets of the Enterprise, wherever located and by whomsoever held, shall be free from discriminatory restrictions, regulations, controls and moratoria of any nature.

(c) The Enterprise and its employees shall respect local laws and regulations in any State or territory in which the Enterprise or its employees may do business or otherwise act.

(d) States Parties shall ensure that the Enterprise enjoys all rights, privileges and immunities accorded by them to entities conducting commercial activities in their territories. These rights, privileges and immunities shall be accorded to the Enterprise on no less favourable a basis than that on which they are accorded to entities engaged in similar commercial activities. If special privileges are provided by States Parties for developing States or their commercial entities, the Enterprise shall enjoy those privileges on a similarly preferential basis.

(e) States Parties may provide special incentives, rights, privileges and immunities to the Enterprise without the obligation to provide such incentives, rights, privileges and immunities to other commercial entities.

5. The Enterprise shall negotiate with the host countries in which its offices and facilities are located for exemption from direct and indirect taxation.

6. Each State Party shall take such action as is necessary for giving effect in terms of its own law to the principles set forth in this Annex and shall inform the Enterprise of the specific action which it has taken.

7. The Enterprise may waive any of the privileges and immunities conferred under this article or in the special agreements referred to in paragraph 1 to such extent and upon such conditions as it may determine.

ANNEX V. CONCILIATION

SECTION 1. CONCILIATION PROCEDURE

PURSUANT TO SECTION 1 OF PART XV

Article 1
Institution of proceedings

If the parties to a dispute have agreed, in accordance with article 284, to submit it to conciliation under this section, any such party may institute the proceedings by written notification addressed to the other party or parties to the dispute.

Article 2
List of conciliators

A list of conciliators shall be drawn up and maintained by the Secretary-General of the United Nations. Every State Party shall be entitled to nominate four conciliators, each of whom shall be a person enjoying the highest reputation for fairness, competence and integrity. The names of the persons so nominated shall constitute the list. If at any time the conciliators nominated by a State Party in the list so constituted shall be fewer than four, that State Party shall be entitled to make further nominations as necessary. The name of a conciliator shall remain on the list until withdrawn by the State Party which made the nomination, provided that such conciliator shall continue to serve on any conciliation commission to which that conciliator has been appointed until the completion of the proceedings before that commission.

Article 3
Constitution of conciliation commission

The conciliation commission shall, unless the parties otherwise agree, be constituted as follows:

(a) Subject to subparagraph (g), the conciliation commission shall consist of five members.

(b) The party instituting the proceedings shall appoint two conciliators to be chosen preferably from the list referred to in article 2 of this Annex, one of whom may be its national, unless the parties otherwise agree. Such appointments shall be included in the notification referred to in article 1 of this Annex.

(c) The other party to the dispute shall appoint two conciliators in the manner set forth in subparagraph (b) within 21 days of receipt of the notification referred to in article 1 of this Annex. If the appointments are not made within that period, the party instituting the proceedings may, within one week of the expiration of that period, either terminate the proceedings by notification addressed to the other party or request the Secretary-General of the United Nations to make the appointments in accordance with subparagraph (e).

(d) Within 30 days after all four conciliators have been appointed, they shall appoint a fifth conciliator chosen from the list referred to in article 2 of this Annex, who shall be chairman. If the appointment is not made within that period, either party may, within one week of the expiration of that period, request the Secretary-General of the United Nations to make the appointment in accordance with subparagraph (e).

(e) Within 30 days of the receipt of a request under subparagraph (c) or (d), the Secretary-General of the United Nations shall make the necessary appointments from the list referred to in article 2 of this Annex in consultation with the parties to the dispute.

(f) Any vacancy shall be filled in the manner prescribed for the initial appointment.

(g) Two or more parties which determine by agreement that they are in the same interest shall appoint two conciliators jointly. Where two or more parties have separate interests or there is a disagreement as to whether they are of the same interest, they shall appoint conciliators separately.

(h) In disputes involving more than two parties having separate interests, or where there is disagreement as to whether they are of the same interest, the parties shall apply subparagraphs (a) to (f) in so far as possible.

Article 4
Procedure

The conciliation commission shall, unless the parties otherwise agree, determine its own procedure. The commission may, with the consent of the parties to the dispute, invite any State Party to submit to it its views orally or in writing. Decisions of the commission regarding procedural matters, the report and recommendations shall be made by a majority vote of its members.

Article 5
Amicable settlement

The commission may draw the attention of the parties to any measures which might facilitate an amicable settlement of the dispute.

Article 6
Functions of the commission

The commission shall hear the parties, examine their claims and objections, and make proposals to the parties with a view to reaching an amicable settlement.

Article 7
Report

1. The commission shall report within 12 months of its constitution. Its report shall record any agreements reached and, failing agreement, its conclusions on all questions of fact or law relevant to the matter in dispute and such recommendations as the commission may deem appropriate for an amicable settlement. The report shall be deposited with the Secretary-General of the United Nations and shall immediately be transmitted by him to the parties to the dispute.

2. The report of the commission, including its conclusions or recommendations, shall not be binding upon the parties.

Article 8
Termination

The conciliation proceedings are terminated when a settlement has been reached, when the parties have accepted or one party has rejected the recommendations of the report by written notification addressed to the Secretary-General of the United Nations, or when a period of three months has expired from the date of transmission of the report to the parties.

Article 9
Fees and expenses

The fees and expenses of the commission shall be borne by the parties to the dispute.

Article 10
Right of parties to modify procedure

The parties to the dispute may by agreement applicable solely to that dispute modify any provision of this Annex.

SECTION 2. COMPULSORY SUBMISSION TO CONCILIATION PROCEDURE PURSUANT TO SECTION 3 OF PART XV

Article 11
Institution of proceedings

1. Any party to a dispute which, in accordance with Part XV, section 3, may be submitted to conciliation under this section, may institute the proceedings by written notification addressed to the other party or parties to the dispute.

2. Any party to the dispute, notified under paragraph 1, shall be obliged to submit to such proceedings.

Article 12
Failure to reply or to submit to conciliation

The failure of a party or parties to the dispute to reply to notification of institution of proceedings or to submit to such proceedings shall not constitute a bar to the proceedings.

Article 13
Competence

A disagreement as to whether a conciliation commission acting under this section has competence shall be decided by the commission.

Article 14
Application of section 1

Articles 2 to 10 of section 1 of this Annex apply subject to this section.

ANNEX VI. STATUTE OF THE INTERNATIONAL TRIBUNAL FOR THE LAW OF THE SEA

Article 1
General provisions

1. The International Tribunal for the Law of the Sea is constituted and shall function in accordance with the provisions of this Convention and this Statute.

2. The seat of the Tribunal shall be in the Free and Hanseatic City of Hamburg in the Federal Republic of Germany.

3. The Tribunal may sit and exercise its functions elsewhere whenever it considers this desirable.

4. A reference of a dispute to the Tribunal shall be governed by the provisions of Parts XI and XV.

SECTION 1. ORGANIZATION OF THE TRIBUNAL

Article 2
Composition

1. The Tribunal shall be composed of a body of 21 independent members, elected from among persons enjoying the highest reputation for fairness and integrity and of recognized competence in the field of the law of the sea.

2. In the Tribunal as a whole the representation of the principal legal systems of the world and equitable geographical distribution shall be assured.

Article 3
Membership

1. No two members of the Tribunal may be nationals of the same State. A person who for the purposes of membership in the Tribunal could be regarded as a national of more than one State shall be deemed to be a national of the one in which he ordinarily exercises civil and political rights.

2. There shall be no fewer than three members from each geographical group as established by the General Assembly of the United Nations.

Article 4
Nominations and elections

1. Each State Party may nominate not more than two persons having the qualifications prescribed in article 2 of this Annex. The members of the Tribunal shall be elected from the list of persons thus nominated.

2. At least three months before the date of the election, the Secretary-General of the United Nations in the case of the first election and the Registrar of the Tribunal in the case of subsequent elections shall address a written invitation to the States Parties to submit their nominations for members of the Tribunal within two months. He shall prepare a list in alphabetical order of all the persons thus nominated, with an indication of the States Parties which have nominated them, and shall submit it to the States Parties before the seventh day of the last month before the date of each election.

3. The first election shall be held within six months of the date of entry into force of this Convention.

4. The members of the Tribunal shall be elected by secret ballot. Elections shall be held at a meeting of the States Parties convened by the Secretary-General of the United Nations in the case of the first election and by a procedure agreed to by the States Parties in the case of subsequent elections. Two thirds of the States Parties shall constitute a quorum at that meeting. The persons elected to the Tribunal shall be those nominees who obtain the largest number of votes and a two-thirds majority of the States Parties present and voting, provided that such majority includes a majority of the States Parties.

Article 5
Term of office

1. The members of the Tribunal shall be elected for nine years and may be re-elected; provided, however, that of the members elected at the first election, the terms of seven members shall expire at the end of three years and the terms of seven more members shall expire at the end of six years.

2. The members of the Tribunal whose terms are to expire at the end of the above-mentioned initial periods of three and six years shall be chosen by lot to be drawn by the Secretary-General of the United Nations immediately after the first election.

3. The members of the Tribunal shall continue to discharge their duties until their places have been filled. Though replaced, they shall finish any proceedings which they may have begun before the date of their replacement.

4. In the case of the resignation of a member of the Tribunal, the letter of resignation shall be addressed to the President of the Tribunal. The place becomes vacant on the receipt of that letter.

Article 6
Vacancies

1. Vacancies shall be filled by the same method as that laid down for the first election, subject to the following provision: the Registrar shall, within one month of the occurrence of the vacancy, proceed to issue the invitations provided for in article 4 of this Annex, and the date of the election shall be fixed by the President of the Tribunal after consultation with the States Parties.

2. A member of the Tribunal elected to replace a member whose term of office has not expired shall hold office for the remainder of his predecessor's term.

Article 7
Incompatible activities

1. No member of the Tribunal may exercise any political or administrative function, or associate actively with or be financially interested in any of the operations of any enterprise concerned with the exploration for or exploitation of the resources of the sea or the seabed or other commercial use of the sea or the seabed.

2. No member of the Tribunal may act as agent, counsel or advocate in any case.

3. Any doubt on these points shall be resolved by decision of the majority of the other members of the Tribunal present.

Article 8
Conditions relating to participation of members in a particular case

1. No member of the Tribunal may participate in the decision of any case in which he has previously taken part as agent, counsel or advocate for one of the parties, or as a member of a national or international court or tribunal, or in any other capacity.

2. If, for some special reason, a member of the Tribunal considers that he should not take part in the decision of a particular case, he shall so inform the President of the Tribunal.

3. If the President considers that for some special reason one of the members of the Tribunal should not sit in a particular case, he shall give him notice accordingly.

4. Any doubt on these points shall be resolved by decision of the majority of the other members of the Tribunal present.

Article 9
Consequence of ceasing to fulfil required conditions

If, in the unanimous opinion of the other members of the Tribunal, a member has ceased to fulfill the required conditions, the President of the Tribunal shall declare the seat vacant.

Article 10
Privileges and immunities

The members of the Tribunal, when engaged on the business of the Tribunal, shall enjoy diplomatic privileges and immunities.

Article 11
Solemn declaration by members

Every member of the Tribunal shall, before taking up his duties, make a solemn declaration in open session that he will exercise his powers impartially and conscientiously.

Article 12
President, Vice-President and Registrar

1. The Tribunal shall elect its President and Vice-President for three years; they may be re-elected.
2. The Tribunal shall appoint its Registrar and may provide for the appointment of such other officers as may be necessary.

3. The President and the Registrar shall reside at the seat of the Tribunal.

Article 13
Quorum

1. All available members of the Tribunal shall sit; a quorum of 11 elected members shall be required to constitute the Tribunal.

2. Subject to article 17 of this Annex, the Tribunal shall determine which members are available to constitute the Tribunal for the consideration of a particular dispute, having regard to the effective functioning of the chambers as provided for in articles 14 and 15 of this Annex.

3. All disputes and applications submitted to the Tribunal shall be heard and determined by the Tribunal, unless article 14 of this Annex applies, or the parties request that it shall be dealt with in accordance with article 15 of this Annex.

Article 14
Seabed Disputes Chamber

A Seabed Disputes Chamber shall be established in accordance with the provisions of section 4 of this Annex. Its jurisdiction, powers and functions shall be as provided for in Part XI, section 5.

Article 15
Special chambers

1. The Tribunal may form such chambers, composed of three or more of its elected members, as it considers necessary for dealing with particular categories of disputes.

2. The Tribunal shall form a chamber for dealing with a particular dispute submitted to it if the parties so request. The composition of such a chamber shall be determined by the Tribunal with the approval of the parties.

3. With a view to the speedy dispatch of business, the Tribunal shall form annually a chamber composed of five of its elected members which may hear and determine disputes by summary procedure. Two alternative members shall be selected for the purpose of replacing members who are unable to participate in a particular proceeding.

4. Disputes shall be heard and determined by the chambers provided for in this article if the parties so request.

5. A judgment given by any of the chambers provided for in this article and in article 14 of this Annex shall be considered as rendered by the Tribunal.

Article 16
Rules of the Tribunal

The Tribunal shall frame rules for carrying out its functions. In particular it shall lay down rules of procedure.

Article 17
Nationality of members

1. Members of the Tribunal of the nationality of any of the parties to a dispute shall retain their right to participate as members of the Tribunal.

2. If the Tribunal, when hearing a dispute, includes upon the bench a member of the nationality of one of the parties, any other party may choose a person to participate as a member of the Tribunal.

3. If the Tribunal, when hearing a dispute, does not include upon the bench a member of the nationality of the parties, each of those parties may choose a person to participate as a member of the Tribunal.

4. This article applies to the chambers referred to in articles 14 and 15 of this Annex. In such cases, the President, in consultation with the parties, shall request specified members of the Tribunal forming the chamber, as many as necessary, to give place to the members of the Tribunal of the nationality of the parties concerned, and, failing such, or if they are unable to be present, to the members specially chosen by the parties.

5. Should there be several parties in the same interest, they shall, for the purpose of the preceding provisions, be considered as one party only. Any doubt on this point shall be settled by the decision of the Tribunal.

6. Members chosen in accordance with paragraphs 2, 3 and 4 shall fulfil the conditions required by articles 2, 8 and 11 of this Annex. They shall participate in the decision on terms of complete equality with their colleagues.

Article 18
Remuneration of members

1. Each elected member of the Tribunal shall receive an annual allowance and, for each day on which he exercises his functions, a special allowance, provided that in any year the total sum payable to any member as special allowance shall not exceed the amount of the annual allowance.

2. The President shall receive a special annual allowance.

3. The Vice-President shall receive a special allowance for each day on which he acts as President.

4. The members chosen under article 17 of this Annex, other than elected members of the Tribunal, shall receive compensation for each day on which they exercise their functions.

5. The salaries, allowances and compensation shall be determined from time to time at meetings of the States Parties, taking into account the workload of the Tribunal. They may not be decreased during the term of office.

6. The salary of the Registrar shall be determined at meetings of the States Parties, on the proposal of the Tribunal.

7. Regulations adopted at meetings of the States Parties shall determine the conditions under which retirement pensions may be given to members of the Tribunal and to the Registrar, and the conditions under which members of the Tribunal and Registrar shall have their travelling expenses refunded.

8. The salaries, allowances, and compensation shall be free of all taxation.

Article 19
Expenses of the Tribunal

1. The expenses of the Tribunal shall be borne by the States Parties and by the Authority on such terms and in such a manner as shall be decided at meetings of the States Parties.

2. When an entity other than a State Party or the Authority is a party to a case submitted to it, the Tribunal shall fix the amount which that party is to contribute towards the expenses of the Tribunal.

SECTION 2. COMPETENCE

Article 20
Access to the Tribunal

1. The Tribunal shall be open to States Parties.

2. The Tribunal shall be open to entities other than States Parties in any case expressly provided for in Part XI or in any case submitted pursuant to any other agreement conferring jurisdiction on the Tribunal which is accepted by all the parties to that case.

Article 21
Jurisdiction

The jurisdiction of the Tribunal comprises all disputes and all applications submitted to it in accordance with this Convention and all matters specifically provided for in any other agreement which confers jurisdiction on the Tribunal.

Article 22
Reference of disputes subject to other agreements

If all the parties to a treaty or convention already in force and concerning the subject-matter covered by this Convention so agree, any disputes concerning the interpretation or application of such treaty or convention may, in accordance with such agreement, be submitted to the Tribunal.

Article 23
Applicable law

The Tribunal shall decide all disputes and applications in accordance with article 293.

SECTION 3. PROCEDURE

Article 24
Institution of proceedings

1. Disputes are submitted to the Tribunal, as the case may be, either by notification of a special agreement or by written application, addressed to the Registrar. In either case, the subject of the dispute and the parties shall be indicated.

2. The Registrar shall forthwith notify the special agreement or the application to all concerned.

3. The Registrar shall also notify all States Parties.

Article 25
Provisional measures

1. In accordance with article 290, the Tribunal and its Seabed Disputes Chamber shall have the power to prescribe provisional measures.

2. If the Tribunal is not in session or a sufficient number of members is not available to constitute a quorum, the provisional measures shall be prescribed by the chamber of summary procedure formed under article 15, paragraph 3, of this Annex. Notwithstanding article 15, paragraph 4, of this Annex, such provisional measures may be adopted at the request of any party to the dispute. They shall be subject to review and revision by the Tribunal.

Article 26
Hearing

1. The hearing shall be under the control of the President or, if he is unable to preside, of the Vice-President. If neither is able to preside, the senior judge present of the Tribunal shall preside.

2. The hearing shall be public, unless the Tribunal decides otherwise or unless the parties demand that the public be not admitted.

Article 27
Conduct of case

The Tribunal shall make orders for the conduct of the case, decide the form and time in which each party must conclude its arguments, and make all arrangements connected with the taking of evidence.

Article 28
Default

When one of the parties does not appear before the Tribunal or fails to defend its case, the other party may request the Tribunal to continue the proceedings and make its decision. Absence of a party or failure of a party to defend its case shall not constitute a bar to the proceedings. Before making its decision, the Tribunal must satisfy itself not only that it has jurisdiction over the dispute, but also that the claim is well founded in fact and law.

Article 29
Majority for decision

1. All questions shall be decided by a majority of the members of the Tribunal who are present.

2. In the event of an equality of votes, the President or the member of the Tribunal who acts in his place shall have a casting vote.

Article 30
Judgment

1. The judgment shall state the reasons on which it is based.

2. It shall contain the names of the members of the Tribunal who have taken part in the decision.

3. If the judgment does not represent in whole or in part the unanimous opinion of the members of the Tribunal, any member shall be entitled to deliver a separate opinion.

4. The judgment shall be signed by the President and by the Registrar. It shall be read in open court, due notice having been given to the parties to the dispute.

Article 31
Request to intervene

1. Should a State Party consider that it has an interest of a legal nature which may be affected by the decision in any dispute, it may submit a request to the Tribunal to be permitted to intervene.

2. It shall be for the Tribunal to decide upon this request.

3. If a request to intervene is granted, the decision of the Tribunal in respect of the dispute shall be binding upon the intervening State Party in so far as it relates to matters in respect of which that State Party intervened.

Article 32
Right to intervene in cases of interpretation or application

1. Whenever the interpretation or application of this Convention is in question, the Registrar shall notify all States Parties forthwith.

2. Whenever pursuant to article 21 or 22 of this Annex the interpretation or application of an international agreement is in question, the Registrar shall notify all the parties to the agreement.

3. Every party referred to in paragraphs 1 and 2 has the right to intervene in the proceedings; if it uses this right, the interpretation given by the judgment will be equally binding upon it.

Article 33
Finality and binding force of decisions

1. The decision of the Tribunal is final and shall be complied with by all the parties to the dispute.

2. The decision shall have no binding force except between the parties in respect of that particular dispute.

3. In the event of dispute as to the meaning or scope of the decision, the Tribunal shall construe it upon the request of any party.

Article 34
Costs

Unless otherwise decided by the Tribunal, each party shall bear its own costs.

SECTION 4.
SEABED DISPUTES CHAMBER

Article 35
Composition

1. The Seabed Disputes Chamber referred to in article 14 of this Annex shall be composed of 11 members, selected by a majority of the elected members of the Tribunal from among them.

2. In the selection of the members of the Chamber, the representation of the principal legal systems of the world and equitable geographical distribution shall be assured. The Assembly of the Authority may adopt recommendations of a general nature relating to such representation and distribution.

3. The members of the Chamber shall be selected every three years and may be selected for a second term.

4. The Chamber shall elect its President from among its members, who shall serve for the term for which the Chamber has been selected.

5. If any proceedings are still pending at the end of any three-year period for which the Chamber has been selected, the Chamber shall complete the proceedings in its original composition.

6. If a vacancy occurs in the Chamber, the Tribunal shall select a successor from among its elected members, who shall hold office for the remainder of his predecessor's term.

7. A quorum of seven of the members selected by the Tribunal shall be required to constitute the Chamber.

Article 36
Ad hoc chambers

1. The Seabed Disputes Chamber shall form an ad hoc chamber, composed of three of its members, for dealing with a particular dispute submitted to it in accordance with article 188, paragraph 1(b). The composition of such a chamber shall be determined by the Seabed Disputes Chamber with the approval of the parties.

2. If the parties do not agree on the composition of an ad hoc chamber, each party to the dispute shall appoint one member, and the third member shall be appointed by them in agreement. If they disagree, or if any party fails to make an appointment, the President of the Seabed Disputes Chamber shall promptly make the appointment or appointments from among its members, after consultation with the parties.

3. Members of the ad hoc chamber must not be in the service of, or nationals of, any of the parties to the dispute.

Article 37
Access

The Chamber shall be open to the States Parties, the Authority and the other entities referred to in Part XI, section 5.

Article 38
Applicable law

In addition to the provisions of article 293, the Chamber shall apply:

(a) the rules, regulations and procedures of the Authority adopted in accordance with this Convention; and

(b) the terms of contracts concerning activities in the Area in matters relating to those contracts.

Article 39
Enforcement of decisions of the Chamber

The decisions of the Chamber shall be enforceable in the territories of the States Parties in the same manner as judgments or orders of the highest court of the State Party in whose territory the enforcement is sought.

Article 40
Applicability of other sections of this Annex

1. The other sections of this Annex which are not incompatible with this section apply to the Chamber.

2. In the exercise of its functions relating to advisory opinions, the Chamber shall be guided by the provisions of this Annex relating to procedure before the Tribunal to the extent to which it recognizes them to be applicable.

SECTION 5. AMENDMENTS

Article 41
Amendments

1. Amendments to this Annex, other than amendments to section 4, may be adopted only in accordance with article 313 or by consensus at a conference convened in accordance with this Convention.

2. Amendments to section 4 may be adopted only in accordance with article 314.

3. The Tribunal may propose such amendments to this Statute as it may consider necessary, by written communications to the States Parties for their consideration in conformity with paragraphs 1 and 2.

ANNEX VII. ARBITRATION

Article 1
Institution of proceedings

Subject to the provisions of Part XV, any party to a dispute may submit the dispute to the arbitral procedure provided for in this Annex by written notification addressed to the other party or parties to the dispute. The notification shall be accompanied by a statement of the claim and the grounds on which it is based.

Article 2
List of arbitrators

1. A list of arbitrators shall be drawn up and maintained by the Secretary-General of the United Nations. Every State Party shall be entitled to nominate four arbitrators, each of whom shall be a person experienced in maritime affairs and enjoying the highest reputation for fairness, competence and integrity. The names of the persons so nominated shall constitute the list.

2. If at any time the arbitrators nominated by a State Party in the list so constituted shall be fewer than four, that State Party shall be entitled to make further nominations as necessary.

3. The name of an arbitrator shall remain on the list until withdrawn by the State Party which made the nomination, provided that such arbitrator shall continue to serve on any arbitral tribunal to which that arbitrator has been appointed until the completion of the proceedings before that arbitral tribunal.

Article 3
Constitution of arbitral tribunal

For the purpose of proceedings under this Annex, the arbitral tribunal shall, unless the parties otherwise agree, be constituted as follows:

(a) Subject to subparagraph (g), the arbitral tribunal shall consist of five members.

(b) The party instituting the proceedings shall appoint one member to be chosen preferably from the list referred to in article 2 of this Annex, who may be its national. The appointment shall be included in the notification referred to in article 1 of this Annex.

(c) The other party to the dispute shall, within 30 days of receipt of the notification referred to in article 1 of this Annex, appoint one member to be chosen preferably from the list, who may be its national. If the appointment is not made within that period, the party instituting the proceedings may, within two weeks of the expiration of that period, request that the appointment be made in accordance with subparagraph (e).

(d) The other three members shall be appointed by agreement between the parties. They shall be chosen preferably from the list and shall be nationals of third States unless the parties otherwise agree. The parties to the dispute shall appoint the President of the arbitral tribunal from among those three members. If, within 60 days of receipt of the notification referred to in article 1 of this Annex, the parties are unable to reach agreement on the appointment of one or more of the members of the tribunal to be appointed by agreement, or on the appointment of the President, the remaining appointment or appointments shall be made in accordance with subparagraph (e), at the request of a party to the dispute. Such request shall be made within two weeks of the expiration of the aforementioned 60-day period.

(e) Unless the parties agree that any appointment under subparagraphs (c) and (d) be made by a person or a third State chosen by the parties, the President of the International Tribunal for the Law of the Sea shall make the necessary appointments. If the President is unable to act under this subparagraph or is a national of one of the parties to the dispute, the appointment shall be made by the next senior member of the International Tribunal for the Law of the Sea who is available and is not a national of one of the parties. The appointments referred to in this subparagraph shall be made from the list referred to in article 2 of this Annex within a period of 30 days of the receipt of the request and in consultation with the parties. The members so appointed shall be of different nationalities and may not be in the service of, ordinarily resident in the territory of, or nationals of, any of the parties to the dispute.

(f) Any vacancy shall be filled in the manner prescribed for the initial appointment.

(g) Parties in the same interest shall appoint one member of the tribunal jointly by agreement. Where there are several parties having separate interests or where there is disagreement as to whether they are of the same interest, each of them shall appoint one member of the tribunal. The number of members of the tribunal appointed separately by the parties shall always be smaller by one than the number of members of the tribunal to be appointed jointly by the parties.

(h) In disputes involving more than two parties, the provisions of subparagraphs (a) to (f) shall apply to the maximum extent possible.

Article 4
Functions of arbitral tribunal

An arbitral tribunal constituted under article 3 of this Annex shall function in accordance with this Annex and the other provisions of this Convention.

Article 5
Procedure

Unless the parties to the dispute otherwise agree, the arbitral tribunal shall determine its own procedure, assuring to each party a full opportunity to be heard and to present its case.

Article 6
Duties of parties to a dispute

The parties to the dispute shall facilitate the work of the arbitral tribunal and, in particular, in accordance with their law and using all means at their disposal, shall:

(a) provide it with all relevant documents, facilities and information; and

(b) enable it when necessary to call witnesses or experts and receive their evidence and to visit the localities to which the case relates.

Article 7
Expenses

Unless the arbitral tribunal decides otherwise because of the particular circumstances of the case, the expenses of the tribunal, including the remuneration of its members, shall be borne by the parties to the dispute in equal shares.

Article 8
Required majority for decisions

Decisions of the arbitral tribunal shall be taken by a majority vote of its members. The absence or abstention of less than half of the members shall not constitute a bar to the tribunal reaching a decision. In the event of an equality of votes, the President shall have a casting vote.

Article 9
Default of appearance

If one of the parties to the dispute does not appear before the arbitral tribunal or fails to defend its case, the other party may request the tribunal to continue the proceedings and to make its award. Absence of a party or failure of a party to defend its case shall not constitute a bar to the proceedings. Before making its award, the arbitral tribunal must satisfy itself not only that it has jurisdiction over the dispute but also that the claim is well founded in fact and law.

Article 10
Award

The award of the arbitral tribunal shall be confined to the subject-matter of the dispute and state the reasons on which it is based. It shall contain the names of the members who have participated and the date of the award. Any member of the tribunal may attach a separate or dissenting opinion to the award.

Article 11
Finality of award

The award shall be final and without appeal, unless the parties to the dispute have agreed in advance to an appellate procedure. It shall be complied with by the parties to the dispute.

Article 12
Interpretation or implementation of award

1. Any controversy which may arise between the parties to the dispute as regards the interpretation or manner of implementation of the award may be submitted by either party for decision to the arbitral tribunal which made the award. For this purpose, any vacancy in the tribunal shall be filled in the manner provided for in the original appointments of the members of the tribunal.

2. Any such controversy may be submitted to another court or tribunal under article 287 by agreement of all the parties to the dispute.

Article 13
Application to entities other than States Parties

The provisions of this Annex shall apply *mutatis mutandis* to any dispute involving entities other than States Parties.

ANNEX VIII. SPECIAL ARBITRATION

Article 1
Institution of proceedings

Subject to Part XV, any party to a dispute concerning the interpretation or application of the articles of this Convention relating to (1) fisheries, (2) protection and preservation of the marine environment, (3) marine scientific research, or (4) navigation, including pollution from vessels and by dumping, may submit the dispute to the special arbitral procedure provided for in this Annex by written notification addressed to the other party or parties to the dispute. The notification shall be accompanied by a statement of the claim and the grounds on which it is based.

Article 2
Lists of experts

1. A list of experts shall be established and maintained in respect of each of the fields of (1) fisheries, (2) protection and preservation of the marine environment, (3) marine scientific research, and (4) navigation, including pollution from vessels and by dumping.

2. The lists of experts shall be drawn up and maintained, in the field of fisheries by the Food and Agriculture Organization of the United Nations, in the field of protection and preservation of the marine environment by the United Nations Environment Programme, in the field of marine scientific research by the Intergovernmental Oceanographic Commission, in the field of navigation, including pollution from vessels and by dumping, by the International Maritime Organization, or in each case by the appropriate subsidiary body concerned to which such organization, programme or commission has delegated this function.

3. Every State Party shall be entitled to nominate two experts in each field whose competence in the legal, scientific or technical aspects of such field is established and generally recognized and who enjoy the highest reputation for fairness and integrity. The names of the persons so nominated in each field shall constitute the appropriate list.

4. If at any time the experts nominated by a State Party in the list so constituted shall be fewer than two, that State Party shall be entitled to make further nominations as necessary.

5. The name of an expert shall remain on the list until withdrawn by the State Party which made the nomination, provided that such expert shall continue to serve on any special arbitral tribunal to which that expert has been appointed until the completion of the proceedings before that special arbitral tribunal.

Article 3
Constitution of special arbitral tribunal

For the purpose of proceedings under this Annex, the special arbitral tribunal shall, unless the parties otherwise agree, be constituted as follows:

(a) Subject to subparagraph (g), the special arbitral tribunal shall consist of five members.

(b) The party instituting the proceedings shall appoint two members to be chosen preferably from the appropriate list or lists referred to in article 2 of this Annex relating to the matters in dispute, one of whom may be its national. The appointments shall be included in the notification referred to in article 1 of this Annex.

(c) The other party to the dispute shall, within 30 days of receipt of the notification referred to in article 1 of this Annex, appoint two members to be chosen preferably from the appropriate list or lists relating to the matters in dispute, one of whom may be its national. If the appointments are not made within that period, the party instituting the proceedings may, within two weeks of the expiration of that period, request that the appointments be made in accordance with subparagraph (e).

(d) The parties to the dispute shall by agreement appoint the President of the special arbitral tribunal, chosen preferably from the appropriate list, who shall be a national of a third State, unless the parties otherwise agree. If, within 30 days of receipt of the notification referred to in article 1 of this Annex, the parties are unable to reach agreement on the appointment of the President, the appointment shall be made in accordance with subparagraph (e), at the request of a party to the dispute. Such request shall be made within two weeks of the expiration of the aforementioned 30-day period.

(e) Unless the parties agree that the appointment be made by a person or a third State chosen by the parties, the Secretary-General of the United Nations shall make the necessary appointments within 30 days of receipt of a request under subparagraphs (c) and (d). The appointments referred to in this subparagraph shall be made from the appropriate list or lists of experts referred to in article 2 of this Annex and in consultation with the parties to the dispute and the appropriate international organization. The members so appointed shall be of different nationalities and may not be in the service of, ordinarily resident in the territory of, or nationals of, any of the parties to the dispute.

(f) Any vacancy shall be filled in the manner prescribed for the initial appointment.

(g) Parties in the same interest shall appoint two members of the tribunal jointly by agreement. Where there are several parties having separate interests or where there is disagreement as to whether they are of the same interest, each of them shall appoint one member of the tribunal.

(h) In disputes involving more than two parties, the provisions of subparagraphs (a) to (f) shall apply to the maximum extent possible.

Article 4
General provisions

Annex VII, articles 4 to 13, apply *mutatis mutandis* to the special arbitration proceedings in accordance with this Annex.

Article 5
Fact finding

1. The parties to a dispute concerning the interpretation or application of the provisions of this Convention relating to (1) fisheries, (2) protection and preservation of the marine environment, (3) marine scientific research, or (4) navigation, including pollution from vessels and by dumping, may at any time agree to request a special arbitral tribunal constituted in accordance with article 3 of this Annex to carry out an inquiry and establish the facts giving rise to the dispute.

2. Unless the parties otherwise agree, the findings of fact of the special arbitral tribunal acting in accordance with paragraph 1, shall be considered as conclusive as between the parties.

3. If all the parties to the dispute so request, the special arbitral tribunal may formulate recommendations which, without having the force of a decision, shall only constitute the basis for a review by the parties of the questions giving rise to the dispute.

4. Subject to paragraph 2, the special arbitral tribunal shall act in accordance with the provisions of this Annex, unless the parties otherwise agree.

ANNEX IX. PARTICIPATION BY INTERNATIONAL ORGANIZATIONS

Article 1
Use of terms

For the purposes of article 305 and of this Annex, "international organization" means an intergovernmental organization constituted by States to which its member States have transferred competence over matters governed by this Convention, including the competence to enter into treaties in respect of those matters.

Article 2
Signature

An international organization may sign this Convention if a majority of its member States are signatories of this Convention. At the time of signature an international organization shall make a declaration specifying the matters governed by this Convention in respect of which competence has been transferred to that organization by its member States which are signatories, and the nature and extent of that competence.

Article 3
Formal confirmation and accession

1. An international organization may deposit its instrument of formal confirmation or of accession if a majority of its member States deposit or have deposited their instruments of ratification or accession.

2. The instruments deposited by the international organization shall contain the undertakings and declarations required by articles 4 and 5 of this Annex.

Article 4
Extent of participation and rights and obligations

1. The instrument of formal confirmation or of accession of an international organization shall contain an undertaking to accept the rights and obligations of States under this Convention in respect of matters relating to which competence has been transferred to it by its member States which are Parties to this Convention.

2. An international organization shall be a Party to this Convention to the extent that it has competence in accordance with the declarations, communications of information or notifications referred to in article 5 of this Annex.

3. Such an international organization shall exercise the rights and perform the obligations which its member States which are Parties would otherwise have under this Convention, on matters relating to which competence has been transferred to it by those member States. The member States of that international organization shall not exercise competence which they have transferred to it.

4. Participation of such an international organization shall in no case entail an increase of the representation to which its member States which are States Parties would otherwise be entitled, including rights in decision-making.

5. Participation of such an international organization shall in no case confer any rights under this Convention on member States of the organization which are not States Parties to this Convention.

6. In the event of a conflict between the obligations of an international organization under this Convention and its obligations under the agreement establishing the organization or any acts relating to it, the obligations under this Convention shall prevail.

Article 5
Declarations, notifications and communications

1. The instrument of formal confirmation or of accession of an international organization shall contain a declaration specifying the matters governed by this Convention in respect of which competence has been transferred to the organization by its member States which are Parties to this Convention.

2. A member State of an international organization shall, at the time it ratifies or accedes to this Convention or at the time when the organization deposits its instrument of formal confirmation or of accession, whichever is later, make a declaration specifying the matters governed by this Convention in respect of which it has transferred competence to the organization.

3. States Parties which are member States of an international organization which is a Party to this Convention shall be presumed to have competence over all matters governed by this Convention in respect of which transfers of competence to the organization have not been specifically declared, notified or communicated by those States under this article.

4. The international organization and its member States which are States Parties shall promptly notify the depositary of this Convention of any changes to the distribution of competence, including new transfers of competence, specified in the declarations under paragraphs 1 and 2.

5. Any State Party may request an international organization and its member States which are States Parties to provide information as to which, as between the organization and its member States, has competence in respect of any specific question which has arisen. The organization and the member States concerned shall provide this information within a reasonable time. The international organization and the member States may also, on their own initiative, provide this information.

6. Declarations, notifications and communications of information under this article shall specify the nature and extent of the competence transferred.

Article 6
Responsibility and liability

1. Parties which have competence under article 5 of this Annex shall have responsibility for failure to comply with obligations or for any other violation of this Convention.

2. Any State Party may request an international organization or its member States which are States Parties for information as to who has responsibility in respect of any specific matter. The organization and the member States concerned shall provide this information. Failure to provide this information within a reasonable time or the provision of contradictory information shall result in joint and several liability.

Article 7
Settlement of disputes

1. At the time of deposit of its instrument of formal confirmation or of accession, or at any time thereafter, an international organization shall be free to choose, by means of a written declaration, one or more of the means for the settlement of disputes concerning the interpretation or application of this Convention, referred to in article 287, paragraph 1(a), (c) or (d).

2. Part XV applies *mutatis mutandis* to any dispute between Parties to this Convention, one or more of which are international organizations.

3. When an international organization and one or more of its member States are joint parties to a dispute, or parties in the same interest, the organization shall be deemed to have accepted the same procedures for the settlement of disputes as the member States; when, however, a member State has chosen only the International Court of Justice under article 287, the organization and the member State concerned shall be deemed to have accepted arbitration in accordance with Annex VII, unless the parties to the dispute otherwise agree.

Article 8
Applicability of Part XVII

Part XVII applies *mutatis mutandis* to an international organization, except in respect of the following:

(a) the instrument of formal confirmation or of accession of an international organization shall not be taken into account in the application of article 308, paragraph l;

(b) (i) an international organization shall have exclusive capacity with respect to the application of articles 312 to 315, to the extent that it has competence under article 5 of this Annex over the entire subject-matter of the amendment;

(ii) the instrument of formal confirmation or of accession of an international organization to an amendment, the entire subject-matter over which the international organization has competence under article 5 of this Annex, shall be considered to be the instrument of ratification or accession of each of the member States which are States Parties, for the purposes of applying article 316, paragraphs 1, 2 and 3;

(iii) the instrument of formal confirmation or of accession of the international organization shall not be taken into account in the application of article 316, paragraphs 1 and 2, with regard to all other amendments;

(c) (i) an international organization may not denounce this Convention in accordance with article 317 if any of its member States is a State Party and if it continues to fulfil the qualifications specified in article 1 of this Annex;

(ii) an international organization shall denounce this Convention when none of its member States is a State Party or if the international organization no longer fulfils the qualifications specified in article 1 of this Annex. Such denunciation shall take effect immediately.

Agreement relating to the Implementation of Part XI of the United Nations Convention on the Law of the Sea of 10 December 1982;

Done at New York, 28th July 1994

Table of Contents

Article 1   Implementation of Part XI
Article 2   Relationship between this Agreement and Part XI
Article 3   Signature
Article 4   Consent to be bound
Article 5   Simplified procedure
Article 6   Entry into force
Article 7   Provisional application
Article 8   States Parties
Article 9   Depositary
Article 10 Authentic texts

Annex

Section 1   Costs to States Parties and institutional arrangements
Section 2   Enterprise
Section 3   Decision-making
Section 4   Review Conference
Section 5   Transfer of technology
Section 6   Production policy
Section 7   Economic assistance
Section 8   Financial terms of contracts
Section 9   The Finance Committee

The States Parties to this Agreement,

Recognizing the important contribution of the United Nations Convention on the Law of the Sea of 10 December 1982 (hereinafter referred to as "the Convention") to the maintenance of peace, justice and progress for all peoples of the world,

Reaffirming that the seabed and ocean floor and subsoil thereof, beyond the limits of national jurisdiction (hereinafter referred to as "the Area"), as well as the resources of the Area, are the common heritage of mankind,

Mindful of the importance of the Convention for the protection and preservation of the marine environment and of the growing concern for the global environment,

Having considered the report of the Secretary-General of the United Nations on the results of the informal consultations among States held from 1990 to 1994 on outstanding issues relating to Part XI and related provisions of the Convention (hereinafter referred to as "Part XI"),

Noting the political and economic changes, including market-oriented approaches, affecting the implementation of Part XI,

Wishing to facilitate universal participation in the Convention,

Considering that an agreement relating to the implementation of Part XI would best meet that objective,

Have agreed as follows:

Article 1
Implementation of Part XI

1. The States Parties to this Agreement undertake to implement Part XI in accordance with this Agreement.

2. The Annex forms an integral part of this Agreement.

Article 2
Relationship between this Agreement
and Part XI

1. The provisions of this Agreement and Part XI shall be interpreted and applied together as a single instrument. In the event of any inconsistency between this Agreement and Part XI, the provisions of this Agreement shall prevail.

2. Articles 309 to 319 of the Convention shall apply to this Agreement as they apply to the Convention.

Article 3
Signature

This Agreement shall remain open for signature at United Nations Headquarters by the States and entities referred to in article 305, paragraph 1(a), (c), (d), (e) and (f), of the Convention for 12 months from the date of its adoption.

Article 4
Consent to be bound

1. After the adoption of this Agreement, any instrument of ratification or formal confirmation of or accession to the Convention shall also represent consent to be bound by this Agreement.

2. No State or entity may establish its consent to be bound by this Agreement unless it has previously established or establishes at the same time its consent to be bound by the Convention.

3. A State or entity referred to in article 3 may express its consent to be bound by this Agreement by:

(a) Signature not subject to ratification, formal confirmation or the procedure set out in article 5;
(b) Signature subject to ratification or formal confirmation, followed by ratification or formal confirmation;
(c) Signature subject to the procedure set out in article 5; or

(d) Accession.

4. Formal confirmation by the entities referred to in article 305, paragraph 1(f), of the Convention shall be in accordance with Annex IX of the Convention.

5. The instruments of ratification, formal confirmation or accession shall be deposited with the Secretary-General of the United Nations.

Article 5
Simplified procedure

1. A State or entity which has deposited before the date of the adoption of this Agreement an instrument of ratification or formal confirmation of or accession to the Convention and which has signed this Agreement in accordance with article 4, paragraph 3(c), shall be considered to have established its consent to be bound by this Agreement 12 months after the date of its adoption, unless that State or entity notifies the depositary in writing before that date that it is not availing itself of the simplified procedure set out in this article.

2. In the event of such notification, consent to be bound by this Agreement shall be established in accordance with article 4, paragraph 3(b).

Article 6
Entry into force

1. This Agreement shall enter into force 30 days after the date on which 40 States have established their consent to be bound in accordance with articles 4 and 5, provided that such States include at least seven of the States referred to in paragraph 1(a) of resolution II of the Third United Nations Conference on the Law of the Sea (hereinafter referred to as "resolution II") and that at least five of those States are developed States. If these conditions for entry into force are fulfilled before 16 November 1994, this Agreement shall enter into force on 16 November 1994.

2. For each State or entity establishing its consent to be bound by this Agreement after the requirements set out in paragraph 1 have been fulfilled, this Agreement shall enter into force on the thirtieth day following the date of establishment of its consent to be bound.

Article 7
Provisional application

1. If on 16 November 1994 this Agreement has not entered into force, it shall be applied provisionally pending its entry into force by:

(a) States which have consented to its adoption in the General Assembly of the United Nations, except any such State which before 16 November 1994 notifies the depositary in writing either that it will not so apply this Agreement or that it will consent to such application only upon subsequent signature or notification in writing;

(b) States and entities which sign this Agreement, except any such State or entity which notifies the depositary in writing at the time of signature that it will not so apply this Agreement.

(c) States and entities which consent to its provisional application by so notifying the depositary in writing;

(d) States which accede to this Agreement.

2. All such States and entities shall apply this Agreement provisionally in accordance with their national or internal laws and regulations, with effect from 16 November 1994 or the date of signature, notification of consent or accession, if later.

3. Provisional application shall terminate upon the date of entry into force of this Agreement. In any event, provisional application shall terminate on 16 November 1998 if at that date the requirement in article 6, paragraph 1, of consent to be bound by this Agreement by at least seven of the States (of which at least five must be developed States) referred to in paragraph 1(a) of resolution II has not been fulfilled.

Article 8
States Parties

1. For the purposes of this Agreement, "States Parties" means States which have consented to be bound by this Agreement and for which this Agreement is in force.

2. This Agreement applies *mutatis mutandis* to the entities referred to in article 305, paragraph 1(c), (d), (e) and (f), of the Convention which become Parties to this Agreement in accordance with the conditions relevant to each, and to that extent "States Parties" refers to those entities.

Article 9
Depositary

The Secretary-General of the United Nations shall be the depositary of this Agreement.

Article 10
Authentic texts

The original of this Agreement, of which the Arabic, Chinese, English, French, Russian and Spanish texts are equally authentic, shall be deposited with the Secretary-General of the United Nations.

IN WITNESS WHEREOF, the undersigned Plenipotentiaries, being duly authorized thereto, have signed this Agreement.

DONE AT NEW YORK, this twenty-eighth day of July, one thousand nine hundred and ninety-four.

ANNEX

SECTION 1. COSTS TO STATES PARTIES AND INSTITUTIONAL ARRANGEMENTS

1. The International Seabed Authority (hereinafter referred to as "the Authority") is the organization through which States Parties to the Convention shall, in accordance with the regime for the Area established in Part XI and this Agreement, organize and control activities in the Area, particularly with a view to administering the resources of the Area. The powers and functions of the Authority shall be those expressly conferred upon it by the Convention. The Authority shall have such incidental powers, consistent with the Convention, as are implicit in, and necessary for, the exercise of those powers and functions with respect to activities in the Area.

2. In order to minimize costs to States Parties, all organs and subsidiary bodies to be established under the Convention and this Agreement shall be cost-effective. This principle shall also apply to the frequency, duration and scheduling of meetings.

3. The setting up and the functioning of the organs and subsidiary bodies of the Authority shall be based on an evolutionary approach, taking into account the functional needs of the organs and subsidiary bodies concerned in order that they may discharge effectively their respective responsibilities at various stages of the development of activities in the Area.

4. The early functions of the Authority upon entry into force of the Convention shall be carried out by the Assembly, the Council, the Secretariat, the Legal and Technical Commission and the Finance Committee. The functions of the Economic Planning Commission shall be performed by the Legal and Technical Commission until such time as the Council decides otherwise or until the approval of the first plan of work for exploitation.

5. Between the entry into force of the Convention and the approval of the first plan of work for exploitation, the Authority shall concentrate on:

(a) Processing of applications for approval of plans of work for exploration in accordance with Part XI and this Agreement;

(b) Implementation of decisions of the Preparatory Commission for the International Seabed Authority and for the International Tribunal for the Law of the Sea (hereinafter referred to as "the Preparatory Commission") relating to the registered pioneer investors and their certifying States, including their rights and obligations, in accordance with article 308, paragraph 5, of the Convention and resolution II, paragraph 13;

(c) Monitoring of compliance with plans of work for exploration approved in the form of contracts;

(d) Monitoring and review of trends and developments relating to deep seabed mining activities, including regular analysis of world metal market conditions and metal prices, trends and prospects;

(e) Study of the potential impact of mineral production from the Area on the economies of developing land-based producers of those minerals which are likely to be most seriously affected, with a view to minimizing their difficulties and assisting them in their economic adjustment, taking into account the work done in this regard by the Preparatory Commission;

(f) Adoption of rules, regulations and procedures necessary for the conduct of activities in the Area as they progress. Notwithstanding the provisions of Annex III, article 17, paragraph 2(b) and (c), of the Convention, such rules, regulations and procedures shall take into account the terms of this Agreement, the prolonged delay in commercial deep seabed mining and the likely pace of activities in the Area;

(g) Adoption of rules, regulations and procedures incorporating applicable standards for the protection and preservation of the marine environment;

(h) Promotion and encouragement of the conduct of marine scientific research with respect to activities in the Area and the collection and dissemination of the results of such research and analysis, when available, with particular emphasis on research related to the environmental impact of activities in the Area;

(i) Acquisition of scientific knowledge and monitoring of the development of marine technology relevant to activities in the Area, in particular technology relating to the protection and preservation of the marine environment;

(j) Assessment of available data relating to prospecting and exploration;

(k) Timely elaboration of rules, regulations and procedures for exploitation, including those relating to the protection and preservation of the marine environment.

6. (a) An application for approval of a plan of work for exploration shall be considered by the Council following the receipt of a recommendation on the application from the Legal and Technical Commission. The processing of an application for approval of a plan of work for exploration shall be in accordance with the provisions of the Convention, including Annex III thereof, and this Agreement, and subject to the following:

(i) A plan of work for exploration submitted on behalf of a State or entity, or any component of such entity, referred to in resolution II, paragraph 1(a)(ii) or (iii), other than a registered pioneer investor, which had already undertaken substantial activities in the Area prior to the entry into force of the Convention, or its successor in interest, shall be considered to have met the financial and technical qualifications necessary for approval of a plan of work if the sponsoring State or States certify that the applicant has expended an amount equivalent to at least US$ 30 million in research and exploration activities and has expended no less than 10 per cent of that amount in the location, survey and evaluation of the area referred to in the plan of work. If the plan of work otherwise satisfies the requirements of the Convention and any rules, regulations and procedures adopted pursuant thereto, it shall be approved by the Council in the form of a contract. The provisions of section 3, paragraph 11, of this Annex shall be interpreted and applied accordingly;

(ii) Notwithstanding the provisions of resolution II, paragraph 8(a), a registered pioneer investor may request approval of a plan of work for exploration within 36 months of the entry into force of the Convention. The plan of work for exploration shall consist of documents, reports and other data submitted to the Preparatory Commission both before and after registration and shall be accompanied by a certificate of compliance, consisting of a factual report describing the status of fulfilment of obligations under the pioneer investor regime, issued by the Preparatory Commission in accordance with resolution II, paragraph 11(a). Such a plan of work shall be considered to be approved. Such an approved plan of work shall be in the form of a contract concluded between the Authority and the registered pioneer investor in accordance with Part XI and this Agreement. The fee of US$ 250,000 paid pursuant to resolution II, paragraph 7(a), shall be deemed to be the fee relating to the exploration phase pursuant to section 8, paragraph 3, of this Annex. Section 3, paragraph 11, of this Annex shall be interpreted and applied accordingly;

(iii) In accordance with the principle of non-discrimination, a contract with a State or entity or any component of such entity referred to in subparagraph (a)(i) shall include arrangements which shall be similar to and no less favourable than those agreed with any registered pioneer investor referred to in subparagraph (a)(ii). If any of the States or entities or any components of such entities referred to in subparagraph (a)(i) are granted more favourable arrangements, the Council shall make similar and no less favourable arrangements with regard to the rights and obligations assumed by the registered pioneer investors referred to in subparagraph (a)(ii), provided that such arrangements do not affect or prejudice the interests of the Authority;

(iv) A State sponsoring an application for a plan of work pursuant to the provisions of subparagraph (a)(i) or (ii) may be a State Party or a State which is applying this Agreement provisionally in accordance with article 7, or a State which is a member of the Authority on a provisional basis in accordance with paragraph 12;

(v) Resolution II, paragraph 8(c), shall be interpreted and applied in accordance with subparagraph (a)(iv).

(b) The approval of a plan of work for exploration shall be in accordance with article 153, paragraph 3, of the Convention.

7. An application for approval of a plan of work shall be accompanied by an assessment of the potential environmental impacts of the proposed activities and by a description of a programme for oceanographic and baseline environmental studies in accordance with the rules, regulations and procedures adopted by the Authority.

8. An application for approval of a plan of work for exploration, subject to paragraph 6(a)(i) or (ii), shall be processed in accordance with the procedures set out in section 3, paragraph 11, of this Annex.

9. A plan of work for exploration shall be approved for a period of 15 years. Upon the expiration of a plan of work for exploration, the contractor shall apply for a plan of work for exploitation unless the contractor has already done so or has obtained an extension for the plan of work for exploration. Contractors may apply for such extensions for periods of not more than five years each. Such extensions shall be approved if the contractor has made efforts in good faith to comply with the requirements of the plan of work but for reasons beyond the contractor's control has been unable to complete the necessary preparatory work for proceeding to the exploitation stage or if the prevailing economic circumstances do not justify proceeding to the exploitation stage.

10. Designation of a reserved area for the Authority in accordance with Annex III, article 8, of the Convention shall take place in connection with approval of an application for a plan of work for exploration or approval of an application for a plan of work for exploration and exploitation.

11. Notwithstanding the provisions of paragraph 9, an approved plan of work for exploration which is sponsored by at least one State provisionally applying this Agreement shall terminate if such a State ceases to apply this Agreement provisionally and has not become a member on a provisional basis in accordance with paragraph 12 or has not become a State Party.

12. Upon the entry into force of this Agreement, States and entities referred to in article 3 of this Agreement which have been applying it provisionally in accordance with article 7 and for which it is not in force may continue to be members of the Authority on a provisional basis pending its entry into force for such States and entities, in accordance with the following subparagraphs:

(a) If this Agreement enters into force before 16 November 1996, such States and entities shall be entitled to continue to participate as members of the Authority on a provisional basis upon notification to the depositary of the Agreement by such a State or entity of its intention to participate as a member on a provisional basis. Such membership shall terminate either on 16 November 1996 or upon the entry into force of this Agreement and the Convention for such member, whichever is earlier. The Council may, upon the request of the State or entity concerned, extend such membership beyond 16 November 1996 for a further period or periods not exceeding a total of two years provided that the Council is satisfied that the State or entity concerned has been making efforts in good faith to become a party to the Agreement and the Convention;

(b) If this Agreement enters into force after 15 November 1996, such States and entities may request the Council to grant continued membership in the Authority on a provisional basis for a period or periods not extending beyond 16 November 1998. The Council shall grant such membership with effect from the date of the request if it is satisfied that the State or entity has been making efforts in good faith to become a party to the Agreement and the Convention;

(c) States and entities which are members of the Authority on a provisional basis in accordance with subparagraph (a) or (b) shall apply the terms of Part XI and this Agreement in accordance with their national or internal laws, regulations and annual budgetary appropriations and shall have the same rights and obligations as other members, including:

(i) The obligation to contribute to the administrative budget of the Authority in accordance with the scale of assessed contributions;

(ii) The right to sponsor an application for approval of a plan of work for exploration. In the case of entities whose components are natural or juridical persons possessing the nationality of more than one State, a plan of work for exploration shall not be approved unless all the States whose natural or juridical persons comprise those entities are States Parties or members on a provisional basis;

(d) Notwithstanding the provisions of paragraph 9, an approved plan of work in the form of a contract for exploration which was sponsored pursuant to subparagraph (c)(ii) by a State which was a member on a provisional basis shall terminate if such membership ceases and the State or entity has not become a State Party;

(e) If such a member has failed to make its assessed contributions or otherwise failed to comply with its obligations in accordance with this paragraph, its membership on a provisional basis shall be terminated.

13. The reference in Annex III, article 10, of the Convention to performance which has not been satisfactory shall be interpreted to mean that the contractor has failed to comply with the requirements of an approved plan of work in spite of a written warning or warnings from the Authority to the contractor to comply therewith.

14. The Authority shall have its own budget. Until the end of the year following the year during which this Agreement enters into force, the administrative expenses of the Authority shall be met through the budget of the United Nations. Thereafter, the administrative expenses of the Authority shall be met by assessed contributions of its members, including any members on a provisional basis, in accordance with articles 171, subparagraph (a), and 173 of the Convention and this Agreement, until the Authority has sufficient funds from other sources to meet those expenses. The Authority shall not exercise the power referred to in article 174, paragraph 1, of the Convention to borrow funds to finance its administrative budget.

15. The Authority shall elaborate and adopt, in accordance with article 162, paragraph 2(o)(ii), of the Convention, rules, regulations and procedures based on the principles contained in sections 2, 5, 6, 7 and 8 of this Annex, as well as any additional rules, regulations and procedures necessary to facilitate the approval of plans of work for exploration or exploitation, in accordance with the following subparagraphs:

(a) The Council may undertake such elaboration any time it deems that all or any of such rules, regulations or procedures are required for the conduct of activities in the Area, or when it determines that commercial exploitation is imminent, or at the request of a State whose national intends to apply for approval of a plan of work for exploitation;

(b) If a request is made by a State referred to in subparagraph (a) the Council shall, in accordance with article 162, paragraph 2(o), of the Convention, complete the adoption of such rules, regulations and procedures within two years of the request;

(c) If the Council has not completed the elaboration of the rules, regulations and procedures relating to exploitation within the prescribed time and an application for approval of a plan of work for exploitation is pending, it shall none the less consider and provisionally approve such plan of work based on the provisions of the Convention and any rules, regulations and procedures that the Council may have adopted provisionally, or on the basis of the norms contained in the Convention and the terms and principles contained in this Annex as well as the principle of non-discrimination among contractors.

16. The draft rules, regulations and procedures and any recommendations relating to the provisions of Part XI, as contained in the reports and recommendations of the Preparatory Commission, shall be taken into account by the Authority in the adoption of rules, regulations and procedures in accordance with Part XI and this Agreement.

17. The relevant provisions of Part XI, section 4, of the Convention shall be interpreted and applied in accordance with this Agreement.

SECTION 2. THE ENTERPRISE

1. The Secretariat of the Authority shall perform the functions of the Enterprise until it begins to operate independently of the Secretariat. The Secretary-General of the Authority shall appoint from within the staff of the Authority an interim Director-General to oversee the performance of these functions by the Secretariat.

These functions shall be:
 (a) Monitoring and review of trends and developments relating to deep seabed mining activities, including regular analysis of world metal market conditions and metal prices, trends and prospects;
 (b) Assessment of the results of the conduct of marine scientific research with respect to activities in the Area, with particular emphasis on research related to the environmental impact of activities in the Area;
 (c) Assessment of available data relating to prospecting and exploration, including the criteria for such activities;
 (d) Assessment of technological developments relevant to activities in the Area, in particular technology relating to the protection and preservation of the marine environment;
 (e) Evaluation of information and data relating to areas reserved for the Authority;
 (f) Assessment of approaches to joint-venture operations;
 (g) Collection of information on the availability of trained manpower;
 (h) Study of managerial policy options for the administration of the Enterprise at different stages of its operations.

2. The Enterprise shall conduct its initial deep seabed mining operations through joint ventures. Upon the approval of a plan of work for exploitation for an entity other than the Enterprise, or upon receipt by the Council of an application for a joint-venture operation with the Enterprise, the Council shall take up the issue of the functioning of the Enterprise independently of the Secretariat of the Authority. If joint-venture operations with the Enterprise accord with sound commercial principles, the Council shall issue a directive pursuant to article 170, paragraph 2, of the Convention providing for such independent functioning.

3. The obligation of States Parties to fund one mine site of the Enterprise as provided for in Annex IV, article 11, paragraph 3, of the Convention shall not apply and States Parties shall be under no obligation to finance any of the operations in any mine site of the Enterprise or under its joint-venture arrangements.

4. The obligations applicable to contractors shall apply to the Enterprise. Notwithstanding the provisions of article 153, paragraph 3, and Annex III, article 3, paragraph 5, of the Convention, a plan of work for the Enterprise upon its approval shall be in the form of a contract concluded between the Authority and the Enterprise.

5. A contractor which has contributed a particular area to the Authority as a reserved area has the right of first refusal to enter into a joint-venture arrangement with the Enterprise for exploration and exploitation of that area. If the Enterprise does not submit an application for a plan of work for activities in respect of such a reserved area within 15 years of the commencement of its functions independent of the Secretariat of the Authority or within 15 years of the date on which that area is reserved for the Authority, whichever is the later, the contractor which contributed the area shall be entitled to apply for a plan of work for that area provided it offers in good faith to include the Enterprise as a joint-venture partner.

6. Article 170, paragraph 4, Annex IV and other provisions of the Convention relating to the Enterprise shall be interpreted and applied in accordance with this section.

SECTION 3. DECISION-MAKING

1. The general policies of the Authority shall be established by the Assembly in collaboration with the Council.

2. As a general rule, decision-making in the organs of the Authority should be by consensus.

3. If all efforts to reach a decision by consensus have been exhausted, decisions by voting in the Assembly on questions of procedure shall be taken by a majority of members present and voting, and decisions on questions of substance shall be taken by a two-thirds majority of members present and voting, as provided for in article 159, paragraph 8, of the Convention.

4. Decisions of the Assembly on any matter for which the Council also has competence or on any administrative, budgetary or financial matter shall be based on the recommendations of the Council. If the Assembly does not accept the recommendation of the Council on any matter, it shall return the matter to the Council for further consideration. The Council shall reconsider the matter in the light of the views expressed by the Assembly.

5. If all efforts to reach a decision by consensus have been exhausted, decisions by voting in the Council on questions of procedure shall be taken by a majority of members present and voting, and decisions on questions of substance, except where the Convention provides for decisions by consensus in the Council, shall be taken by a two-thirds majority of members present and voting, provided that such decisions are not opposed by a majority in any one of the chambers referred to in paragraph 9. In taking decisions the Council shall seek to promote the interests of all the members of the Authority.

6. The Council may defer the taking of a decision in order to facilitate further negotiation whenever it appears that all efforts at achieving consensus on a question have not been exhausted.

7. Decisions by the Assembly or the Council having financial or budgetary implications shall be based on the recommendations of the Finance Committee.

8. The provisions of article 161, paragraph 8(b) and (c), of the Convention shall not apply.

9. (a) Each group of States elected under paragraph 15(a) to (c) shall be treated as a chamber for the purposes of voting in the Council. The developing States elected under paragraph 15(d) and (e) shall be treated as a single chamber for the purposes of voting in the Council.

(b) Before electing the members of the Council, the Assembly shall establish lists of countries fulfilling the criteria for membership in the groups of States in paragraph 15(a) to (d). If a State fulfils the criteria for membership in more than one group, it may only be proposed by one group for election to the Council and it shall represent only that group in voting in the Council.

10. Each group of States in paragraph 15(a) to (d) shall be represented in the Council by those members nominated by that group. Each group shall nominate only as many candidates as the number of seats required to be filled by that group. When the number of potential candidates in each of the groups referred to in paragraph 15 (a) to (e) exceeds the number of seats available in each of those respective groups, as a general rule, the principle of rotation shall apply. States members of each of those groups shall determine how this principle shall apply in those groups.

11. (a) The Council shall approve a recommendation by the Legal and Technical Commission for approval of a plan of work unless by a two-thirds majority of its members present and voting, including a majority of members present and voting in each of the chambers of the Council, the Council decides to disapprove a plan of work. If the Council does not take a decision on a recommendation for approval of a plan of work within a prescribed period, the recommendation shall be deemed to have been approved by the Council at the end of that period. The prescribed period shall normally be 60 days unless the Council decides to provide for a longer period. If the Commission recommends the disapproval of a plan of work or does not make a recommendation, the Council may nevertheless approve the plan of work in accordance with its rules of procedure for decision-making on questions of substance.

(b) The provisions of article 162, paragraph 2(j), of the Convention shall not apply.

12. Where a dispute arises relating to the disapproval of a plan of work, such dispute shall be submitted to the dispute settlement procedures set out in the Convention.

13. Decisions by voting in the Legal and Technical Commission shall be by a majority of members present and voting.

14. Part XI, section 4, subsections B and C, of the Convention shall be interpreted and applied in accordance with this section.

15. The Council shall consist of 36 members of the Authority elected by the Assembly in the following order:

(a) Four members from among those States Parties which, during the last five years for which statistics are available, have either consumed more than 2 per cent in value terms of total world consumption or have had net imports of more than 2 per cent in value terms of total world imports of the commodities produced from the categories of minerals to be derived from the Area, provided that the four members shall include one State from the Eastern European region having the largest economy in that region in terms of gross domestic product and the State, on the date of entry into force of the Convention, having the largest economy in terms of gross domestic product, if such States wish to be represented in this group;
(b) Four members from among the eight States Parties which have made the largest investments in preparation for and in the conduct of activities in the Area, either directly or through their nationals;
(c) Four members from among States Parties which, on the basis of production in areas under their jurisdiction, are major net exporters of the categories of minerals to be derived from the Area, including at least two developing States whose exports of such minerals have a substantial bearing upon their economies;
(d) Six members from among developing States Parties, representing special interests. The special interests to be represented shall include those of States with large populations, States which are land-

locked or geographically disadvantaged, island States, States which are major importers of the categories of minerals to be derived from the Area, States which are potential producers of such minerals and least developed States;
(e) Eighteen members elected according to the principle of ensuring an equitable geographical distribution of seats in the Council as a whole, provided that each geographical region shall have at least one member elected under this subparagraph. For this purpose, the geographical regions shall be Africa, Asia, Eastern Europe, Latin America and the Caribbean and Western Europe and Others.

16. The provisions of article 161, paragraph 1, of the Convention shall not apply.

SECTION 4. REVIEW CONFERENCE

The provisions relating to the Review Conference in article 155, paragraphs 1, 3 and 4, of the Convention shall not apply. Notwithstanding the provisions of article 314, paragraph 2, of the Convention, the Assembly, on the recommendation of the Council, may undertake at any time a review of the matters referred to in article 155, paragraph 1, of the Convention. Amendments relating to this Agreement and Part XI shall be subject to the procedures contained in articles 314, 315 and 316 of the Convention, provided that the principles, regime and other terms referred to in article 155, paragraph 2, of the Convention shall be maintained and the rights referred to in paragraph 5 of that article shall not be affected.

SECTION 5. TRANSFER OF TECHNOLOGY

1. In addition to the provisions of article 144 of the Convention, transfer of technology for the purposes of Part XI shall be governed by the following principles:

(a) The Enterprise, and developing States wishing to obtain deep seabed mining technology, shall seek to obtain such technology on fair and reasonable commercial terms and conditions on the open market, or through joint-venture arrangements;
(b) If the Enterprise or developing States are unable to obtain deep seabed mining technology, the Authority may request all or any of the contractors and their respective sponsoring State or States to cooperate with it in facilitating the acquisition of deep seabed mining technology by the Enterprise or its joint venture, or by a developing State or States seeking to acquire such technology on fair and reasonable commercial terms and conditions, consistent with the effective protection of intellectual property rights. States Parties undertake to cooperate fully and effectively with the Authority for this purpose and to ensure that contractors sponsored by them also cooperate fully with the Authority;
(c) As a general rule, States Parties shall promote international technical and scientific cooperation with regard to activities in the Area either between the parties concerned or by developing training, technical assistance and scientific cooperation programmes in marine science and technology and the protection and preservation of the marine environment.

2. The provisions of Annex III, article 5, of the Convention shall not apply.

SECTION 6. PRODUCTION POLICY

1. The production policy of the Authority shall be based on the following principles:

(a) Development of the resources of the Area shall take place in accordance with sound commercial principles;
(b) The provisions of the General Agreement on Tariffs and Trade, its relevant codes and successor or superseding agreements shall apply with respect to activities in the Area;
(c) In particular, there shall be no subsidization of activities in the Area except as may be permitted under the agreements referred to in subparagraph (b). Subsidization for the purpose of these principles shall be defined in terms of the agreements referred to in subparagraph (b);
(d) There shall be no discrimination between minerals derived from the Area and from other sources. There shall be no preferential access to markets for such minerals or for imports of commodities produced from such minerals, in particular:
(i) By the use of tariff or non-tariff barriers; and
(ii) Given by States Parties to such minerals or commodities produced by their state enterprises or by natural or juridical persons which possess their nationality or are controlled by them or their nationals;
(e) The plan of work for exploitation approved by the Authority in respect of each mining area shall indicate an anticipated production schedule which shall include the estimated maximum amounts of minerals that would be produced per year under the plan of work;
(f) The following shall apply to the settlement of disputes concerning the provisions of the agreements referred to in subparagraph (b):
(i) Where the States Parties concerned are parties to such agreements, they shall have recourse to the dispute settlement procedures of those agreements;
(ii) Where one or more of the States Parties concerned are not parties to such agreements, they shall have recourse to the dispute settlement procedures set out in the Convention;
(g) In circumstances where a determination is made under the agreements referred to in subparagraph (b) that a State Party has engaged in subsidization which is prohibited or has resulted in adverse effects on the interests of another State Party and appropriate steps have not been taken by the relevant State Party or States Parties, a State Party may request the Council to take appropriate measures.

2. The principles contained in paragraph 1 shall not affect the rights and obligations under any provision of the agreements referred to in paragraph 1(b), as well as the relevant free trade and customs union agreements, in relations between States Parties which are parties to such agreements.

3. The acceptance by a contractor of subsidies other than those which may be permitted under the agreements referred to in paragraph 1(b) shall constitute a violation of the fundamental terms of the contract forming a plan of work for the carrying out of activities in the Area.

4. Any State Party which has reason to believe that there has been a breach of the requirements of paragraphs 1(b) to (d) or 3 may initiate dispute settlement procedures in conformity with paragraph 1(f) or (g).

5. A State Party may at any time bring to the attention of the Council activities which in its view are inconsistent with the requirements of paragraph 1(b) to (d).

6. The Authority shall develop rules, regulations and procedures which ensure the implementation of the provisions of this section, including relevant rules, regulations and procedures governing the approval of plans of work.

7. The provisions of article 151, paragraphs 1 to 7 and 9, article 162, paragraph 2(q), article 165, paragraph 2(n), and Annex III, article 6, paragraph 5, and article 7, of the Convention shall not apply.

SECTION 7. ECONOMIC ASSISTANCE

1. The policy of the Authority of assisting developing countries which suffer serious adverse effects on their export earnings or economies resulting from a reduction in the price of an affected mineral or in the volume of exports of that mineral, to the extent that such reduction is caused by activities in the Area, shall be based on the following principles:

(a) The Authority shall establish an economic assistance fund from a portion of the funds of the Authority which exceeds those necessary to cover the administrative expenses of the Authority. The amount set aside for this purpose shall be determined by the Council from time to time, upon the recommendation of the Finance Committee. Only funds from payments received from contractors, including the Enterprise, and voluntary contributions shall be used for the establishment of the economic assistance fund;
(b) Developing land-based producer States whose economies have been determined to be seriously affected by the production of minerals from the deep seabed shall be assisted from the economic assistance fund of the Authority;
(c) The Authority shall provide assistance from the fund to affected developing land-based producer States, where appropriate, in cooperation with existing global or regional development institutions which have the infrastructure and expertise to carry out such assistance programmes;
(d) The extent and period of such assistance shall be determined on a case-by-case basis. In doing so, due consideration shall be given to the nature and magnitude of the problems encountered by affected developing land-based producer States.

2. Article 151, paragraph 10, of the Convention shall be implemented by means of measures of economic assistance referred to in paragraph 1. Article 160, paragraph 2(l), article 162, paragraph 2(n), article 164, paragraph 2(d), article 171, subparagraph (f), and article 173, paragraph 2(c), of the Convention shall be interpreted accordingly.

SECTION 8. FINANCIAL TERMS OF CONTRACTS

1. The following principles shall provide the basis for establishing rules, regulations and procedures for financial terms of contracts:

(a) The system of payments to the Authority shall be fair both to the contractor and to the Authority and shall provide adequate means of determining compliance by the contractor with such system;
(b) The rates of payments under the system shall be within the range of those prevailing in respect of land-based mining of the same or similar minerals in order to avoid giving deep seabed miners an artificial competitive advantage or imposing on them a competitive disadvantage;
(c) The system should not be complicated and should not impose major administrative costs on the Authority or on a contractor. Consideration should be given to the adoption of a royalty system or a combination of a royalty and profit-sharing system. If alternative systems are decided upon, the contractor has the right to choose the system applicable to its contract. Any subsequent change in choice between alternative systems, however, shall be made by agreement between the Authority and the contractor;
(d) An annual fixed fee shall be payable from the date of commencement of commercial production. This fee may be credited against other payments due under the system adopted in accordance with subparagraph (c). The amount of the fee shall be established by the Council;

(e) The system of payments may be revised periodically in the light of changing circumstances. Any changes shall be applied in a non-discriminatory manner. Such changes may apply to existing contracts only at the election of the contractor. Any subsequent change in choice between alternative systems shall be made by agreement between the Authority and the contractor;

(f) Disputes concerning the interpretation or application of the rules and regulations based on these principles shall be subject to the dispute settlement procedures set out in the Convention.

2. The provisions of Annex III, article 13, paragraphs 3 to 10, of the Convention shall not apply.

3. With regard to the implementation of Annex III, article 13, paragraph 2, of the Convention, the fee for processing applications for approval of a plan of work limited to one phase, either the exploration phase or the exploitation phase, shall be US$ 250,000.

SECTION 9. THE FINANCE COMMITTEE

1. There is hereby established a Finance Committee. The Committee shall be composed of 15 members with appropriate qualifications relevant to financial matters. States Parties shall nominate candidates of the highest standards of competence and integrity.

2. No two members of the Finance Committee shall be nationals of the same State Party.

3. Members of the Finance Committee shall be elected by the Assembly and due account shall be taken of the need for equitable geographical distribution and the representation of special interests. Each group of States referred to in section 3, paragraph 15(a), (b), (c) and (d), of this Annex shall be represented on the Committee by at least one member. Until the Authority has sufficient funds other than assessed contributions to meet its administrative expenses, the membership of the Committee shall include representatives of the five largest financial contributors to the administrative budget of the Authority. Thereafter, the election of one member from each group shall be on the basis of nomination by the members of the respective group, without prejudice to the possibility of further members being elected from each group.

4. Members of the Finance Committee shall hold office for a term of five years. They shall be eligible for re-election for a further term.

5. In the event of the death, incapacity or resignation of a member of the Finance Committee prior to the expiration of the term of office, the Assembly shall elect for the remainder of the term a member from the same geographical region or group of States.

6. Members of the Finance Committee shall have no financial interest in any activity relating to matters upon which the Committee has the responsibility to make recommendations. They shall not disclose, even after the termination of their functions, any confidential information coming to their knowledge by reason of their duties for the Authority.

7. Decisions by the Assembly and the Council on the following issues shall take into account recommendations of the Finance Committee:

(a) Draft financial rules, regulations and procedures of the organs of the Authority and the financial management and internal financial administration of the Authority;

(b) Assessment of contributions of members to the administrative budget of the Authority in accordance with article 160, paragraph 2(e), of the Convention;

(c) All relevant financial matters, including the proposed annual budget prepared by the Secretary-General of the Authority in accordance with article 172 of the Convention and the financial aspects of the implementation of the programmes of work of the Secretariat;

(d) The administrative budget;

(e) Financial obligations of States Parties arising from the implementation of this Agreement and Part XI as well as the administrative and budgetary implications of proposals and recommendations involving expenditure from the funds of the Authority;

(f) Rules, regulations and procedures on the equitable sharing of financial and other economic benefits derived from activities in the Area and the decisions to be made thereon.

8. Decisions in the Finance Committee on questions of procedure shall be taken by a majority of members present and voting. Decisions on questions of substance shall be taken by consensus.

9. The requirement of article 162, paragraph 2(y), of the Convention to establish a subsidiary organ to deal with financial matters shall be deemed to have been fulfilled by the establishment of the Finance Committee in accordance with this section.

Index

INDEX

Key to the index:
Arabic numerals standing alone refer to the article numbers of the Convention itself. Articles of the annexes to the Convention are denoted by a capital "A" and a Roman numeral for the annex number, followed by the article number in Arabic numerals. "RI" and "RII" refer to the Final Act, Annex I, Resolutions I and II, respectively (of which the text is not reproduced in the reprint of 2005). References to articles can be used in a similar manner as an access to the "Guide" (pages 21-99).

The word "Page" followed by a number refers to the page number of this book.

Finally, the word "example" in parentheses indicates that a large number of articles contain references to the key word and that the article numbers given are only exemplary.

Access to Port
   land-locked states: 125;126; 131
   research vessel: 255
Accession: 307
   to amendments: 155; 314-317
   Internationals organizations: 305;
   AIX
Accused persons: 73; 97, 230
Activities in the area: 134-153; AIII
   Guide: Page: 54-57, 84
   Commentary: Page 121
   meaning of: 1
   pollution: 145, 209, 215
Ad hoc chamber: 188; AVI/36
Adjacent coasts: 15; 74; 76; 83; 134;
   AII/9
Adverse economic effects: 10, 151;
   162;164
Advisory opinion
   by Sea-Bed Disputes Chamber: 191;
   AVI/40
Agreement: (Examples: 62; 299)
Aids
   navigational: 21; 43
   warning signals: 60; 147; 262
Air space: 2, 34,49,56,78,135
Aircraft
   Commentary: Page: 120
   archipelagic passage: 53, 54
   exclusive economic zone: 58
   government liability: 235-236
   high seas: 87
   military: 107; 110-111; 224; 298
   piracy: 101-107
   pollution: 1; 212; 216;222
   sovereign immunity: 42; 236
   transit passage: 38; 39
   baseline: 47- 49
   closing line: 50
   duties of ships: 53-54

Albacore Tuna: 64; AI
Allowable catch: 61-70; 119
   dispute settlement: 297
Amendments: 155; 311-316
Anadromous stocks: 66
Anchorage
   unsafe: 225
Annual audit
   Authority: 175
   Enterprise: AIV/9
Annual budget
   Authority: 172
Annual fee for mining: 82; AIII/13;
   RII/7
Anti-monopolization in Area: 150;
   155; AIII/6-7
Application for activities
   Guide: Page: 84
Application for pioneer investors
   Guide: Page: 98
Arbitral tribunal
   Guide: Page: 92
Arbitration (commercial)
   award: 188
   binding commercial: 188; AIII/5;
   AIII/13; RII/5
   pioneer investors: RII/5
   UNCITRAL Rules: 188; AIII/5;
   AIII/13; RII/5
Arbitrators: AVII/2-3; AVIII/5;
Archaeological and historical
   objects: 149; 303
   Commentary: Page: 124
Archipelagic
   Guide: Page: 34
   Commentary: Page: 105; 114
   air routes: 53
   offers: 159
   powers and functions: 157; 160; 162
   quorum: 159;

duties of state: 54
innocent passage: 52
internal waters: 50
terms: 46
traditional rights: 51
regime of: 49
sea lane passage: 53
sovereignty: 2; 49
submarine cables: 51
suspension of passage: 44;52;54
traffic schemes: 53
waters: 49
Area: Part XI
Guide: Page: 54-58
Commentary: Page 117
clearly defined: 211
ice-covered: 234
legal status of the Area: 137
marine scientific research: 143; 256
meaning of term: 1
renunciation of Area: AIII/17
reserved area: AIII/8
Arrest
civil proceedings: 229
collision: 97
detention (pollution): 219; 220
notification of detention: 231
of persons: 27; 73; 105; 109
of vessels: 28; 73; 97; 105; 109; 111
release of vessels: 73; 226; 292
Artificial Islands (installations)
Commentary: Page: 122
Area: 147
continental shelves: 79; 80
exclusive economic zone: 56; 60
high seas: 87
legal status: 11;60;147;259
marine scientific research: 246; 258-262
pollution: 194;208; 214
removal: 60; 147
safety of navigation: 60; 147; 262
safety zones: 60; 260
Assembly
Guide: Page: 60
composition of: 159
election power: 160; 166; AIV, 5: AIV, 7
establishment 158
membership: 159, 160

request for advisory opinion: 159; 191
rules of procedure: 159
sessions: 159
suspension of rights: 160;162; 184; 185
voting: 159; 184
Assessment
in accordance with UN budget: 160; AIV/11
environmental: 165;200; 204; 206
marine scientific research data and Results: 249
Assistance
for pollution prevention: 202; 203
scientific research: 249; 254
to persons or ships: 98
to research vessels: 255
to states as producers of minerals: 151; 160; 162; 164
transfer to technology: 144; 274; 275; AIII/ 5
Atmosphere
pollution: 194; 212; 222
Atolls: 6; 47
Audit: 174; AIV/9
Authentic texts: 315; 320
Authority: 156-185
guide: Page: 58
administrative tribunal: 168
borrowing money: 171; 174
commodity arrangements: 151; AIII, 7
contract with operator: 153; AIII/3; AIII/16
contractual obligations: 151;189; AIII/21; AIV/2
contributions by members: 171
control of activities in the Area: 153; AIII/3-4
decisions: 159; 189
establishment: 156
exemption from taxes: 183
expenses: 160; 173
exercise of power: 152; 189
facilities: 156
finances: 171-175
incidental powers: 157
legal status: 176

marine scientific research: 143; 256; 274
meaning of: 1
membership: 156; 157
nature and fundamental
  Principles: 157
non-discrimination: 140; 152; AIII/7
offices: 156
organs: 158; 160; 161; 166; 170
payments of coastal states: 82
powers and functions: 152; 160
principles of: 140; 152; 157
privileges and immunity: 177-183
revenue: 150; AIII/13
seat: 156
secretariat: 84; 158; 166-169; 182; 183
suspension of rights: 184
training programs: 143; 144; AIII/ 2; AIII/15
transfer of technology: 144; 273; 274; 276; AIII/5
Award
  arbitral tribunal: AVII/9-12
  commercial arbitral tribunal: 188; AIII/5; AIII/13
  tribunal decision: 296

Banks: 9; 76
Baselines
  Guide: Page 26
  archipelagic: 47-49
  bays: 10
  charts or co-ordinates:
  contiguous zone: 33
  continental shelf: 76
  exclusive economic zone: 57
  reefs: 6
  territorial sea: 3-16; 48
Bays: 10; 298
Benefit of mankind: Preamble; 140; 143; 149; 150
  Introduction: Page: 5
Bigeye tuna: 64; AI
Binding decision: 282; 296; AVI/ 33
Binding force: 296; AVI/31; AVI/33
Blackfin tuna: 64; AI
Bluefin tune: 64; AI
Board of Enterprise: AIV/5
Boarding of a ship or vessel: 27; 28; 73; 110
Bond: 73; 218; 220; 226; 228; 292

Borrowing power
  Authority: 171; 174
  Enterprise: AIV/6; AIV/11
Breadth
  contiguous zone: 33
  continental shelf: 76; 83
  exclusive economic zone: 57; 74
  territorial sea: 3
  zones of archipelagic states: 48
Broadcasting: 109
  Guide: Page: 46
Budget
  Authority: 160; 162; 172
  Enterprise: AIV/6
  Preparatory Commission: RI/14

Cables and pipelines (submarine)
  Guide: Page: 48
  archipelagic state: 51
  continental shelf: 79
  exclusive economic zone: 58; 112-115
  high seas: 87; 112-115
  settlement of disputes: 297
Captain: 27; 94; 97; 98; 211
Casualties
  measures to avoid pollution: 221
Catadromous species: 67
Catch of fish: 61-62; 119
Centers
  promotion of research: 275-277
Certificate
  of compliance: RII/11
  Master's: 97
  pioneer investor's: RII/2 ; RII/11
  vessels: 91; 217; 226
certifying state
  pioneer investment: RII
Cetaceans: 64; 65; AI
Charges
  production charges: AIII/13
  services rendered: 26; 183
Charter (united Nations)
  Preamble: 19; 39; 138; 279;298; 301; RII/15
Charts
  adequate scale: 16; 47; 75;84
  archipelagic baselines: 47
  Area: 134
  continental shelf: 76; 84
  depositary: 16; 47;75; 76;84; 134
  exclusive economic zone: 75
  publicity: 16; 22; 41; 47; 53; 75; 84; 134

sea lanes/ traffic schemes: 22; 41; 53
    territorial sea: 5; 6; 16
Choice of procedure: 287; 299
Civil jurisdiction: 28; 229
Claims
    area: 137
    non-recognition: 89; 137; 241
    overlapping: RII/5
Closing lines
    archipelagic waters: 50
Coastal state: Part II-Part VI
    Guide: Page 24-41
    Introduction: Page:
    Commentary: Page: 102
    area: 134
    high seas: 116
    dispute settlement: 297- 298
    marine scientific research: 246
    pollution: Part XII
Cobalt: 151; AIII/13
Collision of ships: 21; 39; 94; 97; 98; 221
Commercial arbitration: 188; AIII/5; AIII/13
Commission, Legal and Technical: 163-165
Commission, preparatory
    Guide: Page 96
Commission Continental Shelf Limits
    Guide: Page: 82
    Commodity: 151; AIII/7
    Common heritage of
        mankind: Preamble ; 125; 136; 150; 311
    Introduction: Page: 5
Communications
    Authority: 181
    by states parties: 312-314
    by the Tribunal: AVI/41
    marine research: 250; 252
    pollution regulations: 211; 220; 231
    radio: 19; 39; 94; 109
Compensation (see: damage)
    producer of minerals: 151; 171
    scientists: 249
Competent organization
    Commentary: Page: 110
Compulsory procedures: 186; 286-296
    Guide: Pages: 62; 76; 88-93
Conciliation: AV
    Guide: Page: 88
    council proposal: 161; 162
    submission to: 284; 297; 298

Conference
    commodity: 151
    Review Conference: 155; 312
Confidential information: 163; 168; AIII/14; RII/3
Conflicts
    jurisdiction: 189
    overlapping areas: RII/5
    solving of: 59
Consensus
    amendments: 155; 312; AVI/41
    decisions: 155; 161-162; AIV/11
    Sea Conference: Final Act 21
Consent (of a coastal state): 77; 79 142; Part XIII
Conservation and management of living resources
    Guide: Page: 38; 48
    disputes: 297
    enclosed or semi-enclosed seas; 123
    exclusive economic zone; 61-73
    high seas: 63-66; 117 – 120; 145
    organizations: 61; 64; 65; 119; 120
    regional organizations: 63
    technical assistance: 266; 277
    territorial seas: 21
Constitution of the oceans
    Introduction: Page 9
Consular offers: 27; 231
Consumer of minerals: 150; 151
Contiguous zone: 33
    Guide: Page: 30
    Commentary: Page: 112
    archeological and historical objects: 303
    archipelagic states: 48
    breadth: 33
    hot pursuit: 111
    islands: 121
Continental margin: 76
Continental rise: 76
Continental shelf: Part: VI
    Guide: Page: 40
    Introduction; Page: 3
    Commentary: Page: 115
    archipelagic states: 48
    artificial installations: 80
    charts and lists: 76; 84
    coastal state rights: 77-81
    delimitation: 76
    drilling: 81; 246
    hot pursuit: 111
    laying of cables and pipelines: 79; 112

limits: 76; 84; AII/3
scientific research: 77; 246-253
payments to Authority: 82
pollution: 79; 210; 216
superjacent waters: 78
tunneling: 85
Continental slope: 76
Contingency plans for pollution: 199
Contract (mining)
  Guide: Page: 84
Contributions: 82; 171; AIII/13; AIV/11
Conventions (Geneva)
  Introduction: page 16
  1958 Conventions on Law of the Sea: Preamble; 311
Convenience (Flag of): 92
  Commentary: Page: 104
Co-operation
  Commentary: Page 110
Co-ordinates: 16; 47; 75; 76; 84; 134
Copper: 151; AIII/13; AIV/11
Costs of contractors: AIII/13
Council (of the Authority): 161-162
  Guide: Page: 60
Court
  Guide: Page: 76
  choice of forum: 286-298
  Court of Justice: 74; 83; 287; AIX/7
  local remedies: 295
  national: 105; 109; 232; AIV/13; AVI/39
Crew
  armed forces: 29
  illegal acts: 101
  license, certificate: 97
  mutiny: 102
  release: 73; 292
  training: 94
Criminal jurisdiction: 27; 73; 97; 228
Customs duties
  Authority: 183
  Land-locked states: 127

Damage
  Commentary: Page: 128
  activities in the Area: 139; AIII/4; AIII/22
  applicable law:304
  caused by seizure: 106; 110; 111
  marine environment: 145; 194-199; 211; 218-236; 242
  marine scientific research: 263
  warship: 31; 42; 236
Dangerous or noxious cargo: 22; 23
Data
  fisheries: 61; 62; 119
  geodetic: 16; 47;75-76; 84
  marine scientific research: (example 244)
  mining: (example 151)
  pollution: 2000; 201
  proprietary: 163; 168; 181; AIII/14
Debt guarantee for Enterprise: AIV/11
Decision-making procedure
  amendment conference: 312
  Authority: 159
  Commissions: 163
  Council:161
  Review Conference: 155
  Sea Conference: Final Act 21
Decisions: (examples: 160; 296)
Declarations
  by states: 309-310
  International organizations: AIX/2-5
  Settlement of disputes: 287; 298; 299
Deep sea mining
  Commentary: Page: 121
Default
  financial: AIV/11
  member: 184-185
  non-appearance: 294; AIV/11 AVII/9
Defense: 19
Definitions, meaning of
  activities: 1
  archipelagic
    sea lane passage: 53
    state: 46
  Waters: 49
  archipelagos: 46
  area: 1
  Authority: 1
  continental shelf: 76
  contractual terms: AIII/17
  dumping: 1
  enclosed or semi-enclosed seas: 122
  Geographically disadvantaged States: 70
  innocent passage: 19
  international organizations: AIX/1
  land-locked state: 124
  maritime casualty: 221

means of transport: 124
minerals: 133
passage: 18
pollution: 1
resources: 133
States parties: 1
technology: AIII/5
traffic in transit: 124
transit state: 124
warship: 29
Delimitation
artificial islands: 60; 147; 259
continental shelf: 76; 83; 134; AII
disputes about: 298
exclusive economic zone: 74; 75
internal waters: 8; 50
ports: 11
roadsteads: 12
special circumstances: 15
territorial sea: 15; 16
Delta: 7
Denunciation (of the Convention)
by international organizations: AIX/8
by states: 317
notification: 319
Depositary functions
Secretary – General of the Authority: 84
Secretary – General of UN: 16; 47; 75;76;84;287; 298; 306-320; AV/7; AIX/3-5
Design
installations or services: 194
mining equipment: AIII/17
ships: 21; 94; 194; 211; 217
Detention
notification: 226; 231
release of crew: 73; 292
ships: 73; 97; 220; 292
unseaworthiness: 219; 226
Developing states
Introduction: Page: 12
Commentary: Page: 107, 129
activities in the Area: (example 148)
development and transfer of technology: 143-144; 266-274
fisheries: 69-72; 119
pollution assistance: 202; 203; 207
scientific research assistance: 244; 274-277
Development costs of
Contractors: AIII/13

Development of
living resources: 61-63: 119
mineral resources of the Area: 150
technology: (see technology)
Devices: (example 194)
Diplomatic agents: 27; 231
Diplomatic conferences: (examples 211-222)
Director-General (of the Enterprise): AIV/6; AIV/7
Discharge (Pollution)
Guide: Page: 68-71
Authority (rules): AIII/17
coastal state: 194; 220
flag state: 194; 211; 217
in straits: 42;233
marine casualty: 221
Port state: 218
Disclosure of information: 302
Discretionary power
coastal state: 62; 246; 249; 297
power of Authority: 189
Discrimination, non-
by Authority: 140; 141; 152; AIII/6-7
by enterprise: AIV/12
contract: AIII/13
fishery: 119
ice-covered area: 234
plan of work: AIII/6-7
vessels: 24; 26; 42; 52; 227
Disposal of wastes: 1; 145; 216
Dispute settlement: Part XV
Guide: Page: 76; 88-93
Commentary: Page: 131
Dolphin: 64: AI
Drilling: 81; 145
Drugs: 27; 108
Duping
Commentary: Page: 123
meaning of: 1
minimization of: 194
regulations for the Area: AIII/17
special arbitration: AVIII
state jurisdiction: 210; 216

Economic and Social Council of the UN: 169
Economic Planning Commission: 163-164
Ecosystem: 194; 195

Elections: (example 161)
Enclosed or semi-enclosed seas: 122; 123
  Guide: Page: 50
  Commentary: Page: 114
Energy: 56
Enforcement
  Coastal state
    Guide: contiguous zone: Page: 30
    Guide: continental shelf: Page: 40
    Guide economic zone: Page: 36
    Guide: straits: Page: 32
    Guide: territorial sea: Page: 28
  Flag state
    Guide: Page: 44
  Pollution
    Guide: 64-71
Enterprise: 170; AIV
  Guide: Page: 86
  audit: AIV/11
  borrowing power: AIV/11
  Council directives: 162; 170; AIV/2
  disputes: 187
  legal capacity: 158; 170; AIV
  plans of work: 151; AIII/3; AIII/12; AIV/12
  privileges: 177; AIV/13
  reports: 160; 162; AIV/9
  reserved areas: AIII/8-9
  structure: AIV/4
  transfer of income: 171;AIV/10
  transfer of technology: 144; AIII/5
Entry into force
  Introduction: Page: 13
  Amendments: 316
  Convention: 308
  effect on Preparatory Commission: 308; RI/13
Equipment
  fishing: 62
  navigational: 94
  pollution: 194
  of ships: 21; 94; 194; 211; 217; 226
  regulation in Area: AIII/17
  scientific: 248-249; 258-262
  transfer of technology: 274; 275; AIII/5
Equal Rights
  Introduction: Page: 11
Equitable geographical distribution
  Council: 161

Economic and Legal Commission: 163
  Governing Board: AIV/5
  Sea-bed Dispute Chamber: AVI/35
  training: 274
  Tribunal: AIV/2
Evidence
  pollution: 217-223
Exceptions (Convention): 309; 311
Exchange of information: 200; 244
Exclusive economic zone: Part V
  Guide: 36-39
  Commentary: Page: 116
  artificial installations: 56; 60
  charts: 75
  environment protection: 56; Part XII
  freedoms in: 58
  hot pursuit: 111
  legal regime: 55-58
  living resources: 61-73; 297
  opposite coast: 74
  participation in: 62; 69-70
  resolution of conflicts: 59
  scientific research: 56; Part XIII
Expenditures (for activities): AIII/13; RII/7
Experts
  continental shelf: AII/2
  evidence by: AVII/6
  exchange of: 269; 275
  lists of AVII/2
  scientific research: 254
  tribunal: 289
Exploration: (example 123; 153)
  Guide: Page 56; 84

Facilities
Enterprise: AIV/8; AIV/13
  mineral processing: AIII/17
  pollution reception: 211
  port: 18; 25
  training: 275-277
  transit: 125-132
Fact finding: AVIII/5
  Guide: Page:92
Fair conditions: 144; 266; AIII/5
Fees
  application: AIII/13; RII/7
  conciliation commission: AV/9
  contractor's: AIII/13
  fishing: 62
  pioneer investor's: RII/7

Tribunal: AVI/19.34
Final Act
  Guide: Page: 96
  Introduction: Page: 16
  signatories: 156; RI/2
Final provisions: 305-320
  Guide: Page: 80
Finances
  Authority: 171-175
  Enterprise: AIV/11
  rules: AIII/17
Financial benefits from the area: 140
Financial contributors
  to the Authority: 82; 171; AIII/13
  to the Enterprise: AIV/11
Financial security: 73; 218; 220; 226; 228; 292
Financial statements
  Authority: 175
  Enterprise: AIV/9; AIV/11
Financial terms of contracts: AIII/13
First period of commercial
  production: AIII/13
Fishing
  Guide: Page: 38; 48
  Commentary: Page: 119
  access of states: 62; 87
  artificial structures: 60; 147
  coastal state rights: 56; 116
  disadvantaged states: 69-70
  disputes over law enforcement: 298
  gear: 42; 62; 115
  high seas: 87; 116-120
  laws and regulations: 21; 73
  regulatory measures: 42; 62-66; 119 221
  restoration of populations: 61; 119
  sedentary species: 68; 77
  settlement of disputes: 297
  statistics: 61; 62; 119
  traditional rights: 51
  vessels: 42; 62; 73
Flag
  of convenience: 92
  of international organizations: 93
  right to fly: 91
  showing of: 20, 110
Flag state
  Guide: Pages: 42-45; 66
  Commentary: Pages: 104
  arrest: 97
  duties: 94; 99-109; 113
  enforcement: 217; 220; 222

"genuine link": 91
information to: 94
jurisdiction and control: 94; 97; 217
marine environment: 194; 210-219; 222
notification to: 27; 73; 226; 231
registration: 91; 94
request to the coastal state: 27; 292
responsibility: 31; 42; 217; 235; 236
rights: 90
warships, government ships: 31; 42 95; 96; 236
Food and Agriculture
  Organization: AVIII/2
Force majeure: 18; 39
Foreign ships
  archipelagic passage: 53
  charges for passage: 26
  civil/criminal jurisdiction: 27-28; 73; 97; 99-111; 229-230
  design and manning: 21; 194
  innocent passage: 21-25; 52
  pollution: 194; 211-235
  transit passage: 40; 42
Formal confirmation
  by international organizations: 306; 319; AIX
Freedom of the high seas
  Guide: Page: 42
Free zones: 128
Frigate mackerel: 64; AI
Functions: (examples 157; 160)
Funds
  Authority: 171-175; AIII/13
  Enterprise: 170; 173; AIV/11
  for land-locked producer: 171
  pollution compensation: 235
Future of the convention
  Introduction: Page: 15

Gear (fishing)
  indemnity for loss: 115
  in transit passage: 42
  types of use: 62
General Provisions
  Guide: Page: 78
Generally accepted international
  regulations, etc.: (examples 21; 39; 41; 53; 94)
  rules etc.: (examples 21; 211; 226)
  standards: (examples 60; 262)
Geneva Conventions on the Law of the
  Sea: Preamble; 311

Introduction: Pages: 4; 16
Geodetic data: 16; 47; 75-76; 84
Geographical co-ordinates
  archipelagic baselines: 47
  continental shelf: 84
  deposition, etc.: 16; 47; 75; 84; 134
  exclusive economic zone: 75
  territorial sea: 16
Geographically disadvantaged states
  Commentary: page: 105
  access to living resources: 69; 70
  access to Area: 141; 148
  meaning of: 70
  participation in research
    projects: 254
  promotion of transfer of technology
    to: 266; 269; 272
  representation in the Council: 161
"Gentleman's Agreement"
  Introduction: Page: 8
Good faith: (examples 157-300)
Good order and security: 19; 27
Governing Board of Enterprise: AIV/5
Government ships: 29-32; 96; 110; 236

Harbour
  Commentary: Page 111
  access to: 131; 255
Harmful substances: 22; 23; 194; 246
Harvesting capacity: 69; 70; 297
Hazards
  to human health: 1; 98; 146; 242
  to navigation: 225; 234
  to the marine environment: 145; 195
Hearing
  dispute: 187; 286-296; AVI/17
  of witnesses: 223
High seas: 86-120
  Guide: Page: 42-49
  Commentary: Page: 117
  artificial islands: 87
  exclusive jurisdiction on: 92
  freedoms: 58; 87
  illicit trafic: 108
  immunity of ships: 95-96; 110
  invalidity of claims: 89
  legal status: 87; 135
  living resources: 116-120
  piracy: 100-107
  reserved for peaceful purposes: 88
  right of a hot pursuit: 111
  right of navigation: 90

right of overflight:87
right of visit: 110
right to fish: 87; 116-120
submarine cables and pipelines: 87;
  112-115
unauthorized broadcasting: 109; 110
Highly migratory species: 64-65; 120;
  AI
Guide: Page: 82
Historic bays: 10; 15; 298
  Commentary: Page: 111
Historical objects: 149; 303
  Commentary: 124
Hot pursuit (right of): 111
  Guide: Page: 46
Hydrographic survey: 21; 40

Ice-covered area: 234
Identification marking: 262
Illicit traffic in drugs: 27; 108
Immigration, law: 19; 21; 33; 42; 60
Immunities and privileges
  Authority: 177-183
  Enterprise: 177; AIV/13
  Representatives: 182
  Tribunal for the Law of the
    Sea: AVI/10
Immunity
  aircraft: 42; 236
  Authority: 178;182
  ships: 32; 42; 95-96; 110; 236
Incidental powers: 157; AIV/12
Industrial secrets: 163; 168; 181;
  AIII/14
Information
  disclosure of: 302
  scientific research: 248
  to be given by vessel: 211; 220
Innocent passage
  Guide: Page: 28
  archipelagic waters: 52
  internal waters: 8; 25; 211
  meaning of: 19
  suspention: 25; 45; 52
  territorial sea: 17-26; 211
Inspection
  control by the authority: 153;
    162 (2(z)); AIII/17
  of ships: 73; 94; 217; 219; 220; 226
Installations
  Commentary: Page: 122
  Area: 147; 209
  coastal state: 19;21

continental shelf: 79; 80
exclusive economic zone: 56; 60; 79
high seas: 87
hot pursuit: 111
inquiries into damage to: 94
legal status: 7; 11; 47; 60; 147; 259
marine research: 246; 149; 258-262
pollution from: 145; 194; 208; 209; 214
removal: 60; 147
safety zones: 60; 147; 260
Institution of proceedings
Authority staff: 168; AIII/22
arbitration: AVII/1; AVIII/1
conciliation: AV
pollution violation: 216-229
Sea-Bed Disputes Chamber: 187; AVI
Tribunal: AVI/24
Interest-free loans: AIV/11
Interests: (examples 142; 267)
Intergovernmental Oceanographic Commission: AII/3
Interim period (production): 151
Internal waters
Commentary: Pages: 111
archipelagic states: 50
delimitation: 10; 35; 50
hot pursuit: 111
pollution: 211-218
regime: 2; 8
sovereignty: 2
International agreements: (examples 197; 243)
International Atomic Energy Agency: 93
International Civil Aviation Organization: 39
International Court of Justice: 287
jurisdiction: 287; AIX/7
statute of: 74; 83
International economic
order: Preamble
Introduction: Page: 12
International Hydrographic Organization: AII/3
International Law
delimitation: 74; 83
development of: 160; 235
marine casualties: 221
persuant to: (examples 146; 223)
pollution: 235
principle of: Preamble; 19; 39; 301

responsibility and liability under: 304
International Maritime Organization: AVIII/2
Introduction: Page: 3
Commentary: Page: 109
International organizations
Guide: Page: 94
Commentary: Page: 108-110
competent (examples 211; 271)
co-operation with states: (example 123)
co-operation with the Authority: 143; 151
living resources
management: (example 64)
marine scientific research: 238-265
meaning of: AIX/1
participation of: AIX
protection of the marine environment: 197-222
responsibility and liability: 139; 263
signature by: 305; AIX/2
transfer of technology: 266-278
International Sea Bed Authority: 156-185
Guide: Page: 58
International Tribunal for the Law of the Sea: see: Tribunal
Guide: Page: 90
Commentary: Page: 131
Interpretation of application
of a contract: 187-188; AIII/13
of the Convention: (examples 187; 288; AVI/32)
Intervening party: AVI/31
Investigation
flag state: 94; 97; 217
foreign ships: 27; 97; 216-220; 226
port state: 218; 226
Investment: AIII/13; RII
Investor: RII
Islands: Part VIII
Guide: Page: 50
Commentary: Page: 114
baselines: 6-7; 13; 47; 121
non-islands status: 60; 147; 259
reefs: 7; 47
regime of: 121
rocks: 121

Johnson, Lyndon, Statement of 1966
Introduction: Page: 5

Joint arrangements
  coastal state fishery: 62; 72
  Enterprise: AIII/9; AIII/11
  transfer of marine technology: 269
Judgement: 296: AVI/30; AVII/9-12
Juridical person: (examples 153; 190)
Jurisdiction: (see: Enforcement)
  civil: 28; 229
  coastal state: (examples 56; 220)
  commercial arbitral tribunal: 188 AIII/5; AIII/13
  court of tribunal: 286-298
  criminal: 27
  flag state: 91-97; 109; 110; 113; 211 217; 228
  penal: 97; 230
  pollution: 194-214; 235
  vessel pollution: 218-222

Land-based
  producer states: 150; 151(10)
  sources (pollution): 207; 213
Land-locked states: Part X
  Guide: Page: 52
  Commentary: Page: 106
    activities in the Area: 140-141 148; 152; 274
  freedom for: 58; 87; 90; 1131
  meaning of: 124
  membership in the Council: 161
  participation: 69-70; 254
  transfer of marine technology: 266; 269; 272
Law of the Sea
  Introduction: Page 14
  Commentary: Page: 130
Laws and Regulations
  archipelagic sea lanes passage: 54
  contiguous zone: 33
  customs, immigration, fiscal, and sanitary: 19; 21;33;42;40
  exclusive economic zone: 58
  fishing: 60; 62; 73
  marine scientific research: 255
  pipelines and submarine cables: 113-115
  pollution: 205-234
  straits: 42
  territorial sea: 19-31
Legal status (use of term)
  archipelagic waters: 49
  Area and its resources: 137
  Enterprise: AIV/13

  exclusive economic zone: 55
  installations: 259
  space above Area: 135
  straits: 34-35
  territorial sea: 2
  water above shelf: 78
Legal and Technical Commission: 163-165
  Guide: Page: 60
Legitimate interests
  suppliers, etc., of technology: 267; 274
  transit states: 125
Liability: 31; 42; 139; 187; 232; 235-236; 263; 304; AIII/22
  Commentary: Page: 128
License: see: Certificate
  Transfer of mining technology: AIII/5
Limits of national jurisdiction: 86; 134
Lists
  of arbitrators: AVII/2
  of candidates: 162; AII/2; AVI/4
  of conciliators: AV/2-3
  of experts: 289; AVIII/2-3
  of geographical co-ordinates: 16; 47 75; 84; 134; RII/5
Little tuna: 64; AI
Living resources
  Guide: Page: 119
  Commentary: Page: 119
  access to: 62; 69-70; 87; 116-120
  allowable catch: 61-62; 70; 119
  conservation of: Preamble; 21; 56 61; 73; 117-120; 123
  disputes concerning: 297
  harm to by pollution: 1; 221
  harvesting capacity: 70
  management of: 56;61;118; 120
  maximum sustainable yield: 61;119
  surplus: 62; 69; 70
  training: 277
  utilization: 62
Loans for the Enterprise: AIV/11
Loss
  civil claim due to pollution: 229
  claim for cable protection: 115
  of contractor: AIII/13
  of life: 94-98
  pirate ship nationality: 104
  pollution by warships: 42; 236
  damage to states bordering straits: 42

seizure or stoppage: 106; 110; 232
Low-water mark
   importance of: 5-10; 47

Maintaining peace and
   security: Preamble; 138; 301
   Guide: Page: 79
   Commentary: Page: 129
Majority
   arbitral tribunal: AVII/8
   Assembly: 159
   approval of plan of work: 162; 165
   Continental Shelf Commission: AII/6
   conciliation commission: AV/ 4
   Council: 161
   election of members: AII/2; AVI/4; AVI/35
   Governing Board: AIV/5
   member state: AIX/2-3
   Tribunal decisions: AVI/7; AVI/8; AVI/29
Management of living resources: 56; 61; 118; 120
Manganese nodules: (examples 151; AIII/13
Manning regulations
   ships: 21; 94; 194; 211; 217
Marine environment: *see* Pollution
   Guide: Page: 64
   Commentary: Page: 126
Marine mammals: 65; 120; AI
Marine scientific research: Part XIII
   Guide: Page: 72
   Commentary: Page: 121
   by Authority in Area: 143; 274
   by states in Area: 143; 256
   coastal state consent: 245-265
   communications with coastal state: 250
   conditions for projects: 249
   co-operation: 200; 243-244; 247; 275
   exclusive economic zone: 56; 246; 249
   high seas: 87; 257
   implied consent: 252
   information to the coastal state: 248
   installations: 249-261
   obligations of foreign states: 246; 249; 252
   peaceful purposes only: 143; 240
   principles: 240
   promotion: 239; 242
   publication of results: 244; 249; 277
   research project: (example 246)
   right to conduct: 238
   rights of disadvantaged states: 254
   safety zones: 260
   settlement of disputes: 264-265; 297 AVIII/1
   suspension of project: 253
   territorial sea: 21; 40; 245
   training programs: 143; 268; 277
Maritime conflicts
   Introduction: Page: 2
Maritime casualty
   establishing rules: 211
   high seas: 94
   meaning of: 221
   pollution from: 221
   prevention measures: 194
Maritime traffic: 21; 42
Marketing costs: AIII/13
Marlin: 64; AI
Master of a ship: 27; 94; 97-98; 211
Maximum sustainable yield: 61; 119
Meaning of terms: *see* Definition
   Guide: Page: 22
Measures
   facilitate proceedings: 223
   maritime casualties: 194; 221
   seaworthiness: 94; 219
   provisional: 290; AVI/25
Membership
   states in Authority: 156
   suspension of rights: 184-185
Merchant ships: *see* Ships
   Commentary: Page: 118
Military: *see* Warships
   Commentary: Page: 124
Minerals from Area
   claims to: 137
   commodities produced from: 151
   meaning of: 133
   production ceiling for nickel: 151
   title to: AIII/1; AIV/12
Mining technology: AIII/17
   Commentary: Page: 121
Misuse of power: 187; 189
Monetary penalties
   against contractor: AIII/5; AIII/18
   against foreign vessesls: 228; 230
Monitoring
   pollution: 204-206
   radio frequencies by aircraft: 39
   technical assistance: 202

Monopolization in Area: 150; 155; AIII/6; AIII/7
Mouth of a bay or river: 9-10

Namibia: (example 305)
Narcotic drugs: 27; 108
National liberation movements
  observers: 156; Final Act, Resolution IV
Nationality
  of court/tribunal members: AVI/3; AVII/3; AVIII/3
  pioneer investors: RII/10
  ships: 29; 91-92; 104; 106; 110; 209-217
  warships: 29; 110
Natural of juridical person: (examples 137; 153)
Natural resources
  Area: 145
  continental shelf: 77; 79
  exclusive economic zone: 56
  rights to exploit: 56; 77; 137; 193
Nature and principles of the Authority: 157
Navigation
  Introduction: Page: 2
  Commentary: Page: 119
  channels for: 22; 53
  collision prevention: (examples: 21; 94)
  danger to: 24; 44; 225
  freedom of: 58; 87
  interests of: 27-28
  interference with: 60; 78; 147
  penal jurisdiction: 97
  route for international: 53; 147; 261
  safety aids: 21; 43; 262
  safety of: 60; 147; 261
  safety zones: 60; 147; 260
  special arbitration: AVIII
  traffic separation: 22; 41; 53
Neighbouring (affected) states
  archipelagic state: 47; 51
  co-operation with: 98; 123; 254
  information to: 254
  pollution: 198; 211
Net proceeds: AIII/13
New economic order
  Introduction: Page: 12
Nickel: 151
Nodules: (examples 133; 151)

Non-discrimination
  approval of plans of work: AIII/6
  financial matters: AIII/13
  fishermen: 119
  of foreign vessels: 24-26; 42; 52; 227
  operation by the Enterprise: AIV/12
  pollution control: 234
  use of power of Authority: 140-141; 152
Non-governmental organizations: 169
Non-living resources: (example: 56)
Notification
  coastal state: 73; 198; 226; 231; 253-254
  consular officer: 27; 231
  Enterprise: AIII/9; AIII/11
  inter-governmental organizations: 305; AIX
  marine scientific research: 247; 253
  of regulations: (example 211 (6(c)))
  UN Secretary-General: 313; 317; 319
  Tribunal/conciliation: AV; AVI; AVII; AVIII
Noxious substances
  law in strait: 42
  measures against: 194; 207
  innocent passage: 22-23
Nuclear-powered ships: 22-23

Objections to the Convention
  Introduction: Page: 12
Observers: 155; 319; RI/2
  to Conference: Appendix to Final Act
Ocean floor, space, plateau: Preamble; 1, 47; 76
Oceanic sharks: 64; AI
Oceanography: 277
Oceanology: 165
Off-shore: (examples: 11; 219)
Officer
  of a ship: 29; 94; 110
Office of Authority: 156; AIV/8
Oil and oily wastes: 42
Open market: AIII/5
Operator
  (contractor): (example: AIII/3)
Opposite of adjacent coasts
  delimitation: 15; 74;76; 83; 134; AII/9

Organizations
  commentary: Page 109
  regional
    organizations: (examples: 123; 211)
Outer edge
  continental margin: 76
Outer limits
  continental shelf: 76; 84; 134; AII
  exclusive economic zone: 57; 75
  territorial sea: 4
  "Outer shelf"
  Guide: Page: 40
Overflight
  Commentary: Page: 120
  archipelagic sea lanes: 53
  exclusive economic zone; 58
  high seas: 87
  pollution: 212; 222
  settlement of disputes: 297
  strait: 36; 38; 39; 44
Overlapping claims: RII/5

"Package Deal"
  Introduction: page: 8
pardo, Arvid, Proposal of 1967
  Introduction: Page: 5
Parties to a dispute: Part XV; 59; 264; 301; AV-AVIII
Partnership
  activities in the Area: AIII/4; AIII/6
  joint venture: AII/9-11
Passage
  Guide: Page: 28
  innocent: 19
  land-locked state: Part X
  meaning of: 18
  sea line: 53
  transit: 38
Payments
  Authority: 82; AIII/13
  Enterprise: AIV/10
Peaceful means: 279-281
  Guide; Page: 76
Peaceful purposes
  Guide: Page: 79
  Area: 141; 155
  high seas: 88
  research: 143; 147; 240; 242; 246
Penal jurisdiction: 27; 73; 97; 211; 230
Penalties
  fishery violations: 73

pirate: 105
pollution violations: 217-230
Performance regulations in Area: 151; AII/17
Period of commercial production: 151
Periodic review: 154
Pioneer activities
  Guide: Page: 98
Pipelines and cables: 79; 87; 112-115
  Guide: Page: 48
  Commentary: Page: 123
Piracy: 100-107; 110
  Guide: Page: 46
Plan of work
  Guide: Page: 84
  approval by Council: 162
  Enterprise: AIII/3; 12; AIV/2; 12
  exclusive rights: AIII/ 16
  in form of a contract: AIII/3
  general: 153
  interim period: 151
  particulars: AIII/6
  pioneer: RII/7-8
  review by Commission: 165
Plateau: 47; 76
Political independence: 19; 39; 301
Pollution: Part XII
  Guide: Page: 64-71
  Commentary: Page: 126
  aircraft: 1; 212; 216; 232
  airspace: 212; 222
  applicable rules and standards: 211-230
  Area: 145; 147; 162; 209; 215; AIII/17
  artificial installations: 145; 194; 208-209; 214
  assistance: 202-203; 207; 266;275
  atmosphere: 194; 21; 222
  civil claim: 229
  compensation for damage: 235
  conferences: (example: 197)
  continental shelf: 79; 210; 216
  contingency plan: 199
  damage: 145; 194-235; 242; 263
  developing state: 202-203; 207; 266 275
  discharge: 42; 194; 211-221; 233
  dumping: 1; 210; 216
  enclosed or semi-enclosed seas: 123
  enforcement of law: 213-222; 234; 236
  evidence: 217-223

facilities: 211
funds for compensation: 235
global and regional activities: 123; 197-201
imminent danger: 198
installations: 145; 194; 208- 209
introduction of new species: 196
jurisdiction: *see* Enforcement
land-based sources: 207; 213
law and regulations: 205-234
  liability for enforcement measures: 232
maritime casualty: 221
meaning of: 1
meaning of dumping: 1
monetary penalties: 228; 230
monitoring: 204; 206
oil and oily wastes: 42
penalties: 217; 228; 230
practices recommended: 94; 197-212
proceedings: 218; 220
regulations by coastal state: 21; 42; 54; 211
responsibility for damage: 235
safeguards: 223-233
sea-bed: 208-209; 214-215
serious damage: 94; 221; 233
sources of pollution: 207-212
straits: 42; 233
training: 202
vessels: 194; 211; 217-236(*see* Ships)
Polymetallic nodules: 133
Pomfrets: 64; AI
Port
  Commentary: Page: 111
  entry: 18; 25; 218-219; 255
  facilities: 211
  of registry: 98; 220
  unsafe: 225
Port state jurisdiction: 218
  Guide: Page: 70
Powers and functions: (examples: 152; 157; AVI/14)
Preamble
  Guide: Page: 22
Preparatory Commission: RI; RII
  Guide: Page: 96
Preparatory investment: RII
  Guide: Page: 98
President
  arbitral tribunal: AVII/3
  Assembly: 159

Council: 161-162
  Sea-Bed Disputes Chamber: AVI/35
  Tribunal: AVI/8; AVI/12
Prevention of pollution: *see* Pollution
"Primary Sea-Bed"
  Guide: Page: 40
Privileges and immunities
  Authority: 177-183
  Enterprise: 177; AIV/13
  members of the Tribunal: AVI/10
Procedures
  Authority
  Commissions of Council: 164-165
  Council: 161
  Enterprise: AIV/6
  settlement of disputes: Part XV; AV-AVIII
Proceedings
  arbitral tribunal: AVII
  civil, against vessels: 28, 229
  intervention: AVI/31-32
  Sea-Bed Disputes Chamber: AVI/35
  Sponsoring state in: 190
  special arbitration: AVIII/2-4
  Tribunal: AVI/5; AVI/28
  suspension: 218; 228
Processed
  metals: AIII/13
  substances: AIV/12
Procedures
  of minerals: 150-151
Production authorizations: 151
  AIII/7; AIII/13; AIV/6
Production ceiling: 151
Production charges: AIII/13
Production policies: 151
Promotion: (examples: 239; 266)
Proprietary of
  data: 163; 168;181;AIII/14
Prospecting: (example AIII/2)
Protection of
  coastal state: 25
  environment in Area: 145
  human life: 98; 146; 242
  legitimate interests: 267; 274
Provisional measures
  by court or tribunal: 290; AVI/25
Psychotropic substances: 27; 108
Publication
  charts: 16; 47; 75-76; 84
  of law: 21; 24; 42
  reports: 205
  restricted areas: 24; 52; 211

safety zones: 60
sea lanes: 22; 41; 53

Qualifications of contractors: AIII/4 - 7; AIII/17
Quorum
  Assembly: 159
  Continental Shelf Commission: AII/2
  Council: 161
  Governing Board: AIV/5
  Sea-Bed Disputes Chamber: AIV/35
  Tribunal: AVI/13; AVI/25

Radio communications: 39; 94; 109
Ratification:
  amendments: 315-319
  Convention: 306; 308; 316
  Review Conference (system of Area): 155; 316
Reefs: 7; 47
Régime
  of areas: 33; 49; Part V-VIII; Part XI
  for navigational purposes: 17-26; 37-44; 53-54; 87
Regional organizations
  fisheries: 63; 66; 118; 123
Registrar of the Tribunal: AVI/12
Registry
  Commentary: page: 104
  aircraft: 42; 212; 216; 222
  information on: 98; 220
  installation: 109; 209; 262
  ships: 91-94; 209-222
Regulations
  (*see* Laws and---)
Release
  crew: 73; 292
  ships: 73; 111; 219-220; 226; 292
Remuneration of members
  arbitral tribunal: AVII/7
  Governing Board: AIV/5
  Tribunal: AVI/18
  research scientists: 249
Report
  of Council: 160; 162
  of Enterprise: 160; 162; AIV/9
  Preparatory Commission: RI/11
  UN Secretary-General to states: 319
Representation of states: 160-163; 274; AIV/5; AV/2; AVI/3-4
Research project, or vessel: 246-265

Reservation of areas: AIII/8
Resources
  Guide: Page: 56
  meaning of: 133
Responsibility and liability
  Commentary: Page:128
  Authority-contractor: AIII/22
  for activities: 139; 304; AIII/22
  civil pollution claims: 229
  from enforcement measures: 232
  limitations: AIV/3
  marine scientific research: 263
  of international organizations: AIX/6
  pollution: 31; 42; 54; 235-236
  prevalence of other indemnity law: 304
  unlawful seizure: 107
Revenue: 150; AIII/13
Review Conference: 155; 314
Revision of contracts: AIII/19
Ridges: 76
Right to visit: 110
  Guide: Page: 46
Rivers, mouth of: 9
Roadsteads: 12
Rocks: 121
Routes
  non-interference with shipping: 147; 261
Rules of procedure
  arbitration: VII/5
  Assembly: 159; RI/5
  Council: 162
  Enterprise: AIV/6
  Preparatory Commission: RI/4
  Tribunal: AVI/16
Rules of Authority: 146; 153; 159-168; AIII/17

Safety of ships, aircraft
  Commentary: Page: 125
  aids: 43
  air: 39; 212; 222; 262
  collision: 21; 39; 94; 98
  navigation: 21-22; 41-42; 60; 147; 225
  safety at sea, term: 39; 94; 98; 194; 262
  safety zones: 60; 147; 260
  ship: 94; 217; 219
Sail-fishes: 64; AI

Salmon: 66
Sampling
  fisheries catches: 62
  polymetallic nodules: AIII/8; RII/1
Sanitary Law: 33; 42; 60
Sauries: 64; AI
Scientific criteria:
  fishing: 61; 119
  for regulations: 201
  research project: 249
Scientific research: see Marine Scientific Research
  Guide: Page: 72
  Commentary: Page: 121
Sea lanes
  general: 22; 41; 53
  non-interference with: 60; 147; 261
  shipping routes: 261
Sea-bed and subsoil: 1; 56; 76-77; 194
Sea-Bed Disputes Chamber
  Guide: Page: 62
  access: AVI/37
  ad hoc chamber: 188; AVI/36
  advisory opinions: 159; 191; AVI/40
  applicable law: VI/38
  Authority and the-: 162; 165; 189
  composition: AVI/35
  decisions: AVI/ 39
  establishment: 186; AVI/14
  geographical representation: AVI/35
  jurisdiction: 185-189; 287-288
    AIII/21; AVI/37-40
  President: AVI/35
  provisional measures: 290; AVI/25
  quorum: AVI/35
  term of office: AVI/35
Search and rescue: 98
Seaworthiness of ships: 94; 219; 226
Secretariat of Authority: 166-169
  Guide: Page: 60
Secretary -General of the Authority
  amendment proposals: 314
  annual report: 166
  budget proposal: 172
  contact to organizations: 169
  convocation of sessions: 159
  depositary function: 84
  election: 160; 162; 166
  functions: 166
  as observer: 169
  privileges: 182-183
  responsibility: 168
  terms: 166

Secretary-General of the United Nations
  amendments: 312-313
  appointments: AII/2; AV/3; AVIII/3
  convocation: AVI/4; RI/1
  depositor
    charts: 16; 47; 75-76; 84
    conciliation report: AV/7
    declarations: 287; 298; 306-320; AIX/3-5
    recommendations (Shelf Commission): AII/6
    list of arbitrators: AV/2; AVII/2
  Sea Convention: 287; 298; 319
  transmission by: 287; 298; AII/6; AV/7
  Tribunal: AVI/4 -5
Security
  coastal state: 19; 25; 52
  financial: 73; 218; 220; 228; 292
  state party: 302
  of tenure of contracts: 153; AIII/16
Security Council of the United Nations: 298
Sedentary species: 68; 77
Seizure
  Authority property: 179; AIV/13
  pirate ship: 105-107
Self-governing associated states: 305
Semi-enclosed seas: Part IX
  Guide: Page: 50
Semi-processed metals: AIII/13
Seminars, training: 269; 277
Settlement of disputes
  Guide: Page: 76; 88-93
  Commentary: Page: 130; 131
  applicable law: 293
  choice of procedure: 287
  compulsory procedure: 286
  compulsory conciliation: 297; AV/11-14
  concerning activities in Area: 186-190
  exhaustion of local remedies: 295
  in military matters: 298
  natural/juridical persons: 187; 190; 291
  procedure agreements: 287; 299
  provisional measures: 290; AVI/25
  release of vessels: 292
  rights of state to exclude: 297-298
  use of economic zone: 59

Share of net proceeds: AIII/13
Sharks: 64; AI
Shipping routes
  non-interference with: 147;261
Ships or vessels
  Guide: Page: 44
  Commentary: Page: 118
  access to port for land-locked state: 131
  access to port for research vessel: 255
  arrest: 28; 73; 105-111
  assistance: 18; 98; 255
  boarding of: 27-28; 73; 110; 226
  bond: 73; 218-226
  certificate/documents: 23; 91; 97; 217; 226
  civil proceeding against: 229; 304
  collision: 21; 39; 94; 97-98; 221
  crew: 73; 94; 101-102
  damage by: 220-221; 233
  design, construction: 21; 94; 194; 211; 217
  detention: 73; 97; 219-220; 226
  dumping from: 1; 210; 216
  enforcement: 25; 33; 73; 94; 217-234
  fishing: 62; 73
  flag: 90-93
  flag documents: 91
  flag state: (examples: 94; 217)
  force majeure: 18; 39
  foreign vessel: (examples: 26; 231)
  freedom of navigation: 38; 58; 87; 297
  genuine link: 91
  government ships: 29-32; 42; 96; 236
  hazards, danger to: 24; 44; 225; 234
  information to be rendered by: 211; 220
  inspection: 73; 94; 220; 226
  investigation: 27; 94; 97; 217-226
  loss to: 106; 110-111; 232
  manning of: 21; 94; 194; 211; 217
  maritime casualty: 94; 211; 221
  maritime traffic: 21; 42
  master: 27; 94; 97-98; 211
  nationality: 91
  non-discriminatory: 24-26; 42; 52; 227
  nuclear-powered: 22-23
  officer: 94
  penalties: 73; 105; 217-230
  physical inspection: 226
  pirate, definition of: 101
  pollution: 21; 42; Part XII
  proceedings: 218; 220; 228
  radio communications: 39; 94
  research vessel: 248-249; 255
  register of: 91; 94
  release: 73; 111; 226; 292
  search and rescue: 98
  seaworthiness: 94; 219; 226
  seizure: 105-107
  surveyor of: 94; 217
  tanker: 22
  transfer of ownership: 92
  voluntary in port: 218; 220
  visit of: 110
  warships: 29-32; 42; 95; 102-111; 224; 236
Signature
  Introduction: Page: 13
  amendments: 315
  Convention: 305; AIX/2; RI/1
Size or areas: AIII/8; AIII/17; RII/1(e)
Skipjack tune: 64; AI
Slaves: 99;110
Sources of pollution: 207-212
Southern bluefin tuna: 64; AI
Sovereign immunity
  ships: 32; 42; 95-96; 236
Sovereign rights
  air space: 2; 49; 212; 222
  archipelagic states: 2;49
  Area: 137
  coastal state: 2; Part II-VI; 193; 246; 297
  military activities: 298
  states bordering straits: 34; 39
  status of ships: 92
Special arbitral tribunal: 287; AVIII
  Guide: Page: 92
Special chambers of the Tribunal: 188; AVI/15
Species: 61-67; 119; AI
Sponsoring state: 139; 190; AIII/4; RII/10
Staff of Authority
  general: 166-168
  inspectors: 162; 165
Standards: (examples 211; 230)
State Enterprise: (example: 153; RII/2)
Statement
  declaration: 310; AIX

financial: 175; AIV/9
  reservation: 309
State party
  Commentary: Page: 102
Statute
  of the Enterprise: 170; AIV
    Guide: Page: 86
  of the Tribunal :AVI
    Guide: Page: 90
Stocks
  conservation of: 61-66; 119
  interdependence of: 61; 119
  migratory: 63-64
  research regulations: 62
  settlement of disputes: 297
Straits: Part III
  Guide: Page: 32
Structures, artificial
  Commentary: Page: 122
  dumping from: 1
  economic zone: 246; 258
  flag of: 209
  for activities: 147
  legal status: 60; 147; 259
  marine scientific research: 258-262
  pollution from: 208-209; 214-215
  safety zones: 60; 147; 260
  state of registry: 262
Subsidiary organs
  Guide: Page: 60
  Assembly: 160
  Council: 162
  Enterprise: 170
  Secretariat: 166
Substances
  harmful: 22-23
  psychotropic: 27; 108
  toxic: 194; 207
Superjacent waters
  legal status of outer shelf: 78; 135
  scientific research: 257
Surplus of fish catch
  disputes: 297
  participation: 62; 69-70
Suppliers of technology: 144; 267; 274;
  AIV/12
Survey
  for safety of ships: 94; 217
  research and survey activities: 19;
    40; AIII/17
Suspension
  contracts: AIII/18
  marine scientific research: 253

navigation: 25; 42
states parties' rights: 184-185
Swordfish: 64; AI
Symposia
  training: 269; 275-277

Tankers
  use of in sea lanes: 22
Taxes
  Authority: 183
  traffic in transit:127
Technology (transfer of)
  Guide: Page: 74
  Commentary: Page: 129
  definition of mining-: AIII/5(8)
  development and transfer of: Part
    XIV
  promotion by Authority: 143; 144
    274
  transfer to: 144; AIII/5; RII/12
terms and conditions
  fair and reasonable: 144; 267;
    AIII/5
  fishery: 62; 66
  mining: 153; AIII
  settlement of disputes: 187-188
Territorial integrity: 19; 39; 301
Territorial sea
  Guide: Page: 24
  Introduction: Page: 2-5
  Commentary: Page: 112
  airspace: 2
  artificial installations: 11; 258-262
  baseline: 5-14; 57
  breadth: 3
  charts: 16
  conservation regulations: 21; 194
  delimitation between states: 15
  due publicity: 16
  historic titles: 10; 15
  hot pursuit: 111
  innocent passages: 17-32
  legal status: 2
  marine environment obligation: 192;
    Part XII
  meaning of innocent passage: 19
  meaning of passage: 18
  right of innocent passage: 17
  scientific research: 245
Territories: 305
Third states: (example: 72)
Threat or use of force: 19; 39; 301

Title
   to minerals: 137;AIII/1;AVI/12
Traffic
   in transit: 124;130
   separation schemes: 22;41;53
   with drugs: 27;108
Training
   fishery: 62
   for activities in Area: 143-144;274; AIII/15
   in centres: 275-277
     marine scientific research: 244
     pollution prevention: 202
     seminars: 269; 277
     transfer of technology: 268
Transfer
   Guide: Page 74
   contracts: AIII / 20
   data: AIII / 14
   fishing rights: 72
   ownership of ships: 92
   pollution damage: 195
   technology: *see* Technology
   through national centre: 275
   through regional centre: 276-277
Transit passage: 38-45
   Guide: Page: 32
Transit state
   Commentary: Page: 107
   meaning of: 124
Transporting, processing of minerals
   initial program: AIII / 5
   right of the Enterprise: 170; AIV / 1
Tribunal for the Law of the Sea
   Guide: Page: 76; 90
   Commentary: Page: 131
   access: 291; AVI / 20
   conflict of interest: AVI / 7-8
   costs to parties: AVI 34
   costs by states parties: AVI / 19
   criteria for election: AVI / 2-6
   decision-making procedures: AVI / 29
   decisions of: 290; 292; 296; AVI / 7-33
   establishment: 287; AVI / 1; RI / 10
   finality of decisions: 296; AVI / 33
   institution of proceedings: AVI / 24
   judgement: AVI / 30
   jurisdiction: 2877-298; AVI / 21-23
   majority: AVI / 29
   members in particular case: AVI / 8; AVI / 17

President and Vice-president: AVI/ 12
privileges and immunities : AVI/10
procedure:AVI/24-34
provisional measures:290;AVI/25
quorum: AVI/13;AVI/25
Register:AVI/12
remuneration of members: AVI/18
resignation of a member: AVI/5
rules of procedure: AVI/16
Sea – Bed Disputes Chambers: 187; 288; AVI/35
seat: AVI / 1
solemn declarations: AVI / 1
special chamber: AVI / 15
term of office: AVI / 5;AVI / 6
vacancy: AVI: 6; AVI / 9
Truman Proclamation, 1945
   Introduction: Page 3
Tuna: 64; AI
Tunnelling: 85

UNCITRAL Arbitration Rules: 188; AIII / 5; RII / 5
Underwater vehicles: 20
Unification of the Law of the Sea
   Commentary: Page: 130
United Nations
   Commentary: Page: 108
   Charter of: Preamble; 19; 39; 138; 279; 298; 301; RII / 15
   consultation with Authority: 169
   flying the flag: 93
   scale of UN budget: 160; AIV / 11
   Security Council: 298
UN Council for Namibia: 305
UN Environment Programme: AVIII / 2
Use of Force
   by states: 301
   by vessels: 19, 39
Utilization
   living resources: 62; 119

Vessel-source pollution
   Guide: Page: 66-71
   pollution from: 194; 211; 217-236; AVIII / 1
Vessels
   (*see* Ships)
Violations
   by Authority staff: 168: AIII / 22
   by contractor: AIII / 5; AIII /18

by member state:185
unlawful pollution enforcement: 232
by ships: 27; 73; 111; 217-224
Visit
  Guide: Page 46
  right of: 110
Voting
  Assembly: 159
  Council: 161
  Review Conference: 155
  Tribunals, Commissions: AII, AV-AVIII

Warning signals: 60; 147; 262
Warships
  Commentary: Page: 124
  definition: 29
  dispute settlement: 298
  enforcement by: 224
  hot pursuit: 111
  immunities: 32; 95; 236
  innocent passage: 30-31
  military device: 19
  piracy: 102; 107
  pollution: 236
  right of visit: 110
  submarine: 20
Waste
  Authority regulations: AIII / 17
  disposal of: 1; 145
  loading of: 216
Water column
  rights in: 78; 135
  scientific research in: 257
Whales: 64-65; 120; AI

Yamani, Ahmed Zaki, Statement of 1968
  Commentary: Page: 115

Zone
  contiguous: 33
  exclusive economic: 55
  free:128